CONVIVIUMPRESS

Roland Meynet

A New Introduction to the Synoptic Gospels

Translated by Patricia Kelly

CONVIVIUMPRESS
GREGORIAN UNIVERSITY PRESS

SERIES RHETORICA SEMITICA

2010

A New Introduction to the Synoptic Gospels

Original Title: *Une nouvelle introduction aux évangiles synoptiques*

Translation: *A New Introcution to the Synoptic Gospels*

http://www.conviviumpress.com
sales@conviviumpress.com
ventas@conviviumpress.com
convivium@conviviumpress.com

7661 NW 68th St, Suite 108,
Miami, Florida 33166. USA.
Fax: +1 (305) 8875463

Edited *by* Rafael Luciani
Translated and revised *by* Patricia Kelly
Tables translated *by* Vitus Rubianto Solichin
Designed *by* Eduardo Chumaceiro d'E
Series: *Rhetorica semitica*

ISBN: 978-1-934996-11-9

Printed in Colombia
Impreso en Colombia
D'VINNI, S.A.

Convivium Press
Miami, 2010

PUBLISHED IN COLLABORATION WITH THE SOCIETY FOR THE STUDY OF BIBLICAL AND SEMITIC RHETORIC (RBS)

SOCIETY FOR THE STUDY OF BIBLICAL AND SEMITIC RHETORIC (RBS)

Several learned societies exist whose objective is the study of rhetoric. The «Society for the Study of Biblical and Semitic Rhetoric» (RBS) is the only one

- that is devoted exclusively to the study of Semitic literature, in particular the Bible, but also others texts, for example of Muslim origin;
- that consequently is dedicated to listing and describing the particular laws of a rhetoric that have governed the composition of texts which are of no less importance than those of the Greek and Latin world, of which modern Western civilization is the heir.

It must not be forgotten that this same Western civilization is also heir to the Judeo-Christian tradition, which has its origin in the Bible, that is to say, in the Semitic world.

More broadly, the texts that we study are the foundational texts of the three great monotheistic religions: Judaism, Christianity and Islam. Such academic study, the primary condition for better mutual knowledge, can contribute to a rapprochement between those who belong to these diverse traditions.

Founded in Rome, where its headquarters are situated, the «Society for the Study of Biblical and Semitic Rhetoric» (RBS) is a not-for-profit organization, under Italian law, that promotes and sustains research and publications

- especially in the Biblical field, both the New and Old Testaments;
- but also of other Semitic texts, in particular those of Islam.

The essential objective of the RBS is to promote research projects, exchanges between Universities and publications in the area of Biblical and Semitic Rhetoric, thanks especially to the collection of necessary funds for financing these diverse projects.

The «Society for the Study of Biblical and Semitic Rhetoric» first and foremost welcomes and brings together Scholars and University Professors who, in different Universities and Institutes, both in Italy and abroad, work in the area of Biblical and Semitic Rhetoric. It is open also to those who are interested in research and are intent on supporting it. For more information on the RBS, see:

www.retoricabiblicaesemitica.org

RHETORICA SEMITICA

Series directed by Roland Meynet s.j.

Many people think that classical rhetoric, inherited from the Greeks via the Romans, is universal—this is what seems to govern modern culture, which the West has spread through the whole world. But the time has come to abandon this ethnocentrism—classical rhetoric is no longer alone in the world. We cannot judge everything according to the small village where we were born and which we have never left, whether that little «village» is Paris, Rome, Berlin, or even New York.

The Hebrew Bible, whose texts were mostly written in Hebrew, but also in Aramaic, uses a very different rhetoric from Greco-Roman rhetoric, so we need to acknowledge that there is another rhetoric, which we refer to as «Hebrew Rhetoric».

Other biblical texts from the Old and New Testaments, which were translated into or written directly in Greek broadly follow the same rules; we can therefore rightly talk not just about Hebrew rhetoric but more broadly about «Biblical Rhetoric».

Furthermore, these same laws were later recognized to be at work in Akkadian, Ugaritic and other texts which were earlier than the Hebrew Bible, and then in Arabic texts from the Muslim tradition and the Qur'an, later than the biblical literature. This rhetoric, then, is not only biblical, and we might even say that all these texts, which come from the same cultural sphere, belong within the same rhetorical style which we refer to as «Semitic Rhetoric».

Contrary to the inevitable impression of western readers, these texts from the Semitic tradition, whether the Prophets, the Gospels, or the Qur'an, are carefully composed, providing that they are analyzed according to the rhetorical laws which govern them. We know that the text's form and arrangement is the main gate which gives access to its meaning; although its composition does not directly and automatically provide the meaning. However, when formal analysis leads to a thoughtful division of the text, defining its context more objectively, emphasizing the way it is organized at its different structural levels, then the conditions which allow the work of interpretation come together on less subjective and fragmentary bases.

Contents

3

The passage in its broader context. The sequence *PAGE 265*

1 Oh come to the water all you who are thirsty;
though you have no money, come.

Buy corn without money, and eat,
and, at no cost, wine and milk.

2 Why spend money on what is not bread,
your wages on what fails to satisfy?

Listen, listen to me, and you will have good things to eat
and rich foods to enjoy.

3 Pay attention, come to me,
listen, and your soul will live. (Isa 55:1-3)

Foreword

A New Introduction to the Synoptic Gospels. The reader is entitled to some enlightenment on this title —not about the noun «Introduction», but about the adjective «new». This introduction is new because, coming after so many others, it is the latest one, which it will likely remain for very little time. It is new, particularly, because it aims to offer something new in comparison with those which have gone before it. This does not mean that it claims to replace them; far from it. The proof is that, in my introductory lecture course to the Synoptic Gospels at the Gregorian University, which has given rise to this book, I divided the material into two equal parts. The first half, given over to the students personally, is to study one of the best introductions to the New Testament and the Synoptic Gospels which is on the market[1]. I am therefore freed from dealing with introductory questions during the classes, and can dedicate the 50 or so hours of teaching time to teaching the students how to read the Gospel texts. In some introductions to the Synoptic Gospels, after an initial introductory part, the second part is given over to the study of some pericopes of the triple tradition (that is, those which are reported by the three synoptics), the double tradition (those found in Matthew and Luke), or proper to a single Gospel, but taken from here or there[2].

I preferred to study contiguous pericopes —the 12 pericopes from Mark 10, the 14 from Matthew 19 and 20, and the 17 from Luke 17:11-19:46, or 43 pericopes in total. In this way 21 pericopes common to the three synoptics, 4 common to two of them, 2 proper to Matthew and 5 proper to Luke are studied[3].

The main reason for this choice was to not be limited to the study of a few isolated pericopes, but to show how *the pericopes form structured wholes.* The presupposition of the methodology used here, «biblical rhetorical analysis», is as follows: pericopes are not simply juxtaposed, as might seem the case at first sight, but are rather organized, written —and very well written[4]. Synoptic comparison, therefore, cannot consist solely in putting pericopes in parallel, but also

1 See, for example, BROWN R.E., *An Introduction to the New Testament*; GOOSEN G. - TOMLINSON M., *Studying the Gospels: An introduction*; PERKINS PH., *Introduction to the Synoptic Gospels.*

2 For example, GRELOT P., *Évangiles et histoire.* Following the first part, on the theoretical problems of exegesis, the second part is given to some narrative texts: the multiplication of the loaves, the account of the Annunciation, Jesus' Baptism, and the man born blind. The same happens in his second volume, *Les Paroles de Jésus Christ*, in which, after the first chapter on «guiding principles for the reader», textual analyses are presented according to the following literary genres: sentences which can be isolated, framed sentences, parables, and, finally, Jesus' prayers.

3 This tally is approximate. In reality, it is more complicated —for example, Luke's last two pericopes are only partially shared with Matthew and Mark.

4 See MEYNET R., «Présupposés de l'analyse rhétorique», 69-87; repeated in *Lire la Bible*, 2003, Chap. 8; English translation, «Presupositions of Rhetorical Analysis», *Rhetorical Analysis*, 168-181.

in comparing the wholes made up of pericopes, the «sequences» (and «sub-sequences»).

This is what is the real novelty, and the significant contribution which rhetorical analysis makes to the study of the synoptic question. It is enough to consult any synopsis to see that they are happy to show pericopes in parallel, but never sequences; and exactly the same thing happens in introductions to the Synoptic Gospels.

We should add that, even at the level of pericopes, rhetorical analysis enables synoptic study to progress significantly. Usually, in fact, the similarities and differences between the verses are only listed: traditional synopses and most commentaries do no more than this. It is much more vital to examine the composition of each pericope than the comparison of verses, even when this is exhaustive. Many examples in the pages which follow will demonstrate that the differences between the Gospel recensions converge in the construction of very different structures. This is especially clearly noted when pericopes are composed concentrically—for example, in each Synoptic Gospel the account of the call of the rich man is focused on a different point, which naturally leads to an interpretation which better reflects the specific nature of each of the three versions of the same account.

The choice of sequences I have made aims to emphasize the two basic characteristics of the Synoptics, of their similarity, on the one hand, and their difference, on the other, not just of the pericopes themselves, but also, and above all, in the constructions which they are part of, the sub-sequences and sequences.

The two sequences of Matthew 19-20 and Mark 10 are very similar: the 12 pericopes which the first two Gospels share follow the same order, and their sequences are arranged in three sub-sequences, whose boundaries are identical. However, the pericopes which follow the pericope on divorce are very different —in Matthew, this is about the celibate dedicated to the Kingdom of God, while in Mark it is about faithfulness in marriage. In addition, in the very center of the central sub-sequence, Matthew has inserted a parable which is unique to him, the parable of the laborers in the vineyard. Despite these important differences, the similarity between the two compositions is quite remarkable.

For Luke, on the other hand, five of these contiguous pericopes are shared with Matthew and Mark and follow the same order, but the first three belong to a sequence (Luke 17:11-18:30), of which they are the third and last sub-sequence, while the other two belong to the next sequence (Luke 18:31-19:46), which has five other passages.

Rhetorical analysis therefore enables us to significantly renew the study of the synoptic question. To use what has become a classical metaphor, it does not restrict itself to comparing the stones of three similar buildings, but aims to shed light on the architecture as a whole. It is quite clear that, in the context of a simple Introduction, one cannot claim to study the composition of the whole of each of the three Synoptic Gospels to then compare their respective architecture. It seems, however, essential to enable the reader to have an important experience, to be aware, thanks to some examples, that these texts which seem to us to be picked apart are in fact very coherent; that they follow a rigorous logic; that, although every pericope can and must be studied in itself, it must also be read in its literary context, with which it forms a real discourse.

In a work of this kind, we must be careful to manage a path which is progressively more difficult.

- In terms of a single pericope, the account of the healing at Jericho, the introduction shows how the historical-critical method, and particularly the «literary criticism», which will be used only later, proceed.
- The first chapter is dedicated to the study of two passages shared by the three Synoptic Gospels, «The healing of the blind man (or two blind men) of Jericho» and «The call of the rich man». The analysis of the composition of each version of these two pericopes will be carried out in detail, after which they will be placed in parallel.

In addition, the call of the rich man, where Jesus quotes part of the Decalogue, leads us to study its two recensions in the books of Exodus and Deuteronomy. This initial excursus will lead to a reflection on the fact that there are two, not just one, Decalogues in the Bible.

- In the second chapter, each of these two passages is situated in its close literary context, that is, in the sub-sequences they are part of. In Matthew and Mark, the healing of the blind man or men is part of a very similar construction which also has «The request of Zebedee's sons» and «The discourse on service»; however, there are significant differences, including the fact that there is a single blind man in Mark, while Matthew has two, which requires some explanation. Luke's setting is very different: he does not use the account of the request of Zebedee's sons, and places the discourse on service in a very different place, at the center of the first sequence of the Passion[5]. In the same sub-sequence, Luke doubles the account of the blind man and Zacchaeus, a passage which is unique to him.

5 See *Luc*, 831-876; *Jésus passe*, 113-173.

In Matthew and Mark, the pericope of the call of the rich man is inserted into two very similar sub-sequences, which have five passages; Luke's sub-sequence, on the other hand, has only three passages, and their external boundaries, as well as their internal boundaries, do not at all coincide with those of the two sub-sequences in the first two evangelists.

Matthew's sub-sequence, and, similarly, Mark's, is centered on the short pericope in which we see Jesus welcome the children; and here we make a second excursus to examine the two recensions of the Our Father, Matthew's, which all know by heart and which is used in the liturgy, and Luke's, which enables us to take the reflections cut off at the end of the first excursus a little further and to offer an interpretation on the reasons for there being four Gospels and not just one.

- The third chapter is dedicated to the study of the wider context, the *sequences* into which the two pericopes of the blind man (men) of Jericho and the rich man are integrated. In Matthew and Mark, in fact, these belong to a single sequence. These parallel sequences have three sub-sequences —the call of the rich man is part of the first sub-sequence, the healing at Jericho is the last passage of the final sub-sequence. Since these two sub-sequences will have been examined in the previous chapter, it remains only to examine the central sub-sequence, and then the sequence as a whole.

The composition of Luke is quite different. The two accounts, of the rich man and the blind man are part of two distinct sequences. I have already published these two sequences in my commentary on Luke[6]. Here we add the synoptic comparison between the parallel passages of the two sequences in Matthew and Mark.

- A fourth chapter aims to situate the units studied in the previous chapters (passages, sub-sequences and sequences) in the global context of the section and, finally of the book as a whole. This final chapter will be given over to the Gospel of Luke alone.

The first Italian edition of this book began with some forty pages entitled «As an introduction» which are now part of another publication, called *Reading the Bible.* This book is the natural complement to this introduction to the Synoptic Gospels.

ROME AND PARIS, EASTER 2008.

6 *Luc*, 673-706; 707-754.

Abbreviations

1

Abbreviations

AD	*Anno Domini*
ACFEB	Association catholique française pour l'étude de la Bible.
al.	*alii* (others)
Amos	BOVATI Pietro and MEYNET Roland, *Le Livre du prophète Amos*, Paris, Éd. du Cerf, RhBib 2, 1994.
BJ	Bible de Jérusalem.
Bonnard	BONNARD Pierre, *L'Évangile selon saint Matthieu*, Neuchâtel, CNT(N) 1, 1963, Genève, CNT(N), NS 1, 1982³.
Bovati	*Giustizia e ingiustizia nell'Antico Testamento*, course handout, Rome 1996.
Bovon	BOVON François, *L'Évangile selon saint Luc*, Genève, Labor et Fides, CNT IIIa, IIIb, IIIc, 1991, 1996, 2001.
chap.	chapter
col.	column(s)
etc.	et cetera
ed.	edidit, ediderunt
Éd.	Éditions
EDB	Edizioni Dehoniane Bologna
Ernst	ERNST Josef, *Das Evangelium nach Markus*, Regensburg 1981; Italian translation: *Il vangelo secondo Marco*, Brescia, Morcelliana, Il Nuovo Testamento commentato I (1,1-8,26), II (8,27-16,20), 1991.
f., ff.	following
Gnilka	GNILKA Joachim, *Das Matthäusevangelium*, Freiburg, Herder, HThK 1, 1986-1988; Italian translation, *Il vangelo di Matteo*, Brescia, Paideia, CTNT 1/1-2, 1990, 1991.
Hagner	HAGNER Donald A., *Matthew*, Dallas TX, Word Books, WBC 33, 1993-1995.
Ibid.	*Ibidem*
Id.	Idem

JB Jerusalem Bible, London, Darton, Longman & Todd, 1966.

Jésus passe MEYNET Roland, *Jésus passe. Testament, jugement, exécution, résurrection du Seigneur dans les synoptiques,* Rome/Paris, Editrice Pontificia Università Gregoriana/Éd. du Cerf, RhBib 3, 1999.

Lamarche LAMARCHE Paul, *Évangile de Marc,* Paris, Gabalda, EtB, NS 33, 1996.

Légasse LÉGASSE Simon, *L'Évangile de Marc,* Paris, Éd. du Cerf, LeDiv Commentaires 5, 1997.

Lire la Bible MEYNET Roland, *Lire la Bible,* Paris, Flammarion, Champs 537, 2003.

Luc MEYNET Roland, *L'Évangile de Luc,* Paris, Lethielleux, RhSem 1, 2005.

LXX Septugint

MA Massachusetts

Mazzucco MAZZUCCO Clementina, *Lettura del vangelo di Marco,* Torino, Silvio Zamorani editore, 1999.

n. note, notes

NA^{27} NESTLE-ALAND, *Novum Testamentum Graece,* Stuttgart, Deutsche Bibelgesellschaft, 1993^{27}.

NJB New Jerusalem Bible, London, Darton, Longman & Todd, 1994.

NS Nouvelle series

NY New York

p. page

pp. pages

Pesch PESCH Rudolf, *Das Markusevangelium,* Freiburg, Herder, 1977^2, 1980^2; Italian translation: *Il vangelo di Marco,* I-II, Brescia, Paideia, CTNT II,1-2, 1980-1982.

QC Quebec

Rossé ROSSÉ Gérard, *Il vangelo di Luca,* Roma, Città Nuova, Collana scritturistica di Città Nuova, 1992.

TOB Traduction œcuménique de la Bible

trans. translation

Trocmé	TROCMÉ Étienne, *L'Évangile selon saint Marc*, Genève, Labor et Fides, CNT(N), 2000.
TX	Texas
UBS	United Bible Society
v.	verse
vv.	verses

2 Biblical books

Abbreviations for books of the Bible are those used by *Biblica.*

3 Comentaries

References to commentaries have the author's name, followed by page number, e.g., Bovon, II, 388-391.

4 Abbreviations for journals and collections

AnBib	Analecta Biblica
AncB	Anchor Bible
BETHL	Biblioteca Ephemeridum theologicarum Lovaniensium
Bib	*Biblica*
CBQ	*Catholic Biblical Quarterly*
CEv	Cahiers Évangile
CNT(N)	Commentaires du Nouveau Testament. Neuchâtel
CTePa	Collana di testi patristici
CTNT	Commentario teologico del Nuovo Testamento
DBS	*Dictionnaire de la Bible. Supplément*

DTC	*Dictionnaire de théologie catholique*
EtB	Études bibliques
EThL	Études théologiques de Louvain
Gr.	*Gregorianum*
HThK	Herders theologischer Kommentar zum Neuen Testament
JBL	*Journal of Biblical Literature*
JSNT	*Journal for the Study of the New Testament*
LAPO	Littératures anciennes du Proche Orient
LeDiv	Lectio Divina
LiBi	Lire la Bible
MUSJ	*Mélanges de l'Université Saint-Joseph*
NRTh	*Nouvelle revue théologique*
NTS	*New Testament studies*
RB	*Revue biblique*
ReBib	Retorica biblica
RhBib	Rhétorique biblique
RhSem	Rhétorique sémitique
RThL	*Revue Théologique de Louvain*
RSR	*Recherches de Science Religieuse*
SC	Sources Chrétiennes
ScEs	*Science et Esprit*
StRh	*Studia Rhetorica*
VT.S	Vetus Testamentum Supplement Series
YJS	Yale Judaica Series
WBC	Word Biblical Commentary

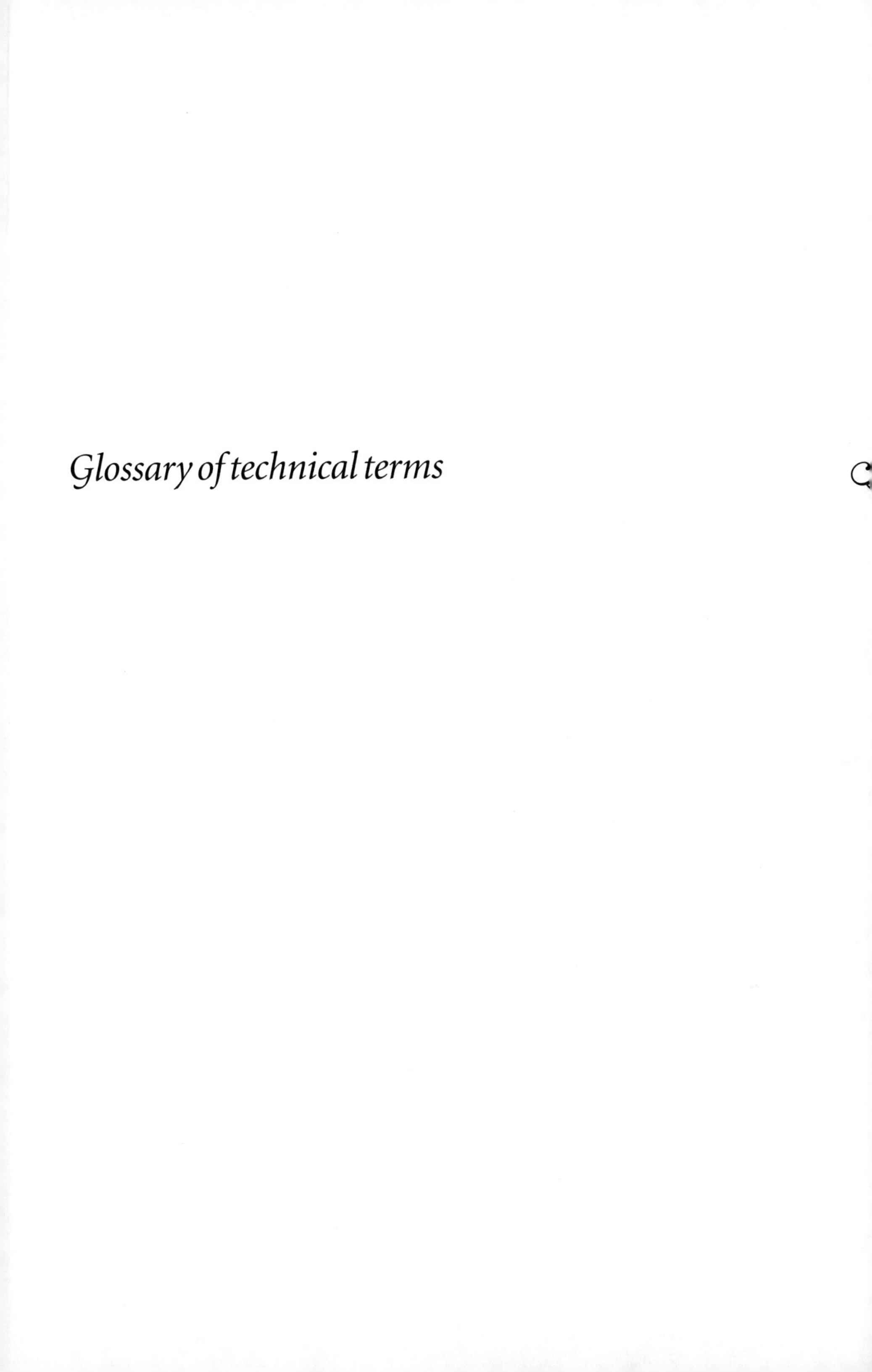

Glossary of technical terms

1

Terms signifying the rhetorical units

Very often, in works of exegesis, the terms «section», «passage» and, especially «piece» and «part» are used unequivocally. Here is a list of terms, which in the present methodological exposition, signify the textual units at each successive level.

THE «INFERIOR» (NON-AUTONOMOUS) LEVELS

Apart from the first and second (Term and Member), the units of inferior levels are formed of *one*, *two* or *three* units of the preceding level.

TERM the term usually corresponds to a lexeme, or word that belongs to the lexicon—noun, adjective, verb, adverb.

MEMBER the member is a syntagma, or group of «terms» linked closely together syntactically. The «member» is the minimal rhetorical unit. Sometimes the member can include only one term (the term of Greek origin is «stich»).

SEGMENT the segment counts one, two or three members, and there are unimember segments (the Greek terms is «monostich»), bimember segments (or «distichs») and trimember segments (or «tristichs»).

PIECE the piece counts one, two or three segments.

PART the part counts one, two or three pieces.

THE «SUPERIOR» (OR AUTONOMOUS) LEVELS

They are all formed of either *one* or *several* units from the previous level.

PASSAGE the passage—the equivalent of the exegetes' «pericope»—is formed of one or several parts.

SEQUENCE the sequence is formed of one or more passages.

SECTION the section is formed of one or more sequences.

BOOK finally, the book is formed of one or more sections. Sometimes it is necessary to use intermediary levels such as the «sub-part», «sub-sequence» and «sub-section»; these intermediary units have the same definition as the part, sequence and section.

SIDE the side is the part of text which precedes and/or follows the center of a construction; if the center is composed of two parts the side corresponds to each of the two halves of the construction.

2

Terms signifying the relations between symmetrical units

TOTAL SYMMETRIES

PARALLEL CONSTRUCTION figure of composition where the elements in paired relations are arranged in a parallel manner: A B C D E | A'B'C'D'E'.
When two parallel units frame a unique element, we talk about parallelism to indicate the symmetry between these two units but the whole (the superior unit) will be considered as a concentric construction: A | X | A'.
«Parallel construction» can also be described as «parallelism» (which is the opposite of «concentricism»).

CONCENTRIC CONSTRUCTION figure of composition where the symmetric units are arranged in a concentric manner: A B C D E | X | E'D'C'B'A', around a central element (which can be a unit of any level of textual organization).
«Concentric construction» can also be described as «concentrism» (which is opposite to «parallelism»).

MIRROR CONSTRUCTION figure of composition similar to concentric construction, but without the central element: A B C D E | E'D'C'B'A'.
When the construction only has four units, we also speak about «chiasmus»: A B | B'A'.

PARTIAL SYMMETRIES

INITIAL TERMS identical or similar terms or syntagmas which mark the beginning of symmetrical textual units; anaphora in classical rhetoric.

FINAL TERMS identical or similar terms or syntagmas which mark the end of symmetrical textual units; epiphora in classical rhetoric.

OUTER TERMS identical or similar terms or syntagmas which mark the outer parts of a textual unit; «inclusio» in traditional exegesis.

MEDIAN TERMS identical or similar terms or syntagmas which mark the end of a textual unit and the beginning of the unit which is symmetrical to it; «link word» in traditional exegesis.

CENTRAL TERMS identical or similar terms which mark the centers of two symmetrical textual units.

PRINCIPLE RULES FOR RE-WRITING

- within the member, terms are usually separated by spaces;
- each member is usually on a single line;
- segments are separated from one another by a blank line;
- pieces are separated by a broken line;
- parts, and sub-parts, are limited by two continuous lines.
- within the passage, the parts are framed (unless they are very short, for instance an introduction or conclusion); the sub-parts are arranged in adjoining frames;
- within the sequence or sub-sequence the passages, re-written in prose, are arranged in frames separated by a blank line;
- within the sequence, the passages of a sub-sequence are arranged in adjoining frames.

For details, see R. MEYNET, *Traité de rhétorique biblique*, Paris, Lethielleux, RhSem 4, 2007. See *Traité*, ch. 5, 283-344 on the rules for re-writing (on the re-writing of synoptic tables, see ch. 9, 471-506).

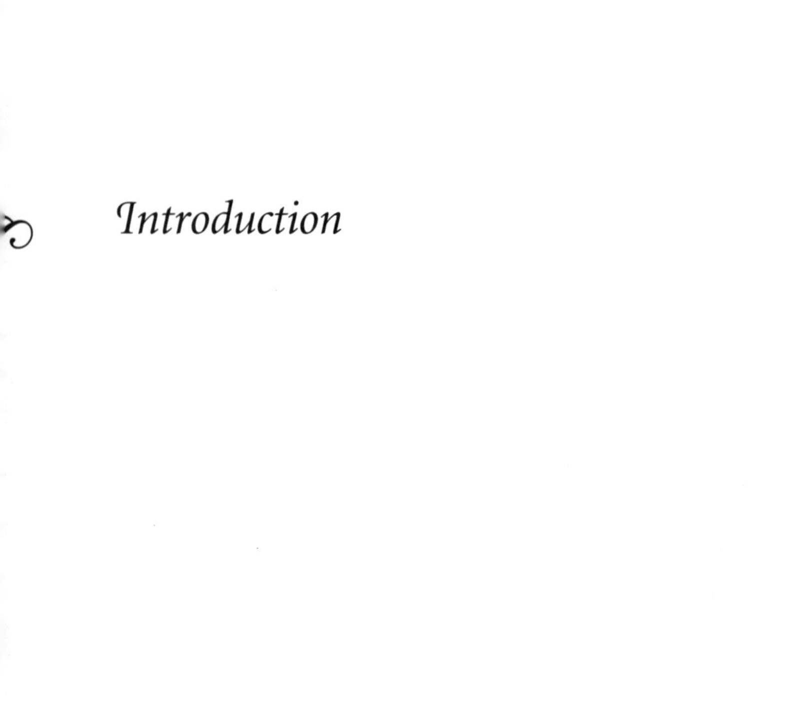

Introduction

The first chapter will be given to the study of two pericopes, «The healing of the blind man (or the two blind men) of Jericho» and «The call of the rich man». Before beginning our rhetorical analysis of these two texts, in this 'Introduction' we will deal with various basic questions about editions, translations and synopses. We will also have to introduce the main aspects of historical-critical exegesis, which has been traditional for a century.

A. EDITIONS AND TRANSLATIONS

In most translations into modern languages, the Synoptic Gospels are presented as collections of short units («pericopes»)[1] to which titles are given. For example, in the *New Jerusalem Bible* Mark 10[2] is divided into nine passages, while in the *New Revised Standard Version* it is divided into six:

NJB	v.
1. The question about divorce	1-12
2. Jesus and the children	13-16
3. The rich young man	17-22
4. The danger of riches	23-27
5. The reward of renunciation	28-31
6. Third prophecy of the Passion	32-34
7. The sons of Zebedee make their request	35-40
8. Leadership with service	41-45
9. The blind man of Jericho	46-52

NRSV	v.
1. Teaching about divorce	1-12
2. Jesus blesses little children	13-16
3. The rich man	17-31
4. A third time Jesus foretells his death and Resurrection	32-34
5. The request of James and John	35-45
6. The healing of blind Bartimaeus	46-52

1. THE TITLES OF PERICOPES ARE NOT PART OF THE TEXT

The titles of pericopes in our translations are very useful, as they enable us to find what we are looking for more quickly when we are flicking through the book; but we need to remember that these titles are not part of the Gospel text, but are the work of the editor, as is clearly shown by the example from Mark 10. They are not revealed, as the biblical text is. They can, therefore, be criticized and, where necessary, corrected, suppressed, or added to.

1 «Pericope» is a technical term in exegesis which comes from the Greek (the prefix *peri-* meaning «around» and the verb *koptō* meaning «to cut»; it can be literally translated as «cut-out»). It means a short literary unit distinguished from others, genrally not in action, time or place. Liturgical readings are most often a single pericope.

2 On the division into chapters, see *Lire la Bible*, 14, n. 1; also *Traité*, 113, n. 1.

An initial example: the TOB calls Luke 13:22-30 «Will Israel enter the Kingdom?». The text as it is printed in the TOB follows:

Will Israel Enter into the Kingdom?

22 He was passing through towns and villages, teaching and making his way to Jerusalem.

(*Matt 7:13-14*)

23 Someone said to him, «Lord, will there be only a few people who will be saved?». He said to them, 24 «Try hard to enter by the narrow door, because many, I tell you, will seek to enter and will not succeed.

(*Matt 25:10-12*)

25 When the master of the house will get up and will close the door, remaining outside, you will start to knock on the door, saying, "Lord, open to us' and he will answer you, 'You, I do not know from where you are".

(*Matt 7:22-23*)

26 Then you will start to say, "We have eaten and drunk in your presence, and in our squares you have taught"; 27 and he will say to you, "I do not know from where you are. Go away from me, all of you evil doers!".

(*Matt 8:12-11*)

28 There will be weeping and grinding of teeth, when you will see Abraham, Isaac and Jacob and all of the prophets in the kingdom of God, and you thrown outside. 29 Then they will come from the rising sun and from its setting, from the north and from the south, to take place at the feast of the kingdom of God.

(*Matt 19:30; 20:16; Mark 10:31*)

30 And thus, there are some of the last who will be first and there are some of the first who will be last».

One interpretation may be that the problem of salvation is not only a problem for Israel—the children of «Abraham, Isaac and Jacob» (28), but also for Jesus' disciples, that is, those who have «eaten and drunk in his presence» (26)! In fact, the contemporary reader understands it in this way[3]. The TOB title therefore imposes *one* interpretation, which, at the very least, is debatable. In addition, the TOB divides the pericope into six distinct paragraphs, following the Matthean parallels (and the Markan parallel for the last verse), giving the reader the impression that this is not a single, composed text, but a collection of *logia* (Jesus' words) coming from the source Q (material which is shared by Matthew and Luke, but absent from Mark) copied in a disordered fashion; in other words, a composite pericope[4].

3 See, for example, Bovon, II, 388-391 (the Church Fathers, *Ibid.*); see too *Luc*, 596-599.

4 The NJB's title forces the same interpretation: «The narrow door; rejection of Jews, call of the gentiles» (see the note in the NJB); the title of the Spanish Casa de la Biblia translation, or the simpler translation into modern Hebrew (UBS), «The narrow door», leaves the interpretation open.

Another example: in the JB Luke 7:36-50 is entitled «The woman who was a sinner», as though there were not another, more important, character, whom Jesus criticizes and with whom he speaks at length to lead him to convert—Simon the Pharisee! The translation of the New Testament into modern Hebrew has a title which better respects the content of the pericope: «Jesus in the house of Simon the Pharisee»[5].

The best-known critical edition of the Greek text[6] does not give titles, just as the manuscripts do not. However, the text is divided into paragraphs, as follows for Mark 10:

Divisions of the NA^{27}, without titles
10:1
10:2-9
10:10-12
10:13-16
10:17-22
10:23-27
10:28-31
10:32-34
10:35-40
10:41-45
10:46-52

Divisions of the NJB, with titles
The question about divorce
Jesus and the children
The rich young man
The danger of riches
The reward of renunciation
Third prophecy of the Passion
The sons of Zebedee make their request
Leadership with service
The blind man of Jericho

In comparing these divisions with the NJB division, we can see that the first pericope, entitled in the NJB, «The question about divorce» (1-12), is divided by NA^{27} into three paragraphs (1; 2-9; 10-12).

2. THE DIVISIONS ARE NOT PART OF THE TEXT!

It is useful to emphasize this again—the divisions of our editions (paragraphs in NA^{27}, divisions with or without titles in the translations) are not revealed, for they are absent from the great majority of ancient manuscripts. They must, therefore, be taken for what they are—an aid—but one which can lead us into error. The same goes for punctuation, which is absent from ancient manuscripts (see the copies of two manuscript texts, pp. 36-37).

5 See MEYNET R., «"Celui à qui est remis peu, aime un peu" (Lc 7,36-50)»; abridged version in MEYNET R., *Tu vois cette femme? Parler en paraboles*, 169-182; see *Luc*, 330-336.

6 Nestle-Aland, *Novum Testamentum Graece*, 27th edition (henceforth NA^{27}).

Beza Codex (D), fourth-fifth century: end of John's Gospel

ϹΗΜΕΝΩΝΠΟΙΩΘΑΝΑΤΩΔΟΞΑϹΕΙΤΟΝΘΝ
ΚΑΙΤΟΥΤΟΕΙΠΩΝΛΕΓΕΙΑΥΤΩΑΚΟΛΟΥΘΕΙΜΟΙ
ΕΠΙϹΤΡΑΦΕΙϹΔΕΟΠΕΤΡΟϹΒΛΕΠΕΙΤΟΝΜΑΘΗΤΗΝ
ΟΝΗΓΑΠΑΙΗϹ ΑΚΟΛΟΥΘΟΥΝΤΑ
ΟϹΚΑΙΑΝΕΠΕϹΕΝΕΝΤΩΔΕΙΠΝΩ
ΕΠΙΤΟϹΤΗΘΟϹΑΥΤΟΥ ΚΑΙΕΙΠΕΝΑΥΤΩ
ΚΕ ΤΙϹΕϹΤΙΝΟΠΑΡΑΔΙΔΩΝϹΕ
ΤΟΥΤΟΝΟΥΝΕΙΔΩΝΟΠΕΤΡΟϹΛΕΓΕΙΑΥΤΩΙΗΥ
ΚΕ ΟΥΤΟϹΔΕΤΙ ΛΕΓΕΙΑΥΤΩΟΙΗϹ
ΕΑΝΑΥΤΟΝΘΕΛΩΜΕΝΕΙΝΟΥΤΩϹ
ΕΩϹΕΡΧΟΜΑΙΤΙΠΡΟϹϹΕ ϹΥΜΟΙΑΚΟΛΟΥΘΕΙ
ΕΞΗΛΘΕΝΟΥΝΟΥΤΟϹΟΛΟΓΟϹΕΙϹΤΟΥϹ
ΑΔΕΛΦΟΥϹ ΚΑΙΕΔΟΞΑΝΟΤΙΟΜΑΘΗΤΗϹ
ΕΚΕΙΝΟϹΟΥΚΑΠΟΘΝΗϹΚΕΙ ΚΑΙΟΥΚΕΙΠΕΝΑΥΤΟ
ΟΙΗϹ ΟΥΚΑΠΟΘΝΗϹΚΕΙϹ ΑΛΛΑΕΑΝΑΥΤΟΝ
ΘΕΛΩΜΕΝΕΙΝ ΕΩϹΕΡΧΟΜΑΙΠΡΟϹϹΕ
ΟΥΤΟϹΕϹΤΙΝΟΜΑΘΗΤΗϹ ΟΜΑΡΤΥΡΩΝ
ΠΕΡΙΤΟΥΤΩΝ ΚΑΙΟΓΡΑΨΑϹΤΑΥΤΑ
ΚΑΙΟΙΔΑΜΕΝΟΤΙΑΛΗΘΗϹΕϹΤΙΝΑΥΤΟΥ
ΗΜΑΡΤΥΡΙΑ ΕϹΤΙΝΔΕΚΑΙΑΛΛΑΠΟΛΛΑ
ΟϹΑΕΠΟΙΗϹΕΝΟΧΡϹΙΗϹ ΑΤΙΝΑ
ΕΑΝΓΡΑΦΗΤΑΙΚΑΘΕΝ ΟΥΔΑΥΤΟΝ
ΟΙΜΑΙΤΟΝΚΟϹΜΟΝΧΩΡΗϹΕ
ΤΑΓΡΑΦΟΜΕΝΑΒΙΒΛΕΙΑ

ΕΥΑΓΓΕΛΙΟΝ ΚΑΤΑ
ΙΩΑΝΗΝ ΕΤΕΛΕϹΘΗ
ΑΡΧΕΤΑΙ ΕΥΑΓΓΕΛΙΟΝ
ΚΑΤΑ ΛΟΥΚΑΝ

At the end of the page:

ευαγγελιον	κατα ιωανην	ετελεσθη	αρχεται	ευανγελιον	κατα λουκαν
That is:					
«The Gospel	of John	is finished,	begins	the Gospel	of Luke».

Anyone who knows Greek can read, from the 2nd line: και τουτο ειπων λεγει αυτω… (John 21:19b). Note that, in ancient manuscripts, not only is the punctuation missing, but there are not even any spaces between words; however, the end of the lines matches the division between words. The abbreviations, indicated by a line above, would also have been recognized: IHS or IHN (according to the case) for ΙΗΣΟΥΣ or ΙΗΣΟΥΝ; ΚΕ for ΚΥΡΙΕ; ΧΡΣ for ΚΡΙΣΤΟΣ. See K. ALAND - B. ALAND, *The Text of the New Testament*, 103-128.

Scroll of Isaiah found in a cave at Qumran: Isa 52:13-53,8

There is no punctuation in this manuscript, but words are separated by spaces. The fourth Song of the Servant begins in the first line: *hinnēh yaśkîl ʿabdî yārûm weniśśāʾ wegābah meʾōd…*

Isa 52 [13] See, my servant will prosper, he shall be lifted up, exalted, rise to great heights. [14] As the crowds were appalled on seeing him —so disfigured did he look that he seemed no longer human— [15] so will the crowds be astonished at him, and kings stand speechless before him; for they shall see something never told and witness something never heard before.

53 [1] «Who could believe what we have heard and to whom as the power of Yhwh been revealed?» [2] Like a sapling he grew up in front of us, like a root in arid ground. Without beauty, without majesty (we saw him), no looks to attract our eyes; [3] a thing despised and rejected by men, a man of sorrows and familiar with suffering, a man to make people screen their faces; he was despised and we took no account of him. [4] And yet ours were the sufferings he bore, ours the sorrows he carried. But we, we thought of him as someone punished, struck by Elohim, and brought low. [5] On him lies a punishment that brings us peace, and through his wounds we are healed. [6] We had all gone astray like sheep, each taking his own way, and Yhwh burdened him with the sins of all of us. [7] Harshly dealt with, he bore it humbly, he never opened his mouth, like a lamb that is led to the slaughter-house, like a sheep that is dumb before its shearers never opening its mouth. [8] By force and by law he was taken; would anyone plead his cause? Yes, he was torn away from the land of the living, for our faults struck down in death.

For the rhetorical analysis of this poem, see R. MEYNET, «Le quatrième chant du Serviteur (Isa 52,13-53,12)»; see too ID., *Mort et ressuscité selon les Écritures*, 125-175.

The two «passages» (or «pericopes») examined in this first chapter belong to the «triple tradition», which means that they are found in the three Synoptic Gospels. In the first case, the limits of the three recensions match exactly. However, if we wished to give a title which would match all three recensions, we would have to choose something fairly vague: «The healing at Jericho». While in Mark and Luke Jesus restores sight to *one* blind man, in Matthew he heals *two*! In the second passage, the title «The call of the rich man» (without clarifying that in Matthew he is «young») suits all three parallel accounts; but we will see that Luke's boundaries are not the same as Matthew and Mark.

B. SYNOPSES

Texts of the triple tradition can be written in three columns in a «synoptic» way (from the Greek *syn-* «together» and *opsis*, «vision»), so that those elements which are identical or similar are horizontally together. Books which present the gospels in this way are called «synopses».

1. TRADITIONAL SYNOPSES

Many synopses limit themselves to printing the text in three columns, making the textual elements match *grosso modo*, and usually separating the verses from one another in so many paragraphs; See, for example, the English text in the fourth edition of Throckmorton's Synopsis (1979; see p. 39)[7]. The most «scientific» Greek synopsis works in exactly the same way[8].

7 The English text is based on *Revised Standard Version* (1952). The arrangement follows the Greek text of the ninth edition of the Huck - Lietzmann's Synopsis of 1936.

8 ALAND K., *Synopsis quattuor evangeliorum.*

B.H. THROCKMORTON, ed., *Gospel Parallels. A Synopsis of the First Three Gospels*, Nashville 1949, 1979[4], § 193, p. 134.

Matt 20:29-34	Mark 10:46-52	Luke 18:35-43
	[46] And they came to Jericho;	[35] As he drew near to Jericho,
[29] And as they went out of Jericho, a great crowd followed him. [30] And behold, two blind men sitting by the roadside, when they heard that	and as he was leaving Jericho with his disciples and a great multitude, Bartimaeus, a blind beggar, the son of Timaeus, was sitting by the roadside. [47] And when he heard that it was	a blind man was sitting by the roadside begging; [36] and hearing a multitude going by, he inquired what this meant. [37] They told him,
Jesus was passing by, cried out, «Have mercy on us, Son of David!».	Jesus of Nazareth, he began to cry out and say, «Jesus, Son of David, have mercy on me!».	«Jesus of Nazareth is passing by». [38] And he cried, «Jesus, Son of David, have mercy on me!».
[31] The crowd rebuked them, telling them to be silent; but they cried out the more, «Lord, have mercy on us, Son of David!». [32] And Jesus stopped and called them, saying,	[48] And many rebuked him, telling him to be silent; but he cried out all the more, «Son of David, have mercy on me!». [49] And Jesus stopped and said, «Call him». And they called the blind man, saying to him, «Take heart; rise, he is calling you». [50] And throwing off his mantle he sprang up and came to Jesus.	[39] And those who were in front rebuked him, telling him to be silent; but he cried out all the more, «Son of David, have mercy on me!». [40] And Jesus stopped, and commanded him to be brought to him;
«What do you want me to do for you?». [33] They said to him, «Lord,let our eyes be opened».	[51] And Jesus said to him, «What do you want me to do for you?». And the blind man said to him, «Master, let me receive my sight».	and when he came near, he asked him, [41] «What do you want me to do for you?». He said, «Lord, let me receive my sight».
[34] And Jesus in pity touched their eyes, and immediately they received their sight and followed him.	[52] And Jesus said to him, «Go your way; your faith has made you well». And immediately he received his sight and followed him on the way.	[42] And Jesus said to him, «Receive your sight; your faith has made you well». [43] And immediately he received his sight and followed him, glorifying God; and all the people, when they saw it, gave praise to God.

In his much older English synopsis, J.M. Thompson used *cursive* to mark the different elements; but note that what is in Roman type is not only what is shared by all three Synoptics (the triple tradition), but also what is shared by Matthew and Luke (the double tradition)[9]:

9 See THOMPSON J.M., *The Synoptic Gospels Arranged in Parallel Columns*, Oxford 1910, 66-67.

Mark 10:46-52	Matt 20:29-34	Luke 18:35-43
46 *And* they *come to Jericho*; and as he went out from Jericho *with his disciples and* a great multitude,	29 And as they went out from Jericho, a great multitude *followed* him.	35 *And it came to pass,* As he *drew nigh unto* Jericho,
	30 *And behold,*	
the son of Timaeus, Bartimaeus, a blind beggar, was sitting by the way side. 47 And when he heard	*two* blind men sitting by the way side, when *they* heard	a *certain* blind man sat by the way side begging; 36 and hearing *a multitude going* *by, he inquired what this meant.*
that it was Jesus of Nazareth,	that Jesus was passing by,	37 *And they told him*, that Jesus of Nazareth passeth by.
he *began* to cry out, and say, Jesus, thou son of David, have mercy on me!	cried out, saying, *Lord* Have mercy on *us*, thou Son of David!	38 And he cried, saying, Jesus, thou Son of David, have mercy on me!
48 And *many* rebuked him, that he should hold his peace; but he cried out the more a great deal,	31 And *the multitude* rebuked *them*, that *they* should hold *their* peace; but *they* cried out the more, *saying*,	39 And *they that went before* rebuked him, that he should hold his peace; but he cried out the more a great deal,
Thou son of David, have mercy on me!	*Lord*, have mercy on *us*, thou Son of David!	Thou son of David, have mercy on me!
49 And Jesus stood still, and *said*, *Call ye him.* *And they call the blind man, saying* *unto him,* *Be of good cheer; rise, he calleth thee.* 50 *And he, casting away his garment,* *sprang up, and came to Jesus.*	32 And Jesus stood still, and *called them*,	40 And Jesus stood, and *commanded him to be brought* *unto him;*
		and *when he was come near*,
51 And Jesus *answered* him, and said, What wilt thou that I should do unto thee? And *the blind man* said unto him, *Rabboni*, that I may receive my sight.	and said, What will *ye* that I should do unto *you*? 33 *They* say unto him, Lord, that *our eyes may* be *opened*.	he *asked* him, 41 What wilt thou that I should do unto thee? And he said, Lord, that I may receive my sight..
52 And Jesus said unto him, *Go thy way*; thy faith hath made thee whole.	34 And Jesus, *being moved with* *compassion, touched their eyes;*	42 And Jesus said unto him, *Receive thy sight*; thy faith hath made thee whole.
And straightway he received his sight, and followed him *in the* *way*.	and straightway *they* received *their* sight, and followed him.	43 And immediately he received his sight, and followed him, *glori-* *fying God; and all the people, when* *they saw it, gave praise unto God.*

Another, much more practical synopsis, was written by two Dominican scholars from the well-known *École Biblique et archéologique française* in Jerusalem[10]. The English translation follows here—the point is not the language, but the lay-out. The major advantage of this synoptic visualization is that the text is divided up into «syntagmas», or small groups of words which are syntactically linked. It is therefore much easier to compare the three recensions in detail. Its limitation is that there is no typographical device (italics, bold, small capitals, etc.) which can enable the visualization of the elements shared by the three Synoptics and those which are shared by only two of them. A further inconvenience of this synopsis is that it does not give the Greek text, only a translation,

10 BENOIT P. - BOISMARD M.-É., *Synopse des quatre évangiles en français*, 230-231.

albeit a very literal one which is very faithful to the original. Fortunately, there is also a Greek edition[11].

Matt 20:29-34	Mark 10:46-52	Luke 18:35-43
		35 Now it happened that,
	46 And they arrived at Jericho.	while he was approaching
29 And while they were going out	And while he was going out	Jericho,
of Jericho,	of Jericho,	
	and his disciples	
a numerous crowd	and a fairly large crowd,	
followed him.		
30 And behold	the son of Timaeus	
	– Bartimaeus –,	
	a beggar	
two blind men	blind,	a blind man
sitting alongside the road.	was sitting alongside the road.	was sitting alongside the road,
		begging.
Hearing	47 And, hearing	36 Hearing
		the crowd passing by,
		he asked what was happening.
		37 They told him
that Jesus	that it was Jesus	that Jesus
	the Nazarene,	the Nazorean
was passing (there),		was coming (there).
they cried out saying:	he began to cry out and to say:	38 He exclaimed, saying:
«Lord,		
	«Son of David, Jesus,	«Jesus, Son of David,
have mercy on us,	have mercy on me!».	have mercy on me!».
son of David!».		
31 The crowd	48 And many	39 And those who preceeded
ordered them	ordered him	ordered him
to be silent;	to be silent;	to keep quiet;
but they cried out	but he cried out	but he cried out
more loudly saying:	all the more:	all the more:
«Lord,		
	«Son of David,	«Son of David,
have mercy on us,	have mercy on me!».	have mercy on me!».
son of David!».		
32 And Jesus, stopping,	49 And Jesus, stopping,	40 Jesus, having stopped,
	said:	ordered
called them	»Call him».	that he be led to hm.
	And they called the blind man, saying to him:	
	«Have courage!	
	Rise, he calls you».	
	50 And he, throwing off his cloak	
	jumping up, came to Jesus.	When he came close to him,
	51 And addressing him the word,	
and said:	Jesus said:	he asked him:
«What do you want me to do	«What do you want me to do	41 «What do you want me to do
for you?».	for you?».	for you?».
33 They said to him:	The blind man said to him:	He said:
«Lord, that our eyes be opened».	«Rabbuni, that I might see».	«Lord, that I might see!».
34 Moved by compassion,		
Jesus	52 And Jesus	42 And Jesus
touched their eyes,		
	said to him: «Go,	said to him: «See;
	your faith has saved you».	your faith has saved you».
and immediately they saw.	And immediately he saw.	43 And instantly he saw.
And they followed him.	And he followed him	And he followed him,
	on the way.	glorifying God.
		And all the people,
		seeing that,
		gave praise to God.

11 BOISMARD M.-É. - LAMOUILLE A., *Synopsis graeca quattuor evangeliorum*, (with Introduction in English, French and German).

The authors explain that:

> [w]hen several gospels attest the same pericope, the text of each column is divided into very short lines, in the tradition of the *cola* and *commata* of the ancients, in such a way that by following the same line in the different columns, the eyes perceive immediately the agreements and disagreements among the gospels[12].

I am often asked which is «the best synopsis»; the answer is the one which everyone makes for himself. This is not a jest! The biblical text must not only be read with the eyes, but needs to be written with the hand. With a computer, this is really not difficult—it requires a certain amount of time, to be sure, but it is not wasted time. It is not even necessary to type out the text—there are several computer programs, such as *BibleWorks*, from which the original text, or various translations, can be copied into text documents.

2. AN INITIAL IMPROVEMENT

The ideal would be to be able to use different colors in the synoptic tables, to emphasize the elements which are identical, those which are different, those shared by the three Gospels, those shared by only two. However, for obvious reasons of economy, in this Introduction the tables will be in black and white[13]. This is not an inconvenience: on the contrary! To leave the reader to color the synoptical tables themselves is to give part of the work to the reader—it will be to the reader's profit to «manipulate» the text, to work on it, just as one works with clay.

Rather than colors, in this work we have used different typographical styles: Roman, italic, bold, small capitals and capitals, in different combinations, as well as different type faces (Times, Arial, Bodoni). This will be our initial contribution to improving the synopses[14].

12 BOISMARD M.-É. - LAMOUILLE A., *Synopsis*, I, p. XI. The «colon» (plural «cola») or «stich» is what I call a «member», or the smallest unit of textual organization (for example, «My soul glorifies the Lord» is one member, «my spirit exults in God my savior» is another); so «comma» (plural «commata») is a shorter unit than a «colon», a syntagma (which would be «in God my savior»). The Ancients wrote *per cola et commata*, that is, a colon or a comma per line.

13 In teaching one can use colors (on overhead slides or PowerPoint); the colors are a very valuable aid for students. To improve visilbity it is best to put the elements shared by two Gospels in bold; and to underline the material shared by the three Gospels, as well as putting them in small capitals (see www.retoricabiblicaesemitica.org, Collections spécialisées, Rhétorique sémitique, *Une nouvelle introduction aux évangiles synoptiques*).

14 See the systems used for the synoptic tables which follow one another: Matt-Mark, 63; Matt-Mark-Luke, 64.

2.1. *A note on the importance of writing the biblical text*

Right at the start, we need to emphasize the importance of writing the biblical text in one's own hand. This cannot be put better than in these lines from Jewish tradition:

> The tradition of the sages of Israel says: «Every man of Israel has the duty to acquire a scroll of the Torah; *and if he writes it himself, he is worthy of praise.* Did not our sages say: *if he has written it himself, it is as though he had received it on Sinai?* If he cannot, he must acquire it from someone who has written it. This is how our sages interpret the verse: «Now write down this song which you must use; teach it to the sons of Israel»[15]: write down the Torah in which this song is found»[16].

Of course, this is not a primary-school exercise of re-writing the biblical text in different colors! But the greatest saints were not ashamed to do this, and with great care. Here is what St Ignatius of Loyola told his secretary: wounded at Pamplona, he recovered in his family castle, where he read the *Vita Christi* and the life of the saints.

> As he very much liked those books, the idea came to him to note down some of the more essential things from the life of Christ and the saints; so he set himself very diligently *to write a book* (because he was now beginning to be up and about the house a bit) with red ink for the words of Christ, blue ink for those of Our Lady, on polished and lined paper, in a good hand because he was a very fine penman[17]. Part of the time he spent in writing and part in prayer[18].

Re-writing the biblical text is one of the most important stages in rhetorical analysis. A «re-writing» which is done well is, without doubt, the best way of making the composition of a text visible. Above all, it enables the person doing it to embody the biblical text. It is good if the text is entered with the eyes, better still if it is with the ears, but best if it is with the hands. This last type of contact is close still, like a caress or a kiss:

15 Deut 31:19.
16 *Sefer Ha-Hinukh*, 508-509 (my emphasis); see MEYNET R., *Études sur la traduction et l'interprétation de la Bible*, 12.
17 «This [book] had nearly 300 pages, all written, quarto size» (marginal note of Gonçalvez de Camara, who wrote Ignatius' memoirs).
18 LOYOLA I. (of), *A Pilgrim's Testament*, 11.

See where he stands behind our wall
He looks in at the window, he peers through the lattice.
My Beloved lifts up his voice, he says to me,
«Come then, my love, my lovely one, come» (Song 2:9-10).

I found him whom my heart loves, I held him fast,
nor would I let him go till I had brought him
into my mother's house, into the room of her who conceived me (Song 3:4).

His left arm is under my head
his right embraces me (Song 2:6).

Anyone who is happy to read the book will be «the bridegroom's friend, who stands there and listens, is glad when he hears the bridegroom's voice» (John 3:29); anyone who writes it will be like the bridegroom: «The bride is only for the bridegroom» (*Ibid.*).

c. «DIACHRONIC» WORK

We must start with an observation of the facts[19]. The typographical system used in this table is explained on p. 64.

Matt 20:29-34	Mark 10:46b-52	Luke 18:35-43
29 *And while* they *were leaving* *from* JERICHO, followed him A *numerous* CROWD.	46b *And while* he *was leaving* *from* JERICHO and his disciples and A *considerable* CROWD,	35 Now it happened that, while he was approaching JERICHO,
	the son of Timaeus, Bartimaeus,	
30 And behold TWO BLIND MEN SEATED ALONG THE STREET.	(a) BLIND *beggar* SEATED ALONG THE STREET.	that a BLIND MAN WAS SEATED ALONG THE STREET *begging*.
HEARING *that*	47 And hearing *that*	36 Now HEARING A CROWD passing by, he asked what this could be. 37 They told him that
JESUS *was passing*, *they cried out* SAYING: «HAVE MERCY ON us, [Lord] SON OF DAVID!».	it was JESUS **the Nazarene**, he began *to cry out* and to say: «SON OF DAVID **Jesus**, HAVE MERCY ON **me**!».	JESUS **the Nazorean** *was coming*. 38 And he called out SAYING: «**Jesus** SON OF DAVID HAVE MERCY ON **me**!».
31 Now *the crowd* REBUKED them SO THAT *they would keep quiet*; BUT they CRIED OUT louder saying: «HAVE MERCY ON us, Lord SON OF DAVID!».	48 **And** REBUKED **him** *numerous*. SO THAT *he would keep quiet*; BUT he CRIED OUT **all the more**: «SON OF DAVID, HAVE MERCY ON **me**!».	39 **And** those who preceded REBUKED **him** SO THAT he would be silent; BUT he CRIED OUT **all the more**: «SON OF DAVID, HAVE MERCY ON **me**!».
32 *And* STOPPING JESUS *called* them	49 *And* STOPPING JESUS said: «*Call* **him**!». And they called the blind man saying to him: «Have courage, rise, he calls you».	40 Now STOPPING JESUS ordered that **he** be led to him.
	50 **Now** he, throwing his cloak, walking again, came towards Jesus.	**Now**, while he was approaching,
and *said*: «WHAT DO YOU WANT ME TO DO FOR you?». 33 THEY SAID *to him*: «***Lord***, THAT our eyes be opened!».	51 And responding to him, Jesus *said*: «WHAT DO YOU WANT FOR **you** THAT I MIGHT DO?». The blind man SAID *to him*: «Rabbunì, THAT **I might see again**!».	he asked him: 41 «WHAT DO YOU WANT FOR **you** THAT I MIGHT DO?». He SAID: «***Lord,*** THAT **I might see again**!».
34 Moved by compassion JESUS touched their eyes.	52 **And** JESUS **said to him**: «Go, **your faith has saved you**!».	42 **And** JESUS **said to him**: «See again, **your faith has saved you**!».
AND *immediately* THEY SAW AGAIN AND FOLLOWED HIM.	AND *immediately* HE SAW AGAIN AND FOLLOWED HIM on the way.	43 AND INSTANTLY HE SAW AGAIN AND FOLLOWED HIM glorifying God. And all the people seeing gave praise to God.

19 The coordinating conjunction *kai* is always translated by «and», while *de* is always «now».

There are many Matt-Mark agreements (in addition to material shared by all three):

Matt	Mark
29: While [...] they were leaving from; *numerous*	46: While [...] he was leaving from; *considerable*
30: that; they cried out	47: that; to cry out
31: *the crowd*; would keep quiet; they	48: *numerous*; would keep quiet; he
32: And; called; said	49: And; Call; 51: said
33: to him	51: to him
34: immediately	52: immediately

There are many Mark-Luke agreements:

Mark	Luke
46: **blind man (singular)**; *beggar*	35: **blind man (singular)**; *begging*[20]
47: the *Nazarene*; Jesus	37: the *Nazorean*; Jesus
48: all the more	39: all the more
51: I might see again;	41: I might see again;
your faith has saved you	your faith has saved you

Very few agreements between Matthew and Luke:

Matt	Luke
30: *passing*	37: *coming*
33: Lord	41: Lord

From a numerical point of view, Matthew is the shortest (79 words in Greek), and Mark the longest (119 words); Luke is in between with 108.

- Mark adds: «and his disciples» (46d); «the son of Timaeus, Bartimaeus» (46f); «began» (47c); and, especially «And they called the blind man» until «And he said» (49c-51a); «the blind man» (51e); «on the way» (52f).
- Luke adds his usual «While he was approaching» (35a); «a-(certain)» (35c); «a crowd passing by asked what this could be. They told him that» (36b-37a); he summarizes Mark's long addition (10:49c-51a) by «ordered that he be led to him» (40bc); in addition, he adds, at the end: «glorifying God. And all the people seeing gave praise to God» (43cde).

Before all else, the traditional questions asked by historical criticism, which follows the «historical-critical» method, need to be examined. In this introduction, we will not follow this method, but we need to have an idea of how it pro-

20 The words translated with «beggar» and «begging» are from the same root, however with a different morphological form and prefix.

ceeds, because most «academic» commentaries on the Gospels, and many specialist articles on pericopes, continue to face this way[21].

At the risk of some simplification, we will try to paint a clear picture of the historical development of research. Two main stages can be distinguished: «Form *criticism*» and «Redaction *criticism*». As these titles imply, these two schools are historical; they are therefore described as «diachronic». Their characteristics, in brief are as follows.

- *Form criticism* holds that the Evangelists were but «compilers». Small units —for example, accounts of miracles, or of Jesus' words and parables— were formed in the communities of the first generation of disciples, following the laws of popular literature (folklore), which is why they follow fixed schemas, called «forms». These brief units were then written down, brought together and juxtaposed, without real composition, in our Gospels[22].
- *Redaction criticism*, on the other hand, thinks that the Evangelists played a more important role, «redactors» or «editors». They did not only intervene to juxtapose small units which were transmitted in isolation in the oral tradition, but to bring them all together, even going as far as amending them editorially and adding whatever was necessary to assemble them[23].

1. FORM CRITICISM

1.1. *Forms*

The historical-critical method's main concern is to identify the «form» of texts: «account of healing», «moral story», «account of calling», «of mission», etc. This is why this school was called «Form criticism» (known by its German name *Formgeschichte*, which notes its geographical and cultural background).

The form is the collection of elements which, in the same order, make up the same type of conventional literary unit. It is often claimed that in traditional societies forms are full of meaning, but they are just as full of meaning in modern cultures: one need only open the newspaper to see that death notices often follow a very strict plan[24].

21 For the history of exegesis, an overview of which is necessary, see the works mentioned in the Introduction (p. 17, n. 1), par ex., LÉON-DUFOUR X., *The Gospels and the Jesus of History*, 221-293; BROWN R.E., *An Introduction to the New Testament*, 20-29.

22 For example, see, ROHDE J.W.A., *Rediscovering the Teaching of the Evangelists*, London 1968;

23 For example, see KOCH K., *The Growth of the Biblical Tradition. The Form-Critical Method*; PERRIN N., *What is Redaction Criticism*?

24 See LOHFINK G., *The Bible: now I get it!: a form-criticism handbook.*

Matt 20:29-34	Mark 10:46b-52	Luke 18:35-43
29 ***And while*** they ***were leaving*** ***from*** JERICHO, followed him *A numerous* CROWD. 30 And behold two BLIND MEN SEATED ALONG THE STREET.	46b ***And while*** he ***was leaving*** ***from*** JERICHO and his disciples and *A considerable* CROWD, the son of Timaeus, Bartimaeus, (a) BLIND ***beggar*** SEATED ALONG THE STREET.	35 Now it happened that, while he was approaching JERICHO, that a BLIND MAN WAS SEATED ALONG THE STREET ***begging***. 1.
HEARING ***that*** JESUS *was passing*, ***they cried out*** SAYING: «*HAVE MERCY ON* us, [Lord] *SON OF DAVID*!». 31 Now *the crowd* REBUKED them SO THAT ***they would keep quiet***; BUT they CRIED OUT louder saying: «*HAVE MERCY ON* us, Lord *SON OF DAVID*!».	47 And hearing ***that*** it was JESUS **the Nazarene**, he began ***to cry out*** and to say: «*SON OF DAVID* **Jesus**, *HAVE MERCY ON* **me**!». 48 **And** *the crowd* REBUKED **him**. SO THAT ***he would keep quiet***; BUT he CRIED OUT **all the more** : «*SON OF DAVID*, *HAVE MERCY ON* **me**!».	36 Now HEARING *A CROWD* passing by, he asked what this could be. 37 They told him that JESUS **the Nazorean** *was coming*. 38 And he called out SAYING: «**Jesus** *SON OF DAVID* *HAVE MERCY ON* **me**!». 39 **And** those that preceded REBUKED **him** SO THAT he would be silent; BUT he CRIED OUT **all the more**: «*SON OF DAVID*, *HAVE MERCY ON* **me**!». 2.
32 ***And*** STOPPING JESUS ***called*** them And ***said:*** «WHAT DO YOU WANT ME TO DO FOR you?». 33 THEY SAID ***to him***: «***Lord***, THAT our eyes be opened!».	49 ***And*** STOPPING JESUS said: «***Call*** **him**!». And they called the blind man saying to him: «Have courage, rise, he calls you». 50 **Now** he, throwing his cloak, walking again, came towards Jesus. 51 And responding to him, Jesus ***said***: «WHAT DO YOU WANT FOR **you** THAT I MIGHT DO?». The blind man SAID ***to him***: «Rabbunì, THAT **I might see again**!».	40 Now STOPPING JESUS ordered that **he** be led to him. **Now**, while he was approaching, he asked him: 41 «WHAT DO YOU WANT FOR **you** THAT I MIGHT DO?». He SAID: «***Lord,*** THAT **I might see again**!». 3.
34 Moved by compassion JESUS touched their eyes.	52 **And** JESUS **said to him**: «Go, **your faith has saved you**!».	42 **And** JESUS **said to him**: «See again, **your faith has saved you**!». 4.
AND ***immediately*** THEY SAW AGAIN AND FOLLOWED HIM.	AND ***immediately*** HE SAW AGAIN AND FOLLOWED HIM on the way.	43 AND INSTANTLY HE SAW AGAIN AND FOLLOWED HIM glorifying God. 5.
		And all the people seeing gave praise to God. 6.

In the account of the healing at Jericho, some see an «account of healing». According to Vittorio Fusco, this kind of account is made up of the following elements: «1. the situation of the sick person; 2. encounter with the wonder-worker (thaumaturge); 3. request; 4. word which works the healing; 5. it is noted; 6. final chorus of acclamation»[25]. There is not universal agreement on either the number or the nature of these elements of the form: for some, the general plan only has three parts: 1. *Introduction*: description of the sickness; 2. *Healing*; 3. *Testimony*.

For Rudolph Pesch, for example, the number of elements in this form is the same as for Fusco, but they are quite different in nature: 1. encounter; 2. indication of the sickness; 3. request for healing; 4. act of healing; 5. the miracle is noted; 6. demonstration[26]. The table below divides the three recensions according to the elements of the form which Fusco suggests.

Other exegetes think that the recension in the Second Gospel is not a healing account, because Mark gives the name of the sick person —which is not usual— and because the final element of the form, the final chorus of acclamation (which is only found in the Lukan recension). This would therefore be a «paradigm» (that is, a moral tale, a tale of the blind man's given as a model to the disciples); others go for a «personal legend», or for an «account of a calling»[27].

1.1.1. *Note on «form» and «literary genre»*

It is important to distinguish between «literary genre», which indicates the global content of a text (for larger units: letter, biography, gospel; for smaller units: account of calling or mission, annunciation, healing, parable, etc.) and «form», which indicates all the elements which make up a literary genre. But it should be noted that, very often, exegetes confuse the two. The study of form consists of emphasizing elements which are shared by all texts which belong to the same literary genre.

Even in recent gospel commentaries, the question of identifying the form of a pericope remains an obligatory stage in textual analysis. In his well-known commentary on the Third Gospel, published in 1981 and 1985, Joseph Fitzmyer writes, about Luke 4:31-37, the exorcism in the synagogue at Capernaum:

25 FUSCO V., «Un racconto di miracolo: la guarigione del cieco Bartimeo», 221. Rather than the traditional term «form», the author uses «structure», which risks creating some confusion.

26 See PESCH, I, 221-222.

27 See ACHTEMEIER P.J., «"And he followed him"»; STEINHAUSER M.G., «The Form of the Bartimaeus Narrative»; see FUSCO V., «Un racconto di miracolo», 224.

> This is the first of the twenty-one miracle-stories in the Lucan Gospel. [...] it has all the characteristics of the typical exorcism story: (a) The demon recognizes the exorcist and puts up a struggle; (b) the exorcist utters a threat or command; (c) the demon departs, making a scene; and (d) the spectators' reaction is recorded. These characteristics will be verified in the three other exorcism stories (8:26-39; 9:37-43; 11:14-15).

Later he adds:

> The exorcism stories are but one of the four kinds of miracle stories in this Gospel; there are, in addition, healing stories (sometimes not easily distinguished from exorcisms), resuscitations, and nature miracles.

All the volumes in the Word Biblical Commentary series which is currently being published begin with a section entitled, «Form, Structure, Setting», in which, among other specific points of the historical-critical method, form is discussed[28].

The concept of «literary genre» is also linked to the problem of historicity and the truth of the accounts. To understand a text, it is essential to know its literary genre. The creation accounts at the start of Genesis do not belong to the historical literary genre or to the scientific literary genre, but to the mythological genre, which attempts to explain what cannot be represented because it deals with the 'first things'. These are theological accounts. In the same way, the account of Jesus' temptations, located by the Evangelists before his public ministry, are not historical in the sense that we would use this adjective. They, too, are theological accounts, which does not mean that they have no historical basis[29].

1.2. *The sociological origins*

Since a form is born in a very specific situation (like the death notices we mentioned above), «Form criticism» tries to identify its *Sitz im Leben* (another German term, which has now become the norm!), the «situation in the life», the real-life context, its sociology, the precise moment in the life of the community which made the form develop. For example, it is said that the *Sitz im Leben* of a

28 For an in-depth morphological study of six kinds of miracles, with their thirty-three possible «motifs», see THEISSEN G., *The Miracle Stories of the Early Christian Tradition.*

29 See *Luc*, 180; see too MEYNET R., *La Bible*, «La Bible raconte des histoires», 65-70.

particular psalm is the harvest festival, of another, military victory, and of another, the prayer of a sick person in the Temple, etc.

In terms of the pericope of the healing of the blind man in Mark, a «baptismal context» has been mentioned, because of the invocation to the *Kyrios* («Lord») and the interrogative («What do you want?»)[30]; or an «etiological account», that is, one which has a particular interest for the city of Jericho or the character of Bartimaeus, known in such-a community, which perhaps even formed around him[31]. As these examples show, there is an attempt to explain the text according to its origin.

1.3. *Seeking the sources*

In the second volume of the French synopses, at the start of the commentary on the account of the blind man/men of Jericho, Marie-Émile Boismard writes: «What is the origin of this account? How can we explain the divergences which are present?»[32]. And this is the perfect expression of what historical-critical exegesis seeks. It is interested in the history of the formation of the text, seeking the explanation for the differences between these parallel texts in the origin of the current texts. By comparing the various gospel recensions of the same event, and by studying their similarities, their differences, and even their contradictions, it aims to identify not only which one of the three is the oldest, on which the others rely, but also to reconstruct the sources which the Evangelists would have drawn on. In other words, historical-critical exegesis tries to resolve what has been called «the Synoptic problem». Many different hypotheses have been advanced to resolve this problem[33].

In terms of the pericope under consideration, it is possible to make a few observations. St Augustine, following Papias, and all traditional exegesis after him, said that Mark was a summary of Matthew. This can be said about the whole of their work—in fact, many pericopes of Matthew are not found in the Second Gospel (for example, the infancy narratives, the parable of the workers in the vineyard, the last judgment). But, if we are looking at this pericope about the blind man/men of Jericho, the opposite must be said, for Mark is longer. Matthew is shortest, particularly in comparison to Mark, but also to Luke.

30 TRILLING W., *L'Annonce du Christ dans les évangiles synoptiques*, 150.158.

31 Voir FUSCO V., «Un racconto di miracolo», 224.

32 *Synopse des quatre évangiles en français*, II: *Commentaire*, 320.

33 See the theories on the Synoptic question in the best-known introductions such as LÉON-DUFOUR X., *The Gospels and the Jesus of History*, 169 ff.; more recently, COULOT C., «Synoptique (Le Problème)».

No reliance or dependency between Matthew and Luke can be envisaged, because, apart from the material shared by all three, they agree on very little. However, the agreements between Matthew and Mark, on the one hand, and Mark and Luke on the other, suggest that Matthew and Luke depend on Mark. This is where the «two-source» theory comes from, the most widely-known: that the First and Third Gospels are inspired by Mark, on the one hand, and by «source Q» (from the German *Quelle*, meaning «source» !) on the other, from which Matthew and Luke drew what they share but what is not found in Mark.

Let us see how one historical-critical exegete, Vernon K. Robbins, works[34]. He, clearly, chose to work on the recension which is considered the oldest, that of Mark. The starting point is always to find contradictions, incoherencies and sutures (that is, Mark's interventions to sew the sources he used to an addition) in the Gospel text; in other words, all those mistakes which enable us to see how the evangelical editing has kept traces of the various interventions along the text's formation. The passage, in its literal translation, begins:

> And they come to Jericho
> and going out he from Jericho
>   and his disciples
>   and a considerable crowd… (10:46)

The double mention of Jericho —the entry into the city, followed immediately by leaving it— betrays Mark's clumsy stitching together: the present and the verb itself («come») are characteristic of Mark, who often uses them, just like the participle (in the genitive absolute) «going out» preceded by «and» (*kai*). It is therefore clear that Mark has worked on the primitive text, because he wished to set the scene in Jericho, even though one can think that, in its pre-history, this account had some link to the city. But there is still something strange —after the participial clause «and going out he from Jericho», two other subjects are added, «and his disciples and a considerable crowd». This grammatical construction is perfectly correct in Greek, but it is typical of Mark to introduce the disciples into many of the scenes, a characteristic which will be ignored by Matthew and Luke. This, too, is redactional, that is, added by Mark to his source, in which neither disciples nor crowd are mentioned. The end of v.46, «the son of Timaeus,

34 ROBBINS V.K., «The Healing of Blind Bartimaeus».

Bartimaeus, a blind beggar, was sitting at the road-side», which the account proper begins with, has nothing typically Markan, but is considered to have an undeniable «secondary» characteristic. There are also other incongruities in the rest of the account, like the tension between the titles the blind man gives Jesus: «Rabbuni» in 51 and «son of David» in 47 and 48; like the fact that the healing itself is centered on the blind man and Jesus, without any final acclamation from the crowd, which played an important role up until then. This is why vv. 47-49 are also considered to be secondary, dependant on the fact that the crowd was introduced at the start, while the rest only mentions the blind man and Jesus.

Following this, Robbins believes he can identify at least two stages of the text earlier than the work of the final redactor, Mark. In the first stage, it would be a simple account of a healing, the elements of which can be seen in vv. 50-51. «It is most likely», that an anonymous blind man, outside Jericho, knowing that Jesus was passing by, called out to him, calling him «Rabbuni», and asked him «to have mercy» on him. Even though this is impossible to prove, the disciples would have been introduced at the next stage of the tradition; and this is why «it is more likely» that it was Jesus himself who called the blind man, saying: «Have courage, stand up!». After Jesus' question comes the blind man's answer and «probably» the people were amazed.

When we reach the second stage of the tradition, the blind man has been given a name and the account has become an «apophthegm», a «paradigm», that is, a «moral legend», which emphasized the blind man's faith, and was given as an example to the reader —the action of healing disappeared, replaced by Jesus' words, «Go, your faith has saved you». After this, the warm reply of the man who had been healed was introduced into the account, and, at this stage in the text's history, the intervention of the disciples and the crowd were added to draw out the difficulties which Bartimaeus had to overcome in his journey of faith.

There follows a long discussion on when the title «son of David» was introduced into the account. «Obviously» it was not in the original account. According to Robbins, *contra* others, Mark himself introduced it. There is no point giving the four reasons he puts forward to support his position; the fact is that, with his intervention, Mark sought to put the main emphasis of his account on this description of Jesus as son of David.

It is not necessary to go any further to demonstrate how this methodology proceeds[35]. The presupposition is that the original text was simple, clear, flowing smoothly with no tension. Its development has not only made it more complex, but has also left it full of incoherencies, contradictions, redactional sutures which have altered its original simplicity and ruined its logic. In other words, the history of a text is the history of its decline.

The same movement is found later in Matthew's and Luke's interventions on Mark's text, which they used as one of the two sources for their own redactions. In Fusco's analysis, already mentioned, one can clearly see how Matthew's and Luke's amendments represent a real process of loss and deterioration compared with Mark's older recension.

2. REDACTION CRITICISM

Historical criticism has its own history. It underwent an evolution which sought to correct the excesses of lacunae of Form criticism, all looking towards the origin, from the Gospel texts to go to back to the historical Jesus. «Redaction criticism» aims to reverse this trend: from the historical Jesus to the canonical Gospels. It starts from the results of earlier historical research, but focuses attention on the interventions of the various «redactors», including the final ones, that is, the Evangelists, to determine what their concerns, intentions and, eventually, their theological vision were. In its more recent developments, it is attentive to the phenomena of redaction which go beyond the pericope alone, studying the position of the pericope in its context, close and remote, and even in the work of the final redactor as a whole.

For example, Robbins' article, used previously to introduce Form criticism, is located within this school of Redaction criticism. After research on the sources, he adds two parts entitled, «The Placement of the Story in the Marcan Narrative» (236-241) and «The Function of the Bartimaeus Story in Marcan Christology» (241-243). But we will now turn to another work, a little more recent, in which its author, Earl S. Johnson Jr, follows the same methodology. In the first part (pp. 191-198) he analyzes Mark's text, to distinguish what comes from tradition from what was added by redaction; it is not helpful to use the first part, which is very similar to Robbins'. It is enough to quote what he writes before beginning his analysis of vv. 47-51: «The question about tradition and redaction in

35 In the same methodological style see, for example, JOHNSON E.S. Jr, «Mark 10:46-52: Blind Bartimaeus»; ACHTEMEIER P.J., «"And he followed him"».

these verses is a complicated one and scholars offer radically different assessments of their tradition history» (194). The second part (pp. 198-204) is specifically about Redaction criticism, entitled, «The Meaning of Mark 10:46-52 to Mark and His Church: Blindness and Sight, Faith, Salvation and Discipleship». From the start, the author states that, «Mark's interpretation of 10:46-52 and its relationship to his theme of blindness and sight is best understood by examining the position of the pericope in the gospel and the redactional emphases in the final verse» (p. 198).

In this initial statement one can see clearly that, to the study of additions and changes which the final redactor has introduced to the pericope, another work is being added—that of determining the place of the pericope in the composition of the Gospel, and the structural links which it has with other pericopes which are related to it by their literary genre and their privileged position in the Gospel's architecture. The healing at Jericho is located «at the last possible moment before the passion» (p. 198); it will, therefore, be connected to the healing of another blind man, the blind man of Bethsaida (8:22-26), which is found at the join of the two halves of the Gospel:

> Just as 8:22-26 terminated a series of pericopes in which the blindness of the disciples is graphically depicted, so the story of Bartimaeus concludes a portion of the gospel which shows that despite Jesus' patient instruction, his disciples are still unprepared for his journey to the cross (see especially 10:35-45) (p. 198).

In this short introduction it is impossible to cite all the parallels which the author establishes with the other strategic points of Mark's Gospel. However, we must emphasize the interest which he has in the Evangelist's redactional work, understood as a true work of composing the whole. Note, too, that this exegete's view is still broadly due to Form criticism; his starting point is that he considers the final verse, into which the only two themes which he takes into consideration in the rest of the article—blindness and light, faith, salvation, and being a disciple— to be a redactional addition:

> By adding 10:52b to the traditional material he found in v 52a, Mark emphasizes the relationship of faith, salvation and discipleship. An examination of his understanding of these concepts will illuminate their connection with his theme of blindness and sight and the central significance of 10:46-52 (p. 199).

Johnson's article, like Robbins' and so many others, is emblematic of Redaction criticism, which is still closely linked to the Form criticism which went before it; despite the undeniable progress which it represents, it remains fundamentally historical.

3. HISTORICAL CRITICISM

Finally, in addition to the reconstructions of the text's history, one of the aims of the historical-critical method is to establish the historical truth, according to the expression which has become classical: to establish «what really happened». In the case of this account, the problem is knowing whether Jesus healed one blind man, as Mark and Luke report, or two, as Matthew says; and whether he did so when he was leaving Jericho, as Matthew and Mark say, or when he was coming towards Jericho, as Luke has it.

As it is closer to the historical event, the oldest text is considered to be the most faithful to «what really happened»; in which case, as Mark is the oldest according to the two-source theory, the historical truth would be that Jesus healed one blind man, not two as Matthew says. The results of research into the sources confirm this. Joseph Fitzmyer writes[36]:

> Many have been the attempts across the centuries to harmonize or explain away the differences of these accounts: Three different cures of blind men; two different towns of Jericho, the Old and the New; one man, Bartimaeus, cured as Jesus entered Jericho, the other as he left. Obviously, the accounts were not composed to exercise the ingenuity of interpreters who would try to defend their historicity. The account of a cure of a blind person in the vicinity of Jericho has given rise to different literary traditions about it.

One can see how the author takes a position which favors the healing of a single blind man; and, in addition, with his generic expression «in the vicinity of Jericho», he does not commit himself to a precise moment for the historical event. Fitzmyer attributes the contradictions between the three Gospel accounts to the diversity of «literary traditions». However, he does acknowledge, even implicitly, that there was a historical event underlying each of these different traditions: «the cure of a blind person in the vicinity of Jericho».

36 *Luke*, II, 1212; see too, for example, Pesch, II, 260.

The problem of the historicity of the Gospels is not only of interest to researchers. Even if the question is now passé for many, it is one of the greatest difficulties for the average reader and the student just starting out. Can we believe what is reported in the Gospels? On what basis? How much? How do we distinguish between what really happened in Jesus' life, and what may have been added, or even invented, by tradition and the final redactors?

In terms of the pericope of the blind man or two blind men of Jericho, I shall say later how I read it, and how I deal with the problem. In an introduction such as this one, it is not possible to truly examine the historicity of the Gospels; we will have to be content with suggesting some reading[37].

4. CRITICAL ASSESSMENT

More recent exegesis no longer gives diachronic study the same importance, and quite often ignores it completely[38].

4.1. *Definition of «the historical-critical method»*

Before expressing an opinion, we must clarify exactly what is covered by what is usually called the historical-critical method. We should not refer to any particular author, but to an official text with authority.

In the well-known document of the Pontifical Biblical Commission, *The Interpretation of the Bible in the Church*[39], the historical-critical method «moves through the following steps»:

A. ***Textual criticism***, which «seeks to establish [...] a biblical text as close as possible to the original».

B. ***Linguistic and semantic analysis***, «using the knowledge derived from historical philology».

C. «***the literary critique*** endeavors then»

37 First of all, the introductory chapters of the works already mentioned, but also some other works, which deal with it in a more developped way, such as THEISSEN G. - MERZ A., *The Historical Jesus;* MEIER J.P., *A Marginal Jew: Rethinking the Historical Jesus.*

38 For example an exegete who has used the historical-critical method all his life gives this opinion in the «additional note» to one of his final articles, dealing with the passage of Bartimaeus the blind man: «Because it follows the account's unity and coherence, our synchronic analysis has not been able to discuss the hypotheses which disect the text, attributing some elements to an account which is earlier than the redaction» (DUPONT J., «L'aveugle de Jéricho (Mc 10,46-52)», *Revue Africaine de Théologie*, 181 (= *Études sur les évangiles synoptiques*, 367).

39 Vatican City 1993; the seven pages on the history, principles, description and evaluation of the method should be read (pp. 28-34).

- to individuate the beginning and the end of the textual units, the large and the small ones,
- and to verify the internal coherence of the texts[40].

The existence of doublets, of irreconcilable differences and of other indicators is a clue to the composite character of certain texts. These can then be divided into small units, the next steps being to see whether these in turn can be assigned to different source.

«Genre criticism» and «tradition criticism» are then cited, followed by (we quote again):

> Finally, redaction criticism
> - studies the modifications that these texts have undergone before being fixed in their final state
> - it also analyzes this final state, trying as far as possible to identify the tendencies particularly characteristic of this concluding process.

We should also quote what follows immediately:

> While the preceding steps have sought to explain the text by tracing its origin and development within a diachronic perspective, this last step concludes with a study that is synchronic: at this point the text is explained as it stands, on the basis of the mutual relationships between its diverse elements, and with an eye to its character as a message communicated by the author to his contemporaries (p. 34).

D. Finally ***«historical criticism»*** is to be applied, but only to those texts «which belong to a historical literary genre or are related to events of history» (p. 34).

4.2. *Indispensable work*

One can see clearly that, according to the Biblical Commission's document, the historical-critical document encompasses many different ways of working, from textual criticism to historical criticism. If one accepts this definition, one must adopt the statement with which it begins: «the historical-critical method is *the indispensable* method for the *scientific* study of the meaning of ancient texts» (p. 28; my emphasis).

40 In the original edition, which is in French, this gets turned on its head. A certain distinction is thus established between the two listed operations (to individuate the limits of the unity and to verify their coherence) and in the following text in which the coherencies are placed in doubt.

No exegete can do without «textual criticism» (a.), nor «linguistic and semantic analysis» (b.); all must «determine the beginning and end of literary units, large and small» and «verify the internal coherence of the texts» (start of c.). «Synchronic work», is certainly not reserved to the historical-critical method, even though, in its later developments, «redaction criticism» gives it a certain importance. The same goes for historical criticism.

4.3. *Critique of «literary criticism»*

We must acknowledge unhesitatingly the service which historical criticism has given to exegesis. Research into the sources was born in reaction to the idea that the Gospels enabled direct access to «what really happened» in Jesus' life; earlier centuries had seen the flowering of a great number of *Lives* of Jesus ingeniously based around the Gospel accounts. Then, apart from some fundamentalists, no one thought it was possible to write a book about Jesus with critical work. The Evangelists were not seeking to write a biography of Jesus, but to announce the Good News to their contemporaries. This is why the canonical Gospels reflect the concerns of the communities in which, and for which, they were written. Everyone is now convinced that the synoptic Gospels are the final point in a long history of redaction, starting from oral traditions which were already circulating during Jesus' life (for example, see Luke 9:7: «Herod the tetrarch had heard all about what was going on»).

Among the various tasks brought together under the umbrella of the historical-critical method, the only which has been questioned, and which has been simply abandoned by many, is «literary criticism», in the restricted meaning of research into the sources or the history of the text's redaction. This is not only thought to be impossible, but also unjustified, even harmful. This opinion is not only based on the results of analysis but, above all, on the methodological presuppositions.

• *The «inconsistent results»*, and their great diversity lead to even greater perplexity. Boismard, one of the best-known representatives of literary criticism, stated this almost thirty years ago:

> If many today are skeptical when one speaks about literary criticism and research into the sources, this is for the most part because of the lack of consistency in the results obtained by those who have believed in literary criticism[41].

41 BOISMARD M.-É.- LAMOUILLE A., *La Vie des évangiles*, 115.

· *The hypothetical nature*, that is, not being scientifically proven, or at least, not supported, of both various synoptic theories —even though the majority support the two-source theory— and of reconstructions of various stages in the history of the texts. This type of study can be carried out on some literary texts whose pre-publication manuscripts have been kept; the problem for biblical texts, including the Gospels, is that we do not have any manuscript attestation earlier than the final redaction and the so-called «sources» of the Gospels are purely hypothetical.

· The many complex hypotheses on the earlier states of the text lead to great suspicion. The well-known exegete Jacques Dupont wrote about the pericope of the blind man of Jericho,

> All records have been broken by Boismard M.-É., *Synopse des quatre évangiles en français*, II. *Commentaire*, Paris 1972, 320-322. This writer is quite sure he can distinguish four stages in the history of this narrative: (1) At the start, the account of the healing of a blind man, which is the basis for both Mark 10:46-52 and its synoptic parallels, and John 9, which has kept the primitive plan better. (2) This initial account brought about the version in Document A, from which the synoptic accounts derive. (3) A series of amendments is made to this document by «intermediary Mark», to whose intervention we should attribute the insertion of 46, 48, 49a, 51-52. (4) Finally «the Evangelical Redactor» introduced the mention of the disciples into v.46, the addition of a «considerable» crowd, and the blind man's double name; he, too, added the picturesque scene in vv.49b-50 and, at v.52, the mention of the «road».

Dupont concludes, «We prefer more certain ground by keeping to the text as it is[42]».

· it is the very *presuppositions* of literary criticism which are criticized[43]. It is not only the results which leave other skeptical, but also, perhaps mostly, the principles on which the whole structure is built.

> If it were only a question of interest given to such or such a method of approaching the text of the Gospels and Acts, it would be relatively easy to reach a certain balance by measuring out research into the sources and analysis of the narratives in their cur-

42 DUPONT J., «L'aveugle de Jéricho (Mc 10,46-52)», 367.

43 Here I am re-writing what I wrote in the «Introduction' to my commentary on Luke, *L'Évangile selon saint Luc*, 1988, 8.

rent form. But the crisis seems much deeper. In fact, it is the very principles of the historical-critical method which are questioned[44].

Literary criticism is based on an inkling: it researches «anomalies», «incoherencies», «contradictions», «omissions», «clumsy turns of phrase», «lack of logic»[45] in the text, the traces of reorganization which the text has undergone in the history of its formation. Thus one reaches a dismembering of texts whose scraps are attributed to different sources. So, for example, John's Prologue has been dismantled in various ways —according to one of these analyses[46], there are four sources at the origin of the text— a primitive hymn, the Evangelist, the redactor and, finally, the editor. A summary of some formulas illustrates the method's pre-suppositions: «The thought continues perfectly between verses 1c and 3; verse 2 seems to be extraneous» (p. 10). «Verses 6-9 appear as an addition. They break the *logical* succession between verses 5 and 10» (p. 13); they «do not fit into the *logical* progression of thought» (p. 15). «As the *succession of ideas* is somewhat muddled» (p. 20), v.12c is considered to be an explanatory addition, as is v.13; but this explanation «which disrupts the economy of the hymn» is «obscure» and «clumsy» (p. 22). «The rupture which verse 15 imposes on the *natural train of thought* between verse 14 and verse 16 shows it to be an addition» (p. 23). And the same goes for vv.17-18. I have emphasized the words and expressions referring to logic, for this is the decisive point[47].

D. «SYNCHRONIC» WORK

1. RHETORICAL ANALYSIS, ONE METHOD AMONG MANY

In addition to the «historical-critical method», there are «new methods of literary analysis» and other «approaches»[48]. I have chosen one among many others, «rhetorical analysis», simply because it is the one I know well and have carried out for years. We shall see that this method comes close to «redaction criticism» in its concern to study the Gospels as works which are composed[49]. However, it

44 BOISMARD M.-É. - LAMOUILLE A., *La Vie des évangiles*, 111.
45 The list of these pejorative descriptiions is not only continued in the work cited in the previous list, but also in most works of this kind.
46 ROCHAIS G., «La formation du Prologue de Jean».
47 See my article «Analyse rhétorique du Prologue de Jean».
48 They are presented in brief in PONTIFICAL BIBLICAL COMMISSION, *The Interpretation of the Bible in the Church*, 34-43 «methods», 44-64 «approaches».
49 «Redaction criticism» was also called «composition history» (*Kompositionsgeschichte*). This name did not impose itself. Biblical rhetorical analysis studies the «composition» of texts, but without any reference to their history; it is not diachronic, but only synchronic.

must be said that biblical rhetorical analysis did not arise in historical-critical circles. Its historical origins are much earlier, going back to the late 18th century at least[50]. We should also add that it is distinguished from Redaction criticism which claims to reconstruct the text's pre-history; it is, therefore, essentially synchronic.

2. BIBLICAL RHETORIC

Rather than attributing a lack of logic to the Evangelists, Rhetorical Analysis, like other synchronic methods[51], prefers to place suspicion on criticism. It is possible, in fact, that biblical texts follow a different logic to the logic in which modern readers have been trained. The anomalies, incoherencies, breaks in the normal progression of thought, could also be opinions brought to bear by our Western logic. What if there were another way of expression and composition? A biblical rhetoric, whose canons would be different from those of modern rhetoric, inherited from classic Greece and Rome? My basic thesis is that there is a biblical and wider Semitic rhetoric—and, therefore, a logic— which is very different from classical rhetoric; and that even the texts of the New Testament, for all that they were directly written in Greek (so that they could be understood in their world), are more dependent on this Semitic rhetoric than on Greco-Latin rhetoric.

3. BIBLICAL RHETORICAL ANALYSIS IS NOT A METHOD

The Biblical Commission's document presents rhetorical analysis as «a method»; and I did the same for a long time. Now, however, I would rather say that it represents one of the many «tasks» of exegetical work. In this introduction it is rhetorical analysis which we will use, but it will not be the only tool which we use on the text. We will not systematically use textual criticism, grammatical analysis, or lexicographical research, even though we will, when necessary, stop at a particularly pertinent point. However, after the rhetorical analysis of each passage, we will turn to the «synoptic comparison», and then to what we call the «biblical context», ending with a theological and spiritual «interpretation» of the text[52].

50 I have traced this history in *Rhetorical Analysis*, 43-166; I return to this history, abridging it slightly, in *Traité de rhétorique biblique*, 31-110.

51 Particularly the analysis of the narrative. See the great classic, ALTER R., *The Art of Biblical Narrative*, 11-36, in which the author shows, in a masterly way, how the episode of Judas and Tamar (Gen 38) is not a strange body which interrupts the story of Joseph, but is one with it.

52 To go further into the links between these different tasks, see my *Traité de rhétorique biblique*.

4. COMPARING THE COMPOSITIONS

Form criticism reduced all the accounts of the healing to a single general plan (see the synoptic table, p. 48). Now, each healing account is different from all the others, just as a person is totally unique. It is, of course, important to recognize the person as belonging to the «human race» (not only to the «animal kingdom»), but one cannot limit oneself to this first stage; we must identify the individual, that is, draw out what differentiates them from the rest. One might say that, with rhetorical analysis, we are completing *the work of Form* with *the work of the composition* specific to each account.

One of the limits of the synoptic work which we have carried out until now on the account of the healing at Jericho is that it only takes into consideration the, as it were, horizontal relationship between the texts—we have only compared the content of the texts in an «atomic» way, that is, considering the similarities and differences of each verse. Already at the level of the pericope, rhetorical analysis is interested in their «composition», and the coherence of their architecture. Synoptic study therefore also has to compare the different compositions, that is, the particular way in which each of the first three Gospels has organized, or constructed, its account.

5. A NEW WAY OF CARRYING OUT A SYNOPTIC COMPARISON

Our synoptic comparison will unfold in two stages.

- for the first recension examined (usually Matthew's) we will make no synoptic comparison. The reason for this is quite simple—a passage of the Gospel can be studied in itself, without any synoptic comparison, as it can for so many other biblical texts which do not have parallels.
- the first synoptic comparison will be carried out after the analysis of the composition of the second recension (usually Mark's). The kind of synopsis we will carry out *between the two recensions* will enable us to emphasize not only the similarities and differences in the detail between the syntagmas, but also the similarities and differences in composition. The typographical system used is as follows:

Identical Elements	Minion		
· in identical position	SMALL CAPITALS		
· in different positions	*SMALL CAPITALS*		*ITALIC*[53]
Different Elements	Minion		
· in identical position	lower-case		
· in different positions	*lower-case*		*italic*
Proper to the First Gospel	**lower-case**	**bold**	
Proper to the Second Gospel	***lower-case***	***bold***	***italic***

· the second comparison will be carried out following the study of the composition of the third recension and will take *all three Synoptics* into account, still with the same aim—to emphasize the specific composition of each recension, in addition to the similarities and differences of syntagmas. We will use the following typographical code:

Common to Matthew, Mark, Luke	Times New Roman		
· identical in the same order	SMALL CAPITALS		
· identical, different order	*SMALL CAPITALS*	*ITALICS*	
Common to Mark and Matthew	Times New Roman		
· identical	***lower-case***	***bold***	***italic***
· synonyms	*lower-case*		*italic*
Common to Mark and Luke	Bodoni Mt Condensed		
· identical	**lower-case**	**bold**	
· synonyms	*lower-case*		*italic*
Common to Matthew and Luke	Arial		
· identical	***lower-case***	***bold***	***italic***
· synonyms	*lower-case*		*italic*
Proper to each	Arial Narrow		
	lower-case Roman		

53 When there are too many identical elements in different positions, it is possible, for improved visibility to distinguish two groups—one in Times New Roman, the other in Bodoni.

Chapter 1

The passage itself

We saw in the Introduction how the historical-critical method deals with the account of the healing at Jericho. Let us now return to the study of this same passage, but from the point of view of rhetorical analysis. We really need to uncover the composition of each of the three recensions of the account so that we can then compare not only the details, but their architecture.

The reader who is not yet accustomed to rhetorical analysis will probably be disorientated to start with. As with any other technique, a certain effort and a minimum of patience are required. Rhetorical analysis is not complicated; it is within everyone's reach. However, it does require some care. A methodological introduction is not essential, because, just as with computers, we learn by doing it.

Some people wish to harvest the fruit of interpretation immediately. It is of course possible to leave the first three sections, the precise analysis of the text's «composition», the «synoptic comparison» and the «biblical context», to one side, and to read only the final section, «Interpretation». Is the meaning not the most important of all? This is undeniable—to limit ourselves to the technique would be quite perverse. It would not even be scholarly, for we would not be respecting the very object of our study, that is, the biblical text, whose function is to transmit a message, and, even more, a call to follow and a definitive call to conversion.

However, the interpretations of the biblical text which are offered here are, above all, the fruit of academic work which is inspired by the procedures of structural linguistics. To really take advantage of this work, and to truly taste its fruits, it is necessary to go back over the various steps of the discovery. To take the text's form seriously is to respect materiality, in other words, the body in which the Word took flesh.

This chapter will not only look at the account of the healing at Jericho, but also the account of the calling of the rich man. We will see the reasons for this choice in due course. We could have followed a chronological order, giving the oldest Gospel priority over the others, in which case we would have had to choose among the many hypotheses about the genesis of the Gospels[1]. It is legitimate to prefer more sure ground, and this is why we will begin with the first Gospel according to the canonical order which the Church has chosen to follow. It also happens that the account in Matthew is the shortest, and its composition the simplest.

1 According to www.ntgateway.com, these are no fewer than 1,488...!

A. THE HEALING AT JERICHO

1. THE HEALING OF TWO BLIND MEN IN MATTHEW (MATT 20:29-34)

COMPOSITION

+ [29] And while they were leaving from Jericho,		**FOLLOWED** him	a **crowd** numerous;
+ [30] and behold	two ***BLIND-MEN***	***SEATED***	along the way.

: Hearing		that **Jesus WAS PASSING BY**,	
-	*they cried out*	*saying*:	
. «HAVE MERCY ON US,		[LORD,]	son of David!».

: [31] And the **crowd** rebuked them		so that they would be silent,	
- but the more	*they cried out*	*saying*:	
. «HAVE MERCY ON US,		LORD,	son of David!».

= [32] And, **STOPPING**,		**Jesus** called them	and *said*:
. «What do you want		THAT I MAY DO FOR YOU?».	
= [33]			They *say* to him:
. «LORD,		THAT MAY BE OPENED	the eyes of us».

+ [34] Then in mercy,		**Jesus** touched	the eyes of them
+ and immediately	THEY SAW AGAIN	and **FOLLOWED** him.	

At the outside are descriptions of the initial situation (29-30a) and the final situation (34). The first part has two bimember segments: the first (29) introduces two groups of «characters», Jesus and his disciples[2] in the first member, and the crowd in the second; the following segment (30a) introduces the other two characters, the two blind men. Note the difference between the two groups —the first groups are walking, «leaving from» and «following»[3], while the blind men are «seated»[4]. — The last part (34) is also made up of two bimember segments, with a verb in each member. The first segment tells us what Jesus does, and the second tells us what the blind men do. — Between these two parts, note, in par-

2 According to the previous context, the plural subject of the first verb, «were leaving», includes Jesus and the Twelve.

3 This verb can also be translated as «followed» (as in the synoptic table, 00); *akoloutheō* does not exactly mean «follow», but «accompany», «walk with» (see BALMARY M., *La divine origine*, Chap. IX, «Un Messie à ne pas suivre», 291-319).

4 A punctuation question: most editions and translations give the whole of v.30 as a single phrase: «And behold, two blind men sitting by the road, when they heard that Jesus was passing by, cried out…». The division suggested here is gramatically possible; other examples of «Behold + participle or noun» making a single phrase include Matt 3:17: «And behold a voice from the heavens, saying: "This is my beloved Son, in whom I am well-pleased"»; 4:1 «Then Jesus…»; 12:10: «And behold a man having a withered hand. And they asked him, saying…»; see too 7:4; 12:41,42; 17:5. The text's composition, in four very regular parts, led to the choosing of this punctuation.

ticular, the opposition between the second members: while at the start the two men are «blind» and «seated», at the end «they saw again» and «followed» Jesus. The final verb refers back to the verb in the first segment of the first part (29)[5]; the two blind men are now part of the one group of those who accompany Jesus, with the Twelve and the crowd.

The second part (30b-31) has two parallel pieces: the blind men's two requests (30d.31c) are identical[6] and act as «final terms»; the last members of the first segments re-use the same verbal syntagmas, «cried out saying». The formal links between the first members (30b.31a) are less obvious, but note the crowd's intervention, trying to stop the encounter between the blind men and Jesus; note too that the first verb of the first member, «hearing» and the final verb of the other segment, «be silent», belong to the same semantic field: «to hear» brings the ears into play, while «to be silent» uses the mouth.

The third part (32-33) also has two pieces: Jesus' question (32) and the blind men's response (33). Note the common phenomenon of abbreviation: the first segment of the first piece is a bimember (32a), while the first segment of the second piece (33a) is unimember.

We have already noted the links between the outer parts; — the three occurrences of the name «Jesus» fulfill the role of initial terms for the last three parts (30b.32a.34a); — the two (Greek) synonyms translated by «eyes» act as median terms between the last two parts (33b.34a); — «have mercy», twice in the second part, and «to do» in the first segment of the third part (32b) are general verbs; the meaning of these verbs will only be explained at the end of the third part (33b); — the titles which the blind men give to Jesus change: in the third part, only «Lord» remains (30d); many manuscripts do not have the first occurrence of «Lord» (30d) and this moral could be in the original: the insistence of the blind men's second cry («but the more they cried out») could be emphasized by the repetition of the vocative («Lord, son of David» in 31c after «son of David» alone in 30d). «Lord» is stronger because the Greek word *kyrios* (which we keep in the *Kyrie eleison*) is the word the Septuagint uses to render the divine name «Yhwh» (pronounced *Adonai*); — finally, «stopping» at the start of the third part

5 In the traditional terminology of exegesis, these two occurrences of «follow» are called «inclusio», because they mark the outer limits of a literary unit; I prefer «outer terms», because this name correlates to my system of «initial terms», «final terms», «central terms» and «median terms» (see *Traité*, 219-221; 269-278).

6 For the choice of the textual variant, see METZGER B.M., *A Textual Commentary on the Greek New Testament*, 43.

(32a) is opposed to «passing by» at the start of the second part (30b); note the inversion between the first half of the passage, where Jesus is walking and the blind men are seated (29-31) and the second half, where Jesus stops and the blind men begin walking (32-34).

BIBLICAL CONTEXT[7]

The blind and the lame in the Old Testament

In the Old Testament, the blind and the lame often go together. The two disabilities are linked—unable to see the way, the blind cannot walk without help (see Ps 26:3: «for your loving kindness is before *my eyes* and I *have walked* in your truth»; see too Ps 18:28; 32:8; 116:8).

Blind or lame animals could not be offered as a sacrifice to the Lord (Deut 15:21; Mal 1:8); similarly, the blind and the lame could not offer the sacrifice (Lev 21:18), they could not even enter the Temple (2 Sam 5:8). But Job says, «I was eyes to the blind, and feet to the lame» (Job 29:15); thus he does as the Lord does, guiding the blind on the «path» (Isa 42:16); «The Lord opens the eyes of the blind, the Lord raises up those who are bowed down» (Ps 146:8).

+ 5 Then	shall be opened	the eyes	*OF THE BLIND*
– and	the ears	*OF THE DEAF*	shall be unclosed.
+ 6 Then	shall leap	like a deer	THE CRIPPLE,
– and	shall sing	the tongue	*OF THE MUTE.*

The blind man (5a) is lame (6a) because he cannot see the way; the deaf man (5b) is dumb (6b) because he does not hear.

Blind and lame people healed by Jesus in the Temple (Matt 21:14)

When Jesus went into the Temple, Matthew mentions his final healings, again of «blind and lame people» (note the repetition of «son of David», as at Jericho):

7 This process or stage of exegetical work is also known as «intertextuality». See *Traité*, Ch. 7: «L'intertexte», 375-415; Ch. 12: «Intertexte et interprétation», 591-621; see too MARGUERAT D. - CURTIS A., ed., *Intertextualités. La Bible en écho*; some recent articles in LEMAIRE A. - SÆBØ M., *Congress Volume. Oslo 1998*.

[14] The *blind and lame* approached him in the Temple and he healed them. [15] But the high priest and the scribes, seeing the wonderful things that he was doing and the children who were acclaiming in the temple: «Hosanna to the *son of David*,» were indignant [16] and they said to him: «Don't you hear what they say?». Jesus answers them: «Yes, have you never read: "From the mouth of the children and sucklings you have brought praise?"» (Matt 21:14-16).

The specific nature of the healing of the two blind men of Jericho

Matt 21:14 mentions collective healings (as at the start of Jesus' ministry in 4:23-24; see too 9:35; 15:29-31). The final personal healing of the first Gospel, just before the entry to Jerusalem, is the opposite of the healing of the two blind men of Jericho, which is also the only time when those who have been cured follow Jesus (34b).

INTERPRETATION

A limited weakness

The two blind men could not walk, due to their blindness, and stayed sitting at the side of the road (30a); they are the exact opposite of the group which leaves Jericho following Jesus on his way (29). However, they were neither deaf nor dumb: they hear Jesus passing by (30b), they hear people talking about him, and they cry out insistently (30c.31b), despite the threats from the crowd, who wish to silence them (31a). The crowd seeks to marginalize them completely, closing them up in total disability. They cannot, of course, stop them from hearing, but they do not want them to speak. Jesus supports the desire they expressed when they used what was still healthy in them: hearing when he calls them (32a), the word when he invites them to express their request precisely (32b).

Testing desire and faith

Matthew does not say why the crowd wished to reduce the blind men to silence. Although the crowd threatened them, they seem to support Jesus and not want him to be disturbed. It is likely that they interpreted the blind men's request according to their daily experience: if a blind man was seated «at the side of the road» and not elsewhere, at home, for example, it was because he hoped that those passing by would give him alms. This interpretation is not surprising; what is surprising, however, is Jesus' question: «What do you want me to do for you?». What can a blind man, sitting at the side of the road, ask for, apart from some small change? Jesus thus puts their request, and their faith in him, to the test. What is their deepest desire, which goes beyond their daily needs? And the response to Jesus' surprising question is even more surprising: they wish to see, that is, to change their lives, radically. Even more, in their request they acknowledge that Jesus has the unheard-of power to restore sight to the blind. It was known that the king, whom the blind men twice call «son of David» (30d.31c) had healing powers[8], but it was also known that he had received them from the only one who deserved to be called by the name of «Lord» (33b).

A total healing

As soon as Jesus touched their eyes, the two blind men saw again (34); they could now see the path, and walk without difficulty, and without help. However, Matthew not only says that they walked, but that they «followed him»; as with the paralytic, (Matt 9:1-8), he could have said that they went home. Their healing was total, but it could have been, as it were, only a healing of the body. «Following» Jesus, like the crowd and the Twelve, they became his disciples in some way, that is, people who have left everything to join the Lord. Their whole being, body and spirit, is now healed: they are saved. They are like Saul at Damascus, whom Ananias laid hands on so that he would recover his sight; having received baptism, he became a disciple of Jesus' (Acts 9)[9].

8 See, for example, Hagner, II, 587 (Bibliography, 584). The kings of France were reputed to be able to heal scrofula: they laid their hands on the sick, saying, «The king touches you, may God heal you!». (*Dictionnaire d'histoire de France Perrin*, 335).

9 The current rite of baptism permits, *ad libitum*, the «Ephata» («Open») gesture for the eyes and mouth (see Mark 7:32-35). In antiquity a rite of opening the eyes at the start of the catechumenate was known (see BAREILLE G., «Catéchuménat»). Baptism was called «illumination» (*phōtismos*); among others, JUSTIN, in the second century, wrote: «And this washing is called *illumination*, as those who learn these things are illuminated in the mind. And he who is *illuminated* is washed in the name of Jesus Christ, who was crucified under Pontius Pilate, and in the name of the Holy Spirit, who through the prophets foretold all things about Jesus» (my emphasis; *Apologies*, First Apology, par. 61, 67).

2. THE HEALING OF THE BLIND MAN IN MARK (MARK 10:46B-52)

COMPOSITION

The Markan «addition» of 49-50 has the effect of making his account not a parallel construction, as in Matthew, but a concentric construction. The passage has five parts.—The outer parts (46b-e and 52c) match; the final part has a bimember segment which is opposed to the last member of the first part. The two occurrences of «the way» (46d.52c) act as final terms.—The second part (47-48) has the same parallel composition as the corresponding part in Matthew (20:30b-31; see p. 68). The penultimate part (51-52b) has three segments which report the dialogue between Jesus and the blind man.—The central part (49-50; only in Mark) is a concentric composition. The first segment reports Jesus' action and the last segment (50) reports the blind man's action: he «came to» the one who has had him «called». In the center are the crowd's words and actions; the central verb, «rise»[10], is opposed to «was seated» at the start (46e) and introduces «walking again» in 50 and «followed» at the end in 52c); note that, with the same prefix, *ana-*, «walking again»[11] introduces «see again»[12] in the last part (end of the first segment, start of the end of the central segment) recalling not only the two occurrences of «cry out» in the previous part, but also «asking» in the first part (46e).

10 S. Légasse writes: «we would usually see [the first term] followed by the third verb of the phrase, since the encouragement is given because Jesus, through the intermediary of his escort, calls the blind man. Finally, normally the order to rise would come, followed by the movement which corresponds to it. Mark does not always write in order.» (*Marc*, 650). This is a typically western view: he is comparing biblical texts, which belong to Semitic culture, against Greco-Latin rhetoric. «The order» which Mark follows emphasises the verb «rise», at the center of the construction, one of the two verbs of the resurrection (*anistēmi*, *egeirō*); this order is thus relevant and logical, even though it is different to our own.

11 *Anapēdaō* is a *hapax legomenon* in the NT, so it needs to be treated with care.

12 The translation of *ana-blepō* by «see again» does not imply that the blind man had been able to see before he became blind. Only John mentions the man born blind (John 9); the synoptics to not say whether the blind man or the two blind men were blind from birth or if they had become blind following an accident or illness (such as trachoma, for example, which is still common in hot countries). This point is not relevant.

+ 46b And while **HE WAS LEAVING** from Jericho,
. and **his disciples** **and a crowd considerable**,

+ the son of Timaeus, Bartimaeus,
. a *BLIND-MAN asking*(for alms) **WAS SEATED** along the *WAY*.

:: 47 And hearing that Jesus the Nazarene it was,
– he started to *cry out* and to say:
. «Son of David, Jesus, **HAVE MERCY ON ME!**».

:: 48 And rebuked him **many** so that he would be silent,
– but he all the more *cried out*:
. «Son of David, **HAVE MERCY ON ME!**».

49 And, stopping, Jesus said: «*Call him*».
And *they called THE BLIND-MAN* saying to him: «Have courage, **RISE**, *he calls* you».
50 And abandoning his mantle, **WALKING AGAIN**, he came to Jesus.

= 51 And answering to him, Jesus *said*:
. «What do you want **THAT FOR YOU I MAY DO?**».
= the blind-man *said to him*:
. «Rabbunì, that I MAY SEE AGAIN!».
= 52 And Jesus *said to him:*
. «Go, your faith **HAS SAVED YOU!**».

. And immediately HE SAW AGAIN and **WAS FOLLOWING HIM** on the *WAY*.

The links between the parts: — «many» in 48a refers to those who accompany Jesus, «his disciples» and «a considerable crowd» (46c); — «Rabbuni» (51d) can be paralleled with the name of the blind man, «son of Timeaus, Bartimaeus», a name repeated as though to emphasize its importance — in effect, the rabbi, or teacher, is considered to be the father of his disciple; — note the two occurrences of Jesus in the second part, in the third part and in the fourth part (47a.47c; 49a.50; 51a.52a). The name «Jesus» means «savior»; and the penultimate part ends with the verb «to save» (52b) whose subject is not «Jesus», but the blind man's «faith».

The link between «blind man» and «seated» at the start, and between «saw again» and «following him» at the end, is the same as in Matthew (see 70).

The mantle

The «mantle» was a piece of clothing which was wide at the top, sleeveless, not sewn up, with an opening for the head (like the chasuble which priests wear now). It protected one from the cold and, at night, acted as a bed-cover or a sleeping bag (see Exod 22:25-26; Deut 24:10-13). The seated beggar could therefore receive alms in the front part of the mantle stretched out over his knees.

The verb *apoballō*, translated by «abandon» (50), is a *hapax legomenon* in Mark; it is only found in one other place in the NT, at Heb 10:35:

> [34] In fact, you took part at the sufferings of the prisoners and you accepted with joy of being stripped of your substance, knowing of possessing better and durable ones. [35] Therefore *do not abandon* your confidence, to which a great reward is reserved. (Heb 10:34-35).

Verse 34 permits our interpretation that, in «abandoning his mantle», Bartimaeus «stripped himself of his substance» to «possess a better and more durable wealth».

The image which Paul uses to talk about conversion may also be relevant in this context: «to strip off the old man (Col 3:9-10; Eph 4:20-24), to «put on Christ» (Rom 13:14). This radical conversion takes place through baptism: «For you are all sons of God, through faith in Christ Jesus» (Gal 3:27)[13].

The disciple is his master's son

In every Ancient Near Eastern tradition, the disciple considers and calls his master father, and the master considers his disciple to be his son, and calls him son. When in the book of Proverbs the author addresses his «son», we have to understand that this son is not his child in the flesh, but his disciple (see Prov 1:8, 10, 15; 2:1; 3:1; and especially 4:1ff, 20ff, etc.).

13 Recall that some exegetes have wondered about a baptismal context for the account of the blind man (see p. 51).

«We shall do and we shall obey» (Exod 24:7)

The NJB translates the account of the concluding of the alliance between the Lord and his people in Exod 24 as follows:

> [3] Moses went and told the people all Yhwh's words and all the laws, and all the people answered with one voice: «*All the words Yhwh has spoken, we will carry out!*». [4] Moses put all Yhwh's words into writing, and early next morning he built an altar at the foot of the mountain, with twelve standing-stones for the twelve tribes of Israel. [5] Then he sent certain young Israelites to offer burnt offerings and sacrifice bullocks to Yhwh as communion sacrifices. [6] Moses then took half the blood and put it into basins, and the other half he sprinkled on the altar. [7] Then, taking the Book of the Covenant, he read it to the listening people, who then said: « *We shall do everything that Yhwh has said, we shall obey!*». [8] Moses then took the blood and sprinkled it over the people, saying: «This is the blood of the covenant which Yhwh has made with you, entailing all these stipulations».

First of all, we need to correct the translation, but only on the point which is relevant to us —the final verb of v.3 is translated by «to carry out» and the penultimate verb in v.7 is translated by «to do», although in Hebrew these are the same verbs. Let us rewrite the literal translation of the words of the people:

[3] All the words	that the LORD	spoke	we will do.
[7] All	that the LORD	spoke	we will do and we will listen.

The final expression is surprising. In the modern western way of thinking, at least, hearing comes before action; we have to understand before we can carry out. It is clear that the translations try to resolve this difficulty[14]. For example, the Italian translation uses two synonyms, «we will do it and we will carry it out». With «we will do and we will obey» the NJB has found another way around the problem[15]. To change the text is not the best solution if we wish to understand. My teacher used to say, «Erasing the bumps in the text is the best way of making it slip through your hands». Jewish tradition, on the other hand, has re-

14 In French, only the Osty translation follows the literal translation, «"we will carry it out and we will hear it"».

15 It is true that «to obey» comes from the Latin *ob-audire*, that is «to listen» preceded by a prefix; however, the meaning of «obey» is rather different from «listen».

flected greatly on the meaning of this strangeness[16], often commenting on the surprising order of the two verbs, the priority of doing over listening or understanding, the priority of praxis over theory; in summary, we do not really understand what it is we do.

We find a similar expression in Ps 103:20. Let us look at the translation in the NJB:

Bless the LORD, all his angels,	mighty warriors who fulfill his commands, attentive to the sound of his words.

And now at a literal translation:

Bless the LORD, all his messengers	servants who *do* his will i*n order to listen* to the sound of his word.

The same verbs, «to do» and then «to listen», appear in the same order; in addition, the expression «in order to» indicates that the listening takes place through the doing. «The verse on which our study depends must be understood as: *We will do in order to understand*»[17].

16 See, for example, PAPERON B., «Na'assé ve-nichma'», «Nous ferons et nous entendrons», 101-109.
17 PAPERON B., «Na'assé ve-nichma'», 107.

SYNOPTIC COMPARISON (see pp. 68 and 74)

Matt 20:29-34	Mark 10:46b-52
29 AND WHILE they WERE LEAVING FROM JERICHO, **followed him** A CROWD numerous. 30 **And behold two** BLIND-MEN WERE SEATED ALONG THE WAY.	46b AND WHILE he WAS LEAVING FROM JERICHO ***and his disciples*** ***and*** A CROWD considerable, ***the son of Timaeus, Bartimaeus,*** (a) BLIND-MAN ***asking (for alms)*** WAS SEATED ALONG THE WAY.
HEARING THAT JESUS was passing by, THEY CRIED OUT SAYING: «*HAVE MERCY ON us*, [**Lord**] *SON OF DAVID*!». - - - - - - - - - - - - - - - - 31 But the crowd *REBUKED them* SO THAT THEY WOULD BE SILENT; BUT they CRIED OUT MORE **saying**: «*HAVE MERCY ON us*, **Lord** *SON OF DAVID*!».	47 ***And*** HEARING THAT JESUS ***the Nazarene*** it was, ***he started to*** CRY OUT ***and to*** SAY: «*SON OF DAVID* ***Jesus***, *HAVE MERCY ON me*!». - - - - - - - - - - - - - - - - 48 And *REBUKED* him *many*. SO THAT HE WOULD BE SILENT; BUT he ***all*** THE MORE CRIED OUT: «*SON OF DAVID*, *HAVE MERCY ON me*!».
32 AND STOPPING JESUS CALLED them AND SAID: «WHAT DO YOU WANT *THAT I MAY DO FOR* you?». - - - - - - - - - - - - - - - - 33 THEY SAID: «**Lord**, THAT may be opened our eyes!».	49 AND STOPPING JESUS ***said***: «CALL him!». ***And they called the blind-man saying to him:*** ***«Have courage, rise, he calls you».*** 50 ***And abandoning his mantle,*** ***walking again,*** ***he came to Jesus.*** 51 AND ***answering to him, Jesus*** SAID: «WHAT DO YOU WANT *FOR* you *THAT I MAY DO*?». ***The blind man*** SAID TO HIM: «***Rabbunì***, THAT I may see again!».
34 Then **in mercy** JESUS **touched their eyes.**	52 And JESUS ***said to him***: «***Go, your faith has saved you***!».
AND IMMEDIATELY THEY SAW AGAIN AND FOLLOWED HIM.	AND IMMEDIATELY HE SAW AGAIN AND WAS FOLLOWING HIM ***on the way***.

We have already noted the similarities and differences of each verse and syntagma (see p. 45); now let us compare the composition.

The passage in Matthew has four parts: the introduction (29-30b) and the conclusion (34) match; the two central parts (30c-31; 32-33) are parallel (see p. 68) and oppose the crowd, who wish to silence the blind men, to Jesus, who invites them to say what they want.

The composition of the passage in Mark, on the other hand, is concentric. The introduction (46b-i) exactly matches that in Matthew (29-30b). The conclusion, however, (52cd) only repeats the end of Matthew's conclusion (34cd); Jesus' words (52ab), only in Mark, which replace the gesture of the miracle-worker in Matthew (34a), are part of the exchange of words between the blind man and Jesus (51-52b). The second part (47-48) and the penultimate part (51-52b), like the two central parts in Matthew, oppose the crowd which wishes to silence the blind man, who continues to cry out, and Jesus, who in turn makes him talk and congratulates him. What is particular to the Markan account is found in the center of the construction, where a long part (49-50) broadly develops the short start of the third part in Matthew (32ab). Thus Mark's composition emphasizes, in the center, the role of the crowd, or, rather, its conversion after Jesus' intervention; in opposition it becomes the adjuvant to Jesus' call. The words of the people, on which the central part is focused, and particularly the central imperative, thus take on a significant emphasis.

INTERPRETATION

Everything which we said about the passage in Matthew can be repeated about Mark. The Markan «additions», particularly the central part (49-50), but also the mention of the disciples at the start (46d), just like the final difference, that is, Jesus' last word (52ab) instead of his gestures of touching the eyes of the blind men (Matt 20:34ab), all lead to a change in and broadening of interpretation. We will start from the center of the passage, which is particular to Mark.

The role of the community

For Jesus, it is not enough to call the blind man directly; he has him called (49) by those who are walking with him, the disciples and the crowd (46). This is how he reacts to the threats of those who wish to reduce Bartimaeus to silence (48). He calls them to change their behavior, inviting them to conversion. He associates them with his mission to make the one who had been seated rise up. And it is in response to their voice that the blind man, too, changes his attitude. He was seated, begging people to throw even the smallest coins into his mantle (46); he abandons his cloak, walks again, and comes to the one who has had him called (50). And Jesus acknowledges «the faith» (52) of one who has believed not only in the power of the son of David, but also in the word of the community of those who followed him. At the end, he has joined their group to follow Jesus.

Strip off the old man

«At the call of the Lord [...], nothing else matters any more, [Bartimaeus] abandons his cloak. The Samaritan woman does almost the same thing when, "putting down her water jar", she ran to the town to announce the Messiah, bringing a more living water than the water from Jacob's well (John 4:28).

For there is a presupposition of effective love, which is detachment from everything which is not the object to which we turn. In making a gift to Jesus of *her* precious nard, and by "pouring" it on him, Mary Magdalene recognizes in him *the* paradise of delights which excludes all other places of pleasure. In this gesture and its equivalents is a profession of faith (resounding in the blind man), which includes a renunciation at the same time as a conversion of the heart»[18].

Walking to see

The blind man does not walk, because he cannot see the path. However, Jesus makes him «rise» (49) and «walk again» (50) before making him «see again» (52). The natural order, to see first and then walk, is reversed. Jesus' order is the order of faith, which demands that we do before seeing, that we do to see. «We shall do everything that Yhwh has said; we shall obey» (Exod 24:7). This is not so strange, if we think about how, in human experience, we verify our relationship with the other, especially in love: the moment comes when we have to trust, take the step of agreeing, without knowing where we will be led, renouncing «knowing the other» to be able to walk alongside them. This is the way of every commitment, be it marriage or religious or priestly consecration. «Joining is an act of love, of trust»[19].

A new filiation

It is not unusual, in the Semitic world, for someone to be known as «son of so-and-so»; however, «son of so-and-so» is often preceded by the person's proper name, as in «Simon son of Jonah» for the man Jesus would later nickname Peter (Matt 16:17)[20]. In the account in Mark, the blind man is only identified by his father's name[21], and, absolutely uniquely, the name is repeated, first in Greek and then in Aramaic. This must grab our attention —for nothing is accidental in a text, and particularly not in a biblical text— the more so since only Mark gives the

18 HAULOTTE E., *Symbolique du vêtement selon la Bible*, 106-107.
19 PAPERON B., «Na'assé ve-nichma'», 102.
20 See too Mark 2:14: «Levi son of Alphaeus»; for Jesus too in Matt 1:1: «Jesus Christ son of God»
21 The only character in Mark identified in this way is «Barabbas», that is, «son of the father» in 15:7ff.

name of the blind man. Furthermore, the name which Bartimaeus gives to Jesus when he questions him is also surprising: «Rabbuni» is not used elsewhere in the Synoptics, but only once in John 20:16, when Mary recognizes the risen Jesus in the garden, having first taken him to be the gardener. The form is different from the more simple «Rabbi», which Mark uses for Judas Iscariot in the garden at Gethsemane (Mark 14:45). This is an affectionate form, like *Abba* in relation to the simple *Abī*, «my father». Mary Magdalene uses it after the resurrection of her Master, after years spent with him, and in shock and surprise. With this vocative, Bartimaeus immediately recognizes the one who, like his father, brings him to life.

2.1. A song from today

Jesus, Son of David, have mercy on me!

The blind man of Jericho was seated along the street, a beggar;
Hearing *a crowd* passing, so he questions.
R/
What is this? — It is Jesus of Nazareth who comes!
So he cries out: Son of David, have mercy on me!
R/
Those who went on before wanted him to close his mouth,
But he cried all the louder at Jesus.

SON OF DAVID, HAVE MERCY ON ME!
OPEN MY EYES, THAT I MIGHT KNOW YOU!
R/ CALL ME TO YOU, THAT I MIGHT FOLLOW YOU!
OPEN MY MOUTH, THAT I MIGHT PRAISE GOD!
SON OF DAVID, HAVE MERCY ON ME!

Jesus stops and asks him to come,
And the blind man approaches, Jesus questions him.
R/
What do you want me to do for you? — Lord, that I might see!
Then Jesus said to him: See, your faith has saved you.
R/
The blind man of Jericho saw and followed Jesus, praising God;
All the people saw this, and gave glory to God.

Brothers, the blind man saw, he knew the power of the Son of God,
The people saw, they knew the power of the Son of God.
R/
You, my brother seated in obscurity, cry out to Jesus,
He will call you to come to him; you will see and walk behind him.
R/
Brothers, Jesus has given us to know him and to follow him,
With those that he has saved, we will walk behind him to give glory to God.

The proper work of a real word is to give rise to another. The strength of a text, whether or not it is poetic, and particularly of an «inspired» text is shown in its ability to beget or «inspire» another text, like this canticle in the Sar language, which the pericope from Luke gave rise to[22] a few years ago in Chad[23].

3. THE HEALING OF THE BLIND MAN IN LUKE (LUKE 18:35-43)

COMPOSITION

+ [35] It happened as	HE	*was approaching*	to Jericho,
+ that	*A CERTAIN BLIND-MAN*	**WAS SEATED**	along the way **ASKING** (for alms).

: [36] Hearing ***a crowd*** going by,			
	– *he inquires*		
		. ***WHAT*** was	this.
- [37] They	*announced* him *that*		
		. **JESUS** **THE NAZOREAN**	comes.
- [38] He exclaimed	*saying*:		
		. «Jesus, son of David,	*have mercy on me!*».

[39] Those going before	*rebuked him*	so that	**HE MIGHT STOP SPEAKING.**
But he all the more	*cried out*:	«**SON OF DAVID**,	*have mercy on me!*».
[40] Jesus stopping	*ordered*	that	**HE MIGHT BE LED** to him.

: As he *was approaching*,			
	– *he asked him*:		
		[41] . «***WHAT*** do you want	that for you I may do?».
- He	*said*:		
		. «**LORD**,	that I MAY SEE-AGAIN!».
- [42] Jesus	*said to him*:		
		. «SEE-AGAIN,	your faith has saved you!».

+ [43] And instantly	HE SAW-AGAIN	**AND WAS FOLLOWING** him,	glorifying	GOD.
+ And ***all the people***	SEEING		**GAVE** praise to GOD.	

22 Based on my analysis of the Lukan account, published in 1981, «Au cœur du texte» (with Amon's prayer; see p. 91).

23 «In numerous Christian communities in Africa—and, among others, those of the Sar country in Chad—an anthology of Gospel songs has been established over a number of years, faithfully following the account. This form of memorizing the Gospel deserves to be encouraged» (FÉDRY J., «La composition selon la symétrie concentrique», 40; the setting of the song reproduced here is found at 42).

The passage has five parts. The outer parts (35.43) match. The two segments of the last part parallel the blind man who «saw again» with all the people who «see»; like the blind man «glorifying God», so the people «gave praise to God». The first segment of the last part (43a) is precisely opposed to the second member of the first part (35b): «saw again» is opposed to «blind man», «was following» is opposed to «was seated», and «asking (for alms)» is opposed to «glorifying God» (the opposition between «ask» and «give» is even more direct in 43b).

In the second part (36-38) the blind man deals with the crowd and tries to establish contact with Jesus; in the penultimate part (40b-42) he is «approached» and speaks with him. The first segments (36.40b-41a) end with a generic question (the first one is indirect). In the second part, the crowd's response, introducing «Jesus» as «the Nazorean» (37b) is opposed by the cry of the blind man, who calls him «son of David» (38b); in the penultimate part, Jesus' response (42b) begins with the same verb, «see-again», with which the blind man's plea ended (41c).

The central part (39-40a) is a concentric construction: the second members of the outer segments (39a.40a) are indirect-type questions; the central segment (39b) repeats the blind man's appeal from the end of the first piece (38; but without «Jesus»); this cry is thus at the center of the whole passage.

«He might stop speaking», in the central part (39a), is opposed to «asking (for alms)» in the first part (35b) and to «glorifying God»/«giving praise to God» in the final part (43a.43b). «A crowd» at the start of the second part (36) matches «all the people» at the end of the part (43b). Before the blind man «approaches» Jesus (40b), it is Jesus who «approaches» the place where the blind man is (35a).

Although the narrator only uses the pronoun «he» to describe Jesus (35a) and the crowd calls him by his place of origin, «Jesus the Nazorean» (37b), the blind man gives him the titles «son of David» (38b.39b) and «Lord» (41c). The progression is clear —in his final reply, «See again, your faith has saved you» (42b), Jesus works a significant inversion. He begins by echoing the end of the blind man's request («that I may see again»); but then he does not say «I am sorry for you» but «your faith has saved you». The subject has changed! And everything takes place as though the blind man received the title of «believer», in response to those of «son of David» and «Lord» with which he acknowledged Jesus. The list of titles continues in v. 43, with the double mention of «God». It is legitimate to acknowledge this extension of names as far as God, for the two occurrences of «God» are situated after verbs which belong to the long list of thirteen verbs, «to say» and synonyms (in italics: 36b.37a.38a.39a. 39b.40a.40c.41b. 42a), four of which immediately precede the names given to Jesus (37a, 38a, 39b et 41b).

BIBLICAL CONTEXT

Crowd and people

What we said about the Matthean and Markan accounts also applies, obviously, to the Lukan account (see pp. 70 and 75f). We should add one point on a detail which is unique to Luke: the «crowd» at the start (36) becomes «people» at the end (43b). In Luke, «the people» does not have exactly the same meaning as «the crowd»; where the latter term is neutral, implying no value judgment (e.g., the crowds which come to be baptized by John, 3:7-10), «the people» either indicates the people of Israel (Luke 1:10.17.21) or the group of those who believe.

SYNOPTIC COMPARISON (*see pp. 68, 74 and 82*)

Matt 20:29-34	Mark 10:46b-52	Luke 18:35-43
29 *And* *while* they *were leaving* *from* JERICHO, followed him *A CROWD numerous.* 30 And behold two BLIND-MEN WERE SEATED ALONG THE WAY.	46b *And* *while* he *was leaving* *from* JERICHO and his disciples and *A CROWD considerable,* the son of Timaeus, Bartimaeus, (a) BLIND-MAN *asking (for alms)* WAS SEATED ALONG THE WAY.	35 Now it happened as he was approaching to JERICHO, that a (certain) BLIND-MAN WAS SEATED ALONG THE WAY. *asking (for alms).*
HEARING *that* JESUS *was passing by,* *they cried out* SAYING: «*HAVE MERCY ON* us, [Lord] *SON OF DAVID*!».	47 And HEARING *that* JESUS **the Nazarene** it was, he started to *cry out* and to SAY: «*SON OF DAVID* **Jesus,** *HAVE MERCY ON* **me**!».	36 Now HEARING *A CROWD* going by, he inquires what this was. 37 They announced him that JESUS **the Nazorean** *is passing by.* 38 And he exclaimed SAYING: «**Jesus** *SON OF DAVID* *HAVE MERCY ON* **me**!».
31 And *the crowd* REBUKED them SO THAT *they would be silent*; BUT they CRIED OUT more saying: «*HAVE MERCY ON* us, Lord *SON OF DAVID*!».	48 **And** REBUKED **him** *many.* SO THAT *he would be silent*; BUT he **all the more** CRIED OUT: «*SON OF DAVID*, *HAVE MERCY ON* **me**!».	39 **And** those who went before REBUKED **him** SO THAT he might stop speaking; BUT he **all the more** CRIED OUT: «*SON OF DAVID*, *HAVE MERCY ON* **me**!».
32 *And* STOPPING JESUS *called* them	49 *And* STOPPING JESUS said: «*Call* **him**!». And they called the blind-man saying to him «Have-courage, rise, he calls you». 50 **Now** he, throwing his mantle, walking again, he came to Jesus.	40 Now STOPPING JESUS ordered that **he** might be led to him. **Now,** while he was approaching,
and *said*: «WHAT DO YOU WANT THAT I MAY DO for you?». 33 *They* SAY *to him*: «***Lord***, THAT our eyes may be opened!».	51 And answering him, Jesus *said*: «WHAT DO YOU WANT **for you** THAT I MAY DO?». The blind-man SAID *to him*: «Rabbuni, THAT **I may see-again**!». 52 **And** JESUS **said to him:** «Go, **your faith has saved you**!».	he asked him: 41 «WHAT DO YOU WANT **for you** THAT I MAY DO?». Now he SAID: «***Lord***, THAT **I may see-again**!». 42 **And** JESUS **said to him:** «See again, **your faith has saved you**!».
34 Then in mercy JESUS touched their eyes. AND *immediately* THEY SAW-AGAIN AND FOLLOWED HIM.	AND *immediately* HE SAW-AGAIN AND WAS FOLLOWING HIM on the way.	43 AND instantly HE SAW-AGAIN AND WAS FOLLOWING HIM glorifying God. And all the people seeing gave praise to God.

Where Matthew's passage has four parts, an introduction (29-30b), conclusion (34) and two other parallel parts (30c-31; 32-33), Luke's passage, like Mark's, is made up of five parts arranged concentrically. In its limits, Luke's introduction (35) exactly matches those in Matthew (29-30b) and Mark's (46b-j). But no mention is made in it either of the crowd, as in Matthew, or of the disciples, as in Mark. Just as in Mark, there is a single blind man, and he is a beggar, but Luke does not give his name.

Luke's conclusion (43) begins at the same point of the narrative as it does in Mark (52d); Luke adds the glorification of God by the healed blind man (43b), and in particular the people's praise (43cd). In this way, while the crowd was not mentioned in the introduction, as in Mark, its —converted— equivalent, «the people», intervene in the conclusion.

«The crowd» is only introduced at the start of the second part (36b); the blind man's indirect question follows (36c), the response is «announced» by the same crowd (37a); all these elements are absent from Mark and Matthew. On the other hand, Luke briefly summarizes the whole of the central part of Mark (49-50) with 40a-e. The result of all these differences is that, while Mark focuses his account on the intervention of those people present (probably the disciples and the crowd from the introduction in 46de), Luke emphasizes the blind man's second acclamation of the «son of David» (39ef), rejected by «those who went before him» (39abc) and encouraged by Jesus (40abc).

Note on the center of concentric constructions

Since the start of the nineteenth century it has been known that the center of a concentric composition is its focal point, the hinge, «the key-stone», or «the heart» of the text[24]. Some have used the metaphor of Russian dolls to describe this phenomenon, but it seems preferable to use a truly biblical metaphor. The *menorah*, the seven-branched candlestick which was in the Jerusalem Temple (Exod. 25:31-39; 37:17-24)[25], enables us to understand the main function of concentric compositions. The central branch of the *menorah* is what holds the other branches together. If one branch were broken, the candelabra would be incomplete and unbalanced, but it would nonetheless remain standing; however, if the central branch were removed, there would no longer be a candlestick, and it could not be used to give light. It would be reduced to a collection of separate pieces, now useless.

24 See *Traité*, 86.417.

25 On the vault of Titus' arch in Rome, can be seen the representation of the golden candelabra taken as booty by Titus, son of the Emperor Vespasian, who took Jerusalem in 70 CE.

We therefore need to always examine the center of a concentric construction with care. However, we should add that this center is very often enigmatic[26]. Identifying the center of a text does not mean that we immediately understand its meaning. If it is enigmatic, this means that its function is to invite and encourage the reader to reflect. We will have plenty of opportunity to note this, for example in the Our Father and the four sequences which will be analyzed in this volume.

We have seen what the function of the center was in the construction of the Markan passage, particularly the weight and significance of the imperative «Rise», at the center of the crowd's central words.

In the Lukan account, we might ask why he has focused on the blind man's second invocation, particularly on the repeated title, «son of David». In this case, we will only understand the importance of this center at a higher level, the level of the «sequence» in which the passage is integrated; we shall have to wait for this until Chapter 3.

INTERPRETATION

In carrying out a synoptic study, we need to try to offer an interpretation of Luke's passage which is «contrastive», that is, which emphasizes what differentiates it from the other two accounts, what is specific about the Lukan recension[27].

A triple healing

In Matthew and in Mark, the sick are not only blind but also «seated», unable to walk, because they cannot see the way. At the start of his account, Luke picks up what Mark has already added to the first Gospel, that is, that the sick man «is asking for» alms. At the end of his account, Luke adds that the healed blind man «glorified God» (43). The function of his mouth has changed—from «asking for» help from humanity, he thanks the Lord for the gift of sight received thank to Jesus' word. The request becomes a gift. The man is healed in three ways— in his eyes, in his feet, in his mouth. This blind man reflects the image of all those who are unhappy in the Psalms, whose cry of supplication, thanks to faith in the one who listens, gives way to the song of praise to his glory.

26 The center is often taken up with a question; see MEYNET R., «The Question at the Centre»; and esp. *Traité*, 417-435. A quotation is often there, too; see MEYNET R., «La citation au centre»; Traité, 436-454.

27 An interpretation which does not take account of the parallel narratives can be found in *Luc*, 712-714.

A universal healing

In Matthew the «crowd» act only as an obstacle —they seek to prevent the two blind men from disturbing Jesus. They wished to impose silence on them, to further increase their weakness, by making them, as it were, dumb in addition to being blind and lame. So Jesus intervenes: «he called them and said» (Mark 20,32). We must not interpret the Gospel by imposing on it what another person says. In Matthew Jesus does not ask the crowd to call the blind men, as he does in Mark and Luke; and we are to understand that, when he comes close to them, he questions them —this is another possible meaning of the verb translated by «call»— to ask them what they want. Whatever they want, in Mark, Jesus intervenes with those who are accompanying him to make them change their behavior —from being an obstacle, they become a help to Bartimaeus, inviting him to rise up and approach Jesus. Luke goes even further, since his account ends with a healing and a conversion which implies, in addition to the blind man healed in three ways, «all the people»; they were in fact walking with Jesus, but now they «see» him in a different way and «give praise to God». So, in an almost explicit way, the reader is implicated, called, too, to join the people not only in praise, but also in following the Lord.

A healing which goes all the way

At the start of the narrative, Jesus is not even named. He is described by a pronoun alone, a «he» (36), which is much less personal! The crowd questioned by the blind man speaks his name, adding the descriptive which expresses his human origins: «Jesus the Nazorean» (37). The blind man, on the other hand, gives him the royal title of «son of David», which can of course be interpreted as the flattery which beggars do not hesitate to use to obtain more regular alms. The fact that the crowd does not succeed in silencing the blind man, and that he starts «crying out», repeating the same title without even using the name of «Jesus», as if «Son of David» was the Lord's very name, allows us to see that it is not flattery at all, but true faith. When Jesus then has him come and asks him what he wants, the blind man calls him «Lord», a title which goes far beyond the ordinary meaning of the word. The narrative ends with the double name of «God». The healed blind man, just like the crowd which has become God's «people» together «see» God's hand in Jesus' work, they see in his person the only one who is worthy of «glory» and «praise».

The origins of love

If man's searching is called «faith» (42) when it is certain to obtain what it is seeking, the movement which leads Jesus towards the unhappy, the desire which moves God towards humanity in his misery is called «mercy» (38.39b), or, to use the concrete bodily language of the Bible, the «innards of mercy[28]». It is to Jesus' heart that the blind man's prayer is addressed, in the very center of the passage. Faith can only be in love, that other name for mercy, and love cannot resist faith; a sign that one has no object without the other, each of the characters does not name his only desire, but his partner's desire: the blind man calls on Jesus' «mercy» (38-39b), Jesus in turn recognizes «the faith» of the supplicant (42). It is faith which saves the blind man, but what can faith do without the pre-existence of love which is its foundation? It is he who is approached first (35a.40b).

3.1. *A thirty-four-century-old poem*

This prayer of a blind man to Amon, god of Thebes in Egypt, a «graffito written on a wall of the tomb on one Pairi[29]» predates the synoptic Gospels by many years—it goes back to the fourteenth century BCE.

The literary genre:

This text's literary genre is very different from that of the texts we have examined hitherto—it is a prayer, while the synoptic texts which report the healing accomplished by Jesus in Jericho are narratives, whether of healing or of calling.

Nonetheless, the theme of this prayer is very close to the theme of the gospel accounts. Of course, the one praying asks for his eyes to be healed: Amon has granted that he «see shadows» (19), he wishes to «see» once again (1-4; 19 and 21) and eventually he recovers his sight (30). But his mouth is also at stake: to pronounce the name of his god is a «sweet» thing for him (9-10). Finally, in symmet-

28 The end of the Canticle of Zecharaiah seems to be a translation, in poetic language, of the account of the blind man of Jericho, sitting in the shadows of his blindness:

By the innards of mercy of our God
In whom the rising star (which comes) from on high will visit us
To give light to those who are SEATED in the SHADOWS and the darkness of death
To guide our FEET in the PATH of peace (Luke 1:78-79).

29 BARUCQ A. - DAUMAS F., *Hymnes et Prières de l'Égypte ancienne*, 203 (a new translation with the help of A. Barucq); «Perseas»= a sacred tree of Heliopolis (see GOYON J.-C., *Rituels funéraires de l'ancienne Égypte*, 347).

rical position (23-24), his feet start to move to «follow» his god, who is «good» for him.

In the same way, the healing of the blind man of Jericho in Luke is threefold: not only does the blind man recover the use of his eyes, but also the use of his legs, to «follow» Jesus; his mouth, too, is healed, when at the end he gives glory to God, while at the start he asked for alms.

We might add the theme of searching (27), or desire, as in the third Gospel.

Note that the composition of the Egyptian text is concentric, just like so many biblical texts. In the center (17), the prayer moves from the singular of the supplicant to the only plural of the whole prayer: «Turn towards *us*». This reminds us that the Lukan account ends with the plural «people» who, like the blind man of old, see and give praise to God.

Prayer of a blind man to Amon, god of Thebes

My **heart** wants you TO SEE, **LORD OF PERSEAS,** when your *throat* brings the northern wind, 1
: you give to be satisfied, without which who could eat, 2
: you give to be happy, without which who could drink. 3
My **heart** wants you TO SEE; then my **heart** *ENJOYS*. 4

AMON, 5
- you, you are the protector of the poor, 6
- father for the motherless, 7
- husband for the widow 8

** **IT IS SO SWEET** 9
— **TO PRONOUNCE YOUR NAME!** 10

. It is like the taste of life. 11
. It is like the taste of bread for the child, 12
. the cloth for one who is naked, 13
. like the taste of the tree of (…) for the summer season, 14
. the breath of the breeze for one who is in the prison 15
. (…) (…) (…) (…) 16

TURN TO US, **ETERNAL LORD!** 17

. You, you were here when there existed nothing, you were here, then there was abundance. 18
. You gave that I *SEE the darkness that you give, you illuminate that I SEE you. 19
. Bending yourself, incline your good and loving face. 20
. You will come from afar; will give that your humble servant *SEE; 21
. Scribe Pawahe, give to you that Ra always stoops himself. 22

— **TO BE YOUR FOLLOWER,** 23
** **IS GOOD,** 24

AMON, 25
- The greatest Lord 26
- For one who seeks him will find him, 27
- Deign to cast away the fear. 28

Give *JOY* to the **heart** of all men. 29
In the *JOY* is my *face* that SEES you, 30
AMON, is in feast every day. 31

B. THE CALLING OF THE RICH MAN

After the successful «calling narrative» (at least, according to some[30]), let us move on to another account of the same kind, but which, at first sight at least, failed.

30 See the discussion on the literary genre of the healing at Jericho, above, pp. 47-50.

Quantitative observations

At 92 words in Greek, Luke (18-23) is the shortest, Matthew (116 words) the longest; Mark has 110. Besides what is common to all three (45 words, representing half of the Lukan text), there are many agreements between Matthew and Mark and Mark and Luke; there is, however, only one Matthean-Lukan agreement: «hearing» in the last verse. Here, then is a further example to support the two-source theory: Matthew and Luke depend on Mark (current Mark or an earlier Markan redaction) in ways independent of one another.

Qualitative observations

The really significant differences, more important than the quantitative differences, are those which we will now examine.

The differences between Luke and Mark

The differences do not change the content of the account greatly: — in the first verse, Mark's scene-setting is more life-like, as often happens; — for Luke the simple «someone» becomes «one of the rulers»; Luke does not have Mark's extra command (19: «do not defraud», which is not found in the Decalogues); — he has also suppressed Jesus' look and his «love» (Mark: 21ab: probably a loving gesture, a caress or a kiss); — the other differences are merely «stylistic» (Luke improves Mark's language or style).

The differences between Matthew and Mark/Luke

These differences change the substance: starting from the end, from the least significant to the most significant — Matthew's rich man is «young» (20a.22a; in opposition to Mark and Luke's «since my/the youth», which suggest that their rich man is already mature); Matthew adds two similar conditionals in 21b as in 17e; — he also adds the rich man's questions (18ab); — Matthew also adds «and: You shall love your neighbor as yourself» (19bc; the verb «love» is used by Mark in 21b) to the list of commandments from the Decalogue; — in particular, the formula of the initial question is different: rather than qualifying «master» as in Mark and Luke, in Matthew «good» qualifies what the rich man does (which explains why «interrogate», used in the narrative phrase in Mark and Luke, is moved to Jesus' reply in Matthew (17b).

Matt 19:16-22	Mark 10:17-22	Luke 18:18-23
16 AND behold *someone* coming-*towards* him ***said***: «MASTER, WHAT *GOOD* SHALL I DO ***so that*** I might have ETERNAL LIFE?».	17 AND while he was going out on the way, running-*towards* (him) *someone* and kneeling before him *HE WAS INTERROGATING HIM*: «*GOOD* MASTER, WHAT SHALL I DO ***so that*** ETERNAL LIFE **I might inherit**?».	18 And *INTERROGATED HIM* one of the rulers ***saying***: «*GOOD* MASTER, WHAT HAVING DONE ETERNAL LIFE **shall I inherit**?».
17 NOW HE SAID TO HIM: «WHY DO YOU *ASK ME* about GOOD? ONE-ONLY is GOOD. If you want to enter into the life, observe THE COMMANDMENTS». 18 He says to him: «Which?». Now Jesus said: «These: "you shall not KILL, you shall not *COMMIT-ADULTERY*, you shall not STEAL, you shall not WITNESS-FALSELY, 19 HONOR THE FATHER AND THE MOTHER» and: "You shall love your neighbor as yourself"».	18 NOW **Jesus** SAID TO HIM: «WHY DO YOU **tell** ME GOOD? **No one** (is) GOOD **if not** THE ONLY **God**. 19 THE COMMANDMENTS **you know**: "**Do not** KILL, **do not** *COMMIT-ADULTERY*, **do not** STEAL, **do not** WITNESS-FALSELY", do not defraud; "HONOUR THE FATHER **of you** AND THE MOTHER"».	19 NOW SAID TO HIM **Jesus**: «WHY DO YOU **tell** ME GOOD? **No one** (is) GOOD **if not** THE ONLY **God**. 20 THE COMMANDMENTS **you know**: "**Do not** *COMMIT-ADULTERY*, **do not** KILL, **do not** STEAL, **do not** WITNESS-FALSELY; HONOR THE FATHER **of you** AND THE MOTHER"».
20 ***Says** to him* the young man: «ALL THESE I KEPT. Of what ***still** I lack*?». 21 Declared to him Jesus: «If you want to be perfect, *go*, SELL your possessions AND GIVE TO THE POOR AND YOU WILL HAVE TREASURE IN HEAVENS AND COME, FOLLOW ME». 22 NOW ***hearing*** the young man *the word, he went away afflicted*; FOR HE WAS *having great wealth*.	20 **Now he** declared *to him*: «Master, ALL THESE I KEPT BY MYSELF **from** my **youth**». 21 **Now Jesus** looking at him Loved him and **said to him**: «**Only one** (thing) **you** *lack*: *go*, **what you have** SELL AND GIVE TO THE POOR AND YOU WILL HAVE TREASURE IN HEAVEN AND COME, FOLLOW ME». 22 Now he gloomy at *the word, he went away afflicted*; FOR HE WAS *having great wealth*.	21 **Now he *said***: «ALL THESE I KEPT **from the youth**». 22 **Now** hearing (this) **Jesus** **said to him**: «***Still* only one** (thing) **you** fall-short: all **that you have** SELL AND GIVE around THE POOR AND YOU WILL HAVE TREASURE IN HEAVENS AND COME, FOLLOW ME». 23 NOW ***hearing*** this, he became sad; FOR HE WAS very rich.
23 ***Now*** JESUS SAID *to his disciples*: …	23 And JESUS looking-around SAYS *to his disciples*: …	24 ***Now*** seeing him JESUS [becoming sad] SAID: «How difficult for those who have wealth to enter into the kingdom of God! 25 It is easier that a camel enters through the eye of a needle than a rich-man enters into the kingdom of God». 26 Now those who heard said: «And then who can be saved?». 27 Now he said: «What is impossible to men, is possible to God».

At the end of their account, Matthew (22) and Mark (22) say that the rich man «went away», after which another narrative follows, in which Jesus addresses «his disciples» (Matt: 23; Mark: 23) who were not mentioned in the account of the rich man. Luke, however, does not say that the rich man went away, only that he «became sad» (23c); neither does he say that Jesus' words, which follow, (24) are addressed to the disciples; while we cannot state that they are addressed to the rich man (he does not say: «he said to him», but only: «he said», without clarifying the audience of the words), the rich man hears them like all «those who heard» (26). The Lukan variant, «Now, seeing him Jesus [became sad] said» (’Ιδών δέ αύτόν ό ’Ιησούς [περίλυπον γενόμενον] ειμεν) further emphasizes that the account of the rich man has not yet finished.

So while Matthew and Mark have removed the verses which follow to add them to another passage, Luke makes it all a single passage (18-27), which is confirmed at the higher level of the text's composition in Matthew and Mark as well as in Luke.

2. THE CALLING OF THE RICH YOUNG MAN IN MATTHEW (MATT 19:16-22)

COMPOSITION

The passage is made up of three parts. The first (16-17) has two pieces: the request by «someone» (16) and Jesus' reply (17). In its repetition of «good», 17bc refers back to 16b; with the repetition of «life», 17d recalls 16c. The last part (21-22) also has two pieces: the young man reacts to Jesus' statement (21) with sadness and by going away (22); «having great wealth» (22b) is opposed to «you will have treasure in heavens» (21e). These two parts reflect one another as in a mirror: the last piece opposes «he went away» (22a) to «coming-towards» (16a) in the first piece; the objects of the same verb «have» are opposed, «eternal life» at the start (16c), «great wealth» at the end (22b). The second piece of the first part (17) matches the first piece of the last part (21): they include two conditionals beginning with «if you wish» (17d.21b); one might say that «perfect» (21b) is a divine attribute, just as «good» (17bc) is.

The central part (18-20) has three pieces: the outer pieces are two questions asked by the young man (18b.20bc). The central piece (18c-19) is made up of biblical texts quoted by Jesus: the moving of the commandment to honor one's parents to after the negative commandments (unlike Exodus 20 and Deuteronomy 5) means that this commandment is in the center[31]. «Which» (18b) refers to «commandments» (17e) at the end of the first part; we can understand «all this» and «what» (20bc) as preparing for «great wealth» at the end of the third part (22b), to the extent that the young man «has held» the commandments like things, like his possessions.

31 The quotation is preceded by the definite article «the»; a bit like we say «the Our Father» (see Bonnard, 288).

+ [16] And behold someone		COMING-TOWARDS him said:
:: «Master,	what **good**	shall I do,
– so that I	***MIGHT HAVE***	**ETERNAL LIFE**?».
= [17] Now he said to him:		
:: «Why do you	ask me about	***good***?
:: Only-one	is	***good***!
– IF YOU WANT	***TO ENTER***	**INTO THE LIFE**,
–	***OBSERVE***	**THE COMMANDMENTS**».

+ [18] He says to him:		
	. «**WHICH**?».	
= Now Jesus said:		
«These: "You shall not kill,		you shall not commit-adultery,
you shall not steal,		you shall not witness-falsely;
[19] **HONOR**		**THE FATHER AND THE MOTHER**"
and: "You shall love		your neighbor as yourself"».
+ [20] Says to him *the young man*:		
	. «*ALL THESE*	***I KEPT***;
	. of *WHAT* still	***I LACK***?».

= [21] Declared to him Jesus:		
– «IF YOU WANT	to be	***perfect***,
:: go,	***SELL***	*YOUR POSSESSIONS*
and	***GIVE***	to the poor
:: and you	***WILL HAVE***	**TREASURE IN HEAVENS**
– and come,	follow	me».
+ [22] Now hearing	*the young man*	the word,
+ HE WENT OUT	afflicted;	
:: for he was	***HAVING***	*GREAT WEALTH*.

BIBLICAL CONTEXT

The two Decalogues

At the center of the passage, Jesus quotes some commandments from the Decalogue, to which he adds, «You shall love your neighbor as yourself» (Lev 19:18); Paul (Rom 13:8-10) says that all the commandments are summed up in this one.

We shall now examine the two versions of the Decalogue. It may seem strange to dedicate so much space to Old Testament texts in an introduction to the Synoptic Gospels. The fact is that one cannot understand the New Testament without the Old, and it is essential to do this work.

2.1. *First excursus: the two versions of the decalogue*

«The Decalogue» is one of the few titles which does not come from modern editions of the Bible[32]. «The Ten Words», in Greek the «Deca-logos», is the original name, in the Scriptures themselves[33], of the famous Exodus passage and its twin in the book of Deuteronomy[34]. Despite, or perhaps because of, its venerable age, this description raises problems. This is why most translations feel the need to supply the division of the Decalogue into the Ten Commandments as a note. As we might expect, the earliest Christian tradition is divided on this matter between the Eastern tradition, following the Greek Fathers, and the Western tradition following St Augustine[35]. The number «ten», rather than indicating the number of different commandments, could symbolize the total, just as, in the first creation narrative in Gen 1:1-2:4a, the world was made in ten words[36]. Scripture also uses another name, with a different number: «the two tablets»[37]. The two titles, «*ten* words» and «*two* tablets», have imposed a division into two on the text, while, from a literary point of view, the text is organized in mirror fashion.

32 This excursus returns to my article, «Les deux Décalogues, loi de liberté». An earlier version of this work appeared in 1984: «Les dix commandements, loi de liberté; analyse rhétorique d'Ex 20,2-17 et de Dt 5,6-21». The analysis here is clearly improved, thanks in particular to comments and suggestions from Pietro BOVATI and to his study of the Decalogue in *Giustizia e ingiustizia nell'Antico Testamento* (henceforth: Bovati). I also acknowledge WÉNIN A., «Le Décalogue. Approche contextuelle, théologie et anthropologie» (see too his «Le Décalogue, révélation de Dieu et chemin de bonheur?».), and BALMARY M., *La Divine Origine*; ID., *Abel ou la traversée de l'Éden*. See especially BEAUCHAMP P., *D'une montagne à l'autre, la Loi de Dieu*, particularly the first part, entitled «Le Décalogue», whose starting-point is the account of «The rich man» in Mark 10:17-22).

33 Exod 34:28; Deut 4:13; 10:4.

34 Modern exegesis tends to attribute the Exodus version to the Priestly school and the Deuteronomy version to the Deuteronomic school, in which case the Exodus version would be the later one.

35 The difference depends on the identification of the first commandment (2-3 for the Jews and the Greek Fathers, whom the Orthodox and Protestants follow, or 3-6 for the Latin Fathers, most of the Syriac tradition, Catholics and Lutherans) and, similarly, the last commandment (17ab for the former, 17b for the latter); see Bovati, 83, n. 34.

36 See FRAENKEL A.A., «'Assarah Maamaroth - 'Assarah Dibberot»; see Bovati, 83-84.

37 Exod 31:18; 32:15; Deut 4:13; 5:22; 9:9-11.15.17; 1 Kgs 8:9; 2 Chr 5:10. P. Bovati (81-83) thinks that this number does not indicate the text's division into two parts, as all the iconography suggests, but the number of copies of the same text, one copy for each of the two parties who have concluded the agreement, as was usual when treaties were made at the time, and as still happens today for all written contracts.

Title page of the manuscript of Orosius' *Histories*, Laon, eighth century.
Courtesy of the Bibliothèque municipale de Laon, Bibliothèque Suzanne-Martinet (France).
See SEPIÈRE M.-C., *L'Image d'un Dieu souffrant (IXe-Xe siècle). Aux origines du crucifix*, 278.

2.2. The Decalogue in Exodus (Exod 20:2-17)

Exod 20:2-17 is a passage made up of four parts organized in mirror fashion (see «The passage as a whole», p. 115). The first part (2-7) deals with duties to God and the last part (13-17) with duties to one's neighbor. All the commandments in these two parts are expressed as negative orders. The two central parts (8-11; 12) are distinguished from the other two parts by the fact that they alone have the only two positive commandments—they begin with «Remember[38]...» (8) and «Honor...» (12).

THE FIRST PART (EXOD 20:2-7)

COMPOSITION

+ [2] I (am)		**YHWH**	**your God**		
	. who brought you	from the land	of Egypt,		
	.	from the house	of ***SERVANTS***:		
– [3]	SHALL NOT	EXIST	*for you*	*other gods*	before me.
– [4] You SHALL NOT		**DO**	*for you*	*sculpture*	
– or			any	*representation*,	
	. of what is in the heavens		above,		
	. and of what is on the earth		under,		
	. and of what is in the waters		under	the earth;	
– [5] You SHALL NOT		prostrate	before	*them*	
– and you SHALL NOT		***BE SERVANTS***	to	*them*:	
+ ***because*** I (am)		**YHWH**	**your God**,		
+ (am)		a God	jealous,		
: who	visits	the iniquity	of fathers on sons		
	- on *third* and on *fourth* (generations)		for those who hate me,		
: [6] and	**DOES**	mercy	to *a thousand* (generations)		
	- for those who	love me	and observe my commands.		
= [7] You SHALL NOT pronounce the name of			**YHWH your God**		in vain:
+ ***because*** DOES NOT hold innocent			**YHWH** who pronounces his name		in vain.

The first part has two short sub-parts (2-3 and 7) which frame a more developed sub-part (4-6). While in the first sub-part the commandment (3) is preceded by the reason for it (2), this is reversed in the other two sub-parts where

[38] In certain contexts an infinitive, in Hebrew can have the meaning of an imperative. This infinitive is followed by two futures with the meaning of an imperative, which are also positive: «you will serve and you will do» (9).

the commandment (4-5b and 7a) is followed by its reason (5c-6 and 7b) both introduced by «because».

The first sub-part (2-3) is made up of two segments. The first segment is a tri-member (2abc) in ABB' form. The first member is the titulator, or what the speaker says about his name and rank (2a); the two members which follow explain what he has done for those whom he is addressing (2bc). The second segment is a unimember—the commandment is a result of the action carried out on behalf of the person to whom it is given (3). The outer members match one another. The name «YHWH» could be translated as «the Existing one», as it is in the Septuagint, to show its lexical relationship to the verb «there will not exist» «other gods» in 3, opposed to «your God» in 2a; «before me», at the end of 3, matches «Me» at the start of 2. Note, too, that the second person singular pronoun is repeated three times (2b.3; translated by the pronominal adjective «your» in 2a).

The second sub-part (4-6) has two pieces. The first (4-5b) is made up of two bimembers (4ab.5ab) which frame a trimember (4cde). At the outer parts, the prohibition is repeated twice. The central trimember lists the three parts of the cosmos —«the earth» (singular) between «the heavens» and «the waters» (plural)[39]. Note that the last term is broadened with the addition of «of the earth». The exhaustive list of elements emphasizes the absolutist nature of the commandment. The second piece (5c-6) is made up of three bimember segments. The first one (5cd) is the titulator which begins with the same «I am» as in 2a, but another title of God is added—«a jealous God». The second (5ef) and the third (6ab) segments parallel one another; the two segments explain the title of «a jealous God» which the first segment (5d) ends with. Note the repetition of the verb «do» at the start of the outer segments (4a and 6a).

The third sub-part (7) only has one bimember segment. The commandment (7a) is followed by the reason for it (7b). The same syntagma «pronounce the name» is repeated in both members. The two occurrences of «in vain» act as final terms.

The links between the sub-parts: In addition to what we have already said about the logical movement found in each sub-part between the commandment and the reason for the commandment, we should note:

39 In Hebrew, both these words only exist in the plural form.

+ [2]I (am)		**YHWH**	**your God**		
	. who brought you	from the land	of Egypt,		
	.	from the house	of ***SERVANTS***:		
– [3]	SHALL NOT	EXIST	*for you*	*other gods*	before me.
– [4] You SHALL NOT		**DO**	*for you*	*sculpture*	
– or			any	*representation*,	
	. of what is in the heavens		above,		
	. and of what is on the earth		under,		
	. and of what is in the waters		under	the earth;	
– [5] You SHALL NOT		prostrate	before	*them*	
– and you SHALL NOT		***BE SERVANTS***	to	*them*:	
+ ***because*** I (am)		**YHWH**	**your God,**		
+ (am)		a God	jealous,		
: who	visits	the iniquity	of fathers on sons		
	- on *third* and on *fourth* (generations)		for those who hate me,		
: [6] and	**DOES**	mercy	to *a thousand* (generations)		
	- for those who	love me	and observe my commands.		
= [7]You SHALL NOT pronounce the name of			**YHWH your God**		in vain:
+ ***because*** DOES NOT hold innocent			**YHWH** who pronounces his name		in vain.

• the repetition of «YHWH your God» at the start at the outer sub-parts (2a and 7a) as well as at the start of the second piece of the central sub-part (5c);

• «other gods» at the end of the first sub-part (3) and «sculpture»/ «representation» at the start of the second sub-part (4ab) take on the role of median terms. The repetition of «for you» (3 and 4a) fulfils the same role, the more so as these are the only occurrences of this syntagma in the whole part;

• «servants» in 2c is taken up by «you will not be servants» in 5b;

• the past being recalled at the center of the first sub-part (2bc) is linked to the preview of the future at the end of the second sub-part (5ef-6); the mention of God's saving acts corresponds to the «historical prologue» of covenantal texts, while the threats correspond to the «curses and blessings» of the same texts[40];

• finally, note the link between the «other gods» at the end of the first sub-part (3; «sculpture» in 4a) and the two occurrences of «in vain» at the end of both members of the last sub-part (7a.7b): idols are vanity (Jer 18:15 : «My people have forgotten me! They burn their incense to a *Nothing*!»).

40 See BEAUCHAMP P., «Propositions sur l'alliance comme structure centrale».

BIBLICAL CONTEXT

Like «the heavens», «the earth» and «the waters» (4cde), the verb «make» («do») with which v.4 begins refers to the first creation narrative —God «makes» the firmament on the second day (Gen 1:7), the lights on the fourth day (1:16), and animals living on the earth on the sixth day (1:25). At the end of the sixth day, having crowned his work by creating man and woman, «God saw all he *had made*, and indeed it was very good» (1:31)[41]. The verb «to be» is used for light: «God said, "*Let there be* light", and *there was* light» (1:3). With the firmament, the two verbs are linked: «God said, "*Let there be* a vault [...]." And God *made* the vault [...]» (1:6-7). Now, it is this same verb «to be» (translated by «to exist») which is used just before the verb «to make/do» in the Decalogue: «There *will not exist* for you other gods before me» (Exod 20:3).

INTERPRETATION

«I the Lord your God who brought you from...» (First Commandment)

None of the three commandments which we can see in this first part (3.4-5b.7a) is an impersonal law, like those we might find in a penal code, where they begin abruptly with: «To ... is forbidden». Before giving any commandment, the speaker introduces himself: «I, The Lord» (2a); but he is not content to introduce himself with his name, he also identifies the person he is addressing: «I the Lord, *your* God»[42]. The «Ten Words» are, first and foremost, words from an «I» to a «You». However, as often happens between people, it is not enough for the one introducing himself to give his name to be recognized. He must recall the circumstances of the previous meeting, to bring his own unique face back to the other person's memory. The liberation from slavery in Egypt worked by the Lord on behalf of the person he is talking to identifies both himself and his interlocutor —in just one Hebrew word, *hôṣētîkā*, «I have brought you out» (2b), the first and second person pronouns (*tî* + *k*) are brought together. The whole history of the relationship between God and the children of Israel is reduced to the leaving of Egypt— this is not one event among many others, or even the first; it is the founding event, the birth by which God's fatherhood and the filiation of his chosen people are recognized. Only the reference to the origins can be the basis of the law's expression.

41 See p. 216.

42 Personal pronouns in Hebrew go to the ends of the clause: «*I*, Yhwh, the God of *you*».

«I, the Lord your God, a jealous God...» (the first commandment with the other two)

The reminder of origins is not limited to the «historical» event of the leaving of Egypt. The mention of «in heaven or on earth beneath or in the waters under the earth» (4cde) refers —albeit indirectly— to the original beginning, to the event which it is impossible to describe except with the language of «myth», to the creation which the reader knows was entirely the work of the Lord. However, it should be recognized that the Lord is not introducing himself as Creator, and he is not giving his law in this capacity, but as the Lord who has intervened in history. At what could be identified as the Second Commandment (4-6), the speaker repeats the same formula he began with, «I, the Lord your God» (5c). This time, however, it is not to recall benefits in the past, but to look towards a future left to humanity's choosing. Making the sins of the fathers fall on their descendents to the third and fourth generation is probably a way of making it understood that this address is not given to an individual, and that the present generation's responsibility involves the future of those generations to come. The huge gulf between the third and fourth generations, who take on the curse, and the thousandth generation, who benefit from the blessing, shows the extent to which God's mercy prevails over his punishment. The Lord God of Israel thus paints himself as the absolute master of history, the savior of the past from the beginning (2-3) and the supreme judge of the future (4-6).

«You shall not...» (Second Commandment)

«Listen Israel: Yhwh our God is the one Yhwh. You shall Yhwh your God with all your heart, with all your soul, with all your strength» (Deut 6:4-5). The whole and total nature of love, emphasized three times in this phrase from Deuteronomy, expresses nothing more than that of the first part of the Decalogue: «everything» for the Lord, that is, nothing for anyone else (3). What the accumulation of these three «all»s expresses in a positive way (Deut 6:4) is impressed here by the insistent reiteration of five negative commands (3.4a.5a.5b.7a). Everything is focused on the repeated prohibition of idolatry (4-5b), which is another way of proclaiming the Lord's absolute uniqueness. In fact, after a brief general commandment (3) forbidding Israel from having any other god except their Lord, the central sub-part forbids them at length from «making» idols, representations or images of any of the world's elements. «To make» a god of what is in the heavens, on the earth or in the seas would be to overturn the order of creation, to instill confusion between the Creator and one of his creatures; this would be «hatred» (5f). Making a god means denying oneself as a creature. In addition to not «loving» the Lord their God and not «observing his commandments» (6), to make a god is to arrogate to oneself God's own place, to play at being God. This initial interpretation of the central sub-part, however, needs to be completed, or corrected, by another one. The Second Commandment (4-6) can be understood, not simply as an amplified repetition of the First (2-3), but as another commandment —what is forbidden is making a «statue» or some other representation of the Lord God of Israel, which is exactly what the children of Israel asked Aaron for and received when they made the Golden Calf, which was not another god— in effect, they were saying, «Here is your God, Israel, who brought you out of the land of Egypt» (Exod 32:4).

«You shall not bow down» (still the Second Commandment)

Having arrived as free men in Egypt, presented to Pharaoh by their brother, Joseph, his governor (Gen 46-47), Jacob's children ended up being reduced to hard labor by the Egyptians (Exod 1). «The land of Egypt» was to become «the house of slavery» for the children of Israel, until the day when Yhwh, having revealed his name to his servant Moses (Exod 3:14), brought Israel out of slavery. Then Moses and the Israelites intoned the hymn to Yhwh which ended with these words: «Who among the gods is your like, Yhwh? Who is your like, majestic in holiness, terrible in deeds of prowess, worker of wonders?» (Exod 15:11). After this, hardly had the covenant on Mt Sinai been concluded than the people were prostrating themselves before the Golden Calf (Exod 32). Idolatry and any representation, even of Yhwh, is slavery[43]. It is a return to the land of Egypt, a denial of the liberation worked by the Lord. Israel is not called to «bow down» (5b) but to «love» the Lord (6b) by keeping his commandments. Obedience is not the servile attitude of one who is forced to carry it out, but the fruit of a free choice by one who knows that he has been saved from slavery.

«You shall not pronounce the Name in vain»

The commandment to adore the one God to the exclusion of all others has its corollary—if one is not to acknowledge the existence of other gods before Yhwh (3), it is also imperative not to treat the only Existing One «in vain» (7), that is, as

43 Verse 5b is usually translated with an active verb: «You shall not bow down», although it is in fact a passive verb (*hofal*; lit. «You shall not be bowed down to them»).

though he did not exist, not to pronounce his name, not to bear witness by swearing oaths in his name, as though he were nothing more than the vain idols and their empty images (4ab). God's punishment, which will come down on the perjurer (7b) will not be in vain, and the guilty party will receive proof both of his sin and of the existence of the one he has offended in this way.

THE SECOND PART (EXOD 20:8-11)

COMPOSITION

This part has two sub-parts —the commandment (8-10) and the reason given for the commandment (11).

---

* [8] To remember of	THE DAY OF SABBATH	to **CONSECRATE IT.**	
+ [9] *Six*	*DAYS*	***you will serve.***	
+ and **you will do**	*all your work*		
– [10] And THE SEVENTH	DAY	is Sabbath	to YHWH your God:
– ***you shall not do***	*any work,*	you,	
: and your son		and your daughter,	
: your **servant**		and your handmaid,	
: and your livestock		and your guest	who is at your gates.
+ [11] Because *in six*	*DAYS*	YHWH	**made**
. the heavens		and the earth	
. the sea		and all	that are in them
– and ***he rested***	THE SEVENTH	DAY.	
* Therefore YHWH blessed	THE DAY OF SABBATH	and **CONSECRATED IT.**	

The first sub-part (8-10) has three pieces. The first piece (8) is made up of a single unimember segment, later developed at length. The other two pieces (9 and 10) oppose what should be done on six days of the week to what should not be done on the Sabbath day. While the second piece (9) has only one bimember segment, the third (10) is made up of a bimember (10ab) followed by a trimember (10cde) which lists, in pairs, all those, in addition to «you» in 10b, who are not to work on the Sabbath. Note the words with the same root, «you shall serve» in 9a and «your servant» in 10d («female servant» has another root in Hebrew).

The second sub-part (11) is made up of two pieces. The first piece (11a-e) includes a trimember (11abc —what God made «in six days»), opposed by a unimember (11d: what he did «on the seventh day»). This piece is constructed concentrically —temporal adverbs at the outside, then the verbs, and finally the list in the center. The last piece (11e) is a unimember which brings the sub-part to a conclusion.

The outer segments parallel one another and are the inclusio (8 and 11e). The first tells humanity what he is to do, and the other one what God has done —humanity is invited to do what God has done— the «consecration» of the «Sabbath day».

The first piece of the second sub-part (11a-d) corresponds to verses 9-10 of the first sub-part: — the opposition between «six days» (9a) and «the seventh day» (10a) is repeated in 11a and 11d; — the clauses in 9-10 are doubled compared to clauses 11a-d — two syntagmas, opposed by negation, «you shall/shall not» + «all (your) work» are added to «you will serve» (9a) and «is Sabbath for the Lord your God» (10a)[44]; — 9-10 is a parallel construction; 11a-d a concentric construction; — at the end of the first sub-part (10cde), and in the middle of the second (11bc), are two lists in three tenses, the first of which is more developed than the second. Each ends with a similar expansion, «who is at your door» and «[all] that are in them», emphasizing their symmetry. These two lists have the same exhaustive nature.

BIBLICAL CONTEXT

The Lord's rest

The reason for the commandment (11) refers to the conclusion of the first creation narrative. Note the many lexical repetitions (in italics):

> [1] Thus were completed the heaven and the earth, with all their hosts. [2] God concluded on *seventh day the work* which he *had done* and, on *seventh day*, he *rested* (*šbt*) after all *the work* which he *had done.* [3] God *blessed* the *seventh day* and *consecrated* it, because on it he had *rested* from *all his work* of creation (Gen 2:1-3).

Divine resemblance

The reason for the commandment to rest on the Sabbath is God's action —in other words, in this commandment, humanity is called to imitate the Lord. In fact, still in the first creation narrative, man was made «in the image» of God. «And God said, "Let us make man in our image, in our resemblance". God cre-

44 «All» in 9b and «not any» in 10b translate the same Hebrew word *kol.*

ated man in his image; in the image of God he created him; male and female he created them» (Gen 1:26-27). We should not gloss over the difference between these two expressions: «in our image and in our resemblance» is God's plan, «in his image» is its realization. «The image» is given, but «the resemblance» is left to humanity's initiative, a vocation to be achieved[45].

INTERPRETATION

The command to work

It is true that this part deals above all with the consecration of the Sabbath —this is, in fact, how the text begins— «Remember the day of the Sabbath» (8a). However, after this initial general commandment, humanity is given the order to work for six days (9). Anyone who has not first «done all his work» cannot respect the rest on the seventh day. Linked to the Lord's creative «doing» (11a), humanity's «doing» (9b) is presented as a collaboration in the work of creation —in fact, the same words «to do work», describe God's work in the creation narrative, and humanity's work in the Decalogue. Created in the image of God (Gen 1:27), humanity is given the vocation of a son who does the same work as his father.

The consecration of the Sabbath

What humanity is commanded to do for the seventh day might seem to be totally negative —it is a «do not», which applies to all the people in the house, and to all the animals. However, before the prohibition (10b-e) is the statement «the seventh day is a Sabbath for the Lord your God» (10a), as though the Sabbath, the «stopping of work», were for the Creator before being for the creatures. «Remember» (8) appears to be mostly aimed at recalling creation, humanity's ultimate origins and the origins of their work, that is, to acknowledge that life is not the fruit of humanity's work, but of the work of the One who gives it. Remembering the Sabbath is thus «to consecrate it» (8), «for the Lord your God» (10a).

The Blessing of the Sabbath

But the Sabbath is not only consecrated to God, it is also a blessing for humanity. It is given for the master of the house, and for all those who make up his household, even including the stranger who works for him. The blessing is in the freedom from slavery —on the seventh day, not only are the «son and daugh-

45 See BALMARY M., *La Divine Origine*, Chap. IV, «Où Dieu ne fait que la moitié de son travail», 109-147 (quoting Origen and Basil of Caesarea, 113-116).

ter» (10c) not to be treated as «servant and handmaid» (10d), like the «livestock» or the «guest» (10e), that us, under the slavery of the work which they do on the days when they «serve» (9a), but, on the contrary, the slave and the servant are to be considered as sons and daughters. Consecration and blessing ensure that all, including animals, become affiliated to the head of the household, who acknowledges that he is begotten by the Father in heaven.

THE THIRD PART (EXOD 20:12)

COMPOSITION

+ [12] Honor	the FATHER	of **you**	and the MOTHER	of **you**,
:: so that	are prolonged		the days	of **you**,
+ on the land	that YHWH THE GOD	of **you**	DONATES	to **you**.

This part is the size of a trimember segment. From the syntactical point of view, the main clause (12a), that is, the commandment, is followed by a final clause (12b) and by a complement of place («on the land»), which is itself completed by a relative clause. The last two members are a double reference to the blessing of time (long life) and space (possession of the land); from this perspective the trimember can be described as ABB'. However, the outer members link parents and «Yhwh» who «gives» the land to the child, as parents do when they pass on an inheritance. Note that the three members end with the pronomial suffix -*kâ* («you»), and that this pronoun is repeated twice more in the outer members.

INTERPRETATION

The life which is given to you

This commandment hides its two wonderful surprises in its brevity. The first is that one would expect the second member to finish with a different pronoun: «so that their days are prolonged»; unconsciously, in fact, this is how we read it[46]. The honor due to father and mother, that is, caring for one's parents, might also be aimed at supporting them so that they might live as long as possible. This is the normal reaction, the dearest wish of children. The biblical text subverts this natural desire to a certain extent—it does not deny it, of course, but the reason given for the commandment is different. The aim is not the parents'

46 See BALMARY M., *La Divine Origine*, 227-230, showing that Freud himself read this incorrectly.

long life, but the children's. «The persecuting law of the Supergo said, "Honor your father and mother so that *their* days may be lengthened". The prophetic law of revelation says, "Honor… so that *your* days may be lengthened"»[47]. Honoring the parents allows the children to live their own life, and it is precisely for this reason that children can honor them.

The land which is given you

But there is a further surprise in the text. One might expect «on the land which your father and mother give you», that is, on the property which you have received or will receive as an inheritance from your parents. Honor would be due to father and mother because they give the children the possibility of living by working their own land[48]. The text, however, says, «the land which *the Lord your God* has given you». The reason for the commandment to honor one's parents is that, with the inheritance which allows them to live as freemen, life itself is passed down to the children like a gift from God. To honor father and mother as the Decalogue commands is for humanity to honor the ultimate origin of life and freedom. The vague and, as it were, empty verb, «honor», can probably be opened up to give different meanings, according to the child's status: as a minor, he is to obey his parents; as an adult, he must ensure that his elderly parents, unable to work, are cared for. Above all, the child is to respect those who have handed on life and, with the descent from Abraham, the faith and promises given to the children of Israel[49].

47 BALMARY M., *La Divine Origine*, 228.

48 The term *ʾădāmâ* tends to indicate land which may be cultivated, while *ʾereṣ* means «country», as in v. 2: «the land of Egypt» (see JENNI E. and WESTERMANN C., *Theological Dictionary of the Old Testament*, I, 88-98). «The fruit of the earth» is *pᵉrî hā-ʾădāmâ*; the syntagma *pᵉrî hā-ʾāreṣ* occurs only four times in the Hebrew Bible, three times to describe the produce of the land of Canaan reported by the explorers sent by Moses (Num 13:20.26; Deut 1:25) and once to describe either the Messiah or the remnant of Israel (Isa 4:2). However, the term *ʾădāmâ* is ambiguous and is sometimes used as a synonym for *ʾereṣ*, for example in Deut 26:15: «Look down from the dwelling place of your holiness, from heaven, and bless your people Israel and the soil (*ʾădāmâ*) you have given us as you sower to our fathers, a land (*ʾereṣ*) where milk and honey flow» (see too Deut 11:9.17), or replacing *ʾereṣ* (Deut 7:13; 11:21; 30:20).

49 See Bovati, 139-142.

THE FOURTH PART (EXOD 20:13-17)

COMPOSITION

+	13	You SHALL NOT	**KILL.**		
::	14	You SHALL NOT	COMMIT-ADULTERY.		
–	15	You SHALL NOT	STEAL.		

+	16	You SHALL NOT	**ANSWER**	against *your neighbor*	testimony of deception.
–	17	You SHALL NOT	COVET	the house	of *your neighbor.*
::		You SHALL NOT	COVET	the wife	of *your neighbor,*
				- and his servant	and his handmaid,
				- and his ox	and his ass,
				- and all that is	to *your neighbor.*

This part is made up of two parallel sub-parts (13-15 and 16-17). The first has three similar unimember segments. Each segment is a commandment[50] which has only one term, a verb modified by the same negative and the same modalities of tense, person and number[51]. The second sub-part (16-17) includes two trimember segments (16a-17b and 17cde); «your neighbor» is repeated four times, in each member of the first segment (16.17a.17b) and at the end of the second trimember.

The first members (13 and 16) match to the extent that false witness in a court could lead to the death of a «neighbor». The link between the other members appears to be inverted—coveting a woman (17b) is clearly linked to the prohibition of adultery (14); coveting a house (17a) could correspond to the prohibition of theft (15). However, the fact that 17a and 17b begin with the same verb might allow us to think that the «house» does not mean the physical building, but the household, which also includes all the people living there as well as the objects in it.

50 The unusual translation of v.14 seeks to follow the brevity of the original and to respect the rhythm, which the usual translation, «You shall not commit adultery» does not do.

51 Unimember segments are rare, but it is even rarer to encounter members with only one term. We could possibly have considered these three verses to be a trimember segment, but it is preferable to follow the Masoretic punctuation, especially because of the parallelism between the first (13-15) and second (16-17) parts.

BIBLICAL CONTEXT

The verb «to covet» (*ḥmd*), used twice (17a.17b), has the same root as the participle «enticing/desirable» (*neḥmād*), used first of all to describe the trees which God made grow in the garden (Gen 2:9: «*enticing* to look at and good to eat»), and, above all, in the eyes of the woman tempted by the serpent, for the tree in the middle of the garden, the only one forbidden by God. «The woman saw that the tree was good to eat and pleasing to the eye and that it was *desirable* for the knowledge that it could give. So she took some of its fruit…» (Gen 3:6).

INTERPRETATION

The triple dimension of the neighbor

The Other must be recognized for what he is, in his physical (13) and social (16) life, in his married (14) and family (17a) life, in his economic (15) and domestic (17c-e)life; in short, in what makes him a person like me, my «neighbor». The three repeated commandments keep in their sights the three basic characteristics of humanity according to the Bible—first of all, the person, both physically (13) and socially (16), as spouse (14) and head of a family (17a), then in charge of a whole household, from his wife (17b) to his livestock (17d) via his servants (17c). The neighbor's life, family and property are sacred—anyone who touches them commits a serious wrong against him.

To deny the other is to deny oneself

Whoever kills another person denies it in himself (13); whoever lies by giving false witness against another denies it before others (16): he behaves as though the other did not exist or makes out that he no longer exists. Taking a neighbor's wife or stealing his property, or even just coveting them, that is, daring to think that they might be taken, is to hold one's neighbor to be nothing, to act as though he doesn't count. Committing adultery (14) or stealing (15), even «wishing» to do so (17), is basically the same as suppressing someone by murdering them (13) or destroying them in the eyes of others by bearing false witness (16). This is all to deny that the other is one's «neighbor»; it is also to deny oneself as a human being, that is, as the other's neighbor.

Covetousness, the root of sin (second sub-part)

On a first reading it might appear strange that false witness and covetousness are mentioned after murder, adultery and theft. One might rather expect the opposite, a progression in order of seriousness, from the desire to the action, from the venial to the mortal. The text's order as it is, is clearly not indifferent, and in any case, not insignificant. In fact, it is not only killing, committing adultery and stealing which are not allowed. The prohibition extends to the root of evil, hoping to root it out —prior to the murder itself, the false word which wounds and can be followed by death; prior to adultery and theft, the covetousness which leads one to touch a neighbor's wife and property. It was covetousness of the eyes which led the first woman to touch the forbidden fruit, and we know what that led to.

THE PASSAGE AS A WHOLE (EXOD 20:2-17)

COMPOSITION

The links between the outer parts (2-7 and 13-17)

2 I (am) YHWH YOUR GOD
who brought you from the land of Egypt, from the **HOUSE** of ***SERVANTS***:
3 ***Shall not*** exist for you other gods before me.

4 You ***shall not*** do for you sculpture or any representation,
- of what (is) in the heavens above,
- and of what (is) on the earth under,
- and of what (is) in the waters under the earth.

5 You ***shall not*** prostrate before them and you ***shall not*** ***BE SERVANT*** to them:

Because I (am) YHWH YOUR GOD,
(am) a God jealous,
who visits the iniquity of fathers on sons on third and on fourth (generations)
for those who hate me,
6 and who does mercy to thousand (generations)
for those who love me and observe my commands.

7 You ***shall not*** pronounce the name of YHWH YOUR GOD **in vain**,
because ***does not*** hold innocent YHWH one who pronounces *his* name **in vain**.

[...]

13 You ***shall not*** kill.
14 You ***shall not*** commit-adultery.
15 You ***shall not*** steal.

16 You ***shall not*** testimony against YOUR NEIGHBOUR **falsely**.
17 You ***shall not*** covet the **HOUSE** of YOUR NEIGHBOUR.
You ***shall not*** covet the wife of YOUR NEIGHBOUR,
: and *his* ***SERVANT*** and *his* ***HANDMAID***,
: and *his* ox and *his* ass,
: and all that is to YOUR NEIGHBOUR.

<table>
<tr><td>2 I (am)
who brought you from the land of Egypt,
3 Shall not exist for you other gods before me.</td><td>YHWH YOUR GOD
from the HOUSE of SERVANTS:</td><td></td></tr>
<tr><td>4 You shall not do for you sculpture or any representation,
- of what (is) in the heavens above,
- and of what (is) on the earth under,
- and of what (is) in the waters under the earth.
5 You shall not prostrate before them and you shall not BE SERVANT to them:
Because I (am)
(am) a God jealous,
who visits the iniquity of fathers on sons on third and on fourth (generations)
for those who hate me,
6 and who does mercy to thousand (generations)
for those who love me and observe my commands.</td><td>YHWH YOUR GOD,</td><td></td></tr>
<tr><td>7 You shall not pronounce the name of
because does not hold innocent YHWH one who pronounces his name</td><td>YHWH YOUR GOD</td><td>in vain,
in vain.</td></tr>
</table>

[...]

<table>
<tr><td>13 You shall not kill.
14 You shall not commit-adultery.
15 You shall not steal.</td><td></td><td></td></tr>
<tr><td>16 You shall not testimony against
17 You shall not covet the HOUSE of
You shall not covet the wife of
: and his SERVANT and his HANDMAID,
: and his ox and his ass,
: and all that is to</td><td>YOUR NEIGHBOUR
YOUR NEIGHBOUR.
YOUR NEIGHBOUR,

YOUR NEIGHBOUR.</td><td>falsely.</td></tr>
</table>

- Each part has six negative verbs (3.4a.5a.5a.7a.7b; 13.14.15.16.17a.17b; all with the same negative *lō'*); these are all imperatives, except the last one in the first part («not justify» in 7b).
- The commandment in 16 ends with a synonym («falsely») of the word which both members in 7 end with («in vain»).
- «House» is repeated in 2b and 17a, but these are two different houses —in the first part it is the «house of servants», and in the last part «the house of your neighbor».
- The name of the «Lord», mentioned four times in the first part, qualified as «*your* God» three times, does not reappear in the last part; however, the word «neighbor» is repeated in that part four times, each time qualified as «*your* neighbor». The third person singular pronoun suffix is only found at the end of 7b and 17cd (translated as «your»).

The Lord God seems to be totally absent from the last part. However, one might think that false witness, with which the second sub-part begins (16), brings the oath on the Lord's Name into play[52]. The link established between the final terms of the two last members of the first part (7a.7b) and the final term of the first member of the second sub-part of the last part (16), with the synonyms «in vain» and «falsely», support this interpretation—it is these two commandments which bring the word into play.

The links between the central two parts (8-11 and 12)[53]

8 **TO REMEMBER** of the ***day*** of Sabbath to consecrate it.	
9 Six ***days*** you will serve and do all your works.	
10 And the seventh ***day*** is Sabbath to you shall not do any work, you,	**YHWH YOUR GOD**:
and **YOUR SON**	and **YOUR DAUGHTER**,
your servant	and your handmaid,
and your livestock	and your guest who is at your gates.
11 **Because** in six ***days*** Yhwh made the heavens and the earth the sea and all that are in them and he rested the seventh ***day***.	
Therefore Yhwh blessed the ***day*** of Sabbath and consecrated it.	

12 **HONOUR** **YOUR FATHER**	and **YOUR MOTHER**,
so that are prolonged your ***days***,	
on the land that	**YHWH YOUR GOD** donates to you.

- Both these parts begin with the only positive commandments in the passage[54]: «Remember» (8) and «Honor» (12a).
- The name of the «Lord your God» appears once in each of the two parts (10a.12c).
- «Day», which appears six times in the second part (8.9.10a.11a.11c.11d), is repeated in the plural once in the third part (12b).

52 See BOVATI P., *Re-establishing justice*, 284-286, n. 62.
53 See TAPIERO M., «"Honore ton père et ta mère"», 289; FRAENKEL A.A., «Du père au Père», 305-307.
54 See p. 98, n. 38. The Sabbath commandment also has a negative imperative (10b).

8 **TO REMEMBER** of the ***day*** of Sabbath to consecrate it.

- -

9 Six ***days*** you will serve
and do all your works.

- -

10 And the seventh ***day*** is Sabbath to you shall not do any work, you,	**YHWH YOUR GOD**:
and **YOUR SON**	and **YOUR DAUGHTER**,
your servant	and your handmaid,
and your livestock	and your guest who is at your gates.

11 **Because** in six ***days*** Yhwh made
the heavens and the earth
the sea and all that are in them
and he rested the seventh ***day***.

- -

Therefore Yhwh blessed the ***day*** of Sabbath and consecrated it.

12 HONOUR	**YOUR FATHER**	and **YOUR MOTHER**,
so that are prolonged your ***days***,		
on the land that		**YHWH YOUR GOD** donates to you.

- The first commandment is followed by the reason for it («because» at the start of 11), a reason which goes back to the beginning; the second is followed by its consequence («so that» at the start of 12b), a consequence which is in the present in 12c and in the future in 12b.
- «Son» and «daughter» (10c) belong to the same semantic field as «father» and «mother» (12a). The former are first-degree descendents and the latter first-degree ancestors. In Hebrew, all four terms have the same suffix pronoun in the second person masculine (*-kā*; «of you»), translated by the pronomial adjective «your». The complementarity of the sexes is found in each of these pairs, in the same order, just as it is in the pair «servant and handmaid», parallel to «son and daughter».

The two commandments thus match one another —the commandment of the Sabbath is address to man as a father, and the following one addressed to him as a son. Both deal with internal family relations within the same place, the home.

The links between the four parts

2 I am — THE LORD *YOUR* GOD
who brought you from the land of Egypt, — from the house of *SERVANTS*:
3 Shall not exist for you other gods before me.

4 You **shall not do** for you sculpture — or ***any*** representation,
- of what is in **the heavens** — above,
- and of what is on **the earth** — below,
- and of what is in **the waters** — under the earth.
5 You shall not prostrate before them — and you shall not *BE SERVANTS* to them:

because I am — THE LORD *YOUR* GOD, — a God ***jealous***,
who punishes the iniquity of **FATHERS** on **SONS** on third and on fourth (generations)
for those who hate me,
6 and who does mercy to thousand (generations)
for those who ***love*** me and observe my commands.

7 You shall not pronounce the Name of — THE LORD *YOUR* GOD — **in vain**,
because the Lord does not hold unpunished — who pronounces ***his*** Name — **in vain**.

8 ***To remember*** — of the day of Sabbath — to consecrate it.
9 Six days you *WILL SERVE* — and you **will do** ***all*** your work.
10 And the seventh day is Sabbath — to THE LORD *YOUR* GOD:
you **shall not do** ***any*** work, you,
: and *YOUR* **SON** — and *YOUR* **DAUGHTER**,
: *YOUR SERVANT* — and *YOUR HANDMAID*,
: and *YOUR* livestock — and *YOUR* guest who is at *YOUR* gates.

11 Because in six days The Lord **made**
- **the heavens**,
- and **the earth**,
- **the sea** — and ***all*** that are in them
and he rested the seventh day.
Therefore the Lord blessed — the day of Sabbath — and consecrated it.

12 ***Honor*** *YOUR* **FATHER** — and *YOUR* **MOTHER**,
so that your days are prolonged
on the land that — THE LORD *YOUR* GOD donates to you.

13 You shall not kill. 14 You shall not ***commit adultery***. 15 You shall not steal.

16 You shall not testimony against — *YOUR* NEIGHBOUR — **falsely**.
17 You shall not covet the house of — *YOUR* NEIGHBOUR.
You ***shall not covet the wife*** of — *YOUR* NEIGHBOUR,
: and ***his*** *SERVANT* — and ***his*** *HANDMAID*,
: and ***his*** ox — and ***his*** ass,
: and ***all*** that is to — *YOUR* NEIGHBOUR.

While the symbolic location of the first part (2-7) seems to be the Temple, the home of the worship of the Lord and the invocation of his Name, the location of the two central parts (8-12) is the home, the place where the children, servants, domestic animals and foreign employees are all gathered around father and mother. The location of the last part (13-17) is outside: «the "gate" (that is the cen-

2 I am — THE LORD YOUR GOD
who brought you from the land of Egypt, — from the house of *SERVANTS*:
3 Shall not exist for you other gods before me.

4 You **shall not do** for you sculpture — or ***any*** representation,
- of what is in **the heavens** — above,
- and of what is on **the earth** — below,
- and of what is in **the waters** — under the earth.
5 You shall not prostrate before them — and you shall not *BE SERVANTS* to them:

because I am — THE LORD YOUR GOD, — a God ***jealous***,
who punishes the iniquity of **FATHERS** on **SONS** on third and on fourth (generations)
for those who hate me,
6 and who does mercy to thousand (generations)
for those who ***love*** me and observe my commands.

7 You shall not pronounce the Name of — THE LORD YOUR GOD — **in vain**,
because the Lord does not hold unpunished — who pronounces ***his*** Name — **in vain**.

8 ***To remember*** — of the day of Sabbath — to consecrate it.
9 Six days you *WILL SERVE* — and you **will do *all*** your work.
10 And the seventh day is Sabbath — to THE LORD YOUR GOD:
you **shall not do *any*** work, you,
: and YOUR **SON** — and YOUR **DAUGHTER**,
: YOUR *SERVANT* — and YOUR *HANDMAID*,
: and YOUR livestock — and YOUR guest who is at YOUR gates.

11 Because in six days The Lord **made**
- **the heavens**,
- and **the earth**,
- **the sea** — and ***all*** that are in them
and he rested the seventh day.
Therefore the Lord blessed — the day of Sabbath — and consecrated it.

12 ***Honor*** YOUR **FATHER** — and YOUR **MOTHER**,
so that your days are prolonged
on the land that — THE LORD YOUR GOD donates to you.

13 You shall not kill. 14 You shall not ***commit adultery***. 15 You shall not steal.
16 You shall not testimony against — YOUR NEIGHBOUR — **falsely**.
17 You shall not covet the house of — YOUR NEIGHBOUR.
You ***shall not covet the wife*** of — YOUR NEIGHBOUR,
: and ***his*** *SERVANT* — and ***his*** *HANDMAID*,
: and ***his*** ox — and ***his*** ass,
: and ***all*** that is to — YOUR NEIGHBOUR.

tral square) of the city could be considered, if not the exclusive location, at least one of the typical places of these public relationships»[55].

55 Bovati, 131.

The Sabbath commandment is joined to the commandments about God which come before it, for «the Sabbath is for the Lord your God» (10a); the commandment to honor father and mother (12) begins the list of commandments about the neighbor (13-17), which follow it and which «father and mother» are part of, in a very special way.

There are particularly close links between the first and second parts. It is only here that God's original action on Israel's behalf is mentioned (2b), and then his action on behalf of all creation (11a-d). It is only here that the list of the «heavens» and the «earth» and the «waters» or the «sea» (4 and 11) are repeated, and only here that the verb «to do», is used, both for humanity (4a.9.10b; although note that 4a and 10b have negative imperatives) and for God (6a and 11a).

The terms «fathers» and «sons» in the first part (5c) are repeated, in the singular, in the second part («son» in 10c) and the third part («father» in 12a).

The two lists of three terms in 10cde and 11bcd in the center are echoed, the latter in the heart of the first part (4bcd), and the first at the end of the fourth part (17cde). The mixing of these elements (A/BA'/B') seems to mark the unity of the whole better.

Words with the root *'bd* are found in the first two parts and the fourth part: «servants» and «bow down» in 2b and 5a; «serve» and «servant» in 9a and 10d; «servants» once more in 17c (accompanied, as in 10d, by «handmaid»).

The Hebrew word *kol*, translated by «not one» or «all», is repeated in 4a in the first part, in 9a, 10b and 11d in the second part, and finally, at the end of the last part in 17e.

While «your» is only used of God in the first part («the Lord *your* God» in 2a, 5b and 7a) and is only used of the neighbor in the last part («*your* neighbor» in 16, 17a, 17b and 17e), in the two central parts it not only describes God («the Lord *your* God» in 10a and 12c) but also the six terms of the list in 10cde («*your* son and *your* daughter, *your* servant and *your* handmaid, *your* livestock and *your* guest») and the parental couple («*your* father and *your* mother» in 12a).

The adjective «jealous» (5b), the two verbs «to love» (6b) and «to commit adultery» (14) and the syntagma «to covet your neighbor's wife» (17b) belong to the same semantic field of marital and extra-marital relationships. We might also view the «and» which acts as a conjunction between «your father *and* your mother» (12a) as another, discreet, expression of the same type of relationship.

BIBLICAL CONTEXT

«Each of you must respect his father and mother and you must keep my Sabbaths»

Thus begins the central chapter of the «law of holiness» (Lev 19:3). The fact that these two commandments are joined together is an external confirmation of the Decalogue's composition, in which the same elements are juxtaposed, the other way around, at the center of the whole. The link between these two commandments is surprising. What do a practice which is particular to the people of Israel, and a point of natural law which seems to belong to all the nations, have in common?

INTERPRETATION

The interpretation offered here will be developed from the center of the text, or from the whole formed by the second and third parts (8-12).

Unicity

Like the Lord God, father and mother are unique. A man can have many sons and daughters (10c), he may rule over a great number of servants and handmaids (10d), possess huge flocks and welcome many strangers to his door (10e), but he will only ever have one father and one mother (12a). The relationship with those who brought him into the world is very special. The couple who begat him will never be replaced by brothers, sisters, wives, sons and daughters, however many of each there may be. Of all the family relationships, however strong, the link with father and mother is the only one which cannot be multiplied, just as God cannot be multiplied. The uniqueness of father and mother is an image and symbol of the divine uniqueness. The Lord God has created everything, and it is from him alone, to the exclusion of all else, that we owe our existence (11a). Our fathers and mothers, created in the image of God, are the route through which life is transmitted to us. In honoring them, we acknowledge in them God's gift which has made us exist on earth (12bc).

Inheritance

Glorifying the Lord in one's father and mother, man acknowledges himself to be an heir. Everything that he is and that he has, servants and handmaids, cattle and donkeys, (10de), the land which feeds him (12c), all this has been left to him by his parents, and it has been «given»to him by God through them (12c). He holds his days (12b) and his land (12c) from Another; in sacrificing the seventh day (10a) which is also a gift from God, he acknowledges that even the work which he is given to do on the six days reserved for work (9), in the image of God who made the heavens and earth and the sea and all that they contain (11a-d). Everything is a gift—what he is, what he has, what he does. His life and happiness are linked to this joyful admission. To deny the gift would be, in the same way, to refuse it—logically this would be to shorten his days (12b) and suddenly to leave this earth (12c).

Filiation

Man is an heir even through his descendents. The children he produces on earth are the most wonderful gift which God can give him. This is why sterility is the supreme curse in the Bible—because the supreme blessing, of becoming, like God, a father and mother, is removed from the person. One can only be a true son, a full heir to God the Father, when one has also had children oneself. The man with no descendents, who has no fruit in flesh or in spirit, is not really a man. The two central commandments of the Decalogue define my existence in this double temporal dimension, in its double ontological truth. I am a son or a daughter, and a father or a mother; I beget and am begotten. Here is the fundamental dimension of my being. The Sabbath commandment is aimed at me as a father, who is to free my children from the slavery of work; the following commandment addresses me as a child, who is to honor my father and mother for the freedom which they have given me to leave them in order to become, in my turn, a father or mother.

Freedom

Man created by God is a free subject. The Sabbath is given to him to acknowledge and practice this freedom, himself first, by freeing himself from the slavery of daily work; and at the same time his son and daughter, his servants and his handmaids. He must not treat his son and daughter as slaves; on the contrary, he is to treat his servants as children. Sanctifying the Sabbath day is considering the son's freedom to be holy, sacred, not to be touched by anyone. The child's freedom is for all—the child that I am, even as my children, servants and employees, even the strangers, representing all humanity, are children. The father's and mother's freedom is to recognize that their son and daughter are free, that they are, like them, heirs. It is to pass on the narrative of the gift which was made to them when God brought them out of the land of Egypt from the house of slavery, along with the land which they received. Glorifying one's father and mother is to honor in them those who have received from God even more than those who give.

«The God of you», «the neighbor of you»

«The neighbor» exists (13-17), just as «God» does(2-7). Both have a proper name which is to be respected and honored. «Pronouncing the Name of the Lord your God in vain» (7) and «testifying falsely against your neighbor» (16) mean treating them as though they did not exist. Behaving in this way would deny that the Lord is my God, that the neighbor is my neighbor; it would be to state that they do not count, that they are nothing *to me*, and thus to treat myself as not existing. To deny the other's name, that is, their personhood, is to refuse the other as a relationship which makes me exist as a person. It is not only the Lord my God who makes me exist, but also my neighbor. The «I» can only subsist next to a «you», in relationship with him.

«The house of servants»

The founding, creative act of the Lord is the bringing of Israel out of the house of slavery. «The Lord» thus defines himself as the one who historically brought the children of Israel «out of the land of Egypt», but he is also the one who calls humanity each day to leave «the house of servants» (2b). In addition, he is the one who calls us to imitate him, by freeing others from slavery. The father who reduces his daughter and son to slavery even during the Sabbath, who does not free his servant and handmaid, makes them live —if such is living— in a «house of servants». On the other hand, the one who does not treat his son as a slave, but treats his slave as a child, bringing him out of Egypt, imitating the Lord's behavior, gives them life. The man who «covets another's house» who steals his servant and handmaid, his cattle and ass, who takes his wife, shuts all of them up in a «house of servants». Deprived of «all which is his», the neighbor will soon himself be reduced to slavery. And, finally, the man who reduces the other to slavery also shows himself, more than his victim, to be a slave of his «covetousness» (17ab) —he kills the other, and kills himself.

Child not slave

Along with the land (12), only the child can receive the Law, the Law distilled here in the Ten Words. Land is not passed on to the slave, and neither is the Law, for then it would be coercion by power. The Law is what one accepts freely, the very substance of freedom. It could not be given in Egypt to those who were simply a bunch of slaves, oppressed by their masters, but in the desert, following the liberation worked by the mighty hand of the Lord (2), to those who had become a people, the actors of their own history. The Law consecrates freedom at the same time as it founds it. The Lord's «mercy» will rest on the links between father and son until the thousandth generation for those who love him and observe his commandments (6). Love is the other name for the freedom given by the Law.

Jealousy, love, adultery

The Lord introduces himself as a «jealous God» (5b). This adjective is surprising, and so needs to be interpreted. As is always the case, it can be understood negatively or positively. It would be negative if we understood that God does not want man to take what he owns. In the text, only God's Name is called «his»; nothing else, neither «what is in the heavens above, nor what is on the earth, nor what is in the waters under the earth» (4bcd) is said to belong to God, and, even more so, to humanity! If God has brought them out of the house of slavery it is certainly not to bow down before him. God is jealous of humanity's freedom. His deepest desire is that humanity bow to no one, not even an image of him (4a.5a). Love is not slavery, but a free belonging in which each respects the otherness of the other. The idolater wants to won he who is totally the Other as a thing. The adulterer does not respect the Other's identity, nor what is his. Each deny the other and themselves. The truly free child is the one to whom authority has been given to honor in his parents the conjunction «and» which both distinguishes and unites them, that is, the love which begat him.

The covenant

The Ten Words are not a Law before all else. They are not a list of commands, imposed by a boss who will make humanity's debts weigh them down for ever. The gift of life and of freedom is not blackmail on God's part, in which humanity is indebted to the divinity. The commandments are a single word, which means commitment, promise, confidence. Whoever «gives his word» makes a commitment and, at the same time, trusts in the other, running the risk of betrayal. Just as in love, like the signing of a marriage contract[56], in which the two

56 On the marriage-type covenant concluded by the giving of the Degalogue, see MESSAS CH., «Les Dix Paroles», 17,19.

contracting the marriage are equal[57], the Ten Words represent the pact which God offers to his people, which will be concluded by the rite of the covenant (Exod 24). The gift of freedom presupposes that God has accepted the possibility of rejection, of being «hated» rather than «loved» (5-6)[58]. The punishment proposed for the one who betrays God's trust is not the vengeance of one who feels wounded by infidelity, but the remedy of the One who wishes to save a life, a «visit» from the One who seeks to offer, alongside forgiveness, the restoration of the loving relationship[59].

2.3. The Decalogue in Deuteronomy (Deut 5:6-21)

Three books further on, the Bible again returns to the Decalogue. According to the biblical account, forty years had passed and the generation of those who had received the Exodus Decalogue had died. Before dying within sight of the Promised Land, Moses repeated the Ten Words to their children, who were preparing to enter the land which the Lord had promised to give them. In narrative terms, therefore, the first Decalogue is situated after the leaving of the land of Egypt and the crossing of the Red Sea, and the second before the crossing of the Jordan which enables the people to enter the Promised Land.

COMPOSITION

THE FIRST PART (DEUT 5:6-11)

The first part of the Decalogue in Deuteronomy is absolutely identical to the Exodus Decalogue[60].

57 Bovati, 135.
58 Bovati, 97-101.
59 Bovati, 119, 121.
60 See p. 98.

THE SECOND PART (DEUT 5:12-15)

The first and last sub-parts (12 and 15de) mirror one another with «the day of the Sabbath» preceded by the verbs «to observe» and «to do» in the outer members (12a and 15e), and «what has commanded you the Lord your God» in the second member at the start (12b) and then in the first member at the end (15d).

The central sub-part (13-15c) lays out exactly what «what has commanded you the Lord your God», that is, what it means «to observe» (12a) or «to do» (15e) «the Sabbath day».

+ 12 ***To observe***	THE DAY	OF SABBATH	to consecrate it,
: according to what	*commanded you*		**YHWH YOUR GOD.**
:: 13 Six	*DAYS*	***you will serve***	
:: and ***you will do***	*all*	*your work*;	
.. 14 and the seventh	DAY	IS SABBATH to	**YHWH YOUR GOD.**
– ***You shall not do***	*any*	*work*,	*you*,
	. and your son	and your daughter,	
	. and your **servant**	and your ***handmaid***,	
	. and your ox,	and your ass and all your livestock,	
	. and your guest	who (is) at your gates,	
= so that ***they rest*** your **servant**		and your ***handmaid***,	like *you*.
:: 15 And you will remember that **servant**		you were	in the land of Egypt
.. and brought you	**YHWH**	**YOUR GOD**	from there
.. with hand	mighty	and arm	extended.
: Therefore	*commanded you*		**YHWH YOUR GOD**
+ of ***doing***	THE DAY	OF SABBATH.	

- The first piece has a single trimember AA'B segment (13-14a) in which the six days are of work are opposed to the seventh day.
- The symmetric piece (15abc) is also a trimember, but this time it is ABB', with slavery opposed to freedom, so the six days of the week during which one «serves» (13a) correspond to the time which the children of Israel spent as «servants» in the land of Egypt (15a), while the Sabbath (14a) corresponds to the freedom (15bc) worked by «the Lord your God» (whose name is repeated in 15b as it is in 14a).

• The central piece (14b-g) is made up of a trimember (14bcd), a bimember, which completes the list (14ef) and a unimember (14g) in which the aim of the cessation of «work» is explained. Note the repetition of «servant and handmaid» (14d and 14g) and the pronoun «you» at the end of the outer members of the piece (14b and 14g).

THE THIRD PART (DEUT 5:16)

+ [16] Honor	the father	of **you**	and the mother	of **you**,
+ according to what	commanded	to **you**	**YHWH THE GOD**	of **you**,
: *so that*	are prolonged		the days	of **you**
: and *so that*	there is happiness			for **you**,
: on the land that	**YHWH THE GOD**	of **you**	donates	to **you**.

The part has two segments. The final trimember (16cde) expresses the reason for the commandment (16ab), indicated by the repetition of the conjunction «so that» (16cd). Note the repetition of the syntagma «the Lord the God of you» in the final members (16b and 16e). Each member ends with the same pronomial suffix, «you», which also appears three other times (in 16a, 16b and 16e).

THE LAST PART (DEUT 5:17-21)

+ 17	You	SHALL NOT	**KILL**			
:: 18 and	you	SHALL NOT	*COMMIT ADULTERY*			
– 19 and	you	SHALL NOT	**STEAL.**			
+ 20 And	you	SHALL NOT	**TESTIFY**		against ***your neighbor***	a testimony in vain,
:: 21 and	you	SHALL NOT	*COVET*		the wife	of ***your neighbor***
– and	you	SHALL NOT	**DESIRE**		the house	of ***your neighbor***,
			:	his field	and his servant	and his handmaid,
			:	his ox	and his ass	
			*	and all	that is to	***your neighbor***.

This part is made up of two sub-parts. The first (17-19) is identical to Exod 20:13-15, but the three commandments are now linked by two «and»s, as though the three sins of murder, adultery and theft were interlinked[61].

The composition of the first segment of the second sub-part (20-21b) is almost the same as the composition of Exod 20:16-17b. The Deuteronomy version inverts the last two members, placing «the wife» before «the house», so that the parallelism between the three commandments in the first sub-part is more regular —not only does false witness correspond to murder, but «coveting the wife of your neighbor» corresponds to «committing adultery» and «desiring the house of your neighbor» to «stealing». Note the addition of «field» in the last segment (21cde), and particularly the play between the coordinating conjunctions which bring the terms together in sub-groups.

61 See BEAUCHAMP P., *D'une montagne à l'autre, la Loi de Dieu*, 43-47. The most well-known and emblematic account of this connection is David, whose covetousness led him to commit adultery with Bathsheba, after which he followed the way of the liar and finally had her husband killed (see too the story of Naboth's vineyard in 1 Kings 21).

THE PASSAGE AS A WHOLE (DEUT 5:6-20)

6 I am THE LORD YOUR GOD
who BROUGHT YOU FROM THE LAND OF EGYPT, from the house of *SERVANTS*:
7 ***Shall not*** exist for you other gods before me.

8 You ***shall not*** do for you sculptures or any image,
of what is in the heavens above,
and of what is on the earth bellow,
and of what is in the waters under the earth,
9 you ***shall not*** prostrate before them and you ***shall not*** be *SERVANTS* to them,
because I am THE LORD YOUR GOD, the God jealous,
who visits the iniquity of the **FATHERS** on **SONS** on the third or fourth (generations)
for those who hate me,
10 and who does mercy as far as a thousand (generations)
for those who love me and ***observe*** *my commands*.

11 You ***shall not*** pronounce the name of THE LORD YOUR GOD **in vain**,
because the Lord ***does not*** hold innocent one who pronounces his name **in vain**.

12 ***To observe*** the day of Sabbath to consecrate it,
according to what *COMMANDED you* THE LORD YOUR GOD.

13 Six days *YOU WILL SERVE* and will do all your work,
14 and the seventh day is Sabbath to THE LORD YOUR GOD.

= You ***shall not*** do any work, you,
. neither your **SON**, nor your **DAUGHTER**,
. neither your *SERVANT*, nor your *HANDMAID*,
. neither your ox, nor your ass, all your livestock,
. nor your guest who is at your doors,
= so that they rest your *SERVANT* and your *HANDMAID*, like you.

15 You will remember that *SERVANT* you were in LAND OF EGYT
and BROUGHT YOU FROM THERE THE LORD YOUR GOD by mighty hand and extended arm.

Therefore *COMMANDED you* THE LORD YOUR GOD
of doing the day of Sabbath.

16 ***Honor*** your **FATHER** and your **MOTHER**,
according to what *COMMANDED you* THE LORD YOUR GOD,
so that your days are prolonged and so that there is for you happiness,
on the land that THE LORD YOUR GOD gives you.

17 You ***shall not*** kill. 18 You ***shall not*** commit adultery. 19 You ***shall not*** steal.

20 You ***shall not*** testimony against YOUR NEIGHBOR **in vain**.
21 You ***shall not*** covet the wife of YOUR NEIGHBOR.
You ***shall not*** desire the house of YOUR NEIGHBOR,
. his field and his *SERVANT* and his *HANDMAID*,
. his ox and his ass,
. and all that is of YOUR NEIGHBOR.

Overall, the composition of the Decalogue in Deuteronomy is the same as in the Exodus version. The first part (6-11) is given to duties towards «the Lord *your* God» and the last part (17-21) to duties towards «*your* neighbor». In the center are the only two positive commandments, the consecration of the Sabbath (12-15) and the honor due to father and mother (16).

The links between the outer parts are the same as in the Exodus version (see p. 111). However, they are even more marked because of the repetition of «in vain» in 20 as in 11a and 11b; in Exodus, the synonyms «in vain» and «false» were used.

The links between the two central commandments are more marked in Deuteronomy than in Exodus, where the same clause is repeated, in an identical position —«according to what has a commanded you the Lord your God» (12b. 16b). Here is confirmation that these two commandments are to be read together.

Note, too, that «the *land* of Egypt» in 15a corresponds to «the *earth* that the Lord your God gives you» (16d), which link could lead us to interpret this «earth» as the land of Israel[62].

The link between the Sabbath commandment and the first part is established through the reminder of the leaving of Egypt (6b.15ab). The repetition of «your servant and your handmaid» at the end of 14 and of «servant» in 15a emphasize the importance of the theme of slavery (along with «serve», these two words are repeated ten times).

The verb and noun of the syntagma «those who observe my commandments» at the end of the central sub-part of the first part (10b) are repeated in the two central parts—«observe» at the start of the second part (12a) and «according to what commanded you» in 12b and 16b (and also in 15c)[63].

The Exodus and Deuteronomy Decalogues are both very similar and very different. Their similarities might lead us to think that they are not two different texts, but two versions of the same text. The Bible calls both «the Ten Words»[64] or «the Two Tablets»[65].

62 The term *ʾădāmâ* is used with this meaning in, for example, Deut 30:20: «[19] I call heaven and earth to witness against you today: I set before you life or death, blessing or curse. Choose life, then, so that you and your descendents may live, [20] in the love of Yhwh your God, obeying his voice, clinging to him; for in this your life consists, and on this depends your long stay *in the land* which Yhwh swore to your fathers, Abraham, Isaac and Jacob, he would give them» (see too Deut 32:47; see p. 108, n. 48).

63 The verb «to remember» at the start of the Sabbath commandment in Exodus has not disppeared from the Deuteronomy version, but appears at the start of 15.

64 See p. 96, n. 33.

65 See p. 96, n. 37.

Exod 20:2-17	Deut 5:6-21
2 I AM YHWH YOUR GOD WHO BROUGHT YOU FROM THE LAND OF EGYPT, FROM THE HOUSE OF SERVANTS: 3 SHALL NOT EXIST FOR YOU OTHER GODS BEFORE ME.	6 I AM YHWH YOUR GOD WHO BROUGHT YOU FROM THE LAND OF EGYPT, FROM THE HOUSE OF SERVANTS: 7 SHALL NOT EXIST FOR YOU OTHER GODS BEFORE ME.
4 YOU SHALL NOT MAKE FOR YOU SCULPTURE OR ANY REPRESENTATION, OF WHAT IS IN THE HEAVENS ABOVE, AND OF WHAT IS ON THE EARTH BELOW, AND OF WHAT IS IN THE WATERS UNDER THE EARTH; 5 YOU SHALL NOT PROSTRATE BEFORE THEM AND YOU SHALL NOT BE SERVANTS TO THEM: - BECAUSE I AM YHWH YOUR GOD, THE JEALOUS GOD, WHO VISITS THE INIQUITY OF FATHERS ON SONS ON THIRD AND ON FOURTH GENERATIONS FOR THOSE WHO HATE ME, 6 AND WHO DOES MERCY TO THOUSAND GENERATIONS FOR THOSE WHO LOVE ME AND OBSERVE MY COMMANDS.	8 YOU SHALL NOT MAKE FOR YOU SCULPTURE OR ANY REPRESENTATION, OF WHAT IS IN THE HEAVENS ABOVE, AND OF WHAT IS ON THE EARTH BELOW, AND OF WHAT IS IN THE WATERS UNDER THE EARTH; 9 YOU SHALL NOT PROSTRATE BEFORE THEM AND YOU SHALL NOT BE SERVANTS TO THEM: - BECAUSE I AM YHWH YOUR GOD, THE JEALOUS GOD, WHO VISITS THE INIQUITY OF FATHERS ON SONS ON THIRD AND ON FOURTH GENERATIONS FOR THOSE WHO HATE ME, 10 AND WHO DOES MERCY TO THOUSAND GENERATIONS FOR THOSE WHO LOVE ME AND OBSERVE MY COMMANDS.
7 YOU SHALL NOT PRONOUNCE THE NAME OF YHWH YOUR GOD IN VAIN: BECAUSE YHWH DOES NOT HOLD INNOCENT ONE WHO PRONOUNCES HIS NAME IN VAIN.	11 YOU SHALL NOT PRONOUNCE THE NAME OF YHWH YOUR GOD IN VAIN: BECAUSE YHWH DOES NOT HOLD INNOCENT ONE WHO PRONOUNCES HIS NAME IN VAIN.
8 Remember of THE DAY OF SABBATH TO CONSECRATE IT.	12 Observe THE DAY OF SABBATH TO CONSECRATE IT, *According to what commanded you Yhwh your God.*
9 SIX DAYS YOU WILL SERVE AND WILL DO ALL YOUR WORK. - 10 AND SEVENTH DAY IS SABBATH TO YHWH YOUR GOD: YOU SHALL NOT DO ANY WORK, YOU, AND YOUR SON AND YOUR DAUGHTER, YOUR SERVANT AND YOUR HANDMAID, AND YOUR LIVESTOCK AND YOUR GUEST WHO IS AT YOUR GATES.	13 SIX DAYS YOU WILL SERVE AND WILL DO ALL YOUR WORK; 14 AND SEVENTH DAY IS SABBATH TO YHWH YOUR GOD. - YOU SHALL NOT DO ANY WORK, YOU, AND YOUR SON AND YOUR DAUGHTER, *and* YOUR SERVANT AND YOUR HANDMAID, AND *your ox, and your ass and all* YOUR LIVESTOCK, AND YOUR GUEST WHO IS AT YOUR GATES, *so that they rest your servant and your handmaid as you.*
11 Because in six days Yhwh made the heavens and the earth and the sea and all that are in them and he rested the seventh day.	15 You will remember that servants you were in land of Egypt and Yhwh your God brought you from there with mighty hand and extended arm.
THEREFORE YHWH blessed *THE DAY OF SABBATH* and consecrated it.	THEREFORE YHWH *your God* commanded you of doing *THE DAY OF SABBATH.*
12 HONOR YOUR FATHER AND YOUR MOTHER, SO THAT YOUR DAYS ARE PROLONGED, ON THE LAND THAT YHWH YOUR GOD GIVES YOU.	16 HONOR YOUR FATHER AND YOUR MOTHER, *according to what commanded you Yhwh your God,* SO THAT YOUR DAYS ARE PROLONGED *and so that there is happiness for you,* ON THE LAND THAT YHWH YOUR GOD GIVES YOU.
13 YOU SHALL NOT KILL 14 YOU SHALL NOT COMMIT ADULTERY 15 YOU SHALL NOT STEAL. - 16 YOU SHALL NOT TESTIFY AGAINST YOUR NEIGHBOR falsely. 17 YOU SHALL NOT COVET *THE HOUSE* OF YOUR NEIGHBOR. YOU SHALL NOT COVET *THE WIFE* OF YOUR NEIGHBOR, AND HIS SERVANT AND HIS HANDMAID, and HIS OX AND HIS ASS AND ALL THAT IS OF YOUR NEIGHBOR.	17 YOU SHALL NOT KILL 18 *and* YOU SHALL NOT COMMIT ADULTERY 19 *and* YOU SHALL NOT STEAL. - 20 *And* YOU SHALL NOT TESTIFY AGAINST YOUR NEIGHBOR in vain, 21 *and* YOU SHALL NOT COVET *THE WIFE* OF YOUR NEIGHBOR, *and* YOU SHALL NOT desire *THE HOUSE* OF YOUR NEIGHBOR, *his field* AND HIS SERVANT AND HIS HANDMAID, HIS OX AND HIS ASS AND ALL THAT IS OF YOUR NEIGHBOR.

As we have already seen, the first parts of the two versions (Exod 20:2-7 and Deut 5:6-10) are absolutely identical.

The Sabbath commandment in Deuteronomy (12-15) is quite different from the one in Exodus, not only in its more emphasized concentric composition but, in particular, in the justification which is given in it —no longer creation, but freedom from the land of Egypt.

The third part of the Deuteronomy Decalogue is extended —two additional members are inserted in between the three members of the Exodus version.

In the last part of the Deuteronomy version, the first piece (17-19) is identical to Exod 20:13-15, but here the three commandments are coordinated by two «and»s, as though the three sins of murder, adultery and theft were correlated[66]. The composition of the first segment of the second piece (20-21b) is almost identical to that of Exod 20:16-17b. Deuteronomy reverses the last two members («wife» before «house»), so that the parallelism with the three commandments in the first piece is more regular —not only does false witness correspond to murder, but «coveting the wife of your neighbor» corresponds to «committing adultery» and «desiring the house of your neighbor...» corresponds to «stealing». Note in the last segment (21cde), the addition of «field» and, in particular the play of the coordinating conjunctions which group the terms into sub-groups.

2.4. *Why are there two versions of the Decalogue?*

We may wonder why such a fundamental text has been handed down in two different versions.

Historical explanations

It is possible to look for an explanation in the texts' origins, that is, by trying to trace the texts' history. The two versions are due to two different traditions or theological schools, the Priestly school (Exodus), and the Deuteronomic school (Deuteronomy), and, therefore, from different periods —the Deuteronomic school after Josiah's reforms (622 BCE), and the Priestly school after the Exile (538 BCE); but we will not go into these questions[67].

The functions of doublets

Rather than examining the roots, we can examine the fruits, in order to reflect on the effects of the repetition of this text. The first thing to note is that this is not the only case of «doublets» in the Bible, where things are very often said twice. This is the fundamental law of biblical texts —there are two creation accounts at the start of the Old Testament (Gen 1:1-2,4a and Gen 2:4bff); there are

66 See n. 34 above.

67 See WÉNIN A., «Le Décalogue», 9-10, and, in particular, 76-78 (with Bibliography).

the two dreams, of the cup-bearer and the baker (Gen 40), and then two of Pharaoh's dreams (Gen 41)[68], which Joseph interprets from his prison, two Decalogues, two similar and different infancy accounts for Jesus at the start of the New Testament, in Matthew and Luke.

Even at the most basic level of the composition of texts, the «parallelism of members» —synonymy, antithesis, synthesis[69]— is a general characteristic of not only all poetic texts, including prophetic oracles, but also of many prose texts. For example, Ps 44 has 28 *bimember* segments —the reader can try to distinguish the three kinds of parallelisms.

1 To the choir master. By the son of Korah. A Poem.

2 God, with our ears we have heard,	our fathers have recounted to us,
That which you did in their days,	in the early days, 3 you, your hand:
The nations you disposed to plant them,	you destroyed the people to set them free.
4 Not with the sword they conquered the land	and their arm did not save them,
But your right hand and your arm	and the light of your face, for you love them.
5 You are my king, God,	who decides the salvation of Jacob,
6 In you, our adversaries we push down	in your name we tread down our aggressors.
7 For not in my bow did I trust	and my sword did not save me.
8 For you saved us from our adversaries	and our enemies you confused.
9 In God we praise every day	and your name we glorify for ever.
10 Yet you rejected us and abased us	and you no longer go out with our armies;
11 You make us retreat before the adversary	and our enemies stripped us.
12 You handed us like sheep for slaughter	and among the nations you scattered us;
13 You sold your people for nothing	and you have not gained by their price.
14 You have made us an insult for our neighbors,	scorn and reproach of those around us;
15 You have made us laughing-stock among people,	a shaking head among the nations.
16 Every day my disgrace is before me	and the shame covers my face;
17 For the voice of insults and of blasphemies,	for the face of enemy and one who avenges.
18 All this comes to us without forgetting,	without having betrayed your covenant,
19 Our heart has not turned back	not turned aside our steps from your way.
20 You have smitten us in the place of jackals,	you covered us over with darkness.
21 If we have forgotten the name of our God	and stretch our hands towards a foreign god,
22 Perhaps would God not have discovered this,	for he knows the secrets of heart?

68 See MEYNET R., *Introduction pratique à l'analyse rhétorique*, sixth stage.
69 These are R. Lowth's categories (see *Traité*, 32-37).

23 For you we are massacred every day, we are treated as sheep for slaughter.
24 Rise up, why do you sleep, Adonai? Awake, do not cast us out for ever!
25 Why do you hide your face, do you forget our misery and oppression?
26 For our soul is bowed down to the dust, our body is cleaved to the earth.
27 Arise, come to our help and redeem us because of your mercy.

The function of emphasis

The first function of binarity is emphasis. Repetition is rhetoric's strongest figure, the basic technique of the art of explaining oneself well. Every teacher knows that it is not enough to say or explain something only once. It might have been badly explained, one or other pupil might have been distracted, or might not have heard, or not have understood. The teacher must therefore say the same thing at least twice; but the second time, he will not simply repeat what he has already said—he will used other words, expand what he said, or summarize.

The «model» for this first function of binarity is clearly illustrated in the story of Joseph, Jacob's son. Pharaoh had had two dreams, the dream of the seven fat and the seven lean cows, and then the dream of the seven meager and seven full ears of grain (Gen 41). Joseph's wisdom is revealed in his ability to interpret the dreams, that is, to understand first of all the link between them. Here are Joseph's words:

> «*The dream of Pharaoh is one:* God has announced to Pharaoh what he is about to accomplish. 26 The seven good cows represent seven years, and the seven good ears of grain represent seven years, the dream is only one. 27 The seven thin and bad cows that came after them represent seven years and also the seven empty ears, blasted with an east wind: it is that there will be seven years of famine. 28 It is the thing that I told Pharaoh; God has shown to Pharaoh what he is about to accomplish: 29 behold, seven years are coming, in which there will be great abundance in the land of Egypt, 30 then seven years of famine will arise and all the abundance in the land of Egypt will be forgotten; the famine will consume the land 31 and no one knows any more that there was abundance in the lands, in front of the famine which comes afterwards, because it is very grievous. 32 *And if the dream of Pharaoh is repeated twice, signifies that this thing is decided by God and God is hastening to accomplish it*».

Joseph's final sentence clearly indicates the function of emphasis that he recognizes in the repetition of the dream.

The function of totalizing

Binarity does not only have a function of emphasis, but is also often used to indicate totality. Its simplest form is that of the merisma: «the heavens and the earth» is one way of describing the whole cosmos, «night and day» of describing how long something lasts. Let us look at one example among many[70], Luke 11:31-32[71]:

\+ 31 **THE QUEEN** OF THE SOUTH ***will rise*** in the judgment
– with the men of *this generation*
:: and will condemn *these*;

. **Because** she came from the ends of the earth
: to *HEAR* the *WISDOM* of Solomon.

= And behold, greater than Solomon is here.

- -

\+ 32 **THE MEN** OF NINEVEH ***will arise*** in the judgment
– with *this generation*
:: and will condemn *this*;

: **because** *THEY REPENTED* to the *PROCLAMATION* of Jonah.

= And behold, greater than Jonah is here.

The second piece (32) could appear to be simply a repetition of the first (31), a redundant, or even useless, «doublet». But to the undeniable function of emphasis, we can add complementarity, added to at every opportunity:

- complementarity of gender between a woman («the queen») and «men» is a way of indicating all human beings;
- we might add that complementarity is also found between the one who rules («the queen») and those who are ruled over, «men», which is another way to describe totality;
- geographical complementarity between the «South» and the North («Nineveh») which also indicates totality as all the pagans will judge this generation of the children of Israel;
- there is also, in particular, chronological and necessary complementarity between «listen» and «convert»;

70 See Ps 148: framed by the same acclamation, the first part is about the heavens, while the second deals with the earth (see *Traité*, 270).

71 See *Luc*, 530; *Traité*, 227, 558.

• there is further complementarity between the «wisdom» of the king («Solomon») and the «proclamation» of the prophet («Jonah»), which is one way of saying that Jesus is both king and prophet;
• finally, there is complementarity between the centripetal movement which leads the Queen of the South «from the ends of the earth» to Israel, and the centrifugal movement which brings Jonah from Israel to Nineveh.

«Poetic efficiency»

Binarity's effects are not only emphasis or totalization. There is also a further function, even more important, which has been called «poetic efficiency». The law of binarity allows a play on words:

> Thus we can understand that it is the pressure of a law, at the risk of calling up a repulsive rigidity, which provides the indispensable conditions for *a game, that is, a freedom.* This system of echoes always, even in prose, keeps poetical efficiency, and always directs the gaze towards a meaning which can only exist «between the lines». This is true at the simplest level of mere parallelism: «You will tread on the lion and the adder; the young lion and the serpent you will trample under foot» (Ps 91:13): this leads me to the *idea* of a threat, distinct from its materializations but inseparable from them. Energy is born out of the image, but it has to get free from it. This is probably why the biblical texts offer so much food for thought to the most demanding mind, without doing its thinking for him. They propel their reader towards the fearsome moment when he will have to do the interpretation by himself[72].

The meaning, that is, the author's presence, is not obvious to the reader—it is hidden and, at the same time, revealed «between the lines». This space calls the reader to risk interpretation, that is, not to fill in the gaps, but to dare to make themselves present with their own, personal words. A text's efficiency is measured by its ability to bring forth other texts, to make the reader feel called to write his or her own poem. Biblical binarity represents its openness, the essential condition of its fruitfulness.

72 BEAUCHAMP P., preface to MEYNET R., *L'Analyse rhétorique*, 11-12 (my emphasis).

Theological function

Pushing the reflection further would risk offering not an «explanation», but a further «interpretation» of biblical doublets, a function we might call theological. It appears that we might say that binarity's main function is to avoid being a text which is considered to be absolute, to prevent it becoming idolized in some way. If there were only one text, only one Decalogue, or one Our Father, one might be tempted to worship it, like the Golden Calf. Once duplicated, both similar and different, they are like the cherubim on the ark of the covenant—facing one another symmetrically, their function is to mark the empty space which both separates and unites them, to indicate the location of the divine Presence:

> There I will meet you right at that place. It is above the propitiatory, between the two cherubim which are upon the ark of the Testimony, I will give you my commands concerning the Israelites (Exod 25:22; see also Num 7:89).

Let us try to imagine how great would be the temptation to touch Jesus, to idolize his words, if we had not four, but only one Gospel. Traditional iconography represents the evangelists with four different faces—the man for Matthew, the lion for Mark, the bull for Luke, the eagle for John[73]. According to Ezekiel (Ezek 10:14), these are the four faces of the cherubim, which are not to be confused with the Presence they are the sign of: «The glory of Yhwh came out from the Temple threshold and passed over the cherubim» (Ezek 10:18).

This is why the Church has always, with great determination, refused every attempt at reducing the four Gospels to a single text, whether that of Marcion, who kept only the third Gospel and rejected the others, or that of Tatian, who composed the *Diatessaron*, a work combining the four Gospel recensions into a single narrative. The fact that the canon kept four different Gospels leads the reader not to succumb to the temptation to wish to touch Jesus, as though he were a fixed statue. Difference calls us to follow a person, beyond each of the texts, as Jeremiah says (Jer 20:7). The Gospel is four-faced; Jesus is unique. The fact that the Decalogue has been handed down to us in two different forms leads us to listen to the one God beyond the texts.

The illustration on p. 97 is a beautiful representation of what I have just attempted to explain. At each end of the four arms of the cross are the four evan-

73 See BOGAERT P.-M., «Les Quatre Vivants, l'Évangile et les évangiles».

gelists. On the left, Matthew is identified with his name. It is easy to recognize the others —the bull is traditionally the attribute of Luke, at the bottom, the eagle of John, at the top, and Mark's lion on the right. All four have the book of their own Gospel in their hand. In the center, Christ is represented as the image of the Lamb of God carrying the haloed crucifix; the image is accompanied by the inscription, «Ecce Agnus Dei» («Behold the Lamb of God»); Jesus' name is inscribed, in abbreviation, in the upper two quarters. Matthew's gaze is turned to Jesus, as is Mark's. Note too a difference between the Synoptic Gospels and the Fourth Gospel —the first three show Christ with arrows (only one for Matthew and Mark, two for Luke), which John does not do.

INTERPRETATION OF THE CALL OF THE RICH YOUNG MAN IN MATTHEW

The man's desire

The man who approaches, whom Jesus, like the reader, knows nothing about to start with, is moved by a great unlimited desire. Unlike the blind men of Jericho he is not asking for alms, or even to be healed of an infirmity. He wants nothing less than «eternal life» (16c). He is quite praiseworthy for wanting this kind of life, which is nothing ephemeral but which lasts for ever. With this request he expresses what is in the heart of every person —not just «long days on earth», as promised in the Decalogue (Exod 20:12), but, as had been coming to light for some centuries among the Jewish people of Jesus' day, the fullness of a life unlimited by death.

A corrected request

However praiseworthy this man's deep desire, it is, as his way of making his request shows, contaminated. The words which he uses betray a completely wrong attitude; and this is why Jesus corrects him. The man says he is ready «to do what is good» (16b); Jesus, replying that «only one is good» (17c), invites him to come out of the narcissism of the one who only sees himself and to look towards the Other, towards his God, the only source of all that is good. His desire to «do» good must be converted to the service of the one who knows that good is no real good if it is not received from another. «Eternal life» is not something which one can «have» (16c), acquire, possess, appropriate to oneself; it is not possible to assimilate it and, as it were, eat it as our first parents wished to eat the fruit of the tree in Eden. Jesus realigns the man's expression and desire by saying, rather than «*have* eternal life» (16c): «*enter* into life» (17d). Here are two expressions which are diametrically opposed to one another. «To enter into life» means «to be born»; it means to come out of one-self, to be reborn. Another way of saying this in the Gospels is «to enter into the kingdom of God». «To enter into life» means to enter into the life of another, in the sense which we give that expression to say «to fall in love» with another person and to be loved by them.

To observe or hold the commandments

Jesus invites the man to «observe the commandments» (17e) and, having heard them, he says, (18d-19), «All these I *held*» (20b). These two verbs might, on a first reading, seem to be synonymous, and they may even be so in Greek[74]. However, the objects governed by the two verbs change their connotations. On the one hand it is a question of «observing» the commandments, that is, listening to the voice of another, while on the other it is «holding» things (the neuter plural can be translated as «all these things»). Now we only need to hear the question added by the young man: «what do I still lack?» (20c). We have the feeling that, for him, the commandments are not a word which is spoken to him, a call addressed to him, but something which he possesses. If the commandments are thought of as things, we should not be surprised that he is still missing nothing. Wealth is never enough for the one who has plenty to live on, as daily experience shows. If the Law is idolized—and this is Jesus' basic complaint about the Pharisees— there are never enough commandments, others must always be added—the idol is insatiable.

«Anguish is born when a need is not support for a lack is missing» (J. Lacan)

It is only when the man is about to state that he has held «all» and to express at the same time the emptiness of a lack (20c) that the reader realizes that this is «a young man» (20a). Dissatisfaction is probably the most significant characteristic of adolescence, and the nature of this dissatisfaction is being unable to precisely define what is missing, and to give it a name. This is an indefinite and at the same time an infinite thing: «eternal life». Jesus understands that the young man «wishes to be perfect» (21b); this description can also be translated by «complete», «finished», «mature», even «adult». To a certain extent, the test Jesus puts him to is an initiation test, to make him move from childhood to adulthood.

74 Note that the second verb, *phylassō*, is only used by Matthew here, but the noun with the same root, *phylakē*, with the meaning of «prison» appears seven times (Matt 5:25; 14:3; 18:30; 25:36.39. 43.44).

Being mature means being able to tolerate emptiness, lack, the necessary distance to establish an authentic relationship with the other, while knowing that love presupposes giving up knowing the other, possessing them, assimilating them or consuming them like an object to be eaten. This is also of course true for the woman the young man will one day meet; it is also true for the one whom he is to meet, while observing his commandments, in love.

Father of the poor

If he wishes to be perfect, completed, adult, Jesus invites this young man to be open to others; but not only to those whom the Decalogue mentions: in addition to the father and mother whom he has always honored (19a), he has already learned to respect «his neighbor», that is the person who has a wife, reputation, house and property (18d) and whom he is to «love as himself», according to what Leviticus says (19b). He is called to perfection in the commandment, to open himself to «the poor», to those who have nothing and therefore cannot be stolen from. He does not say to him to abandon the property which he has received from his parents, the property which enables him to live without stealing and make it very easy for him to honor father and mother, he tells him to give it to the poor. Everything which he has received as an inheritance from his parents, without having had to do anything at all to deserve it, is to be handed on to those who have received nothing. In this way he is called to fatherhood, as he is making the poor the heirs to his property. It is only on this condition that he, too, can inherit «a treasure in heaven» (21e), that is, «eternal life» (16c), and, thus, become a son of God.

«And come, follow me!»

Jesus is not content to call the young man to abandon his inheritance on behalf of the poor, but he also invites him to follow him. He does not call him to himself, but to accompany him on the way; not to join him in a dual relationship, closed in on itself, which would be another form of narcissism[75]. Jesus' path is the one which leads to the Father: «only one is good» (17c). Not to consider

75 Here I cannot resist quoting a poet: «He does not speak to draw a dust of love on himself. What he wants he does not want for himself. What he wants is that we tolerate one another to live together. He does not say, love me. He says, love each other. There is a gulf between these two phrases. On the one hand there is the gulf, and we rmain on the other side. This is perhaps the only man who has ever really spoken, broken the ties of words and of seduction, of love and of complaints» (BOBIN C., *L'homme qui marche*, 16-17).

Jesus essentially in how he relates to the Father would be to worship him idolatrously. It is not a question of denying Jesus' divinity, but of seeing in him the image of the Father, honoring him as the only Son of God. It is only in this way that we, too, can become children of the Father.

Sadness, a motif of hope

At the end of the narrative, the young man «goes away» (22a); he does not accept Jesus' invitation to accompany him on his path. The text adds that he goes away «sad». Sadness is a sign of interior malaise. He had come to express his dissatisfaction, in the hope of being able to overcome it, ready to «do» whatever was needed to fulfill it; and now he goes away with more, deeper, dissatisfaction, because he has felt unable to rise to the challenge, to do what Jesus said he should to be «perfect». It is true that he holds the property which he has, but he goes away with something extra which he did not have when he came onto the scene—sadness. This can perhaps open up a path for him, if he is able to recognize the sign of a call to come out of himself to find the path of love for his neighbor (19b).

Note on the conditionals in Matthew 19:17 and 21

The first conditional —«If you wish to enter life»— is clearly linked to observance of the Law («the commandments»); the second—«If you wish to be perfect» (or «adult»), implies following Jesus, conditioned by the abandonment of all wealth, including the trust put in the observance of the Law. «Perfection» in the Gospel, or through grace, can, therefore be understood as the real completion of the Law[76].

76 See, for example, Bonnard, 288.

3. **THE CALLING OF THE RICH YOUNG MAN IN MARK (MARK 10:17-22)**

COMPOSITION

– 17 And while he	was going out	on the way,	
– RUNNING SOMEONE		AND KNEELING-TOWARDS	HIM,
– HE WAS ASKING			HIM:
	. «***Good*** Master,	what	shall I do,
	. so that	**ETERNAL LIFE**	***I MIGHT INHERIT***?».

+ 18 NOW JESUS	SAID TO	HIM:	
: «Why	do you tell me	***good***?	
: No one	is ***good***	if not ***THE ONLY*** God!	
- 19 You know	the commandments:		
	.. «Do not kill,	do not commit-adultery,	
	.. ***DO NOT STEAL***,	do not testimony-falsely,	***DO NOT DEFRAUD***;
	:: *Honor your father and your mother*"».		

– 20 He declared to him:			
«Master,	ALL THESE	***I KEPT BY MYSELF***	from my youth».

+ 21 NOW JESUS	LOOKED AT	HIM,	
+ LOVED HIM	AND SAID TO	HIM:	
: «***ONLY ONE*** thing you lack:			
	.. Go,	WHAT YOU HAVE	***SELL***
	.. and	***GIVE TO***	the poor
	.. and	***YOU WILL HAVE***	**TREASURE IN HEAVEN**
	:: *and come, follow me*».		

– 22 *GLOOMY*	AT THE WORD,		
– HE WENT AWAY	*AFFLICTED*;		
	. for he was	***HAVING***	GREAT WEALTH.

Mark's passage is organized in three parts, two long parts (17-19 and 21-22) around a very short central part (20). The main reason for this division is that 17b and 21a (Markan additions) fulfill the function of initial terms for the outer parts —these members correspond very precisely to one another.

The commandments of the Decalogue (19bcd) are paralleled with Jesus' orders (21cde). At the center of the construction the rich man's declaration (20) is the pivot which balances the two series of commandments. Note that the first series ends with the honor due to father and mother (19d) and that the second ends with the invitation to follow Jesus (21e).

The outer pieces (17 and 22) are opposed to one another—the initial enthusiasm (two participles and a main clause in 17b) give way to sadness (two participles and a main clause in 22a). In addition, in the final members, «having great wealth» is opposed to «I might inherit eternal life».

BIBLICAL CONTEXT

Job

Like Job, the rich man says that he has always remained faithful to the law of the Lord (see, among many other texts, Job 13:18-28; 16:17; 23:10-12; 27:6). God has allowed Job to be tested by losing all his wealth. The man who comes to Jesus is invited to give up all his wealth; he will be compensated for such abandon by the gift of an incomparably greater wealth, «treasure in heaven», that is, close to God:

24 If you throw the gold in the dust,	and the Ophir among the stones of the brooks,
25 the Shaddai shall be your gold	and shall be for you plenty of silver.
26 Then in the Shaddai you shall delight	and you shall lift up your face to Eloah (Job 22:24-26).

Here true wisdom is found (Job 28). Job defends himself for having loved gold and wealth to the point of making them idols (31:24-28); conversely, he used his great wealth to become «the father of the poor» (29:16; see 30:24).

«Do not defraud»

This verb means to deprive the poor man of what is due to him, for example, Deut 24.14 (Alexandria Codex):

> 14 Do not defraud the salary of the poor and needy, whether he is one of your brethren or one of the sojourners who is in your land at your city-gates. 15 You shall give him his salary on the day itself, before the sun sets; because he is poor and sets his desire on it. So that he may not cry out against you to the Lord. Otherwise you will be held guilty (Deut 24:14-15; see also Sir 4:1)[77].

«From my youth»

This expression is repeated twice in Ps 71:5.17. The whole psalm, a long song of confidence in God alone, needs to be re-read:

> 5 For you are my hope, Lord, my trust, Adonai, *from my youth.*
> 6 On you I have my support *from the womb,* you my portion *from the belly of my mother,*
> in you my praise continually.

77 See Légasse, 518, n. 26.

SYNOPTIC COMPARISON (see pp. 95 and 139)

Matt 19:16-22	Mark 10:17-22
[16] AND **behold** SOMEONE coming-TOWARDS him said: «MASTER, WHAT *GOOD* SHALL I DO SO THAT I might have ETERNAL LIFE?».	[17] AND ***while he was going out on the way***, running- TOWARDS (him) SOMEONE ***and kneeling before him*** asked ***him***: «*GOOD* MASTER, WHAT SHALL I DO SO THAT ETERNAL LIFE I might inherit?».
[17] NOW HE SAID TO HIM: «WHY DO YOU ask ME about GOOD? ONLY-ONE is GOOD. **If you want to enter into the life,** **observe** THE COMMANDMENTS».	[18] NOW ***Jesus*** SAID TO HIM: «WHY DO YOU tell ME GOOD? ***No one*** (is) GOOD ***if not*** THE ONLY ***God***.
[18] **He says to him:** **«Which?».** **Now Jesus said:** **«These**: "You shall not KILL, you shall not COMMIT-ADULTERY, you shall not STEAL, you shall not TESTIMONY-FALSELY; [19] HONOR THE FATHER AND THE MOTHER" and: **"You shall love your neighbor** **as yourself"**».	[19] THE COMMANDMENTS ***you know***. «Do not KILL, do not COMMIT-ADULTERY, do not STEAL, do not TESTIMONY-FALSELY, ***do not defraud***; HONOR YOUR FATHER AND YOUR MOTHER"».
[20] Says TO HIM **the young man**: «ALL THESE I KEPT. Of what **still** I LACK?».	[20] ***Now he*** declared TO HIM: «***Master***, ALL THESE I KEPT by myself ***from my youth***».
[21] **Declared to him Jesus:** «**If you want to be perfect,** GO, SELL your possessions AND GIVE TO THE POOR AND YOU WILL HAVE TREASURE IN HEAVENS AND COME, FOLLOW ME».	[21] ***Now Jesus looked at him, loved him*** ***and said to him***: «Only one (thing) ***you*** LACK: GO, what you have SELL AND GIVE TO THE POOR AND YOU WILL HAVE TREASURE IN HEAVEN AND COME, FOLLOW ME».
[22] NOW **hearing** the young man THE WORD, HE WENT AWAY AFFLICTED; FOR HE WAS HAVING GREAT WEALTH.	[22] NOW he ***gloomy at*** THE WORD, HE WENT AWAY AFFLICTED; FOR HE WAS HAVING GREAT WEALTH.

The ends of the outer pieces (Matt 16:22; Mark 17:22) are identical. The first piece of Mark, however, is more developed, as he adds two subordinate clauses (17a.17c). The main difference is that, while in Matthew «good» qualifies deeds, in Mark it qualifies the «Master».

Matthew adds two conditionals (17d.21b) in symmetrical position, which frame the central part; he also adds the young man's comment in 18ab, and the quotation from Leviticus in 19bc. Mark adds a commandment (19f) to the quotation from the Decalogue, and changes the young man's question (Matt 20c) so that it is Jesus who speaks of lacking (21b). The sentence in the narrative which introduces this statement by Jesus (21ab) recalls the introduction (17bc) with which it forms the initial terms of the outer parts. Finally, and notably, Mark develops Matt 19:20ab, which in his construction becomes the central part of the passage.

While Matthew's passage is focused on the quotations from the commandments, Mark's balances on the rich man's statement in which he affirms his faithfulness to the law[78]. These two very different centers illustrate the initial difference well—for Matthew, the rich man's question is totally centered upon the right thing to do, and that is why the center of the passage is occupied by the commandments which have to be «done», while for Mark the emphasis of the rich man's first question seems to rest on the person to whom it is addressed, which is why the apostrophic «Master» is repeated in the center (20b) and the man's behavior is emphasized.

INTERPRETATION

It is very clear that many aspects noted in the interpretation of the parallel passage in Matthew (see pp. 135-138) can be repeated for Mark's account. However, the interpretation here will try to emphasize the specific traits of the second Evangelist's recension.

So much love!

Like Matthew, Mark waits until the final words of his account to say that the man who had come towards him was rich (22b). However, unlike Matthew, he does not say that he was young. However, we see this from the start. Only a young man has these enthusiasms and this kind of unlimited desire. Even if he were not that young, he had kept the spontaneity which belongs to adolescence: «he ran and knelt» (17b), he calls Jesus «good Master» (17c). Having, as it were, kept his distance with his first reaction (18-19), then seeing that he has now stopped calling him good and noting how he has always been faithful to the command-

78 Note that the central part of the passage in Mark ends with a quotation from Ps 71:5.17.

ments (20b), Jesus responds fully to his affection—he gazes at him and «he loved him», probably expressing his love with an affectionate gesture (21a). After Jesus' second comment, however, (21b-e), everything changes radically. A great sadness, just like his enthusiasm, submerges him. Mark emphasizes this strongly—he went away «gloomy» and «sad».

A voracious love

However, the way in which he had formulated his initial question (17c) might allow us to think that he was on the right path. The young man in Matthew wished «to have» eternal life; in Mark he wished to «inherit» it; but there is a gulf between these two verbs. He seems to have understood that life is not owned, but is received, freely, like the property a father leaves to his children without any merit on their part. When he says, «All these I kept by myself from my youth» (20), he is perhaps not very humble, but he is certainly not lying. His faithfulness gives rise to Jesus' affection reaction (21a). And it was with the same love that the Lord tested his desire for eternal life and his faithfulness to the commandments. His reaction revealed his heart and shone light on his true motive. If he were ready to leave everything he had to the poor, he would see where his treasure really lay. The only thing he lacks (21b) is, precisely, acceptance of lack. This «one thing» which Jesus introduces is clearly opposed to what he has just said: «All these I kept by myself from my youth» (20b). Still attached to his «great wealth» (22), as he had jealously kept, or held onto the commandments (20), he shows that he covets eternal life with the same voracious love which does not leave any room for the other. This other is, of course, God himself, the only good, the one who has given him the commandments and could make him inherit eternal life; but the other[s] are the poor with whom he refuses to share his inheritance, to whom he refuses the food which they need and which he wishes to hold for himself alone. It should be no surprise that, having never pronounced the name of God, he does not wish to hear the poor mentioned. «No one who fails to love the brother whom he can see can love God whom he has not seen. Indeed, this is the commandment we have received from him, that whoever loves God also loves his brother (1 John 4:20-21).

«From my youth»

When, at the very heart of the passage, the rich man declares that, «All these I kept by myself from my youth» (20b), we can certainly understand that he is telling the truth, that he has never disobeyed the commandments of the Law which deal with the neighbor. However, if we can see an echo of Psalm 71, it is also possible to expect that his attachment does not correspond to the psalmist's faith, who confesses, «You are my hope, Lord, my trust, Adonai, since my youth» (Ps 71:5), «I will tell of your justice alone» (16). He seems rather to place his trust in his own observance of the Law and, thus, in a certain way, in himself and not in God alone.

Follow the Son

When Jesus quotes the Decalogue, it may seem strange that he limits himself to the duties to one's neighbor, as though he passed over the duties to God, the commandments forbidding any idolatry, in silence. However, he reveals that the rich man is unfaithful to the first of all the commandments: if he is unable to give up his wealth, this means that he lives only for his wealth —he lives for his wealth, his wealth makes him live. This is the idol he refuses to be separated from. It might seem strange that this Jesus, who, from the start refuses so clearly to be called «good», for «no one is good but God alone», is the same Jesus who invites the rich man to follow him, from the point where this is the only thing he lacks. So who is unique, God or Jesus? Jesus himself might become an idol, if he were considered outside of his relationship to his Father. If he is able to impose such a demand without blasphemy, it is because he has totally entered the kingdom of God, because, for him, God is the only good, the supreme good. Following him is to enter the same movement. Following Jesus as the Son is to go with him, as with all sons, to the only Father.

The inheritance passed on to the child

While God alone is good, wealth is not bad. Jesus does not demand that the wealth is rejected, or even sold cheaply, but sold and a just price given to the poor. By making those who lack everything his heir, the rich man, like Job, will become «the father of the poor». Rather than enslaving them, which is the fate of their condition, he will treat them as his own children. Only the one who has acknowledged himself to be a child can become a father. The one who was wealthy in property will become wealthy in children, because he will have made the poor inherit what he received from his father and mother. Just as Jesus can call the disciples to whom he has given everything which he has received from his Father «my children» (Mark 10:24), to whom he has passed on the one «good» there is, God, who reigns over them as over him.

Why does Jesus not recall the «duties» to God? We know that these are in fact prohibitions: *no* other gods; *no* images either of those gods or of the God of Israel; *no* worship of these images; *no* use of God's name in swearing oaths or, more literally, «in vain» (Deut 5:11; Exod 20:7). A historian might suggest that, in New Testament times, it was unheard of for a Jew to worship both the God of the covenant with Israel and «Baal», or to worship any image. What had angered the prophets, from Elijah to Jeremiah, was no longer found in Israel at the time of the Gospels. So, in such conditions, what use would it have been to recall these offences? The historian's comment is very useful, particularly since it gives a new turn to the question. It makes us, or should make us, ask, what form does idolatry take when a society is no longer syncretist (Yhwh synthesized with Baal), when representations of the divinity are not seen? Alerted by this question, our attention will not stop in Jesus' time, but will turn to our own culture. The Gospel, in Matt 6:24 and Luke 16:13, gives a partial response (Matt 6:24), with the formula: «You cannot serve God and money». This is clearly about the first tablet of the Decalogue, since it deals with a choice between God and God's substitute. It is also about the characteristics our society and society in Jesus' time have in common. Finally, the theme of money, that idol, is not foreign —this is the least we can say— to the episode we are commenting on, since wealth is what prevents the hero from responding to Jesus' call.

(Cf. Beauchamp P., *D'une montagne à l'autre, la Loi de Dieu*, Paris 1999, 16-17).

4. THE CALLING OF THE RICH MAN IN LUKE (LUKE 18:18-27)[79]

COMPOSITION

This passage is composed concentrically around Jesus' words in v. 22. The outer parts (18-19 and 26-27) have two segments, the first members of which, ending with the verb «to say», introduce the words of the speakers. The first segments (18 and 26) are questions addressed to Jesus, which pose the same question about salvation (26) or «eternal life» (18). The second segments give a similar response from Jesus —only God is good, only with God can the impossible be achieved (the two occurrences of «God» act as final terms).

The second and penultimate parts (20-21 and 23-25) are made up of two pieces. This outer pieces (20 and 24-25) have a unimember segment (20a and 24a) introducing a trimember. The five commandments quoted by Jesus seem to be arranged concentrically: «do not testimony falsely» corresponds to «do

79 See *Luc*, 694-697.

\+ 18 A ruler questioned him *saying*:
– «***Good*** Master, *WHAT* ***must*** I do *TO INHERIT* **ETERNAL LIFE?**».

\+ 19 *Said* to him Jesus:
– «Why do you tell me ***good***? No one is ***good***, if not the only GOD.

* 20 You know *the commandments*:
: "Do not commit-adultery, do not kill,
: ***DO NOT STEAL***,
: do not testimony falsely, honor your father and your mother"».

• 21 He said: «*All these* ***I KEPT*** from my youth».

22 Having heard, Jesus *said* to him:
«You lack still only one thing:
all that ***YOU HAVE***
SELL (IT) and ***GIVE*** *(IT)* to the poor
AND YOU WILL HAVE **A TREASURE IN HEAVENS;**
then come and follow me».

• 23 He having heard that, became very sad: ***FOR HE WAS VERY RICH.***

* 24 Seeing him [that he became sad] *Jesus said*:
: «How difficult for ***THOSE WHO HAVE WEALTH*** to enter into the kingdom of GOD.
: 25 For it is easier that a camel enters through the eye of a needle
: than ***A RICH MAN*** enters into the kingdom of GOD!».

\+ 26 Those who heard *said*:
– «Then *WHO* ***can*** **BE SAVED?**».

\+ 27 He *said*:
– «What is ***impossible*** to men, is ***possible*** to GOD».

not kill», because false witness in a court can result in the death penalty[80]; in central place, the commandment «do not steal». The trimember 24b-25 is ABA' type. The most obvious relationship between these two trimembers is found between «do not steal» and «those who have wealth» and «a rich man». The final segment of the second part (21) and the first segment of the fourth part (23) match —they begin in the same way with «He», but, especially, they oppose what the rich man has done in relation to the commandments of the Law (21)

80 Note that Luke has changed the order of the first two commandments compared to the text of the Decalogue (see p. 109); the reason for this change could be precisely to reinforce the concentric construction.

and what he will not do in relation to Jesus' invitation (23; «very» seems to correspond to «all»).

The central part, after the narrative phrase (22ab), is concentrically composed. At the edges are two unimember segments: the «only thing» which he lacks» (22c) is to follow Jesus (22g). The central trimember is ABA' type: the first and third members oppose «all that *you have*» and «*you will have* a treasure in the heavens»; in the center is the gift to the poor (22e).

Between the two parts, «only one thing» in the center recalls «the only God» at the end of the first part (19b). In the same way, «me» at the end of the central part (22g) introduces «the kingdom of God» in 24b and 25b, for both are equally opposed to wealth.

BIBLICAL CONTEXT (see pp. 70 and 139)

Just as in Matthew and Mark, the essential reference point is the Decalogue (see p. 95) and Job (see p. 140). To Job 29:2-17 (particularly v.16: «I was the father of the poor») we can add Sir 4:1-10, which ends with these words:

> Be like a father to the fatherless
> and as good as a husband to their mothers.
> And you will be like a child to the Most High
> who will love you more than your own mother does (10).

The camel and the eye of a needle

We wanted to seek «reasonable» explanations for this image, by saying, for example, that the «camel» is not an animal, but a piece of cord or thread, or that the eye of a needle was a very narrow gate into Jerusalem. Apparently such explanations are not indispensable[81].

SYNOPTIC COMPARISON

Having studied the composition of each of the three versions, we can compare not only the syntagmas and the verses, but the way in which they have been composed, for what is crucial to understand is that the differences between the

81 See for instance Légasse, 522, n. 58 (a similar image is found in Rabbinic literature, with the difference being that the camel is replaced by an elephant).

Matt 19:16-22	Mark 10:17-22	Luke 18:18-23
16 AND behold *someone* coming-*towards* him ***said***: «MASTER, WHAT *GOOD* SHALL I DO ***so that*** I might have ETERNAL LIFE?». --- 17 NOW HE SAID TO HIM: «WHY DO YOU *ASK* ME about GOOD? ONLY-ONE is GOOD. If you want to enter into the life, observe THE COMMANDMENTS».	17 AND while he was going out on the way, running-*towards* (him) ***someone*** and kneeling before him *HE WAS INTERROGATING HIM*: «*GOOD* MASTER, WHAT SHALL I DO ***so that*** ETERNAL LIFE **I might inherit**?». --- 18 NOW **Jesus** SAID TO HIM: «WHY DO YOU **tell** ME GOOD? **No one** (is) GOOD **if not** THE ONLY **God**.	18 AND *INTERROGATED HIM* one of the rulers ***saying***: «*GOOD* MASTER, WHAT HAVING DONE ETERNAL LIFE **shall I inherit**?». 19 NOW SAID TO HIM **Jesus**: «WHY DO YOU **tell** ME GOOD? **No one** (is) GOOD **if not** THE ONLY **God**.
18 He says to him: «Which?». --- Now Jesus said: «These: "You shall not KILL, you shall not *COMMIT-ADULTERY*, you shall not STEAL, you shall not TESTIMONY-FALSELY, 19 HONOR THE FATHER AND THE MOTHER" and: "You shall love your neighbor as yourself"». --- 20 ***Says*** *to him* the young man: «ALL THESE I KEPT.	19 THE COMMANDMENTS **you know**: «**Do not** KILL, **do not** *COMMIT-ADULTERY*, **do not** STEAL, **do not** TESTIMONY-FALSELY", do not defraud; «HONOR THE FATHER **of you** AND THE MOTHER"». 20 **Now he** declared *to him*: «Master, ALL THESE I KEPT BY MYSELF **from** my **youth**».	20 THE COMMANDMENTS **you know**: --- "**Do not** *COMMIT-ADULTERY*, **do not** KILL, **do not** STEAL, **do not** TESTIMONY-FALSELY; HONOR THE FATHER **of you** AND THE MOTHER"». 21 **Now he** ***said***: «ALL THESE I KEPT **from the youth**».
Of what ***still*** *I lack*?». 21 Declared to him Jesus: «If you want to be perfect, *go*, SELL your possessions AND GIVE TO THE POOR AND YOU WILL HAVE TREASURE IN HEAVENS AND COME, FOLLOW ME». --- 22 Now ***hearing*** the young man *the word, he went away afflicted*; FOR HE WAS *having great wealth*.	21 **Now Jesus** looking at him loved him and **said to him**: «**Only one** (thing) **you** *lack*: --- *go*, **what you have** SELL AND GIVE TO THE POOR AND YOU WILL HAVE TREASURE IN HEAVEN AND COME, FOLLOW ME». --- 22 Now he gloomy at *the word, he went away afflicted*; FOR HE WAS *having great wealth*.	22 **Now** hearing (this) **Jesus** **said to him**: «***Still*** **only one** (thing) **you** fall short: all **what you have** SELL AND GIVE around THE POOR AND YOU WILL HAVE TREASURE IN HEAVENS AND COME, FOLLOW ME». 23 Now ***hearing*** This he became sad; FOR HE WAS very rich.
23 ***Now*** JESUS SAID *to his disciples*: …	23 And JESUS looking around SAYS *to his disciples*: …	24 ***Now*** seeing him JESUS [became sad] SAID: --- «How difficult for those who have wealth to enter into the kingdom of God! 25 It is easier that a camel enters through the eye of a needle than a rich man enters into the kingdom of God». 26 Now those who heard said: «Then who can be saved?». 27 Now he said: «What is impossible to men, is possible to God».

three Synoptic Gospels together have as their function the effect of significantly changing the architecture of each.

The most remarkable point is that the center moves:

- in Matthew, the narrative is focused on quotations from the Old Testament, that is, on the «commandments» of the Law (18b-19c);
- in Mark, conversely, the center is taken up by the rich man's declaration about his observance of the commandments (20); the commandments in the Decalogue are placed in parallel with Jesus' «commandments» (21dg);
- in Luke, as the passage also includes vv. 24-27 (whose parallel in the first two Gospels is a distinct passage), the center moves further still and includes Jesus' «commandments» (22).

If our analysis of the composition of the three passages is correct, this must be interpreted. In fact, as we have already said (see p. 86), the center of a construction is always a point of emphasis, which is the pivot on which the rest of the text balances.

Let us try to give an explanation:

Matthew: we know that according to ancient tradition Matthew was writing in and for Jewish-Christian communities, made up essentially of Jews who had become disciples of Jesus. This is why we should not be surprised by the place given to the Torah and its commandments, which remained so central for them.

Mark: tradition tells us that Mark was Peter's interpreter, particularly during his stay in Rome, and that he wrote his Gospel for Roman communities, made up of Jewish Christians and Gentile Christians, pagans who had converted to faith in Christ. Here, then, Jesus' commandments are placed in parallel with those in the Torah.

Luke: finally, Luke addresses communities made up particularly of Greeks, that is, Gentile Christians, so it is natural that, for them, Jesus' commandments would be the center of attention.

«You cannot serve God and Mammon» (Luke 16:13)

The rich man in Matthew was a young man, and the one in Mark was very similar to him. Luke, however, introduces «a ruler», that is, one of the leaders of the people[82]. He was probably a Pharisee[83], but Luke does not say this explicitly. However, at the end this man shows that, like the Pharisees, he is very attached to his property. Luke has already described the Pharisees as «loving money» (16:14), people for whom wealth was Mammon, that is, an idol. As a gift from God or from men, wealth was a good thing. When it is the fruit of plundering or theft, defrauding one's neighbor (20c), it is clearly a bad thing. But it is not necessary that wealth is acquired wrongly for it to be perverse; it is enough for it not to be considered the gift it really is. It is a gift to be received, gratefully, from the hand of God via father and mother who must be honored for this (20d); a gift to make generously to others, to those who have nothing, to the «poor» (22h), for the only objective way of knowing whether wealth is a gift of God to us is to share it. For the one who is attached to it (23) and places all his faith in it, not in the Giver, wealth becomes the idol to which everything else is sacrificed, an idol in the image of the rich man, who receives everything and never gives anything. In other words, according to the first commandment quoted by Luke, to idolize wealth is adulterous. It is to abandon one's proper spouse for another; to leave the true God for an idol who is unable to make one «inherit eternal life» (18b), who cannot «save» (26b).

God and wealth

Even more than the young man in Matthew and Mark, the rich ruler understood the lesson which Jesus opposes to his first question (18-19): not only will he now give up calling him «good», but he will not even call him «Master» (21) any more. Only God is «good». He is the one «Master». He alone can enable him to «inherit eternal life», beyond anything humanity can «do». The same lesson is repeated at the end of the account, in reaction to the question of those who took part in

82 Jairus is called the «synagogue leader» (Luke 8:41); in 12:58 a magistrate appears, a leader who exercises the function of judge. During the Passion the «high priests» (23:13; 24:20), along with «the people» whose political and religious leaders they are (23:13.35), are called *archontes*, which is translated as «leaders» («leaders of the people»).

83 We will see in due course that, in the composition of the whole sequence, the Pharisees are continually paralleled with the disciples (as also happens elsewhere); we might therefore think that this «leader» is from the Pharisees party.

the action (26): God is the only one who can «save» (27). We could not be clearer on this matter—the reader has the impression he is reading Paul. However, Jesus sends the rich man to the Law (20); would it be enough to observe the commandments quoted by Jesus to obtain the inheritance of eternal life? These commandments all deal exclusively with relating to one's neighbor, as though Jesus had left the first of the Decalogue, which deals with man's relationship with God, to one side. However, we should not forget that Jesus' first response to the rich man already referred to the first commandments which forbade idolatry and called for respect for the one God to the exclusion of all others: «No one is good but God alone» (19b). Exactly symmetrical in its position to the quotation of the last commandments of the Decalogue (20), observing the first commandment of the Law is twice called «entering into the kingdom of God» (24b.25b). Whoever does not observe the last commandments cannot say that he observes the first commandment, but the same must be said for the one who «holds» them (21) like a rich man holds his wealth—like a personal possession which will ensure him «eternal life». The only criterion of a just observance of the commandments is explained at the center of the passage (22): the one who wishes to «inherit eternal life» (18b), that is, «to be saved» (26b), must make the poor the heirs to his own wealth, and save them from lack. In other words, whoever wishes to become a child of God must behave as a father to the poor. «Following» Jesus means nothing more, for it is he who has enriched us by his poverty: «You are well aware of the generosity which our Lord Jesus Christ had, that, although he was rich, he became poor for your sake, so that you should become rich through his poverty» (2Cor 8:9). In this way he showed his love for God.

> In referring to God alone, he has opened up for us the commandments dealing with God in a more radical and direct way than by reciting them. He only came into this world to be the perfect worshipper of the Father. He shares all with the Father, without any confusion with him. All that the Father has which is good, the Son has received, and he has nothing which he has not received from the Father. At the same time, he will not allow his interlocutor to confuse himself with him in a suffocating relationship, and he demonstrates that neither is this his relationship with the Father. He is the «Son», that is, other than the Father.
>
> Following Jesus is, from now on, to follow him in the essential movement which calls him to the only good, his Father. Of course Jesus is «good», but the only «goodness» he has in himself is that through which he comes from the Father and goes to

the Father. What is goodness in him is only what is loved and what loves. It is in the name of this that he calls the one who has just spoken to him. He did not suspect him; he criticizes him. He criticizes him, and, we read, «he loved him». Of course the Gospel is not describing the hero's' ambiguous behavior towards Jesus as idolatry; that would be an accusing violence out of tune with his subtlety, which is the subtlety of life. However, through all these allusions, we see drawn in these verses the precise possibility of an idolatrous worship of Jesus, which would be what happened if we managed to go to him without allowing ourselves to be led to the Father.

(Cf. Beauchamp P., *D'une montagne à l'autre, la Loi de Dieu*, Paris 1999, 19).

Increasingly, exegetes insist that, in order to truly understand a pericope from the Gospels, it should be placed in its «context». However, most academic commentaries, even the most recent, study the pericopes one after the other, contenting themselves with occasional observations on the links between the pericope under examination and those around it, without these links being used in the slightest way for interpretation.

It is essential to start by explaining the notion of context. Generally, it is extremely vague. As the word itself indicates, the context of a pericope is made up by the pericope which precedes it and the one which follows it. Usually one distinguishes between the «immediate context», that is, the two pericopes which frame the pericope under examination, and the «wider context», that is a certain, imprecise, number of pericopes which go before and after it.

This definition is not enough to satisfy the linguist. This is used for working on precise «pertinent» units —s/he has learned to distinguish sentences, propositions and words in the movement of words or the «spoken chain». We offer two examples:

- *Firstly, the level of the word.* The word «medal» has five letters (which in this case correspond to five sounds or phonemes). The graphical context of the /d/ is formed by the previous two letters (/me/) and the two which follow (/al/). However, the context of the /m/ only includes the four letters which follow it (/edal/) and the context of the /l/ only includes the previous four letters (/meda/).
- *Secondly, the level of the sentence.* Let us look at the first sentence of this paragraph: «This definition is not enough to satisfy the linguist». This sentence has nine words. The context of the word «enough» is made up of the four words which come before it and the four which follow it; however, the syntactical context of «this» is only formed by the eight words which follow it and the context of «linguist» only by the eight words which precede it. The first word of the following clause, («This») is not part of the syntactical context of the word «linguist», even though it is contiguous to it on the written page.

Meaning is greatly dependent on context. Let us take as an example the word «veil». Out of context, it is impossible to know what it means — we might have a broad idea, or unconsciously choose one possibility among all the possible ones, without even noticing that there are others. If the word «veil» is *out of context*, we cannot know if it is a noun or a verb. If we add the article «the» in front of «veil», the context enables us to understand that this is a noun, «the veil», and not a verb, as it would be if we put «I» in front of «veil»: «I veil». However, even with the veil we do not know what kind of veil this is. If we broaden the context, for example by adding a supplementary noun, we can distinguish several meanings: «the veil of a nun» is different from «the veil of the temple». If we add a verb, we would have «take the veil», which is what female religious do when they join a religious community; or «wear the veil» as some Muslim women do, and so forth.

The same rules apply for the organization of a text at a higher level than the level of the «passage». The context of a passage cannot simply be defined by the pericopes which go before it or follow it. The context of a passage will only be those pericopes which precede and follow it if it is at the center of the construction; if the passage under consideration is the last in the construction, its context will be made up of one or more previous pericopes; and if it is at the start, its context will be one or more passages which follow it. The clearest example is that of the first passage in a Gospel, whose context can only be made up by what follows it, and the same goes for the last passage in the book, whose context will obviously have to be made up of all that goes before it. All this presupposes that the biblical text is organized in «discrete» units, whose limits are not arbitrary, but which can be identified by objective procedures. I call these units, which are higher units than the passage, «sequences», and they can also include «sub-sequences». The second chapter of this book is given to the study of three sub-sequences, from Matthew, Mark and Luke, which the accounts of the healing in Jericho are part of, and then those into which the accounts of the calling of the rich man have been inserted[1].

A. THE ACCOUNTS OF THE HEALING AT JERICHO IN THEIR IMMEDIATE CONTEXT

1. THE SUB-SEQUENCE IN MARK 10:35-52

We shall begin with Mark, not because it is the oldest, and therefore the closest to the historical events, but purely for didactical purposes —we will better understand the reasons why Matthew had two blind men, rather than just one, by comparing the Markan sub-sequence to the Matthean sub-sequence.

This sub-sequence includes two quite developed accounts, «James and John make their request» (35-40) and «The healing of the blind man Bartimeaus» (46b-52), which frame a brief discourse by Jesus (41-46a).

1 On «context», see *Traité*, especially 346-355.

1.1. *James and John make their request (Mark 10:35-40)*

COMPOSITION

35 And come near	to him	James and John, the sons of Zebedee,		saying to him:
+ «Master,	WE WANT			
	that **what we will ask you**		you may do	for us».
36 He said	to them:			
+ «What	DO YOU WANT			
	that		I may do	for you?».
37 They said	to him:			
: «**GRANT**	to us that	*ONE AT YOUR RIGHT*	*AND ONE AT YOUR LEFT*	
= we may	***sit***	in your glory!».		

38 *Jesus said to them:* «You do not KNOW **what you ask!**

–	CAN YOU			
. drink of	the cup	of which	I drink	
.. or	the baptism	in which	I am baptized	to be baptized?».
39 *They said to him:*				
+ «WE CAN».				
– *Jesus said*	*to them:*			
.	«The cup	of which	I drink	you shall drink
.. and	the baptism	in which	I am baptized	you shall be baptized.
= 40 But to	***sit***	*AT MY RIGHT*		*OR AT MY LEFT*
: is not mine to **GRANT** it,				
: but it is for those to whom it has been prepared».				

Two parallel parts (35-37; 38b-40) are joined by a very brief central part (38a). The first and last parts are each made up of two pieces (35-36 and 37; 38b-39 and 40). The piece 35b-36 has two parallel segments, while the symmetrical piece (38b-39) has three segments, arranged concentrically. These first pieces are followed by two shorter pieces (37 and 40) which parallel one another; v.40 ends with a member in which the «mine» in 40b is opposed to the agent of the divine passive, «it has been prepared», that is God («left» translates two synonyms: *aristerōn* in 37b and *euōnymōn* in 40a). Between the two parts, «can you» (38b) and «we can» (39b) recall, in mirror fashion, «we want» (35b) and «[do] you want» (36b); «the cup» and «the baptism» (38cd.39de) are opposed to «glory» (37c). In the center (38a), «you do not know» ensures the connection between «want» and «can»; «what you ask» repeats «what we will ask you» in 35c. These two «ask»s correspond to the two «give»s in 37b and 40b.

BIBLICAL CONTEXT

The cup and baptism

In the Old Testament the image of the cup represents testing and suffering (Ps 60:5; 75:9; Isa 51:17, 22). The cup reappears at the Last Supper (14:23) and at Gethsemane (14:36). The waters in which humanity is submerged are one of the main metaphors for agony and death (Ps 69:2-3, 15-16; Jonah 2:3-10: the song of the prophet swallowed up by the waters).

Sons of Thunder

Only Mark recounts that Jesus gave a name to Zebedee's sons: «James the son of Zebedee and John the brother of James, to whom he gave the name Boanerges, or "Sons of Thunder"» (Mark 3:17).

«At Jesus' right and his left»

It is only in 15:27 that the same expression, «And they crucified two bandits with him, one on his right and one on his left *(euōnymōn)*», reappears.

INTERPRETATION

The two brothers' wish

James and John seem to have really deserved the name Jesus gave them when he chose them to be among the Twelve: they really are «Sons of Thunder!» Just like a flash of lightning in a calm sky, their request appears unexpectedly, to the detriment of the other ten. Their impetuous nature gives them the audacity to ask first of all for a blank check, and then to demand nothing less than first rank. In response to Jesus' question, they show absolutely no hesitation—they can drink his cup and be baptized with his baptism. They are confident in themselves, just as they are confident in their master's absolute power. They know what they are worth, and they do not draw back before the necessary conditions to reach the goal they have set themselves. Their ambition and determination are surely a model for every disciple.

Jesus' wish

Jesus does not in fact tell the two brothers off, but supports their wish (36). They wish to share his glory (37); this is clearly also their master's wish. But, when Jesus starts by revealing the total lack of wisdom (38a), this means that their request is seriously distorted. Above all, Jesus wishes to check whether his disciples are ready to accompany him on the way of his Passion; and he confirms their commitment when he announces that they will drink his cup and share his baptism. But the main distortion in their request is not found here. Jesus seems to refuse to promise what they have asked for (40), while he has noted that they will fulfill the conditions to reach glory (39de). In effect, he denies the omnipotence which the two brothers attribute to him (37) and refers them to the only one who has the authority to «give» the glory which they sought. He does not wish to be confused with the Father; the disciples must recognize him as the Son, who is expecting glory to be given to him by another. In so doing, he invites the sons of Zebedee to become, like him, sons of God.

1.2. *Called to Serve (Mark 10:41-46a)*

COMPOSITION

41 *And having heard,*	*the ten*	*began to be indignant*	*at James and John.*
42 *And having called them to him,*	*Jesus*	*says*	*to them:*

«You know that					
. those considered	**to command**	the *NATIONS*	**exercise lordship**		over them
. and	the **GREAT-ONES**	among them	**exercise authority**		over them
43 Not so shall it be	among you,				
+ but who wants	**GREAT** to become	among you,	shall be	of you	*the servant*
+ 44 and who wants	among you to be	the **first**,	shall be	of **ALL**	*the slave.*
45 For the Son of Man	did not come				
. to	**be served**		but to *serve*		
. and	*to give his own life*		*a ransom*		for **MANY**».

46 *And they come to Jericho.*

Two parts of the narrative (41-42a; 46a) frame a discourse made up of three pieces. The commandment given to the disciples (43-44), opposed to the law which governs relations of authority among the pagans (42bcd), is motivated by Jesus' behavior (45). Every piece is made up of a unimember and two bimembers. The parallelism between the last two segments of the first two pieces is obvious. The last segment of the third piece (45c) develops and clarifies the second member of the previous segment (45b: «to serve»). The movement from «servant» to «slave» in the second piece is repeated and enveloped in the last piece, where «serve» corresponds to «servant», but «give his own life a ransom» («give himself as a ransom», taking on the place and condition of the slave) is much stronger and means to sacrifice his life, to die. «Many» at the end of the last piece (45c) takes up «all» at the end of the second piece and can be considered to be making an inclusio with «the nations» at the start of the first piece (42c), particularly if we take into account the link between this text and the Songs of the Servant in Isaiah (see «Biblical Context»).

BIBLICAL CONTEXT

Humanity's dominion over the animals

The first two verbs which describe the attitude of the leaders of the nations (42c) are those which the Septuagint uses to translate Gen 1:28: «God blessed them, saying to them, "Be fruitful, multiply, fill the earth and *subdue it. Be masters* of the fish of the sea, the birds of heaven and all the living creatures that move on earth"». The first verb was already used when God decided to create man: «Let us make man in our own image, in the likeness of ourselves, and let them *be masters* of the fish of the sea, the birds of heaven, the cattle, all the wild animals and all the creatures that creep along the ground» (1:26). The same verb «to be masters» is also used for the new creation after the Flood: «Be fruitful, multiply, fill the earth; *be masters of it*» (Gen 9:1).

The Servant of the Lord

Jesus' discourse echoes the Song of the Servant, in which the theme of universal salvation thanks to the Servant were already to be found, for example in Isa 49:6: «It is not enough for you to be my servant, to restore the tribes of Jacob and bring back the survivors of Israel. I shall make you a light to the nations so that my salvation may reach the remotest parts of earth». The whole of the fourth Song of the Servant (Isa 52:13-53:12) is given to the account of the ransom worked by the Servant of the Lord on behalf of those who have persecuted him[2].

2 See MEYNET R., «Le quatrième chant du Serviteur (Is 52,13-53,12)».

INTERPRETATION

The very first law

For the pagan nations relationships of authority are most often governed by the desire for power and domination (42cd). It is enough to open one's eyes to see it: «everyone knows this» (42b). The leaders crush those they are charged to protect; they are served by those they are commanded to serve. Although their role is to procure food for their flock, and to defend it against predators, shepherds rarely resist the temptation to become voracious wolves themselves (Ezek 34). This law of the jungle, which governs relationships between animals, is opposed by the law which the Son of Man recalls (45). These are animals which man has been charged by God with being masters over, not with being similar to. It is man's animal nature which is to be domesticated, not his neighbor, created, like him, in the image of God.

The law of slavery

If we understand that those who exercise power are to be careful not to reduce those in their care to slavery, if it is already more difficult to accept that leaders are at the service of those they rule, it seems quite mad to claim that they have to make themselves their «slaves» (43b-44). By definition, the slave is the opposite of his master —deprived of his own freedom, he is quite dependent on his master; and yet, according to Jesus, the master does not belong to himself, but is totally dedicated to others. He does not have his own plans, but is governed by his community. He is at the service of his people at any time, just like a slave at the feet of his master.

Ready to sacrifice one's life for one's children

Just like the mother-hen confronting the sparrow-hawk to defend her chicks, the true leader does not hesitate to risk death to safeguard his children's life (45c). He is ready to give up his own body to satisfy the enemy's appetite, provided that the life of his people be spared. True service goes this far —it accepts slavery at the price of freedom for another, it does not refuse to go as far as giving up one's own life to snatch others from slavery. This is what the Son of Man is preparing to do (45) and what will be the model which his disciples are to follow (43-44).

Giving his life as a ransom for sinners

The Son of Man is not content to give his life as a ransom for his own people. He will give it «for many» (45), «as a ransom» for their wickedness. If the «many» at the end of the discourse refers to the «nations» at the start (42c), it is certainly not impossible to imagine that, at the end of the Son of Man's life, «This is my blood, the blood of the covenant, poured out *for many*» (14:24). They represent a much larger group than the Twelve who «all drank from it» (14:23). These are all the sinners whom he intends to redeem by his poured-out blood, not only the disciples who will abandon him, but also those, Jews and pagans both, who will condemn him to death.

«For many»

We might ask why Jesus' last word is not «all» but «many»: «to give his own life as a ransom *for many*» (45c). Jesus uses the same word at the Last Supper (14:24). This choice is not merely fortuitous. Salvation is not imposed, it is offered freely to all humanity—of course, it is offered to «all», to all those who will accept it. The Eucharistic Prayer of the Roman Rite says «shed for you and for *all*». This final word is not found in any of the Gospel accounts, nor even in 1Cor 11:24-25, nor even in the official Latin text: *qui pro vobis et* pro multis *effundetur*. It cannot be said that the translation in various languages is an error of translation; it is an interpretation[3].

3 The French translation says, «pour la multitude», the English, «for all». The Greek, clearly, follows the Gospel texts (*pollois*).

1.3. *Jesus opens his disciples' eyes (Mark 10:35-52)*

COMPOSITION OF THE SUB-SEQUENCE

35 And **COME towards** him James and John, the **sons of Zebedee**, saying to him: «Master, we
want that what we ***will ask*** you, you may do for us». 36 He said to them:

«WHAT ***DO YOU*** ***WANT*** THAT I MAY DO FOR YOU?».

They said to him: 37 «Grant to us that we may ***SIT*** at your right and at your left in your glory».
38 Jesus said to them: «YOU DO NOT KNOW what you ***ask***. Can you drink of the cup that I drink of or be
baptized with baptism in which I am baptized?». 39 They said to him: «We can». Jesus said to
them: «The cup of which I drink you shall drink and the baptism in which I am baptized you shall
be baptized. 40 But to ***SIT*** at my right or at my left, is not mine to grant it; it is for those whom it
has been prepared».

41 And having heard, the ten began to be indignant at James and John.
42 And having summoned them, Jesus says to them:

«YOU KNOW that those considered to command the nations dominate them and their great-ones subdue them. 43 But it shall not be so among you,

but who ***WANTS*** to be great among you will be your servant
44 and who ***WANTS*** to be first among you will be slave of all.

45 For **the Son of Man** did not come to be served, but to serve and to give his life a ransom for many».

46 And they come to *Jericho*.

And while **COMING out** of *Jericho*, he, his disciples and a considerable crowd, **the son of Timaeus**,
Bartimaeus, a BLIND-MAN, ***WAS SITTING*** along the way, ***asking*** (for alms). 47 And having heard
that it was Jesus the Nazarene, he started to cry out and to say: «**Son of David**, Jesus, have
mercy on me!». 48 Many rebuked him so that he would be silent, but he cried out all the more:
«**Son of David**, have mercy on me!». 49 Stopped, Jesus said: «Call him». And they called the
blind saying to him: «Have courage! ***RISE***, he calls you!». 50 Having abandoned his mantle,
walking again, he came to Jesus. 51 Answering him, Jesus said:

«WHAT ***DO YOU*** ***WANT*** THAT I MAY DO FOR YOU?».

The blind-man said to him: «Rabbuni, that I may see again!». 52 Jesus said to him: «Go, your
faith has saved you». And immediately he saw again and ***WAS FOLLOWING*** him on the way.

The links between the first two passages are so obvious that many consider them to be a single pericope[4]. The second passage is the lesson which Jesus draws for the Twelve from what happened in the first passage. The third passage takes place in another place and another time, because the stay in Jericho is situated between the two accounts (46a and 46b).

The strongest formal mark of the unity of this sub-sequence is probably the symmetrical repetition of an identical question (as well as the movement from

4 So, for example the *Jerusalem Bible* and the *New Jerusalem Bible* split the text at the same point with the same titles for the pericopes, «The sons of Zebedee make their request» and «Leadership with service», while the *Catholic Study Bible* links the two into one, entitled «Ambition of James and John».

the plural to the singular) at almost the start of the first passage (36) and almost at the end of the third (51); in the original, these two questions, both asked by Jesus, reflect one another in mirror fashion:

«*What* ***do you want*** *that I may do*	*for* YOU*?».*
«*For* YOU	*what* ***do you want*** *that I may do?».*

The verb «to want» is re-used twice at the center of the second passage (43-44); and in this way the center and the outer parts match[5].

The characters relating to Jesus in the outer passages are «the sons of Zebedee» and «the son of Timaeus» named at the start of each passage (35 and 46b)[6]; Jesus, meanwhile, calls himself «Son of man» in the central passage (45) and he is called «Son of David» in the final passage (47.48).

«You do not know», at the center of the first passage (38) is opposed to «you know» at the start of the second (42); «blind man» in the third passage (46) can be linked to this verb, as we will see in due course.

«To be seated» is found in the first and third passages (37.40 and 46), and, in the central passage, this is also the position of the commanders and the great ones, who make others serve them.

The two occurrences of «James and John» (35.41) act as initial terms for the first two passages. Two verbs with the same root, *pros-poreuontai* and *ek-poreuomenou,* both translated as «come» (35.46b), act as initial terms for the first and third passages; two other verbs with the same root follow them, *aitēsōmen* and *pros-aitēs,* translated by «we will ask» (35.38) and «asking-for-alms» (46). The two occurrences of «Jericho» act as median terms between the two last passages (46).

BIBLICAL CONTEXT

Blindness and misunderstanding

The first account is focused on the misunderstanding of Zebedee's sons; the second introduces the son of Timaeus, who is blind. The link between blindness and misunderstanding is well-known in the Bible. In Isa 56:10-11, for example:

5 This is one of the laws of composition of biblical texts; see LUND N.W., *Chiasmus in the New Testament.*

6 Mark is the only one of the synoptic authors to name the blind man.

+ [10] His *WATCHMEN* are	all **blind,**	they KNOW nothing.
– All of them are	**dumb** DOGS,	they can not bark.
They dream,	*LYING DOWN,*	they love to slumber.
– [11] These DOGS are	**greedy,**	they do not KNOW to be satisfied.
+ And they are	*SHEPHERDS,*	they do not KNOW to understand.

Blindness is paralleled with lack of intelligence from the very first segment. The «watchmen» (10a) or «shepherds» (11b) who should be guarding the flock are the people's leaders who are not doing their work—they are not using their mouths to warn of danger (10b), but to consume (11a). The whole piece turns on 10c which describes them as «lying down». Eyes, mouth, feet, and intelligence—all are still, just as in Mark.

The Son of Man

The title which Jesus uses to describe himself comes from Dan 7, which talks about a glorious character to whom the Lord will give eternal kingship:

> [13] I gazed into the visions of the night. And I saw, coming on the clouds of heaven, someone like a *son of man.* He came to the one of great age and was led into his presence. [14] On him was conferred sovereignty, glory and kingship, and men of all peoples, nations and languages became his servants. His sovereignty is an eternal sovereignty which shall never pass away, nor will his empire ever be destroyed (Dan 7:13-14).

However, before being glorified, «the Son of man» must undergo the test of suffering and humiliation.

INTERPRETATION

Seated or standing

The blind man seated at the roadside receives the command to get up (49) and ends up following Jesus on the way (52). James and John, who wished to be seated in the glory of their Master (37), are referred to the Passion, their Passion being identical to that of Jesus (38-39). Jesus presents his own Passion to the Twelve as a service, «for the Son of man did not come to be served but to serve» (45). To be served is to be seated, like the king on his throne; to serve is to remain standing as a servant does. The sons of Zebedee, just like the other ten apostles, who demanded to be seated in the glory of the king, are called to remain standing just as servants and slaves do (43-44). As for Bartimaeus, everything takes place as though the miracle were not so much that he recovers his sight, but that he gets up to follow the Son of man, like the Twelve (52). Seated on the ground, expecting his bread and clothing to come from others (46), seated on thrones (37) expecting others to serve them (42): neither is the attitude of a disciple (43). Jesus' disciple is to get up to serve his brothers (43-44), following his Master (45).

Blind unawareness

The blindness of Timaeus' son refers back to the unawareness of Zebedee's sons[7]. James and John do not know what they are asking for (38), they do not see the path which they will have to take to be seated in the King's glory. Jesus opens their eyes: they will have to drink the same cup and be baptized in the same baptism as him, and go through the Passion (38-39). They know perfectly well what the world's law is (42), the more so since they have just proved that they follow it themselves, and just as the ten others, who get angry, do (41). But they still do not know the law of the kingdom of God which Jesus will teach them (43-44). Like beggars, they ask to be given the first places, although they are asked to give their own lives, just like the Son of man, in ransom for the many (45). Bartimaeus, too, who asked for alms, abandons all his alms with his mantle (50) to give himself to the Lord (52).

Son of man, son of David

Timaeus' son twice calls out to the «Son of David» (47.48); Jesus describes himself as the «Son of man» (45). He uses this *name* each time he talks about his Passion. Here, the Son of man is the one who serves, the slave who will give his life as a ransom for the many. «Son of David» is a royal title. Jesus does not give this title to himself—it is not for him to give it to himself—but he is recognized as such by the Son of Timaeus as well as by the Sons of Zebedee, those who wish to be seated on either side of this king of glory. Jesus, who gives himself the title of Son of man, and who does not reject the title of Son of David, is both king and servant. These two titles, which might appear to be opposed to each other, are in fact complementary: there is no glory without the cup and baptism (37-38), there

7 This is noted, for example, by Ernst, 501: «The disciples' blindness, who do not wish to understand the meaning of the *sequela* of the cross, is in strong contrast with the fact that the beggar can [now] see».

is no greatness without service (43-44), there is no resurrection without going through suffering and death.

2. THE SUB-SEQUENCE IN MATT 20:20-34

The sub-sequence in Matthew presents the same montage of three passages, but the first Evangelist has not used the same means to produce it.

2.1. *The mother of Zebedee's sons makes her request (Matt 20:20-23)*

COMPOSITION

+ [20] *Then came to him*	*the* MOTHER OF *Zebedee's sons*		with her SONS,
– prostrating	and ***ASKING*** for something from him.		
+ [21] *Now he said to her*:			
– «What	DO YOU WANT?».		
Now she said to him:			
: Say that	***they may sit***		these two SONS of mine
: one *AT* [your] *RIGHT AND* one *AT YOUR LEFT*			in your *kingdom*».

[22] Now answering Jesus said: «**You do not KNOW** what you ***ASK***!

–	CAN YOU	drink of the *cup*	that I am about to drink of?».
+ *They say to him*:			
– «WE CAN».			
+ [23] *He says to them*:		«My *cup*,	you shall drink of.
= But	***to sit***	*AT MY RIGHT OR AT MY LEFT*	
: is not mine	to give,		
: but is for those	to whom it has been prepared		by my FATHER».

Two parallel parts (20-21; 22b-23) are linked by a very short central part (22a).

The first and last parts (20-21b and 21cde; 22b-23a and 23bcd) are made up of two pieces which match. The piece 20-21b has two parallel segments, while its symmetrical piece (22b-23a) has three segments, arranged concentrically. These first pieces are followed by two other, shorter, pieces (21cde and 23bcd). Between the two parts, «you can» (22b) and «we can» (22d) recall «do you want» (21b), to which «asking» (20b) corresponds; «the cup» (22b.23a) is opposed to «kingdom» (21e); «my Father» at the end (23d) is opposed to «the mother of Zebedee's sons» at the start (20a; the three occurrences of «sons» in 20 [twice] and 21d belong to the same semantic field).

At the center of the passage (22a), «you do not know» acts as a hinge between «want» and «can»; «what you are asking» refers back to «asking for something» in 20b.

SYNOPTIC COMPARISON (*see pp. 169 and 159*)

Matt 20:20-23	Mark 10:35-40
20 Then came TO HIM **the mother of** *ZEBEDEE'S SONS* **with her sons, prostrating** **and** *ASKING* **for something from him.** 21 NOW HE SAID to her: «WHAT DO YOU WANT?».	35 And come near TO HIM ***James and John,*** *THE SONS OF ZEBEDEE* ***saying to him: «Master, we want*** ***that what we*** *WILL ASK* ***you*** ***you may do for us***». 36 NOW HE SAID to them : «WHAT DO YOU WANT ***That I may do for you***?».
NOW she SAID TO HIM: «Say THAT *MAY SIT* these two sons of mine ONE AT [your] RIGHT AND ONE AT YOUR LEFT in your kingdom».	37 NOW they SAID TO HIM: «Grant to us THAT ONE AT YOUR RIGHT AND ONE AT YOUR LEFT *WE MAY SIT* in your glory!».
22 NOW **answering** JESUS SAID: «YOU DO NOT KNOW WHAT YOU ASK!	38 NOW JESUS SAID ***to them***: «YOU DO NOT KNOW WHAT YOU ASK!
CAN YOU DRINK OF THE CUP THAT **I am about to** DRINK OF?». THEY SAY TO HIM: «WE CAN». 23 HE SAYS TO THEM: «As for **my** CUP, YOU SHALL DRINK OF.	CAN YOU DRINK OF THE CUP THAT I DRINK OF ***or the baptism in which I am baptized*** ***to be baptized***?». 39 ***Now to him*** THEY SAID: «WE CAN». ***Now Jesus*** SAID TO THEM: «THE CUP ***that I drink of*** YOU SHALL DRINK OF ***and the baptism in which I am baptized*** ***you shall be baptized.***
BUT TO SIT AT MY RIGHT OR AT MY LEFT, IS NOT MINE TO GIVE, BUT IT IS FOR THOSE TO WHOM IT HAS BEEN PREPARED **by my Father**».	40 BUT TO SIT AT MY RIGHT OR AT MY LEFT IS NOT MINE TO GIVE, BUT IT IS FOR THOSE TO WHOM IT HAS BEEN PREPARED».

As often happens, Matthew is much more concise than Mark—the long request at the start of Mark (35def) is summarized by a brief indirect question in Matthew (20de); Jesus' question is also shorter in Matt 21b than it is in Mark (36b); in the first sub-part of the last part, Matthew does not return to the image of baptism (Mark: 38ef.39de) and neither does he use «Now to him» and «Now Jesus» (Mark: 39ab).

On the other hand, Matthew adds some words: «answering» (22a), «I am about to» (22d), «as for» (Greek: *men*) and «my» (23b), and, especially, «by my Father» at the end (23g) which corresponds to his essential amendment: while in Mark it is Zebedee's sons who make their request (and they are called by their name in 35b), in Matthew it is their mother who intervenes on behalf of her two sons (20b).

Despite all these differences, the composition of the two passages is the same.

BIBLICAL CONTEXT

The cup

We can say the same about «the cup» as we did in Mark (see p. 160). In Matthew, too, the cup is found twice in the first Passover sequence, at the Last Supper (26:27) and during the prayer in Gethsemane (26:39.42)[8].

At Jesus' right and left

In Matthew this expression appears only once in 27-38 at the point of Jesus' execution—this is the place of the two bandits crucified with him.

The mother's request

Just as Bathsheba knelt and prostrated herself before David, so the mother of Zebedee's sons «prostrated herself» (Matt 20:20) before Jesus. The two mothers make a similar request: Bathsheba implored the king that he designate her son Solomon to be his successor on the throne of Israel, in the place of another of the king's sons, Adonijah son of Haggith (2Sam 3:4) who had set his sights on the kingdom (1Kgs 1:1-10).

INTERPRETATION

The disciples and their mother

The two disciples are called «Zebedee's sons» and their mother calls them «my sons». No-one, not even the narrator, calls them by their proper names. The mother «bows low and asks» (20b); she replies to the question Jesus asks her (21). The two brothers are there, of course (20a) and she shows them to Jesus, but still as «these two sons of mine» (21d), as though they only existed through their relationship to their father and, particularly, her, as though they had not yet sepa-

8 See *Jésus passe*, 62-63, 67.

rated from her. The mother is not even described as Zebedee's wife, but with an expression whose strange nature is notable: «the mother of Zebedee's sons» (20a). Note too that, with other women, she is present, even «at a distance», when Jesus dies, crucified between the two bandits, while her two sons have abandoned him (27:56).

Jesus and his Father

No sooner has the mother expressed her request than Jesus cuts her short and turns to his two disciples: «You do not know what you are asking» (22a). He separates them from their mother and treats them as adults with their own wishes. From this moment the dialogue, which in the first part of the account, took place between the mother and him, is now between the master and the two sons. Jesus thus plays the role of the father, whose function is precisely to separate the sons from their mother. The two brothers express their determination to share their master's fate, when they drink his cup. However, Jesus does not swap one disordered attachment for another. He does not take the mother's place; on the contrary, he refers them to the ultimate origin on whom he himself depends, «his Father» (23d). In this way he totally fulfils the function of parents to their children, sending them to the only one from whom all good comes, the only one to whom judgment belongs.

2.2. *The discourse on service (Matt 20:24-28)*

COMPOSITION

24 *And*	*having heard,*	*the ten*	*were indignant*	*at the two brothers.*
25 *Now Jesus*	*having called*	*them*	*to him,*	*said:*

«You know that			
. **the rulers**	of the *NATIONS*,	**exercise lordship**	over them
. and **the GREAT-ONES**		**exercise authority**	over them;
26 it shall not be so	among you,		
+ but who wants **GREAT**	among you to become	shall be *OF YOU*	*the servant*
+ 27 and who wants to be	among you **the first**	let be *OF YOU*	*the slave*,
28 As the Son of Man did not come			
. to **be served**		but to *serve*	
. and to *give his life*		*a ransom*	for *MANY*».

After a short narrative introductory part (24-25a), Jesus' discourse has three pieces. The commandment given to the disciples (26-27), in opposition to the law which governs relations of authority for the nations (25bcd), is motivated by the Son of Man's behavior (28).

The parallelism between the final two segments of the first two pieces is clear (25cd; 26b-27), with some variation in the order of words in the second piece. The last segment in the third piece (28c) develops and explains the second member of the previous segment (28b: «to serve»). The progression from «servant» to «slave» in the second piece (26b.27) is repeated and developed in the second piece: «to serve» matches «servant» precisely, but «give his life as a ransom» seems to be much stronger and to mean «to sacrifice one's own life», that is, «to die». The «many» at the end of the last piece (28c) could be considered to make an inclusio with «the nations» at the start of the first piece (25c), particularly if we consider the links between this text and the Songs of the Servant (see the second point of «Biblical Context» in Mark, p. 162).

SYNOPTIC COMPARISON (see pp. 173 and 161)

Matt 20:24-28	Mark 10:41-46a
[24] AND HEARD, THE TEN WERE INDIGNANT AT the two brothers. [25] Now JESUS, CALLED THEM TO HIM, SAID:	[41] AND HEARD, THE TEN ***began to*** BE INDIGNANT AT James and John. [42] and CALLED THEM TO HIM, JESUS SAID ***to them***:
«YOU KNOW THAT the rulers of THE NATIONS EXERCISE LORDSHIP OVER THEM AND THE GREAT-ONES EXERCISE AUTHORITY OVER THEM ;	«YOU KNOW THAT those considered to command THE NATIONS EXERCISE LORDSHIP OVER THEM AND ***their*** GREAT-ONES EXERCISE AUTHORITY OVER THEM.
[26] IT SHALL NOT BE SO AMONG YOU, BUT WHO WANTS GREAT *AMONG YOU TO BECOME* SHALL BE OF YOU THE SERVANT [27] AND WHO WANTS *TO BE AMONG YOU* THE FIRST let be OF **you** THE SLAVE,	[43] IT SHALL NOT BE SO AMONG YOU, BUT WHO WANTS GREAT *TO BECOME AMONG YOU* SHALL BE OF YOU THE SERVANT [44] AND WHO WANTS *AMONG YOU TO BE* THE FIRST shall be OF ***all*** THE SLAVE.
[28] as THE SON OF MAN DID NOT COME TO BE SERVED BUT TO SERVE AND TO GIVE HIS LIFE A RANSOM FOR MANY».	[45] For THE SON OF MAN DID NOT COME TO BE SERVED BUT TO SERVE AND TO GIVE HIS LIFE A RANSOM FOR MANY».
	[46a] ***And they come to Jericho.***

The most notable difference between the two versions is that Mark makes the start of v.46 the conclusion of his passage, which has no corresponding piece in Matthew. As usual, Matthew is shorter than Mark. He does not repeat «began to» (Mark 41a), he shortens «those considered to command» (Mark 42c) to «the rulers» (25c) and «their great ones» (Mark 42e) with simply «the great ones», he emphasizes the parallelism of 26-27, changing Mark's «all» (44b) to «you» (27b, as in 26c). Finally, he makes the last piece subordinate to the previous piece, using «as», rather than Mark's simple coordination («For», 45a).

BIBLICAL CONTEXT

Matthew's text is so similar to Mark's that the biblical context is the same (see p. 162).

INTERPRETATION

The differences between Matthew and Mark are so minimal that we can re-use the interpretation of the Markan passage for the Matthean passage (see p. 174).

The Discourse on Service in Luke

Luke does not report Zebedee's sons' request, and integrates discourse on service into the first Passover sequence, which I refer to as «Jesus' testament». While Matthew and Mark make the account of the Last Supper the center of their sequence, Luke focuses his sequence on the discourse on service[9].

Matt 26:1-56	Mark 14:1-52	Luke 22:1-53
Jesus announces his Passion 1-2		
= The authorities decide to kill Jesus 3-5	= The authorities decide to kill Jesus 1-2	= The authorities decide to kill Jesus
The anointing at Bethany 6-13	*The anointing at Bethany* 3-9	and
= Judas the disciple decides to sell Jesus 14-16	= Judas the disciple decides to hand over Jesus 10-11	Judas the disciple decides to hand him over 1-6
Preparation of the Passover 17-19	Preparation of the Passover 12-16	= Preparation of the Passover 7-13
		: Celebration of the Passover 14-20
Prediction of the betrayal by Judas 20-25	Prediction of the betrayal 17-21	Prediction of the betrayal 21-24
CELEBRATION OF THE PASSOVER 26-29	CELEBRATION OF THE PASSOVER 22-25	*DISCOURSE ON SERVICE* 25-30
Prediction of Peter's denial 30-35	Prediction of Peter's denial 26-31	Prediction of Peter's denial 31-34
		: *Swords of the apostles* 35-38
+ Gethsemane 36-46	Gethsemane 32-42	= Agony of Jesus 39-46
+ Arrest 47-56	= Betrayal by Judas Ear is cut = Fight of the disciples 43-52	= Arrest 47-53

9 See *Jésus passe*, 113-173; *Luc*, 831-876.

2.3. *Jesus Opens His Disciples' eyes (Matt 20:20-34)*

COMPOSITION OF THE SUB-SEQUENCE

[20] Then came to him the mother of the SONS OF ZEBEDEE with her sons, prostrating and asking for something from him. [21] He said to her:

«**WHAT *DO YOU WANT*?».**

She said to him: «Say that these my **two** sons ***MAY SIT*** one at your right and one at your left in your KINGDOM». [22] Answering, Jesus said: «YOU DO NOT KNOW what you ask. Can you drink of the cup that I am about to drink of?». They say to him: «We can». [23] He says to them: «My cup, you shall drink of; but to ***SIT*** at my right or at my left is not mine to give, but it is for those to whom it has been prepared by my Father».

---

[24] Having heard, the ten were indignant at the **two** brothers.
[25] Now Jesus having summoned them, said:
«YOU KNOW that
: the rulers of the nations exercise ***lordship*** over them
: and the great-ones exercise authority over them;
[26] it shall not be so among you;
but who ***WANTS*** among you to become great, shall be your servant,
[27] and who ***WANTS*** among you to be the first, shall be your slave,
[28] as THE SON OF MAN did not come
: to be served but to serve
: and to give his life a ransom for *many*».

---

[29] And while they were leaving from Jericho, followed him a *numerous* crowd. [30] And behold, **two** BLIND-MEN ***SITTING*** along the way, having heard that Jesus was passing by, they cried out, saying: «Have mercy on us, ***Lord***, SON OF DAVID!». [31] The crowd rebuked them so that they would be silent; but the more they cried out, saying: «Have mercy on us, ***Lord***, SON OF DAVID!».
[32] And stopped, Jesus called them and said:

«**WHAT *DO YOU WANT* that I may do for you?».**

[33] They say to him: «Lord, that our eyes may be opened!». [34] Moved with pity, Jesus touched their eyes and immediately they saw again and they were ***FOLLOWING*** him.

In the outer passages (20-23; 29-34) Jesus' first (21b) and last (32b) questions, which are very similar, act as outer terms (or «inclusio») for the sub-sequence as a whole. In addition, «seated» re-appears in 21c, 23b and 30b (which is opposed by «accompany» at the end of the last passage in 34b); «reign» (21d) matches the two occurrences of «son of David» (30c.31b).

The three passages of the sub-sequence are linked by the series «sons of Zebedee» (20a), «Son of man» (28a) and «son of David» (30c.31b), by the repetition of «two» (21c.24c.30b); «to want» is found once in the outer questions (21b.32b) and twice at the center of the sub-sequence (26b.27); «you do not know» in 22a in the first passage is opposed to «you know» in 25d in the second passage, which «blind men» in 30b in the third passage (the blind man is one who does not see, or does not understand) matches.

«Many» in 28c and «numerous» in 29, which translate words with the same root in Greek (*pollōn* et *polys*), act as median terms (or «link-words») for the last two passages. The verb translated by «exercise lordship over» at the start of Jesus' discourse (25e) is from the same root as «Lord» (30c.31b).

SYNOPTIC COMPARISON

Matt 20:20-34	Mark 10:35-52
[20] Then came to him the mother of the sons of Zebedee with her sons, prostrating and asking for something from him. [21] He said to her: « WHAT DO YOU WANT?». She said to him: «Say that these my **two** sons ***MAY SIT*** one at your right and the other at your left in your kingdom». [22] Answering, Jesus said: «YOU DO NOT KNOW what you ask. Can you drink of the cup that I am about to drink of?». They say to him: «We can». [23] He says to them: «My cup, you shall drink of; but ***TO SIT*** at my right or at my left is not mine to give, but it is for those to whom it has been prepared by my Father».	[35] And come to him James and John, the **sons of Zebedee**, saying to him: «Master, we want that what we will ask you, you may do for us». [36] He said to them: «WHAT DO YOU WANT THAT I MAY DO FOR YOU?». They said to him: [37] «Grant to us that we ***MAY SIT*** one at your right and the other at your left in your glory». [38] Jesus said to them: «YOU DO NOT KNOW what you ask. Can you drink of the cup that I drink of or be baptized with the baptism in which I am baptized?». [39] They said to him: «We can». Jesus said to them: «The cup of which I drink you shall drink and the baptism in which I am baptized you shall be baptized. [40] But ***TO SIT*** at my right or at my left, is not mine to give; it is for those to whom it has been prepared».
[24] Having heard, the ten were indignant at the **two** brothers. [25] Having summoned them, Jesus said: «YOU KNOW that the rulers of the nations dominate them and the great-ones subdue them; [26] it shall not be so among you, but who WANTS to become great among you, shall be your servant [27] and who WANTS among you to be the first, shall be your slave, [28] as the ***Son of Man*** did not come to be served but to serve and to give his life a ransom for many».	[41] Having heard, the ten began to be indignant at James and John. [42] Having summoned them, Jesus said to them: «YOU KNOW that those considered to command the nations dominate them and the great-ones among them subdue them. [43] It shall not be so among you, but who WANTS to be great among you shall be your servant [44] and who WANTS to be the first among you shall be the slave of all. [45] For the ***Son of Man*** did not come to be served, but to serve and to give his life a ransom for many». [46] And they come to Jericho.
[29] And while they were leaving from Jericho, a numerous crowd followed him. [30] And behold **two** BLIND-MEN, ***BEING SEATED*** along the way, heard that Jesus was passing by, they cried out, saying: «Have mercy on us, Lord, ***son of David***!». [31] The crowd rebuked them so that they would be silent; but the more they cried out, saying: «Have mercy on us, Lord, ***son of David***!». [32] Stopped, Jesus called them and said: «WHAT DO YOU WANT THAT I MAY DO FOR YOU?». [33] They say to him: «Lord, that may be opened our eyes!». [34] Moved with pity, Jesus touch their eyes and immediately they saw again and they were ***FOLLOWING*** him.	And while coming out of Jericho, he, his disciples and a considerable crowd, the **son of Timaeus**, Bartimaeus, A BLIND-MAN, ***WAS SEATED*** along the way, asking for alms. [47] Heard that it was Jesus the Nazarene, he started to cry out and to say: «***Son of David***, Jesus, have mercy on me!». [48] Many rebuked him so that he would be silent, but he cried out all the more: «***Son of David***, have mercy on me!». [49] Stopped, Jesus said: «Call him». And they called the blind-man, saying to him: «Have courage, rise, he calls you!». [50] Having abandoned his mantle, walking again, he came to Jesus. [51] Answering him, Jesus said: «WHAT DO YOU WANT THAT I MAY DO FOR YOU?». The blind-man said to him: «Rabbuni, that I may see again!». [52] Jesus said to him: «Go, your faith has saved you». And immediately he saw again and he was ***FOLLOWING*** him on the way.

Matt 20:20-34	Mark 10:35-52
[20] Then came to him the mother of the sons of Zebedee with her sons, prostrating and asking for something from him. [21] He said to her: « WHAT DO YOU WANT?». She said to him: «Say that these my two sons ***MAY SIT*** one at your right and the other at your left in your kingdom». [22] Answering, Jesus said: «YOU DO NOT KNOW what you ask. Can you drink of the cup that I am about to drink of?». They say to him: «We can». [23] He says to them: «My cup, you shall drink of; but ***TO SIT*** at my right or at my left is not mine to give, but it is for those to whom it has been prepared by my Father».	[35] And come to him James and John, the sons of Zebedee, saying to him: «Master, we want that what we will ask you, you may do for us». [36] He said to them: «WHAT DO YOU WANT THAT I MAY DO FOR YOU?». They said to him: [37] «Grant to us that we ***MAY SIT*** one at your right and the other at your left in your glory». [38] Jesus said to them: «YOU DO NOT KNOW what you ask. Can you drink of the cup that I drink of or be baptized with the baptism in which I am baptized?». [39] They said to him: «We can». Jesus said to them: «The cup of which I drink you shall drink and the baptism in which I am baptized you shall be baptized. [40] But ***TO SIT*** at my right or at my left, is not mine to give; it is for those to whom it has been prepared».
[24] Having heard, the ten were indignant at the two brothers. [25] Having summoned them, Jesus said: «YOU KNOW that the rulers of the nations dominate them and the great-ones subdue them; [26] it shall not be so among you, but who WANTS to become great among you, shall be your servant [27] and who WANTS among you to be the first, shall be your slave, [28] as the ***Son of Man*** did not come to be served but to serve and to give his life a ransom for many».	[41] Having heard, the ten began to be indignant at James and John. [42] Having summoned them, Jesus said to them: «YOU KNOW that those considered to command the nations dominate them and the great-ones among them subdue them. [43] It shall not be so among you, but who WANTS to be great among you shall be your servant [44] and who WANTS to be the first among you shall be the slave of all. [45] For the ***Son of Man*** did not come to be served, but to serve and to give his life a ransom for many». [46] And they come to Jericho.
[29] And while they were leaving from Jericho, a numerous crowd followed him. [30] And behold two BLIND-MEN, ***BEING SEATED*** along the way, heard that Jesus was passing by, they cried out, saying: «Have mercy on us, Lord, ***son of David***!». [31] The crowd rebuked them so that they would be silent; but the more they cried out, saying: «Have mercy on us, Lord, ***son of David***!». [32] Stopped, Jesus called them and said: «WHAT DO YOU WANT THAT I MAY DO FOR YOU?». [33] They say to him: «Lord, that may be opened our eyes!». [34] Moved with pity, Jesus touch their eyes and immediately they saw again and they were ***FOLLOWING*** him.	And while coming out of Jericho, he, his disciples and a considerable crowd, the son of Timaeus, Bartimaeus, A BLIND-MAN, ***WAS SEATED*** along the way, asking for alms. [47] Heard that it was Jesus the Nazarene, he started to cry out and to say: «***Son of David***, Jesus, have mercy on me!». [48] Many rebuked him so that he would be silent, but he cried out all the more: «***Son of David***, have mercy on me!». [49] Stopped, Jesus said: «Call him». And they called the blind-man, saying to him: «Have courage, rise, he calls you!». [50] Having abandoned his mantle, walking again, he came to Jesus. [51] Answering him, Jesus said: «WHAT DO YOU WANT THAT I MAY DO FOR YOU?». The blind-man said to him: «Rabbuni, that I may see again!». [52] Jesus said to him: «Go, your faith has saved you». And immediately he saw again and he was ***FOLLOWING*** him on the way.

Matthew's setting is the same as Mark's. The greatest, or at least, the most obvious difference, is that while in Mark Jesus heals only one blind man, in Matthew he heals two. We should ask, why there is this difference.

Again we find the same inclusio of Jesus' questions, even though the parallelism is less obvious in Matthew, because he does not have the subordinate clause in the first question (Matt 21b). «Seated» (Matt 21c.23b.30b; Mark 37a.40a.46d), the connection between «you do not know» (Matt 22a; Mark 38a), «you know» (Matt 25a; Mark 42b) and «blind man/men» (Matt 30a; Mark 46d), etc, are also repeated. Mark uses the repetition of «son of...» to link the three passages in his construction: «son of Zebedee» (35b) and «son of Timaeus» (46c), which is a way of paralleling characters; and we should add to these the titles to describe Jesus, «Son of man» (45a) and «son of David» (47b.48c), which link the last two passages. Matthew does not use the same method, as he, conversely uses the repetition of the figure «two»: their mother calls James and John «my two sons» (21c) in the first passage, and at the start of the second passage they are called «the two brothers» (24a). Finally, at the start of the third passage there is not one blind man, as in Mark, but «two» (30a).

In the past, exegetes wondered which, Matthew or Mark, reported the authentic historical truth —how many blind men did Jesus really heal at Jericho? This kind of question is a type of false question— on the pretext of academic work (historical work, in this case), we stop ourselves from listening to and welcoming what the text is seeking to transmit —this can blind the reader!

The first reason for such a difference might be literary (or «rhetorical» to use the terminology of the exegetical methodology which I employ). This variation is only one way of drawing the reader's attention to the links between the characters in question —as we have already seen, we need to understand that Bartimaeus' blindness, or the two blind men in Matthew, refer back to the blindness of the two brothers, Zebedee's sons.

We should add that Matthew likes to double his characters: in 8:28 he has two demoniacs in the place of one in Mark 5:2 and Luke 8:27; in 9:27 he has two blind men, just as in this sub-sequence; in addition, in 4:18.21, in the account of the first disciples, he is the only one to use the expression «the two brothers» for Simon and Andrew as well as for James and John; in Gethsemane, in 26:37, he is the only one to use «the two brothers» to mention James and John; during Jesus' trial in 26:60, he alone mentions «two» false witnesses. It is therefore a style which is characteristic of Matthew.

However, these literary explanations, which we call rhetorical or stylistic, are still external explanations. The difference in numbers between «one blind man» and «two blind men» may lead the reader to reflect, as will other numbers in the text.

We have already emphasized that the blind man, or the two blind men, refer back to the two brothers James and John —in Matthew this is four people. But there are also «the ten others», who are also blind, like the two brothers and the two blind men —now we have fourteen... without mentioning the «numerous» or «considerable crowd» who accompany the Lord (Matt 29b; Mark 46c) and which does not understand, who do not see what those who are physically blind see; and, finally, the «many» for whom the Son of man will give his life as a ransom (Matt 28c; Mark 45c).

If the believing reader does not see that he, too, is part of this «numerous crowd», that he resembles «the ten apostles», the «two» brothers, Bartimaeus or the «two blind men», s/he risks remaining shut up in his or her own blindness. Matthew's text, just like Mark's, invites the reader to rise up, to see again, to walk on the way to Jerusalem with Jesus.

2.3.1. *Another look at «traditional» exegesis*

It is no exaggeration to say that the type of reading which we have carried out is still new. In fact, «rhetorical analysis» is based on presuppositions which are different from, and even opposed to, those of the historical-critical method, particularly form criticism (*Formesgeschichte*) and «literary history», but also redaction criticism.

As we have explained[10], the main presupposition of that method is that the Gospels are broadly inorganic collections of small units handed on through oral tradition, later compiled by redactors whose intervention was limited to retouching to link these units to one another, in a more or less artificial way.

This is why in commentaries pericopes are studied and interpreted independent of one another. At best, such-and-such a link between passages is indicated, but this is rare, and, in any event, not systematic. For example, in his 1963 commentary on Matthew, Pierre Bonnard is content to indicate a single link between the account of the healing of the two blind men in Jericho with the context which comes before and after it:

> This account is found in the three Synoptics, in the same place in Mark and Matthew, soon after the vital declaration, «the Son of man has come to serve» (20:28; Mark 10:45); and in Luke directly after the third prediction of the Passion. It is therefore well-integrated into the structure of the Gospel. In this context, we can give it a double significance: firstly, the one going up to Jerusalem to suffer is still the Son of David, as the two blind men publicly profess [...] In addition, and this second meaning does not contradict the first: about to enter his city, the Son of David does not disdain stopping to help a poor blind man seated at the side of the road, for this David has «come to serve and not to be served» (v. 28)[11].

10 See pp. 45-61.
11 Bonnard, 298-299.

Paul Lamarche's commentary is much more recent (1996), and he also emphasizes a link with what comes before and after the account of the blind man Bartimeaus:

> In some ways this account is linked to what has preceded it (for example 10:51 evokes 10:36); however, in other ways (we are on the way to Jerusalem, and compare 10:47.48 to 11:10) the narrative is linked to what follows[12].

About 10:36 and 10:51, that is, about the two almost identical questions in which we recognized an inclusio for the whole sub-sequence, Lamarche is happy merely to say that:

> The parallelism between Jesus' question to the blind man («what do you want me to do for you?».) and the question he addresses to Zebedee's sons does not emphasize the importance of the disciples' will, but, by this question, Jesus forces men to be aware of their deepest desire, and to express it (p. 262).

As for the double apostrophic «son of David» (10:47-48), he notes merely that it is repeated at 11:10 with the acclamation with branches: «Blessed is the coming kingdom, the kingdom of our father David» (pp. 263-264) and makes no link to the passage with Zebedee's sons' demand.

The same goes for Camille Focant's 2004 commentary. He is content with briefly indicating the links between the passages at the end of his interpretation of Mark 10:35-45, which he considers to be a single pericope: «In contrast with the disciples' blindness, the pericope which follows will describe the healing of the blind man Bartimaeus»[13]. When he then studies the pericope of the blind man, he notes that, «Jesus asks the blind man a question (v. 51) whose terms are almost identical to those in the question asked to Zebedee's sons some verses above (10:36). The effect is to bring out for the reader the contrast between the two responses»[14].

These examples illustrate the essential difference between traditional exegesis and rhetorical analysis. In rhetorical analysis, the formal links between the passages carry a meaning which not only goes beyond the total meaning of all the passages taken individually, but enables them to be better understood.

12 Lamarche, 263; see too S. Légasse, 646, n. 3.
13 Focant, 399.
14 Focant, 406.

Other commentaries, even recent ones, do not note any link between the pericope of the blind man and the pericope of Zebedee's sons. For example, in his commentary on Matt, Donald Hagner notes that the title «son of David» is repeated at the welcome with branches at 21:9 and that, in the Temple, Jesus will again heal the blind and the lame (21:14)[15], but he says nothing about the links between the first and third passages of the sub-sequence[16].

Others resist what they think of as a «symbolic» reading, which, they say, is impossible to prove. At the end of his commentary, Rudolph Pesch writes about Bartimaeus' healing:

> *It is not possible to establish* whether now, at the start of the fourth main part (8:22-26), Mark intends to give a symbolic meaning to the healing of a blind man (10:46-52), by referring back to the victory over the disciples' incomprehension. His composition indicates, however, that the healing faith which restores sight, leads one to follow Jesus' way in the community of service of the disciples. For the community, Zebedee's sons show, in an exemplary fashion, that Jesus' suffering opens their eyes: their positive response to the question, confirmed by Jesus, presupposes that their incomprehension is overcome[17].

Earlier, Pesch adds, «If we do not sufficiently take *Mark's respectful attitude to tradition* into account, it is easy to over-evaluate the account's *symbolic content which is not demonstrable* (p. 267; my emphasis).

In his analysis of the account of the blind man at Jericho[18], Vittorio Fusco emphasizes the ancient difference between historical exegesis and symbolic exegesis (pp. 213-214); he does not hide his reluctance for the latter type:

15 Hagner, II, 584.

16 Other commentaries, such as Gnilka II 277-94, may also be consulted.

17 Pesch, II, 255. My emphasis.

18 In the introductory volume to the Synoptics: LÀCONI M. *et al.*, ed., *Vangeli sinottici e Atti degli Apostoli*, 213-225.

Less certain, but possible, other links with earlier scenes[19] : the beggar Bartimaeus, by abandoning his cloak (the inalienable property of the poor man: cf. Exod 22:25f; Deut 24:12f), takes the place of the rich man who refuses to *follow Jesus* (10:17-31); he is also opposed to James and John (10:35-45), who, in answer to Jesus' question, «What do you want me to do for you?». asked for the first places in the Kingdom (p. 216; I have emphasized the first words, which are so cautious).

Finally, note Jean Radermakers' commentary on Mark, in which he gives great importance to the book's composition, but unfortunately does not identify the sub-sequence which we have examined[20].

3. THE SUB-SEQUENCE IN LUKE 18:35-19:10

Mark and Matthew integrate their account of the healing at Jericho in a very similar, three-passage setting. We will now see what the Third Gospel does with the parallel passage of the blind man of Jericho. Luke does not link this scene to Zebedee's sons' request; conversely, he has joined the account of the blind man (18:35-43) to the account of Zacchaeus, a passage which is only found in Luke (19:1-10).

19 Interesting references to B. Standaert, J. Dupont and L. Di Pinto.

20 RADERMAKERS J., *La Bonne Nouvelle de Jésus selon saint Marc.* Note his hesitation on the text's structure, II, 281-286.

3.1. *The conversion of Zacchaeus (Luke 19:1-10)*

COMPOSITION

+ [1] And having entered,
+ he WAS PASSING *through Jericho.*

: [2] And behold a man
: by name called Zacchaeus,

- and he was a chief-of-the tax-collectors
- and he (was) rich.

---

[3] And he *was seeking* to SEE Jesus **WHO HE WAS.**

- And he was unable because of the crowd,
- for in stature he was small.

: [4] And running forward before,
: he climbed upon a sycamore

+ to SEE him
+ because *through that (way)* he was about to PASS BY.

+ [5] When he arrived at the place,
+ HAVING LOOKED UP, *Jesus said to him:*

- «Zacchaeus, in haste come down!
- **For today in your house I must stay**».

: [6] And in haste he came down
: and received him by rejoicing.

= [7] HAVING SEEN it,
= all were murmuring, saying:
= «With a *SINNER* **HE WENT IN** *to lodge*!».

---

[8] *Having stood, Zacchaeus said to the Lord*:

. «Behold: *the half of my goods*, **LORD**,
.. to the poor I *give*;

. and if I have defrauded anything from anyone,
.. I will *give back fourfold*».

+ [9] *Jesus said to him:*

- «**Today salvation to this house has come**,
: because he is also a son of Abraham;

= [10] For **HAS COME** the Son of Man
= *to seek* and *save* what was *LOST*».

This passage is made up of two parts: Zacchaeus looks for Jesus (1-4), and Jesus finds Zacchaeus (5-10). The boundary of the first part is formed by the inclusio «passing through» (1a.4b). The first piece describes the place first (1), and then Zacchaeus[21] (2). The very short central piece (3a), expresses Zacchaeus' desire. The third piece (3b-4) recounts how the chief tax-collector managed to overcome his disability to obtain what he wanted. The final member (4b) refers back to the center (3a) and to the first member of the part (1a).

The second part (5-10) is also concentric: two sub-parts (5-7 and 9-10) frame Zacchaeus' declaration (8). The four tenses of each of the outer sub-parts are parallel, but the last part saves the first member of each segment. The symmetry between the end of 5a and 9a is total, it is significant between the end of 5b and 9b, and it is still clear between the end of 7 and 10[22], which consequently leads us to place the third segments (6 and 9c) in parallel, even though from the linguistic point of view they have nothing in common.

In the center (8), introduced by a narrative phrase, are Zacchaeus' only words. The main verbs share the same root, have the same subject and the same moods; at the outer parts are two fractions (1/2 and 1/4), the beneficiaries being «the poor», and then those whom Zacchaeus has wronged.

The joining of the parts is achieved by the end of 4 and the start of 5:

because	through there	*he was about* TO PASS BY,
When HE ARRIVED		at that place.

If in the first part Zacchaeus is identified in detailed fashion (2ab.3b), the whole text, like the character described, is focused on Jesus. The problem, for the chief tax-collector, is how to «see» Jesus (twice: 3a.4b), how to identify him (3a). Conversely, the second part is focused on Zacchaeus' new identity, which is opposed to his former identity («sinner» in 7, «lost» in 10b), or, more precisely, on his decision to convert which makes him move from his former identity to his

21 *Zakchaios* is the Hellenized form of the Hebrew name *Zakkai*. According to Fitzmyer (1223), this name means «pure», «innocent». Is this irony on Luke's part? But the *piel* of the verb means «to make innocent» or «to declare to be innocent», «to acquit», and it is probably this meaning which we should understand, since after Zacchaeus' confession, Jesus declares him to be «a son of Abraham».

22 The first verb, *eis-elthen* (lit. «come-into»), is usually rightly translated by «enter»; the translation «came» as the *elthen* in v. 10 better shows, albeit by reinforcing it, the similarity of the two verbs in the original.

new description as a «son of Abraham». Jesus' identity («me» in 5b), presented as the savior («salvation» in 9b and «to save» in 10b) is in the second part—Zacchaeus, who wanted to see «who Jesus was», in the center of the first part (3a), acknowledges him as «Lord» in the center of the second part (8d). Note, too, the lexical repetition of «seek», where the subject in Zacchaeus in 3a, and Jesus in 10.

BIBLICAL CONTEXT

The symmetrical position of 9c («because he is also a son of Abraham») and 6 («And in haste he came down and received him rejoicing») was indicated above. Here we can see a reference to the account in Genesis 18 where Abraham offers hospitality to the three men who appear to him at the oak of Mamre. Here we find the same haste: like Zacchaeus (Luke 19:4), Abraham «runs» (Gen 18:2.7), like Zacchaeus (Luke 19:5b.6), he «hastens» (Gen 18:6) as do his wife (6) and servant (7). Note the presence of a tree in both accounts (an oak and a sycamore, both sacred trees) and, above all, that the three men in the Genesis account are identified from the beginning as «Lord» (Gen 18:1; the same word is used twice in Luke 19:8).

INTERPRETATION

A mutual quest

Two characters are each seeking one another: Zacchaeus, the chief tax-collector, «looks» to see who Jesus is (3ab) and Jesus, «the Son of man», declares that he has come «to seek» those who are lost (10), «tax-collectors and sinners». Seeking to see Jesus, Zacchaeus uses the means he needs (4ab). He is small in stature, which stops him seeing Jesus (3b). He does what he needs to to turn the situation around—he climbs a tree to see the one he is looking for (4). But, having arrived under the sycamore, it is not Zacchaeus who see Jesus, but the other way around—it is Jesus who «raises his eyes» towards him (5), for he, too, searches him. To see Jesus, Zacchaeus had climbed a tree (4); at Jesus' request, he quickly comes down (6), always ready to do what he has to, ready for any change, to meet the one seeking him, and this time to meet him closer.

Who is Jesus?

Who is Jesus? This is the question which bothers Zacchaeus (3a). He has heard people speaking about Jesus, and desperately wants to see him. Not only will he see him, but he will speak to him, receive him in his home, offer him food and shelter (6). Like Abraham his father (9c), he recognizes God visiting in his guest.

He calls him «Lord» (8) and treats him as such. He will hear Jesus declare himself to be both «Son of man» (10a) and Savior (10b). Zacchaeus' expectation is satisfied beyond anything he could have hoped for.

Who is Zacchaeus?

And yet, we might say that the real question is not who Jesus is, but who this man is. Zacchaeus wants to know who Jesus is (3), but he is referred back to himself (8). The first word Jesus speaks is his name (5b). He calls him to do something immediately (5b) which leads him back to the house he left to seek the one he had heard people talking about. The chief tax-collector, who lost himself in the anonymity of the crowd, is led into the full light of his status as public sinner (7). Jesus does not say that all those who see Zacchaeus as a sinner are wrong. For Jesus, too, he is a sinner, since it is precisely these lost people, like him, whom «the Lord» (8) has come to find (10); to find, and to save, since Zacchaeus will definitively become a «son of Abraham» (9c).

The conversion of a man of money

Here we see Zacchaeus, standing up, making a solemn declaration of conversion to Jesus (8), but not a beautiful declaration of principles, rather a tax declaration. Zacchaeus remains a man of money even at the very heart of his conversion —he pays, not in words, but in figures. His words are percentages —he will give «half» (8d), he will give back «a quarter» (8e). The change, or conversion, is not an affair of the heart, but a financial matter —the heart changes, money changes hands. With the same movement he expresses a double judgment, what he has stolen and what he will give back, a judgment which is both on the past and on the future, joined together in conversion from this moment on, in the today of salvation.

Salvation

«Today salvation has come to this house» (9b). It is salvation in person which has come to Zacchaeus' house, Jesus, the one who «has come to save» (10b). This is, of course, salvation for Zacchaeus, but also, as a consequence of this, for the poor and for those he has defrauded. Zacchaeus sought to see Jesus (3a); Jesus' entire action consists in opening his eyes to other people. Referred back to himself, he is also referred to his brothers, «the poor» (8d), and to those whom he «had defrauded» (8e) of what they had to live on; in summary, those who, like him, need to be saved (10b).

3.2. *The Blind man and Zacchaeus (18:35-43 and 19:1-10)*

COMPOSITION OF THE SUB-SEQUENCE

[35] It happened as he was approaching to **Jericho**, that a BLIND-MAN was seated along the way, asking (for alms).
[36] Heard a **crowd** going by, he was inquiring **WHAT THIS WAS.** [37] They announced to him: «Jesus the Nazorean comes here!». [38] He exclaimed saying: «Jesus, SON OF DAVID, have mercy on me!». [39] Those who were going before rebuked him so that he might stop speaking.

But he all the more cried out: «SON OF DAVID, have mercy on me!».

[40] Jesus, having stopped, ordered that he might be led to him. While he was approaching, he asked him: [41] «What do you want that I may do for you?». He said: «LORD, that I may **see again**». [42] Jesus said to him: «**See again**! Your *FAITH* has **SAVED** you».
[43] Instantly he **saw again** and was following him, glorifying God; and **all the people**, ***having seen***, gave praise to God.

19 [1] Having entered, he was passing through **Jericho**. [2] And behold a man by name called Zacchaeus, and he was a chief of the tax-collectors and he was rich.

[3] He WAS SEEKING TO **see** Jesus **WHO HE WAS.**

BUT HE COULD NOT because of the **crowd**, for in stature he was small. [4] And running forward before, he climbed upon a sycamore to **see** him because he was about to pass by there.
[5] When he arrived at the place, **having looked up**, Jesus said to him: «Zacchaeus, come down quickly! For today I must stay at your house». [6] And he came down quickly and received him joyfully. [7] ***Having seen*** it, **all** murmured saying: «It is with a sinner that he went in to lodge!».

[8] Stood up, Zacchaeus said to the LORD: «Behold: the half of my goods, LORD, to the poor I give; and if I have defrauded anything from anyone, I will give it back four-fold».

[9] Jesus said to him: «Today **SALVATION** has entered into this house, because he is also *SON OF ABRAHAM*! [10] For the SON OF MAN has come to seek and **SAVE** what was lost».

Both accounts begin by noting a similar place—the first scene takes place on the outskirts and the second, shortly afterwards, within the same city of «Jericho» (18:35 and 19:1).

Even though the blind man is poor (he is «asking for alms»; 18:35b) and Zacchaeus «rich» (19:2b), the two characters are similar. Like the blind man, Zacchaeus «cannot see» Jesus (19:3); one «inquires» about what is happening (18:36), the other «seeks» to see it (19:3-4); a similar question moves them: «what was this?». (18:36), «who Jesus was?». (19:3).

Jesus recognizes the blind man as a believer (18:42), and Zacchaeus as a son of Abraham (19:9), the father of believers. Their faith «saves» them both (18:42 and 19:9).—Jesus is called «son of David» by the blind man (18:38-39); he calls himself the «Son of man» (19:10). The second title does not usually refer to his glory, but to his humiliation and Passion. The two titles are complementary.—Jesus is describes as the one who «comes»: he says about himself that he «has come to seek and save what was lost» (19:10). This might seem fortuitous if Luke were not the only of the Synoptic writers to use the same word (with the prefix *para-* in 18:37) in the account of the blind man.

There are frequent verbs of seeing: *ana-blepō*, translated by «to look up» in 19:5 and «see-again» in 18:41.42.43a (that is, three times in the first passage and once only in the second); *oraō*, translated as «see» in 18:43b and 19:3.4.7 (that is, only once in the first passage, and three times in the second).

Both characters call Jesus «Lord» (18:41a; 19:8a), from where comes the title given to the sub-sequence.

INTERPRETATION

The wish of the blind man and the tax-collector

The two characters might seem to be opposed to one another in every way—the former is poor and has to beg to survive (18:35), the chief tax-collector is rich (19:2); the former is anonymous, while all know the name of the second; like all the unfortunates of those times, despite of his disability the blind man had the pity of people, who helped him with their alms, while the chief tax-collector was despised and rejected. And yet, despite appearances, the two also in a strange way resemble one another. Both live at the margins: the blind man, seated at the roadside, was considered to be impure by the Law, which did not allow him to make an offering at the Temple, and did not even allow him to enter it; the tax-collector was also impure, because he dealt with the pagans for whom he collected taxes. Furthermore, both are unable to see. The first is blind, and does not see Jesus but has to ask passers-by what is happening (18:36); Zacchaeus is small and, like the blind man, cannot see Jesus (19:3). Both are moved by the same desire and take the necessary steps to get what they want—the blind man cries out (18:38-39) and gets up to go towards Jesus (40), while the tax-collector runs to climb a tree (19:4). Both wish to see, and both get for more than they could have hoped for at the start.

The crowd's blindness

As he moves about, Jesus is always surrounded by the «crowd» (18:36 and 19:3). Luke does not say why so many people accompany him all along the journey. Rather, he emphasizes the fact that they form a barrier around him, as though to protect him from, or to stop him coming into contact with people it would not be appropriate for him to be in touch with. Whether they mean to or not, the crowd prevents Zacchaeus from seeing Jesus (19:3). They do, of course answer the blind man's question, and inform him (18:36-37), but when he starts imploring for Jesus' mercy, the crowd threatens him to silence him (38-39). When Jesus decides to go to the home of the chief tax-collector, they condemn Zacchaeus' sin as much as Jesus' choice, as though they think that Jesus is blind to the extent that he cannot identify his host. But who is really blind —those who only see Jesus as «the Nazorean» (18:37) or the one who calls him «son of David» (38-39), those who only «see» Zacchaeus as a «sinner» (7) or the one who recognizes him as a «son of Abraham» (9)?

Jesus opens the eyes of the blind

Jesus restores sight to the blind man who asks him for this (18:42-43); he is also led to acknowledge Jesus not only as «son of David» (38-39) but also as the «Lord» (41), the son of the one who will finally «glorify» him (43). Jesus also opens the eyes of «the crowd» (36), which is led to become the «people» of God (43). All call the one they are accompanying «the Nazorean» (37); at the end, like the blind man, they «see» God's work in him, and they «give [God] praise» (43). In the meantime, Jesus had called them to change the way in which they see the blind man, who is no longer an inconvenience who should be pushed away, but a person who is to be invited to encounter his savior —and theirs. In the same way, Jesus invites the crowd who «murmur» against Zacchaeus and him (19:7) to convert in its way of seeing, and, like him, to acknowledge the conversion of the chief tax-collector, who has become a «son of Abraham» (9), and the coming of «salvation» (9); not only Zacchaeus «was lost», but all those who had made themselves, rather than God judges—and blind judges at that. Jesus restores sight to all.

Note, in reference to what we have said (see pp. 180-183) about the hesitation of traditional exegesis about what it calls «the symbolic meaning», which cannot be «demonstrated» or «established».

Let us say clearly that this meaning, even it relies on the text and on links between different passages, cannot be «proven», as a theorem can be proven, or as a mathematical demonstration can be given, which imposes itself and forces one to follow.

The symbolic meaning is, on the contrary, «felt», as a sentiment is felt, for example, faced with the beauty of a landscape, a work of art, and existential truth. With biblical texts, this experience is not only understanding what *the text says about my own truth, and what it reveals to me personally* intellectually, with the brain, but with what the Bible calls «the heart»[23].

23 See *Lire la Bible* (2003), 240-242; *Traité*, 630-635.

B. THE ACCOUNTS OF THE CALLING OF THE RICH MAN IN THEIR IMMEDIATE CONTEXTS

1. THE SUB-SEQUENCE IN MATT 19:1-26

Following a short introduction the length of a piece (1-2), this sequence has five passages. In the table below the headings follow those in the *Jerusalem Bible.*

The penultimate passage, «The rich young man», was already studied in the first chapter. Now we need to analyze and comment on each of the other passages in themselves, following which we will study the composition of the sub-sequence as a whole. However, before starting out, it would be useful to glance at a roadmap, so here is the general plan of the sub-sequence:

Introduction	1-2
THE QUESTION ABOUT DIVORCE	3-9
Continence	10-12
JESUS AND THE CHILDREN	13-15
THE RICH YOUNG MAN	16-22
The danger of riches	23-26

The «Question about divorce» and «The rich young man» are long (seven verses each), while the other three passages are short (three or four verses).

SYNOPTIC COMPARISON

We shall leave the synoptic comparison until the point where we have examined the parallel sub-sequence in Mark, for the synoptic study must be undertaken at the right moment. Each Gospel has its own coherence which will be drawn out without taking the others into account, otherwise there would be a risk of projecting the characteristics of one Gospel onto another. However, at a later point, the synoptic comparison will be indispensable for drawing out the specific points of each, as we saw for the two parallel sub-sequences in Matthew and Mark which include the request of Zebedee's sons, the discourse on service and the healing of the blind man or men. We should add that the synoptic comparison, as we do it, is carried out not only at the level of the passages, but also at the higher levels, of sub-sequences, (in this chapter) and sequences (in Chapter Three).

1.1. *The question about divorce (Matt 19:3-9)*

COMPOSITION

The passage is organized into two parallel parts (3-6; 7-9): a short question from the Pharisees (3.7), to which Jesus responds at length (4-6 and 8-9).

– [3] *And came near to him* *some Pharisees,*
– *tempting him* *and saying:*

: «Is it lawful for A MAN
: to REPUDIATE HIS WIFE *for any motive?»*.

• [4] And he answering said:

+ «Have you not read
+ that *the Creator* FROM THE BEGINNING "male and female made them"
+ [5] and he said:

. "For this man will leave the father and the mother
- and ***BE JOINED*** to **HIS WIFE**
- and the two will be *one flesh only?"*.

– [6] So, they are no more two
– but one flesh only.

+ Therefore what *God* ***HAS JOINED***,
+ let **not** *MAN* SEPARATE».

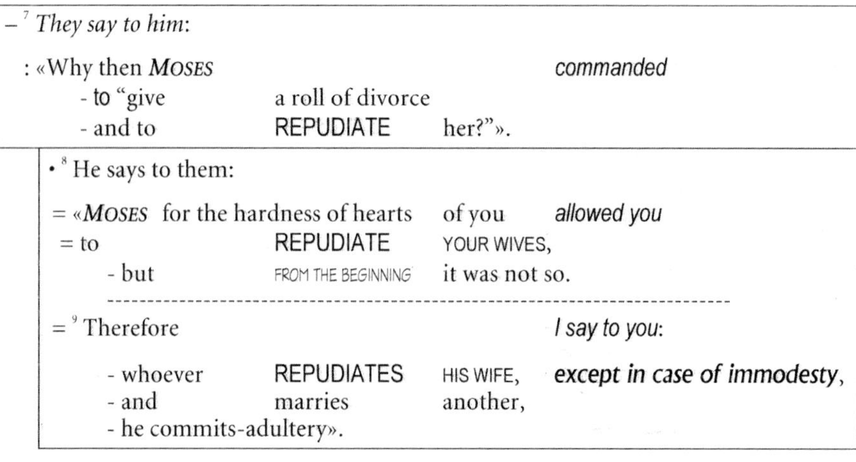

– [7] *They say to him:*

: «Why then *MOSES* *commanded*
- to "give a roll of divorce
- and to REPUDIATE her?"».

• [8] He says to them:

= «*MOSES* for the hardness of hearts of you *allowed you*
= to REPUDIATE YOUR WIVES,
- but FROM THE BEGINNING it was not so.

= [9] Therefore *I say to you:*

- whoever REPUDIATES HIS WIFE, ***except in case of immodesty***,
- and marries another,
- he commits-adultery».

In the second sub-part (4-6) of the first part, Jesus' words are in a concentric construction around the quotation of the words of God (5bcd). The outer pieces match one another in mirror fashion: «God» in 6b matches «the Creator» in 4b; «two» in 6a matches «male and female» in 4c. The last segment (6b) answers the Pharisees' question directly (3b) with the repetition of «man» and the connection between «repudiate» and «separate».

In the second sub-part of the second part (8-9), Jesus opposes his position and Moses': «I say to you» in 9a is opposed to «allowed you» in 8a.

The exception, «except in case of immodesty» in Jesus' final statement (9b) is opposed to «for any motive» in the Pharisee's initial question (3b). In the first part, Jesus opposes the Pharisees' question to the words which originated with God; in the second part he explains Moses' concession (8b) to oppose it again to the same words of God (the link is indicated by the repetition of «in the beginning» in 4b and 8c), after which he gives his own interpretation of the divine words in the account of the beginning (9).

BIBLICAL CONTEXT

The account of creation

Matthew quotes Gen 1:27 in v.4c, and Gen 2:24 at the center of the first part (5bcd).

The Mosaic Law of divorce

> [1] Supposing a man has taken a wife and consummated the marriage; but she has not pleased him and he has found some *impropriety of which to accuse her;* so he has made out a writ of divorce for her and handed it to her and then dismissed her from his house; [2] she leaves his home and goes away to become the wife of another man. [3] If this other man… (Deut 24:1-3).

Strictu sensu, this text is not expressing a law, but describes a normal case of divorce. The law followed this introduction, and did not allow anyone who had repudiated his wife to take her back after she had been repudiated and married by another man.

The Greek word grec *porneia,* which translates the Hebrew expression «a vice» (*'erwat dābār;* literally, «something shameful») means «fornication», that is, either «adultery» or «prostitution»[24].

24 See BJ, note b.

In Jesus' time, the legitimacy of divorce was in not in question, but scholars of the Law did not agree on the extension of the reason allowing divorce. The School of Hillel was very broad and accepted any reason of complaint from the husband (even burning the dinner!), while for the School of Shammai, only scandalous behavior by the wife or being unfaithful to her husband could be a reason for divorce[25].

The opposition to divorce in Judaism

Even before Christ, there was a tendency which clearly opposed divorce. So, Mal 2:13-16 says:

> 13 And here is something else you do: you cover the altar of Yhwh with tears, with weeping and wailing, because he now refuses to consider the offering or to accept it from your hands. 14 And you ask, «Why?». It is because Yhwh stands as witness between you and the wife of your youth, the wife with whom you have broken faith, even though she was your partner and your wife by covenant. 15 *Did he not create a single being that has flesh and the breath of life?* And what is this single being destined for? God-given off-spring. Be careful for your own life therefore, and do not break faith with the wife of your youth. 16 For I hate divorce, says Yhwh the God of Israel, and I hate people to parade their sins on their cloaks, says Yhwh Sabaoth. Respect your own life, therefore, and do not break faith like this.

Mal 2:15 alludes to this same text in Gen 2:24 which Matthew quotes literally in v. 5.

Jesus and the Law

The Matthean version of the passage, with its opposition between «what Moses allowed» (8) and what Jesus «says» (9) recalls the long series of «You have heard it said...» [...] But I say to you...» in the Sermon on the Mount (Matt 5:21-47), and particularly the second of the so-called «antitheses»[26].

25 See BENOIT P. - BOISMARD M.-É., *Synopse*, ii, 306.

26 On the incorrect name of «antitheses», see KOT T., «Accomplir la justice de Dieu. Mt 5,17-48», 18; Jesus' words are not to be considered as opposing the law, but as a commentary, a reading, the proper interpretation.

Opposition between the Law of Moses and the earlier account

In the letter to the Galatians, Paul uses the argument of the earlier promise to Abraham, which he declares superior to the law of Moses:

> But my point is this: once God had expressed his will in due form, no law that came four hundred and thirty years later could cancel that and make the promise meaningless (Gal 3:17).

+ 27 *You have heard that it was said:*				
. «YOU SHALL NOT	COMMIT-ADULTERY».			
= 28 *Well then, I tell you:*				
:: everyone who	***looks at***	**a woman**	to desire her,	
– already	COMMITED-ADULTERY	with her	in his heart.	

.. 29 If	***your right eye***	scandalizes	you,	
. pluck	it			
. and cast	it	(away) from	you:	
	: for it is good for		you	
	- that perishes			one of your members,
	- and not your whole body		be cast away	**in Gehenna.**
.. 30 And if	***your right hand***	scandalizes	you,	
. cut	it			
. and cast it		(away) from	you:	
	: for it is good for		you	
	- that perishes			one of your members,
	- and not your whole body			**in Gehenna** goes away.

+ 31 *It was also said:*			
. «Who	repudiates	**his woman,**	
.	let him give	to her	***a bill of divorce***».
= 32 *Well then, I tell you:*			
:: everyone who	repudiates	**his woman,** [except in case of immodesty],	
– makes	her	COMMIT-ADULTERY	
:: and whoever	***marries***	a repudiated,	
–		COMMITS-ADULTERY.	

INTERPRETATION

This passage has been greatly studied and discussed, not only by exegetes, but particularly by theologians and ethicists, for it deals with the very concrete and sensitive matter of the indissolubility of marriage. The various Christian Churches have adopted different practices: the Orthodox Churches, and the Protestant Churches allow divorce in the case of adultery, while the Catholic

Church is more inflexible and does not accept any breaking of the marriage contract. To a certain extent, in brief, the former Churches follow Matthew and the exception he gives, while the Catholic Church follows Mark's radical direction. This is not the place to enter into this discussion: we will limit ourselves to a few points of reflection on Jesus' attitude in relation to the Pharisees and the Law as Matthew presents it.

Temptation

When, at the start, Matthew says that the Pharisees only came to Jesus to «tempt» him (3a), he is interpreting their behavior. For him, the Pharisees are not moved by a desire for the truth; what interests them is putting Jesus to the test to make him stumble. In their malice, they can find no better subject-matter than the highly sensitive and much discussed one of the reasons for divorce. Their question is a trap, just like the hunter's trap: a lure whose aim is to catch the victim in a net, to capture or kill. According to their expectations, Jesus will not be able to escape, but will be forced to take one side or the other. To use Matthean terminology, he will have to choose between right and left. If he goes to the right, to the House of Shammai, which only accepted divorce in the case of adultery or prostitution by the woman, he would be accused of being hard and merciless; if, however, he went to the left, to the House of Hillel, which allowed the husband to repudiate his wife for any reason, he would be accused of laxity. There is no escape route for him!

Going back to the beginning

Jesus escapes the trap in his reply; but this is not a crafty trick, as a first, superficial reading might suggest. It is not that he seeks to avoid the problem by extricating himself. On the contrary, he shows a sure path for anyone who would risk remaining the prisoner of an incorrect problem, which does not give a satisfactory solution for anyone; the path of returning to the beginning. This is exactly what one does, spontaneously, in any group—a religious order, for example—when a difficult problem arises and trips us up. One turns back to one's basic intuition, to the source which is not yet polluted by the passing of centuries and the possible deviations and inevitable flagging. Jesus sends those talking to him back to the first pages of the Scriptures and thus to the «Creator» himself (4b), «God» in person (6b). Jesus does not go either to the right with the House of Shammai, or to the left with the House of Hillel, but turns to the heavens, towards God (Psalm 124).

The hardened heart

Despite the lesson they are given, the Pharisees do not see themselves as beaten. Jesus refers them to the first two chapters of Genesis, and they do not even attempt to discuss the scriptural reference; it seems, therefore, that they accept it. However, they note a contradiction between the first law, and Moses' law allowing divorce (7). Jesus does not deny that the Teacher of Israel granted this possibility, but he interprets it as a concession to the weakness of the children of Israel, «because of the hardness of your hearts». It is probably significant that Jesus does not use the first person plural, but the second person plural, in an insistent way, three times, in each of the three members of the phrase, when he could have left it out: «It was because of the hardness of *your* hearts that Moses allowed *you* to repudiate *your* wives» (8b). In this way, returning again to the «beginning» which he has already developed at length (4-6), he keeps his distance.

The Matthean exception

Along with the great majority of exegetes, we can see in the formulation of Jesus' final statement (9) the intervention of the final Matthean redactor, who would have added «except in the case of immodesty» (9b), to take account of the practice of the Judeao-Christian Churches for which the first Gospel was written. These communities had kept the rules which the most demanding of their Jewish brethren followed: like the House of Shammai, divorce was only allowed if the wife was adulterous or prostituted herself. This was a very restrictive interpretation of the Mosaic law, which reflected Jesus' basic attitude in his faithfulness to God's original desire. However, even if the exception does not go back to the historical Jesus, the final canonical text has it and it seems that it is legitimate to think that the Matthean Church would not have accepted it, had they thought that it did not faithfully represent the message of Christ.

1.2. *Voluntary continence (Matt 19:10-12)*

COMPOSITION

+ [10] *The [his] disciples say to him:*				
: «If this is the condition of man with respect to the wife,				
: **it is not good**			**to marry!»**.	

+ [11] *And he said to them:*				
- «Not all	**understand** [this] word,		but only those to whom (it) **is given**.	
. [12] For	**there are**	**eunuchs**	who from the mother's womb	are born so
. and	**there are**	**eunuchs**	who are made eunuchs	by men
. and	**there are**	**eunuchs**	who are made themselves eunuchs	for the kingdom of Heavens.
- Who can	**understand**,		let him **understand!»**.	

This passage has two parts, the disciples' declaration (10), followed by Jesus' declaration (11-12). Jesus' words are in a concentric composition. In the center there is a piece made up of three bimembers which result from the disciple's choice (12c); the two bimember segments which frame this piece (11b.12d) match, with the triple occurrence of the verb «to understand».

BIBLICAL CONTEXT

«The kingdom of Heavens»

The expression «the kingdom of heavens» is typical of Matthew; the other synoptic authors never use it. Even now, the Jews avoid pronouncing the ineffable Name, also know as the sacred tetragram, which we transliterate as Yhwh. When it appears in biblical texts it is read as «Adonai» which the Septuagint translated as *Kyrios*, «Lord». Other names are also used through respect for the name of God: «the Name» (in Hebrew, to say «Blessed be the Lord!», one says «Blessed [be] the Name!»), «the Power» (see, for example, Matt 26:64, «Then you will see the Son of man seated at the right hand of the Power»; the Douay-Rheims translates it as «at the right hand of the power of God»), «the Heavens», in the plural only because in Hebrew the word is always in the plural. This is why we use a capital letter.

Only the High Priest was allowed to pronounce the name, when, one day a year, on the day of Yom Kippur, he entered the Holy of Holies.

The eunuch excluded from worship

Like all those with disabilities—the blind, the lame, and others (see p. 70), eunuchs were excluded from the priesthood and from worship (Lev 21:16-24)[27].

Eunuchs welcomed into the House of the Lord

The third part of the book of Isaiah begins with the following proclamation, which announces the coming of the time of salvation for all, including those who are excluded, foreigners and the marginalized among the people of Israel, symbolized by the eunuchs:

> [1] Thus says Yhwh:
> Have a care for justice, act with integrity, for soon my salvation will come and my in-
> tegrity be manifest. [2] Blessed is the man who does this and the son of man who clings
> to it: observing the sabbath, not profaning it, and keeping his hand from every evil
> deed [...]
> +[3C] Let no **eunuch** say:
> «And I, I am a dried-up tree».
> [4] For Yhwh says this:
> + To **the eunuchs** who observe my sabbaths, and resolve to do what pleases me
> and cling to my covenant, [5] I will give, in my house and within my walls, a monument
> and a name better than sons and daughters; I will give them an everlasting name that
> shall never be effaced (Isa 56:1-2.3c-5).

INTERPRETATION

The disciples' dismay

Having heard Jesus' reply to the Pharisees about the indissolubility of marriage, the disciples are horrified: if the husband is to tolerate an intolerable wife for his whole life, it would be better not to marry! Here we can see an echo of some of the wisest proverbs: if it is true that «a prudent wife is [an inheritance] from the Lord» (Prov 19:14), it is also clear that «It is better to dwell in a corner of the housetop, than with a contentious woman, and a house in common» (Prov 21:9; 25:24); «It is better to dwell in a desert land than with a contentious and irritable woman» (Prov 21:19). The disciples' dismay suggests that the practice of divorce was very different from what the Master had just said.

27 This law is in force in the Catholic Church, where a disabled man may only be admitted to Holy Orders with a dispensation.

Something even more incomprehensible

In his reply, Jesus seems to accept his disciples' conclusion. It is better to make oneself a eunuch (12c) than to marry (10c). However, the reason he gives for such a choice is rather different from theirs. It is better not to marry, not to avoid putting up with an impossible woman, but to give oneself entirely to God. Celibacy is not a refuge «in a desert», «in the corner of the roof», but a dedication «for the kingdom of Heavens» (12c)[28]. Matthew does not report the disciples' reaction to this statement, but Jesus himself, aware of the difficulty they have in accepting this, is careful to solemnly warn them twice that only those who have been given this gift by God will be able to understand his words (11b.12d).

1.3. *Jesus and the Children (Matt 19:13-15)*

COMPOSITION

+	13 Then	*were presented*	to him	**children**	
::	that	HE MIGHT LAY	THE HANDS	**on them**	and pray.
=	Now	***the disciples***	rebuked	**them.**	
		14 Now Jesus said:			
		.	«Leave	**the children**	
		.	and do not prevent	**them**	
			: to ***come*** to	**ME!**	
=	For	**to such as these**	is	**THE KINGDOM OF HEAVENS».**	
::	15 And	HAVING LAID	THE HANDS	**on them,**	
+		*he departed*		from there.	

This short passage is made up of three parts. The members of the outer segments (13ab.15) mirror one another. The syntagma «laid the hands» + object appears in 13b and 15b; «left» in 15b matches «were presented» in 13a. The central part has three pieces: in the center (14bcd), Jesus' command; the final phrase of 14 matches 13c, for Jesus oppose those who are «like» children to the «disciples» who «rebuke» them.

28 See MEYNET R., «*Tu vois cette femme?*», «La parabole de l'arbre de la vie», 123-131.

BIBLICAL CONTEXT

This passage is very enigmatic. It says absolutely nothing about the special qualities children have which are needed to reach the kingdom of God.

Being like little children

The comparison with Matt 18:1-4 shows that the quality those who are to become like children should have is «humility» (*tapeinōsis*):

> [1] At this time the disciples came to Jesus and said: «Who is the greatest in the kingdom of Heaven?». [2] So he called a little child to him and set the child in front of them. [3] Then he said, «I tell you solemnly, unless you change and become *like little children*, you will never enter the kingdom of Heaven. [4] And so, the one who makes himself as little *as this child* is the greatest in the kingdom of Heaven».

INTERPRETATION

If this passage is so enigmatic, this suggests that we need to wait until we have completed our study of the sub-sequence as a whole to understand the role and meaning it has in its context.

We should also recall that this brief passage is found at the center of the construction. Now, it is very common that the center of a composition is taken up by a question, a proverb, or a parable, that is, by something which is problematic or enigmatic. The solution can only be found by relating the center to the rest of the literary unit: see, for example, Ps 113, focused around the question: «Who is like the Lord our God?»[29] or the Song of the Sea (Exod 15), focused on a very similar, although much more developed, question[30].

1.3.1. *Second excursus: the lord's prayer*

Many Christians, even those who are most faithful in their religious practice, have not the slightest idea that the text of the Our Father which they recite every day is not the only version of the Lord's prayer in the New Testament. Matthew is not the only one to locate this prayer at the center of the Sermon on the Mount. Luke also tells us that, in response to his disciples' request, Jesus gave them a prayer, the text of which is quite different to that of Matthew.

29 See *L'Analyse rhétorique*, 273; *Traité*, 199-201, 572-573.

30 See MEYNET R., «Le cantique de Moïse et le cantique de l'Agneau», 54; ID., *Called to freedom*, 78. On the center, see ID., «The Question at the Center»; *Lire la Bible* (2003), chap. 7, 121-144; *Traité*, 417-435.

1.3.2. *The Lord's Prayer according to Matthew (6:9-13)*[31]

The Our Father according to the Matthean version (Matt 6:9-13) is probably the best-known text of the whole of the New Testament. This is the one which Christians know off by heart, and it is the prayer they say most often. The habit of reciting it antiphonally has imposed a division of the prayer into two parts, which is now deeply engrained in the mind, similar to the division of the Decalogue, also known as «the two tables», most often interpreted as: 1) a table of duties towards God and 2) a table of duties towards one's neighbor. A clear analysis of the Decalogue showed, on the contrary that «the ten words» are arranged concentrically[32], and the same is true of the Our Father.

COMPOSITION

How many petitions are in the Our Father?

Some are of the opinion that this prayer has six petitions[33], with the final clause effectively being joined to the previous one by «but», giving a single clause: «and lead us not into temptation, but deliver us from evil»[34]. As the «temptation» comes from «the Evil one»[35], the final phrase is just a sort of repetition, with different words, of the previous phrase.

However, we should note that, from a purely syntactical point of view, these final two clauses are independent phrases (that is, they are main clauses, without subordinate clauses), joined by «but» (the opposing weight of «but» should not intervene in the syntactical analysis). Note, too, that the penultimate clause, «lead us not into temptation» is itself joined to the previous main clause by «and»: «Forgive us our trespasses, as we forgive those who trespass against us, *and* lead us not into temptation». Strictly speaking, we should consider these three clauses as forming a single phrase, made up of the first main clause, «Forgive us our

31 Here I am returning to my article «La composition du Notre Père».

32 See above, pp. 96-126.

33 On the history of the composition of the Our Father, see ANGÉNIEUX J., «Les différents types de structure du Pater dans l'histoire de son exégèse»; for a list of those who think it has six or seven requests, see J. Carmignac (*Recherches sur le «Notre Père»*, 312 ff) is more precise than Angénieux (44, n.11). Of the Fathers, Gregory of Nyssa, Ambrose and John Chrisostom appear to blend the last two sentences into a single request; Tertullian, Cyprian, Cassian and Augustine, on the other hand, list seven requests. Luther opted for the figure seven, while Calvin held that there were only six requests. Carmignac's demonstration (312-317) supporting seven requests appears to be decisive; I could only add an additional argument. One might also look at BAUDOZ J.-F. - DAHAN G.- GUINOT J.-N., *La Prière du Seigneur.*

34 For the moment we will follow the official liturgical translation.

35 See p. 211.

trespasses»[36] to which the other two main clauses, «lead us not into temptation» and «deliver us from evil» are joined:

Ø. **Forgive** us our trespasses,
    1. as we forgive those who trespass against us,
  and
Ø. **Lead us not** into temptation
  but
Ø. **deliver** us from evil.

If we wanted to follow through the syntactical analysis, we should also add that in Greek the clause «forgive us our trespasses» begins with the coordinator *kai* («and»), just as the next phrase does, and that it can thus be considered to coordinate with the previous clause, «Give us today our daily bread». We must go back to the precise nature and function of the *kai* which precedes «forgive us»[37]. Suffice to note that no one dreams of making these last four main clauses of the text, from «give us» to «deliver us», into a single petition. «Lead us not into temptation, but deliver us from evil» are two petitions, purely because they coordinate two commands which, from the syntactical point of view, are of the same order.

The Our Father, then, has seven petitions. This should not surprise us; on the contrary, once we know the value of this figure in the Bible, from the seven days of creation at the start of Genesis to Revelation, which is full of sevens (the seven churches, the seven seals, the seven trumpets, the seven golden bowls, etc.): it is well known that the figure seven symbolizes totality. Matthew is particularly fond of it[38]: even his genealogy is organized into three groups of «fourteen», which is the first multiple of seven; chapter 13 has even parables; chapter 23 has the seven curses spoken against the scribes and the Pharisees. To these we can add the seven petitions of the Our Father, and the seven Beatitudes at the start of the Sermon on the Mount, to which we will return.

The «classical» division into two

The custom of reciting the psalms antiphonally was applied to the recitation of the rosary, and so the «Our Father» as well as the «Hail Mary» were thus divided into two parts:

36 This clause is the «main» clause because a comparative («as we forgive those who have trespassed against us»; lit. «our trespassers») is subordinate to it.
37 See p. 207.
38 See too CARMIGNAC J., *Recherches*, 315.

Our Father who art in heaven,
1. hallowed be **thy** name
2. **thy** kingdom come
3. **thy** will be done, on earth as it is in heaven.

---

4. Give ***us*** today our daily bread,
5. and forgive ***us*** our trespasses, as we forgive those who trespass against us
6. and lead ***us*** not into temptation
7. but deliver ***us*** from evil.

The criteria for the division of the Our Father is clear to all —it is based on pronouns. The first part includes the first three petitions, which use «you», the second has the last four petitions which use «us». This is the opinion of, among other modern scholars, M. Dumais who, in his article in the *Supplément au Dictionnaire de la Bible*, reflects the popular opinion[39]:

> The structure of the Our Father in Matthew is well balanced. After a solemn invocation («Our Father who art in heaven»), the first part has three petitions in the form of desires addressed to the second person singular (you). These end with a hinge-formula («on earth as it is in heaven»). Next, this time addressed to the first person plural (us) come three petitions in the form of a request (or four, if we consider the antithetical petition which continues the petition about temptation and linked to it by *alla*)[40].

If we quote an authoritative document which represents the most common opinion, the *Catechism of the Catholic Church* presents it as follows:

> After we have placed ourselves in the presence of God our Father to adore and to love and to bless Him, the Spirit of adoption stirs up in our hearts seven petitions, seven blessings. The first three, more theological, draw us toward the glory of the Father; the last four, as ways toward him, commend our wretchedness to his grace. (§ 2803).
>
> The first series of petition carries us toward Him, for His own sake: *thy* Name, *thy* kingdom, *thy* Will (§ 2804).

39 DUMAIS M., «Sermon sur la montagne»; ID., *Le Sermon sur la montagne.*
40 «Sermon», 878.

The second series of petitions [...] go up from us and concern us from this very moment, in our present world: 'give *us* (...) forgive *us* (...) lead *us* not (...) deliver *us*'. The fourth and fifth petitions concern our life, as such — to be fed and to be healed of sin; the last two concern our battle for the victory of Life — that battle of prayer (§ 2805)[41].

Of course, it is not incorrect to note the difference in the second-person-singular pronouns in the first three petitions, and the first-person-plural pronouns in the last four petitions; but this is only one indicator of the composition. There are others which are just as important. By sticking to just one indicator there is a strong chance of missing the text's real organization, and, thus, losing much of its meaning. To be sure, the text's composition must always be based on a body of convergent criteria.

J. de Fraine offers another criteria to support the same division into two parts (3 + 4 petitions): «The first group has no grammatical link, while in the second, the petitions follow one another with the link-word *kai*»[42]. We will have to return to this to see if it is possible to interpret it in another way.

Concentric composition

Internal criteria

In addition to the play on pronouns which we have just discussed, we should also note several other facts.

1 First of all, the last three petitions are directed towards freedom from bad things, «trespasses», «temptation», «evil» (or «the Evil One»). Conversley, «the bread» of the fourth petition is not a bad thing, but a good thing, like the first three petitions, «the name» (of God), his «kingdom», his «will». So we can see that, while from the morphological point of view the fourth petition belongs with the last three (in «us»), from the semantic point of view it belongs with the first three (good things).

2 In addition, the third and fifth petitions are the only ones which finish with an expansion which in Greek begin with the same «as» (Greek *hōs*): «in earth *as* it is in heaven» and «*as* we forgive those who trespass against us». In technical terms, these two petitions are bimember segments, while the first two

41 *Catechism of the Catholic Church*, commentary on the Our Father, §§ 2803-2806. Note the subdivision of the last four petitions into two groups.

42 FRAINE J. DE, «Oraison dominicale», 598.

Father	hallowed be		your	NAME,			1
of us	come		your	KINGDOM,			2
who	be done		your	*WILL*,	AS in heaven	so on earth;	3
				the BREAD	of *us*	the daily	4
				give	to *us*	today;	
in	and forgive	to	*us*	our *DEBTS*,	AS we also forgive	our debtors	5
the	and lead not		*us*	into TEMPTATION			6
heavens,	but deliver		*us*	from EVIL.			7

and last two petitions are each only one member. The third and fifth petitions therefore form a frame for the fourth.

3 To this, we should add evidence which is blindingly obvious, although not often seen: the fourth petition is the one which is numerically central.

4 This is not all. Like those which frame it, the fourth petition is also a bimember segment; however, it is distinguished from the other two by the fact that, in the literal translation, its two members are strictly parallel:

THE BREAD	of	**us**	*the daily*
GIVE	to	**us**	*today*

Each phrase begins with the two main terms (the direct object and the verb), followed by the indirect objects «of us» and «to us», and then the two synonyms[43], the adjective «daily» and the adverb «today».

5 In addition, the central petition is different from all the others in that it is the only one which begins with an object, rather than a verb[44].

43 Synonyms in this translation; on the meaning of the adjective translated by «daily» (we are following the liturgical translation which follows the *vetus latina* translation), see p. 208, n. 50.

44 I owe this criterion, which had escaped me, to CARMIGNAC J., *Recherches sur le «Notre Père»*, 192.

6 Again, it is the only petition where a material thing is requested, which distinguishes it clearly from the petition for the hallowing of the Name, the kingdom, God's will, the forgiveness of sins, and the avoidance of temptation and evil/the Evil One.

7 Last but not least, the petition for daily bread is the one which agrees best with the name of the One to whom the «Our Father» prayer is addressed[45]. If we had to begin each of the first and last three petitions with the most appropriate divine name, the second petition would clearly begin with «Our *King*» («your *kingdom* come»); the first probably with «the *Holy One*» («*hallowed* be thy name»); the third with «our Lord» or «our Teacher», as here it is «doing his will»; the fifth with «God of Mercy and Compassion», «slow to anger, abounding in love», the sixth with «our Aid», and the seventh with «our Liberator» or «our Savior». Strictly speaking, however, it would only be the central petition which required the name «Father», for the common experience of children, at that time at least, was that it was the father who earned and gave out the daily bread.

8 In terms of the coordinators, «and», at the start of the fifth and sixth petitions, and «but» at the start of the final, it is clear that the second «and» coordinates the fifth and sixth petitions, and that «but» coordinates the last two. What about the first «and», at the start of the fifth petition? It is possible to interpret it as coordinating the fourth and fifth petitions (as J. de Fraine does). It is also possible to consider it to be a coordinating conjunction[46], as it appears so often in the text of the Gospels. To give but three examples among so many, and only in Matthew, the two accounts of the controversy about divorce (Matt 19:3-9; see p. 192) and the healing of the two blind men of Jericho (Matt 20:29-34; see p. 68) each begin with *kai*; the whole of the sequence which makes up chapters 19 and 20 of Matthew also begins with *kai* (see p. 307). The fact that only the last three petitions begin with a real coordinator can therefore be understood as a higher indicator of their unity. The last three petitions are coordinated, just as the first three are juxtaposed.

45 In our re-writing of the text, this single vocative is put on the side to demonstrate that it introduces both the prayer as a whole, and each of the seven petitions.

46 See BLASS F. - DEBRUNNER A., *A Greek Grammar of the New Testament*, § 442.

Given the convergence of all these indication, a concentric organization, rather than a division into two, imposes itself[47], reproducing the form of the seven-branched candelabra[48]. This should not surprise us, given that we know how many biblical texts are composed in this way[49].

External criteria

Until now we have only looked at criteria which are internal to the Our Father itself. They were, it seemed, more than enough to prove the text's concentric composition. However, it is also helpful to support them using some external criteria.

The first is surely that Luke's version of the Our Father, even though it has only five petitions in place of Matthew's seven, is also a concentric construction, as we will see below (see p. 221). The central petition, as in Matthew, is the request for bread.

The discussions which the description next to «bread» has given rise to are well known. *Epiousion* is a hapax legonmenon: in the whole of the New Testament, it is only found in Luke's Our Father (11:3) and it is used but once in the Septuagint. The problem of identifying the «bread», material and/or spiritual bread, finds a partial response, which is probably decisive, in another text which is structurally linked to the Our Father[50].

47 I myself discovered the concentric composition of the Our Father, and was then delighted to discover that I had not been the first; far from it. See in particular ANGÉNIEUX J., «Les différents types de structure du Pater dans l'histoire de son exégèse». According to this scholar, it was Theodore of Mopsuestia (d. 428) who, in the patristic era, was the first to recognize the concentric composition of the Our Father in Matthew (52); in the scholastic period (start of the twelfth century) Pseudo-Anselm of Laon returned to it (59-62), followed by others, particularly Alexander of Hales, St Albert the Great, St Bonaventure and, in modern times, different authors, but E. Lohmeyer in particular (339-342).

48 The text which describes the candelabra (Exod 25:31-37 = 37:17-22) is itself a wonderful example of concentric construction; see the analysis of this text in MEYNET R., *Quelle est donc cette Parole? Analyse «rhétorique» de l'Évangile de Luc (1-9 et 22-24)*, LeDiv 99, Les Éditions du Cerf, Paris 1979, vol. A 135-137, vol. B, planche 1; ID., «Au cœur du texte. Analyse rhétorique de l'aveugle de Jéricho selon Lc», *NRTh* 103 (1981) 696-697.

49 It is enough to refer to *Luc* and *Amos*. See too MEYNET R., *Traité*, 266-268. We should add that many note that the «heaven» at the end of the third petition recalls the «heaven» of the initial address and conclude that these two occurrences make an incluiso, which would prove the prayer's division into two parts. It is true that the inclusio in question marks the boundaries of the first side (9b-10), but this does not prevent the prayer being a concentric construction; the second side is made up of the last three petitions, the four being the pivot for the whole.

50 For the various interpretations of *epiousion*, see CARMIGNAC J., *Recherches*, 121-143; 214-220. Let us recall some of the solutions he offers: «of tomorrow», «of the time to come», «of always», «necessary», «sufficient», «substantial», «supersubstantial», etc. Carmignac concludes that «Whether we examine the Fathers, Greek philology or Semitic philology, until now no irrefutable argument has been able to truly establish the meaning of the mysterious *épiousios*» (143). Rather than deplore our ignorance, we would be better to rejoice!

It is acknowledged that the heptameter of the Lord's prayer sits at the center of the whole Sermon on the Mount (Matt 5-7)[51]. But there is another heptameter at the very start of the sermon. Elsewhere I have shown that the long blessing on those who are persecuted (5:10-12) is not an integral part of this heptameter, but that it makes up the center of the first sequence of the address as a whole (5:3-16)[52]. The first seven beatitudes, according to the order given in the Beza Codex and some other manuscripts, and accepted by most translations including Osty, the JB, are organized concentrically:

+ [3] **BLESSED**	the poor	*in spirit*	for theirs	is the kingdom of	**HEAVENS!**
+ [4] **BLESSED**	the meek		for they	***WILL INHERIT***	the earth!
[5] **BLESSED**	the mourners		for they	**will be comforted!**	
[6] **BLESSED**	the hungry and thirsty	FOR JUSTICE	for they	**will be satisfied!**	
[7] **BLESSED**	the merciful		for they	**will be done mercy!**	
+ [8] **BLESSED**	the pure	*in heart*	for they	will see	**GOD!**
+ [9] **BLESSED**	the peacemakers		for they	will be called ***SONS*** of	**GOD!**

Contrary to what many authors say, the repetition of «for theirs is the kingdom of heaven» in verses 2 and 10 does not make an «inclusio». The inclusio is not the only figure of biblical rhetoric. Of course, this repetition does have a function in Matthew's composition of the text, but it is the function of «initial terms» (anaphora, if one prefers the Greek terminology): it marks the start of different units, the heptameter of verses 3-9 and the long beatitude of those who are persecuted (10-12). The central three beatitudes (5-7) are the only ones which end with a single lexeme. In addition, all three are divine passives, where God is the real, but unspoken, subject. The segments of the first piece (3-4) end with two complementary terms, «heavens» and «earth»; in the last piece (8-9) God is the penultimate word of each segment. At the end of the first segments of the outer pieces (3.9) «God» corresponds to «heavens». In the second members of the second segments (4-9) «sons» recalls «will inherit», for sons inherit. The central beatitude is the one in which the first member is most developed. The first

51 For example, see LUZ H., *Matthew 1-7. A Commentary*, Minneapolis: Augsburg 1989, 212 (German original, 1985); DUMAIS M., *Le Sermon*, 87-90.

52 MEYNET R., «Les fruits de l'analyse rhétorique», www.retoricabiblicaesemitica.org: *StRh* 14 (13.02.2004; 19.06.2006).

members of the outer pieces (3.8) are the only ones in which the subjects have an object (the dative in Greek: «the poor in spirit», «the pure in heart»).

The concentric composition of this passage, made up of the first seven beatitudes, is, therefore, similar to the composition of the Our Father. The similarity in construction between the first passage of the Sermon on the Mount (Matt 5-7) and its central passage are a weighty external criteria.

In addition, the central beatitude (5,6) corresponds to the central petition of the Our Father. Here the subject of food also arises, for those who are «hungry and thirsty» just like for those who ask for «bread». This typically «structural» connection should lead us to reflect on the nature of the «bread» which is asked for in the Our Father, the more so since, in the long beatitude about those who are persecuted, which follows the heptameter, «justice» is closely linked to the person of Jesus.

+ [10] **Blessed** THE PERSECUTED		*BECAUSE OF JUSTICE*
:: FOR theirs is the kingdom of		HEAVENS!
+ [11] **Blessed are you**		
	when they insult *you* and PERSECUTE	
	and say all kind of evil against *you*	*BECAUSE OF ME*
+ [12] **Rejoice and be glad**		
:: FOR your reward (is) great in		HEAVENS!
+ For THUS THEY PERSECUTED *the prophets before you.*		

The two beatitudes in vv.10 and 11 shed light on one another. Those who are persecuted are persecuted «because of justice» (10a) and «because of me» (11d); thus Jesus is identified with justice. The «bread» which is asked for at the center of the Our Father therefore has something to do with «justice» and, if Jesus is identified with «justice», we are right to understand this «bread» as «the bread which comes from heaven» (John 6:32). Jesus' words reported in the Fourth Gospel, «I am the bread of life. He who comes to me *will never be hungry;* he who believes in me *will never thirst*» (John 6:35), are effectively a direct echo of the central beatitude, «Happy are *those who hunger and thirst* for righteousness, for they will be satisfied».

As we might expect, of course, there are other connections between the two heptameters of the Beatitudes and the Our Father. St Augustine viewed them as paralleling one another[53]. It is plenty to note two connections: the «kingdom» of God[54], in the first beatitude, is repeated in the second petition in the Our Father; the verb «inherit» in the second beatitude announces the «sons of God» in the seventh —because only sons inherited— and refers to the apostrophe in the Lord's prayer, «Our Father, who art in heaven» (note that this last word already appeared at the end of the first beatitude).

Connections between the symmetrical petitions

Returning to the Our Father, we should examine the links which unite the first three petitions, on the one hand, with the last three petitions, on the other. Most commentators do so and it is unnecessary for our thesis to return to this. On the contrary, we should examine, in brief, the connections between the petitions which mirror one another on either side of the central petition; the concentric construction invites us to do so quite naturally.

The first and last petitions

The last word of the last petition, *ponēron*, is ambiguous, as we have already indicated. It can be interpreted as the neuter common noun, «evil», but also as the masculine proper name, «the Evil One». In addition to the reasons which support this latter interpretation[55], the symmetry between the outer petitions leads us to hear that this proper name is opposed to the divine «Name» of the first petition[56]. It is true that, generally, «evil» is directly opposed to «good» (e.g., Matt 5:45; 7:11), but it is possible to see an oblique opposition between «evil» and «holy» («be hallowed»). In 1Macc 1:15, «they abandoned the *holy* covenant, submitting to the heathen rule as willing slaves of *impiety*», «impiety» is clearly opposed to the holiness of the covenant (see too Isa 1:4). Luke does not have the final petition of the Our Father which Matthew has, but at the end of the commentary which he adds to the Lord's prayer, he repeats the adjective «evil» which is opposed in some way to the «Holy Spirit»: «If you, then, who are *evil*, know how

53 AUGUSTINE, *Commentary on the Lord's sermon on the mount*, II,11,38, 146-148; St Augustine parallels the two central petitions.

54 «The heaven» is a traditional Jewish way of indicating God without pronouncing his ineffable name. This is why, unlike the other evangelists, who only use the expression «the kingdom of God», Matthew mostly prefers «the kingdom of heaven(s)» (32 times, against «the kingdom of God» three times).

55 See CARMIGNAC J., *Recherches*, 306-312.

56 Carmignac presents a similar argument (*Recherches*, 310, n. 12), but he links the last petition to the initial apostrophe.

to give to your children what is good, how much more will the heavenly Father give the *Holy Spirit* to those who ask him!» (Luke 11:13)[57].

The second and penultimate petitions

The relation between the «kingdom» of God and «temptation» (by the «Evil One») does not seem immediately obvious. However, in the Gospel, these two opposite realities are realities into which one does or does not enter. In the Sermon on the Mount itself, «if your righteousness does not surpass that of the scribes and Pharisees, *you will never get into* the kingdom of Heaven» (Matt 5:20)[58]. In Gethsemane, Jesus warned the disciples, «Watch and pray *that you enter not into temptation*» (26:41). «To enter into temptation» is to enter the designs of the Evil One, to enter his company, to submit to his authority, while «entering the kingdom of Heaven» is totally opposed to this. Note, too, that these are the only two petitions which begin with a verb of movement: «to come» (*erchomai*) and «to enter» (*eispherō*; *eis-erchomai* in 26:41).

The third and fifth petitions

The two petitions which frame the center are similar in form, with their second member beginning with the same «as», which distinguishes them from all the others. This «as» obviously indicates an equivalence, in the first case between «heaven» and «earth», where the person praying asks that «God's will» be done; in the second case between asking God («in heaven») to forgive trespasses and the forgiveness of trespasses carried out by «us», that is, humanity («on earth»). The movement in the two petitions is parallel, «heaven» and «earth» in one, God, and «us» in the other. This leads us to ask whether God's «will», which the third petition mentions, would not be the forgiveness of sins, the forgiveness which human beings grant to one another as much as the forgiveness the Father wishes to offer. The only commentary which Matthew offers on the Our Father relates precisely to the forgiveness of sins:

> For if you forgive men their trespasses, your heavenly Father will also forgive you; but if you forgive not men their trespasses, neither will your Father forgive your trespasses (Matt 6:14-15).

57 In Matt 4:5, «the devil» takes Jesus to «the Holy City»; in 24:15, «disastrous abomination» is established in «the holy place».

58 See too Matt 7:21; 18:3; 19:23-24; 23:13.

In addition, the first and last passage of the commentary which Jesus gives on the Law, just before the works of justice at the heart of which we find the Our Father (Matt 5:21-26; 43-47) also deal with reconciliation and forgiveness[59]; and chapter 5 ends with this summary order, «You must therefore be perfect *as* your heavenly Father is perfect» (5,48), where the «as», which recalls the two petitions of the our Father, indicates that humanity, created «in the image of God» (Gen 1:26-27) is called to realize its original vocation.

It is, therefore, possible to interpret the third petition in the light of the fifth petition. We do not ask God to do his will on earth as in heaven, but humanity to accomplish God's will on earth, as he accomplishes it in his home, heaven.

Why is the request for bread at the center of the Our Father?

The center of concentric constructions is often taken up by a question, a proverb, or a parable; in other words it is always enigmatic[60]. The center of the Our Father does not deviate from this law of biblical rhetoric. The reader will not fail to be astounded that the request for bread is at the center of the Lord's prayer[61]; this is not usually what one would expect to find here. «The kingdom of God» is what constitutes the center of the Our Father. This is more noble, more theological, than «bread». This is what one often hears, and what can be read in authorized commentaries[62].

Working on a text while expecting to find in it what one already knows—or imagines one knows— is certainly not a good methodology. A formal analysis, which demands technical skill and rigor, is the guarantor of greater objectivity. This is the condition *sine qua non* of the respect of the other who is addressing me through the text. A text is not a mirror in which we contemplate our own image. Formal analysis supposes a total renunciation; it demands that, temporarily, we place the meaning in parenthesis (I refer to this as the ascesis of meaning),

59 See KOT T., «Accomplir la justice de Dieu. Mt 5,17-48».

60 See *Traité*, chap. 8, 417-469.

61 «In the past people were often scandalized by the fact that physical demands were mentioned first [...] The request for bread thus presents itself as the most provocative of all those found in the Our Father» (GNILKA J., *Il vangelo di Matteo*, 333.335).

62 For example, SCHÜRMANN H., *La prière du Seigneur, à la lumière de la prédication de Jésus*. From the very first page he states that, «it is the prayer of those who are vowed body and soul to the "seeking" of the kingdom of God, who have made it their only raison d'être» (7); the first part of his work is entitled «The one great wish of the prayer» and essentially focuses on the second petition (40-47); «The preoccupation with translating the ardent desire for the comoing of the Kingdom is such that it seems impossible to add others to it. This desire, like a giant, rises, solitary and sovereign, to heaven» (63).

in the certainty that an unexpected meaning will be given at the end, far richer than I might have been able to imagine to begin with. This kind of reading, stripped, as far as it can be, of any preconceived ideas, inevitable leads us to allow ourselves to be moved, dislodged. A reading which does not shake up the reader, which does not change him or her, runs a strong risk of being nothing more than a projection.

To read, truly read, a text, is not a cozy fireside chat between well-brought up people, in which one shares information, recalls memories, has a good time. Reading a text is a confrontation, a row, hand-to-hand fighting, which one can only leave marked and changed. It is Jacob wrestling with the angel (Gen 32:23-33), a bloody fight, which went through the night «until daybreak»; an obstinate battle which refused to give up until it had obtained what it wanted: «I will not let you go until you bless me»; a fight which left its mark, as it did on the patriarch's hip; a fight, at the end of which, while the reader is not allowed to know the angel's name, Jacob still receives an unexpected revelation, in addition to the blessing, a new name which marks a change of identity:

> He asked, «What is your name?». «Jacob», he replied. He said, «Your name shall no longer be Jacob, but Israel, because you have been strong against God, you shall prevail against men» (Gen 32:28-29).

The constant discussions which have been going on since Christian antiquity on the nature of the bread of the fourth petition bear witness to the huge difficulty which it harbors. Theodore of Mopsuestia, the main representative of the Antiochene school, characterized by its attachment to the literal meaning, held that it meant only the material bread which is necessary to our bodily subsistence[63], while Origen, who developed the fourth petition at length, clearly privileged the spiritual meaning, almost passing in silence over material bread[64].

INTERPRETATION

Bread is never simply material

Anyone who suffers from hunger and lives with the constant preoccupation of subsistence, in the agony of tomorrow to feed himself and support his family, will probably be more aware than the well-fed of the material meaning of bread.

63 THEODORE OF MOPSUESTIA, *Les Homélies cathéchétiques*, 309-315.
64 ORIGEN, *Treatise on Prayer*, 166-183.

The millions of Christians who today still find themselves in this position, are right to ask the Father in heaven to help them to survive from day to day. However, it is not at all clear that it is they who are most closed to any spiritual interpretation. The poorest know, probably better than anyone else, that «man does not live on bread alone», that he hungers for words as much as for a crust of bread, for respect and dignity more than for help in satisfying those needs which we call basic[65]. Having said this, the literal meaning is certainly not to be excluded; on the contrary.

But limiting oneself to the literal meaning is to reduce the text unduly. The first reason is that what is requested is «bread», not, for example «fruit», which is there to be gathered, as in the garden of Eden. Bread is part of nature, from the wheat produced by the earth; but even the wheat, before the transformation which makes it into bread, is not given directly from nature, it is not a wile grass, but a cereal, the fruit of humanity's work. The human input into bread presupposes not only the long work of sowing and harvesting, threshing and flailing, but also the grinding, the kneading and the baking; all these actions imply the cooperation of several men and women, who unite their efforts for a common aim. Once baked, bread is also something one does not eat alone, but which one shares with family and friends, with guests, with the hungry. So bread is never simply just a material object; it is pre-eminently a symbolic food, in the original meaning of the word «symbol», which indicates relationship and recognition. This primary dimension of bread is anthropological. It is from here that we have to begin, before any truly biblical or theological consideration. Let us add that is called «our bread», not «my bread»; it is the bread of an «us», made by us and for us. Nor is it called «your bread», for it is not first of all God's bread, but the bread of our bodily subsistence, which humanity makes with their own hands.

Bread and blessing

For the Jews, bread is also what the blessing at the start of the meal is spoken over, in a particularly solemn way at the start of the Sabbath, before sharing it among all those present. «Blessed are you, Lord our God, king of the universe, who has brought this bread from the earth!». Note, first of all, in this line, that the Lord is called «our God», in the plural. In addition, the brevity of the formula

65 This is what Fr Joseph Wresinski, founder of ATD-Quart Monde continually proclaimed; see, for example, *Les pauvres sont l'Église*; *Heureux vous les pauvres.*

is surprising. It acknowledges God as the only giver of the bread, passing in silence over the human intermediaries, as though the essential part which humanity plays in making its food was the blessing alone.

It is known that the Jewish blessing over the bread, as well as that over the wine which is parallel to it («Blessed are you, Lord our God, king of the universe, who has ripened the fruit of the vine!») is taken up and amplified at the Offertory prayer of the Mass. By doing this, Jesus' disciples merely take up the gesture which their Master made and repeat his words, in memory of him. So, for a Christian, the gift of bread necessarily refers to the Last Supper and the Eucharist. But let us not go too fast; or, rather, let us go back, as far as the beginnings.

The first words which God addressed to the humans he had just created, male and female, were a double blessing, of which this is the first side:

> God blessed them, saying to them:
>
> «Be fruitful, multiply, fill the earth and subdue it. Be masters of the fish of the sea, the birds of heaven and all living animals on the earth» (Gen 1:28).

The first of the six hundred and thirteen commandments of the Torah is the command to be fruitful, to give life, to become a parent, «in the image of God» (1:27). God is the Father and the first gift which he gives humanity is parenthood. God gives the gift of giving. God's second word, which includes the verb «to give», concerns food:

> God said, «See, I *give you* all the seed-bearing plants that are upon the whole earth, and all the trees with seed-bearing fruit; this shall be [as] your food.
>
> To all wild beasts, all birds of heaven and all living reptiles on the earth I give all the foliage of plants for [as] food» (Gen 1:29-30).

God gives; and he gives «all». The text emphasizes this «all», seven times, the very figure of totality, just like the seven days of the first week, which has just ended: to humanity, «*all* plants [...] upon the *whole* earth and *all* trees»; to *all* beasts, *all* birds, *all* which moves, *all* foliage. What God is giving is «food» for both humanity and animals. Food is life which maintains itself and evolves. In giving food, God thus behaves like a father, as much to the animals as to the man and the woman.

God's blessing is part of his creative act. It immediately follows on from the three formula which separate each of the first five days of creation, now joined for the first time:

> And so it was. God saw all he had made, and indeed it was very good. Evening came and morning came: the sixth day (Gen 1:30-31).

It is only on the sixth, final day of creation, that the narrator modifies the second refrain by adding «all he had made» and the adverb «very».

The curse is turned into a blessing

But humanity was not slow to make itself and all creation unhappy, by paying attention to the voice which made them believe that God was jealous and did not wish to give them everything. This is what brings the second creation account into play, which is nothing more than the testing of faith in God's gift (Gen 2-3). It is surely not coincidence that the test of tests is linked to «eating», and more precisely to the gift of food; and it will end with the cursing of the soil, and with these words from God to Adam: «With sweat on your brow shall you eat your bread» (Gen 3:19). This is the first time that the word «bread» appears in the Bible. We might wonder whether the central petition of the Our Father is responding in some way to this; as though the curse were, not erased, but overturned, transformed into a blessing. This implies that the petition for bread is because no longer will humanity eat bread «with sweat on their brow», but will receive it freely from the hand of God. The manna in the desert was already a gift from heaven; but it only lasted for a while, for the time that the people crossed the desert to settle in the promised land where they cultivated the earth. The bread which Jesus has us ask for in the Our Father, the bread that he himself will give, is his body, «given» with his blood, poured out «for the forgiveness of sins» (Matt 26:28). Jesus is the new Adam, who gives himself rather than wishing to take, and in this way he redeemed the first sin. In the Fourth Gospel, John, who leaned against the Lord during the Last Supper, will explain at length that the bread which has come down from heaven, the new and definitive manna, which gives eternal life, is none other than Jesus (John 6). Recall, too, that, from his very birth, Jesus was placed «in a manger»; if Luke's account (2:1-20) emphasizes the manger by repeating it three times, it is doubtless to indicate that the new-born is a food, which will be realized at the other end of the Gospel in the gift of his body during the Paschal meal[66]; we should also add that Jesus was born in Bethlehem, which means, «the house of bread».

Bread and the «works of righteousness»

We do not wish to go over hackneyed arguments about the nature of bread. We recall, for instance, that the first of the devil's temptations is, precisely, about «bread» (Matt 4:3); the words Jesus opposes him with recall that what makes humanity live, its true bread, are «the words which come from God's mouth».

What is perhaps less clear, is the connection between the Our Father and the three works of righteousness which form the central sequence of the Sermon on the Mount (Matt 6:1-18). The petition for bread is not only the key-stone of the Lord's prayer, but also represents the key to the reading of the group made up of prayer, fasting, and almsgiving. An initial question could be phrased in these terms, like an enigma: what do fasting and almsgiving have in common? These two religious practices must be correlated, since they are symmetrical, they are matching one another on either side of the prayer which frames them; in addition, they are constructed on precisely the same model.

In both cases, there is an acceptance of something lacking. The person giving alms and the person who fasts give up the bread which they have, which they have petitioned the Father for and obtained from him. Alms are the bread which one gives up to give it to those who are poor and hungry. In giving alms, humanity does God's work, imitating the generosity of the Father and showing that we are his children. As Job said, «I was the father of the poor» (Job 29:16). The person who is fasting also gives up eating bread, for a while. In this way he indicates that he does not owe his origin to himself, that he does not subsist through his own work, that life does not come to him from bread, but from the One who gives it —in other words, before God— before God alone, Jesus says —he recognizes his sonship. In brief, to give alms is to be a parent, to fast is to be a child. «To practice righteousness» is therefore to find one's proper place in the line of sonship, the place one receives and the place one gives, like the bread which symbolizes it[67].

66 See MEYNET R., «La Nativité de Jésus (Lc 2,1-20)».

67 On the theme of food in the Bible as a whole, see A. WÉNIN's lovely book, *Pas seulement de pain… Violence et alliance dans la Bible.*

AS A CONCLUSION, AN ILLUMINATING COMPARISON

The connections between the heptameter of the Our Father and the heptameter of the Beatitudes have given an external criterion which confirms the validity of the analysis which we have carried out of the Lord's Prayer.

Another comparison, with a text which is outside the biblical corpus, will enable us to draw the specificity of the Our Father out still further, in its essential dimensions. Muslim tradition has a prayer which is very similar to the one which Jesus taught[68]. The literal translation is:

...of Fadâla ben 'Ubayd al-Ansârî who said: the prophet taught me a prophylactic prayer and commanded me to use it for whom I want, saying to me: Say:

Our **LORD** who art	*in heaven*,		1
: Sanctified be	your name		2
: YOUR-COMMANDMENT (be)	*in heaven*	and the earth	3
+ *O God*,			4
– as YOUR-COMMANDMENT	(be)	*in heaven*,	5
– so place	***your mercy***		6
:: *ON* us		on the earth	7
+ *O God*, **LORD** of goods,			8
– forgive us	our sins, our faults and our trespasses		9
– and let come down	***your mercy*** and a healing of your healings		10
:: *ON* what A such suffer of	and heal him.		11

The similarities are striking, from the apostrophe in line 1. The first petition (2) is identical to the first petition in the Our Father, the second (3) is very similar to the start of the third petition of the Our Father; the petition for forgiveness is found in line 9. We will not carry out a precise analysis of this text, but simply note what differentiates it, in essence, from the Our Father.

From the first word, the person who is addressed is not called «Our Father» but «Our Lord»; the whole difference is already here. Many Christians, so used to considering God as their Father, cannot even imagine that he could be considered otherwise by other believers. Islam is distinguished from Christian belief on the fundamental point of divine filiation. For Islam, Jesus is not in any way the Son of God; his disciples certainly are not! So we can understand why the central petition

68 IBN HANBAL, *Musnad*, n° 23839; the same text, with minor variants, is to be found in ABÛ-DÂWÛD, *Sunan*, Book 22, *Tibb*, 19 *bâb kayfa al-ruqy*.

of the Our Father, which is the child's specific petition, should be totally absent from the prayer which Muslim tradition says goes back to Mohammad himself. We can also understand that, while this prayer asks for God's forgiveness, it is careful not to repeat «as we forgive». Note that an «as» is found in the third petition (5), later matched by a «so» (6); but this «as» only indicates the work of the one God «in heaven» and «on earth». In the Our Father, on the other hand, God's will is granted to humanity, so that it can be accomplished «on earth as it is in heaven».

1.3.3. *The Lord's Prayer according to Luke (11:2b-4)*

The version of the Our Father in Luke is markedly shorter than that in Matthew (see the re-writings pp. 201 and 216).

Matt 6:9b-13	Luke 11:2b-4
FATHER **of us who (art) in heavens,**	FATHER,
HALLOWED BE YOUR NAME, [10] COME YOUR KINGDOM, **be done your will,** **as in heaven, so on earth.**	HALLOWED BE YOUR NAME, COME YOUR KINGDOM.
[11] THE BREAD OF US THE DAILY *give* TO US *today.*	[3] THE BREAD OF US THE DAILY *give* TO US *every day.*
[12] AND FORGIVE TO US THE *debts* OF US, *as we also forgive* TO THE DEBTORS OF US [13] AND LET NOT US ENTER INTO TEMPTATION **but deliver us from Evil.**	[4] AND FORGIVE TO US THE *sins* OF US, *because we ourselves forgive* TO ***everyone*** WHO IS INDEBTED TO US AND LET NOT US ENTER INTO TEMPTATION.

In Luke, the apostrophic address is reduced to Matthew's first word. The last words of the central petition are different, but synonyms. Luke uses the synonymous «sins» (4a) rather than Matthew's «debts» (12a). Matthew has an «as» instead of Luke's «because» (4b), which matches the «because» in the symmetrical petition (10c). Also, where Matthew talks about «debtors» in the plural (12c), Luke uses the singular and adds «every» (4c)[69].

69 For completion, we should also note that the same «give» in the central petition translates a present imperative in Matthew and an aorist imperative in Luke, just as the same «we forgive» translates a perfect in Matthew (12b) and a present in Luke (4b).

Those of Matthew's petitions which are not repeated, the third and the seventh, are precisely those which are at the end of the two groups each of three petitions which frame the central petition. In this way the concentric construction around the petition for bread is maintained.

Luke's composition is certainly slightly imbalanced, to the extent to which the second member of the petition for pardon (4b) does not have a corresponding member in the first part; however, the essential structure of the composition is respected, particularly the central position of the petition for bread.

<table>
<tr><td rowspan="5">FATHER,</td><td>hallowed be</td><td></td><td>the NAME</td><td>of you,</td><td></td></tr>
<tr><td>come</td><td></td><td>the KINGDOM</td><td>of you;</td><td></td></tr>
<tr><td></td><td>3</td><td>THE BREAD
GIVE</td><td>of us
to us</td><td>the daily
every day;</td></tr>
<tr><td>4 forgive
for we also forgive</td><td>us</td><td>the SINS
every debtor</td><td>of us
of us,</td><td></td></tr>
<tr><td>and let not enter</td><td>us</td><td>into TEMPTATION.</td><td></td><td></td></tr>
</table>

Just as with the Decalogue, the fact that Lord's Prayer has been handed down in two similar, but still quite different, forms, leads us not to let the text tyrannize. Through these words, and beyond their material nature, is the voice of the one who gave us his prayer, who places his own words in our mouths, like a delicious morsel, to which we are invited to listen; just like the voice of God which comes out of the space which simultaneously separates and unites the two cherubim framing it.

1.3.4. *The two cherubim*

Here it is worth pausing briefly at the sequence which begins with the description of the temple which God orders Moses to build, after having given him the Decalogue (Exod 20) and made a covenant with the people (Exodus 24). This first sequence (Exod 25:10-40), which describes four objects, is in a concentric construction[70]. The first two objects have several points in common. The most obvious is that the mercy-seat is placed on the ark like its cover, which is what the

70 See PAXIMADI G., *E io dimorerò in mezzo a loro*, 78; see too MEYNET R., «Es 25,10-40. A proposito del libro di G. Paximadi».

last verse of this pair of passages says, v.21. The same v.21 obviously matches the last verse of the passage on the ark (16).

The last two passages are also twinned: among others, they end in the same way, with the description of the accessories, those of the table in 29, and of the candlestick in 37-28. We also know that these two objects were placed together in the first room of the Dwelling.

The most surprising thing, for those who do not know the laws of biblical rhetoric, is that the passages match remotely, the first matching the fourth, that is, the ark matching the table, and the second with the penultimate, that is, the mercy-seat with the candelabra. Note in particular that the candlestick and the cherubim are arranged symmetrically as objects. The two cherubim are facing one another at either side of the mercy-seat, while from the central trunk of the candlestick were three arms on each side, matching in pairs.

Let us come to the significance of the whole, the meaning of the composition, or rather the meaning which the composition points to.

The center is the not just the physical focal point, but also the semantic, that is, theological focal point. The ark and mercy-seat, just like the table and candlestick are objects, and only objects. But the ark with its cover, the mercy-seat, contain «the witness», that are the tablets of the Law, the Decalogue, that is, the words written by the Lord himself on the stones; these are the divine words of the past, even though that past is very recent. We should not forget that all the words of this text (Exod 25:10-40) are pronounced by God, addressed to Moses; these are the divine words of the present. Then in the center of the sequence the future words are spoken—the Lord foresees and promises to continue to speak in the future. His word will not be shut up in the objects described, not even in the ark of the covenant or the Decalogue; his words will come out from the space between the two cherubim placed facing one another on the mercy seat: «from between the two cherubim», says the text, at the very heart of the central passage, the place of the *Shekhina*, the Presence.

[10] THEY SHALL MAKE AN ARK OF ACACIA WOOD.
Two and a half cubits long and one and a half cubits wide and one and a half cubits high.
[11] **AND YOU SHALL OVERLAY IT WITH PURE GOLD;** inside and outside you shall plate it. **AND YOU SHALL MAKE A MOLDING OF GOLD AROUND IT.**
– [12] And you shall cast for it *FOUR RINGS OF GOLD*, and you shall fix them on *its four feet*, and two rings on it first side and two rings on its second side.
– [13] AND YOU SHALL MAKE POLES OF ACACIA WOOD AND YOU SHALL OVERLAY THEM WITH GOLD. [14] And you shall put the poles into the rings, on the side of the ark, ***to carry*** the ark ***with them***. [15] In the rings of the ark shall be the poles; they shall not be removed from it.
[16] AND YOU SHALL PUT INTO THE ARK THE TESTIMONY *WHICH I WILL GIVE YOU.*

[17] YOU SHALL MAKE A MERCY-SEAT OF PURE GOLD;
two and a half cubits long and one and a half cubits wide.
[18] And **you shall make** two cherubim OF GOLD. ***Hammered work* shall you make them** at the two ends of the mercy-seat.
[19] **And make one cherub at the one end and one cherub at the other end.** Of one piece with the mercy-seat you shall make the cherubim on its two ends. [20] And the cherubim shall have their wings stretched out above, covering with their wings the mercy-seat; and their faces one towards another, towards the mercy-seat are *THE FACES* of the cherubim.
[21] And you shall put the mercy-seat on the top of the ark,
AND INTO THE ARK YOU SHALL PUT THE TESTIMONY *WHICH I WILL GIVE YOU.*

+ [22] And I will meet *you* there, and I WILL SPEAK *with you*
- from **above** the mercy-seat,
- BETWEEN THE TWO CHERUBIM
- that (are) **above** the ark of the Testimony,
+ all that which I COMMAND *you* *for the Sons of Israel.*

[23] YOU SHALL MAKE A TABLE OF ACACIA WOOD.
Two cubits long and a cubit wide and one and a half cubits high.
[24] **AND YOU SHALL OVERLAY IT WITH PURE GOLD.** **AND YOU SHALL MAKE A MOLDING OF GOLD AROUND IT.**
[25] And you shall make a frame of a handbreadth around it, and you shall make a molding of gold to its frame round about.
– [26] And you shall make for it *FOUR RINGS OF GOLD* and you shall put the rings on the four corners which are on its *four feet*. [27] Over against the frame shall the rings be placed for the poles to carry the table.
– [28] AND YOU SHALL MAKE THE POLES OF ACACIA WOOD AND YOU SHALL OVERLAY THEM WITH GOLD and ***one shall carry with them*** the table.
[29] And **you shall make** its plates, and its cups, its covers, and it bowls by which they pour libations; of pure gold you shall make them.
[30] AND YOU SHALL PUT ON THE TABLE THE BREAD OF THE PRESENCE before me always.

[31] YOU SHALL MAKE A CANDELABRA OF PURE GOLD.
Hammered work* shall you make** the candelabra; its base and its branch, its calyxes, its buds and its flowers shall be one peace with it. [32] And six branches shall come out of its sides. **Three branches of candelabra on its first side, and three branches of candelabra on its second side.** [33] **Three calyxes made like almonds in the one branch, with a bud and a flower, and three calyxes made like almonds in the other branch, with a bud and flower.** So for the six branches that are coming out from the candelabra. [34] And in the candelabra shall be FOUR calyxes made like almond, with their buds and flowers. [35] **And a bud under two branches of one piece with it, and a bud under the second pair of branches of one piece with it.** So for the six branches that are coming out from the candelabra. [36] Their buds and their branches shall be one piece with it. All of it shall be one ***hammered work, PURE OF GOLD.
[37] And **you shall make** its lamps, seven; and the lamps shall be mounted so that it will shed light on its front side. [38] And its snuffers and its fire pans shall be pure of gold. [39] Of a talent of pure gold shall one make it with all these utensils. [40] Notice and make them according to the pattern which was shown you on the mountain.

1.4. *The danger of wealth (Matt 19:23-26)*

COMPOSITION

+ [23] *Jesus said to his disciples*:

. «Truly	I say to you				
: that	a rich-man	WITH DIFFICULTY	***shall enter***	***into the kingdom of HEAVENS!***	
. [24] Again	I say to you:				
: it is	EASIER	for a camel	through the eye of a needle		to pass
: than for	a rich-man		to ***enter***	***into the kingdom of GOD!***».	

[25] *Hearing, the disciples were greatly amazed saying*:

« Who then CAN	***be saved?***».

+ [26] *Looking at, Jesus said to them*:

: «For	men	***this***	is IMPOSSIBLE;
: for	**GOD**	**all**	is POSSIBLE».

The disciples' question (25) is framed by two of Jesus' sayings (23-24 and 26). In the first sentence, Jesus' statement is repeated and emphasized in each case by a formula of emphasis, «truly I say to you» and «again I say to you».

«With difficulty» (23c), «easier» (24b), «can» (25b), «impossible» (26c) belong to the same semantic field. The interrogative pronoun «who» at the center (25b; a further example of the law of the question in the center) refers to «a rich man» in 23c and 24c in the first part and to «men» in the last part (26b). «God» (24c), matching «Heavens» (23c), is repeated at the end (26c). «Being saved» (25b) matches «enter into the kingdom of heavens» (23c) and «enter into the kingdom of God» (24c) in the first part, and is then repeated with the pronoun «this» in the last part (26b).

BIBLICAL CONTEXT

«The kingdom of heaven»

As was said above (see p. 198), the expression «the kingdom of heaven(s)», which Matthew is fond of, is the equivalent of «the kingdom of God». Here, the two expressions are in symmetrical positions, acting as final terms for the two segments 23bc and 24abc.

Wealth is a blessing from the Lord

In the Old Testament, wealth, along with heirs, is one of the clearest signs of God's blessing. The servant sent by Abraham to find a wife for his son Isaac introduces himself in these terms:

> He said: «I am the servant of Abraham. [35] Yhwh has overwhelmed my master with blessings, and Abraham is now very rich. He has given him flocks and herds, silver and gold, men slaves and women slaves, camels and donkeys (Gen 24:34-35)[71].

INTERPRETATION

Only difficult for the wealthy, or impossible for everyone?

The disciples were not «amazed» without reason (25a)! What Jesus stated with such conviction and force (23-24) was radically opposed to what all the people of Israel had always believed —that wealth was a sign of God's blessing. The wealthy, blessed by the Lord, were to be considered as already being part of the kingdom of God. The disciples were therefore right to ask, if it would be so difficult for a rich man to enter the kingdom of Heaven, «who can be saved?» (25b). And Jesus does not reply that it will be easier for the poor to reach salvation. In reply to the disciples' question, he states that it is not only difficult for the rich to enter the kingdom of God, but for «men» (26b), that is, for all; and what is more, he does not mention difficulty any longer (23c) but rather impossibility (26b). Salvation is beyond human ability, and can only be God's work—for him alone are «all things possible» (26c).

1.5. *The Sub-Sequence as a Whole (Matt 19:1-26)*

COMPOSITION

Leaving the introduction (1-2) to one side for the moment, *the first two passages* (3-9 and 10-12) are closely linked. With their question (10b), the disciples react to what Jesus has just said; note the repetition of «condition» and «woman» at the start of the two passages (3b and 10b).

• In *the last two passages* (16-22 and 23-26), the dialogue between Jesus and his disciples after the rich young man had gone deal with the same subject, wealth which risks preventing «entering» (17b and 23b.24b) «into life», that is, «in the

71 For example, Gen 24:1; 26:13-14; 30:43; 32:6; 33:11; Deut 28:3-6.11-12; Lev 26:3-10; Ps 112:3; 1Kgs 3:13; 10:14-25 (see Légasse, 617, n. 51).

kingdom of Heaven» (which refers back to «treasure in heaven» in 21b); «having heard that» in 25 matches «having heard this word» in 22a.

The first two passages (3-9 and 10-12) match the last two (16-22 and 23-26) in parallel; at the center (13-15), is the scene with the children.

· *The first and fourth passages* have the same composition: a question addressed to Jesus (3b.16b) by people who «approach him» (3a and 16a; these terms act as initial terms); — Jesus' reply quoting the Torah (4b-6 and 18b-19); in both cases the syntagma «father and mother» is at the center of the quotation; — there follows a question from the interlocutors (7 and 20), — and a last reply from Jesus (8-9 and 21-22). Note, too, that «to commit adultery» is repeated at the end of the first passage (9b) and at the center of the other one (18b).

· *The second and last passages* (10-12 and 23-26) introduce «the disciples» (10a and 23a.25a), who were not mentioned in the previous passages. «The kingdom of heaven» is repeated in 12c and 23b.24b; note too, at the end of the passages, words from the family «can/be able to» (12c and 25), «impossible» and «possible» (26ab), which act as final terms.

· *The central passage* (13-15) begins like the first and fourth passages, but the verb is different, for the children do not approach on their own initiative, but «are presented to him» (13a). Here too are «the disciples» (13b) and also «the kingdom of heaven» (14b), as in the second and the last passages. «The children» at the center of the construction (14a) match «father and mother» at the center of the first and fourth passages (5a.19a). «Come to me» (14b) matches «follow me» in the fourth passage (21b) which takes up «followed him» in the introduction (2). This passage is thus linked to all the other passages of the sub-sequence, including the introduction.

The introduction: we have already noted that «to follow» (with the same object) is used in the introduction and in the fourth passage 2 and 21b; note that, leaving Galilee to go into Judea, Jesus leaves the region of his father and mother.

[1] It happened when Jesus had finished these words,
He departed from Galilee and came into the territory of Judea beyond the Jordan.
[2] And a large crowd FOLLOWED HIM and he healed them there.

– [3] Some Pharisees CAME NEAR TO HIM to tempt him, saying:
«Is it lawful for a man to repudiate his ***wife*** for any ***condition*** whatsoever?».
+ [4] Answering he said:

«Have you not read that the Creator from the beginning
"male and female made them" and he said:
[5] "For this man will leave **THE FATHER AND THE MOTHER**
and be joined to his wife and the two will be one flesh only?".
[6] So they are no more two, but one flesh only.
Therefore what God has joined, let not man separate».

– [7] They said to him: «Why then Moses commanded to «give a roll of divorce and to repudiate her»?».
+ [8] He says to them: «Moses because of the hardness of your hearts allowed you to repudiate your wives, but from the beginning it was not so. [9] Therefore I say to you, whoever repudiates his wife, except in the case of immodesty, and marries another **COMMITS-ADULTERY**».

[10] The ***disciples*** say to him:
«If this is the ***condition*** of man with respect to the ***wife***, it is not good to marry». [11] He said to them: «Not all understand this word, but only those to whom it is given. [12] For there are eunuchs who from the mother's womb are born so; and there are eunuchs who are made eunuchs by men; and there are eunuchs who are made themselves eunuchs for **THE KINGDOM OF HEAVENS**. Who ***can*** understand, let him understand!».

[13] Then children WERE PRESENTED TO HIM that he might lay the hands on them and pray; and the ***disciples*** rebuked them. [14] But Jesus said: «Leave **THE CHILDREN** and do not prevent them to COME TO ME; for to such as these belongs **THE KINGDOM OF HEAVENS**». [15] And having laid the hands upon them, he departed from there.

– [16] And behold someone COMING TO HIM, said:
«Master, what good shall I do so that I might have **ETERNAL LIFE**?».
+ [17] He said to him: «Why do you interrogate me on good? Only one is good. If you want to ***enter*** into the **LIFE**, observe the commandments». [18] He says to him: «Which?». Jesus said:

«These: "You shall not kill, you shall not ***COMMIT-ADULTERY***,
you shall not steal, you shall not testimony falsely,
[19] honor **THE FATHER AND THE MOTHER**",
and "love your neighbor as yourself"».

– [20] The young man says to him: «All these I kept; of what still I lack?».
+ [21] Jesus declared to him: «If you want to be perfect, go, sell your possessions and give to the poor and you will have **TREASURE IN HEAVENS**; and come, FOLLOW ME». [22] **Heard this word**, the young man went away afflicted; for he was having great wealth.

[23] Jesus said to his ***disciples***:
«Truly, I say to you, that a rich-man shall with difficulty ***enter*** into the **KINGDOM OF HEAVENS**. [24] Again I say to you, it is easier for a camel to pass through the eye of e needle than for a rich-man to ***enter*** into the **KINGDOM OF GOD**». [25] **Heard this** the disciples were greatly amazed saying: «Who then ***can*** BE SAVED?». [26] Looking at, Jesus said to them: «For men this is ***impossible***, but for God all is ***possible***».

BIBLICAL CONTEXT

Like angels in heaven

To the Sadducees who questioned him on the ultimate fate of the woman who had married seven brothers one after the other, Jesus replied, «At the resurrection men and women do not marry; no, they are like the angels in heaven» (Matt 22:23-33)[72]. What defines man at the very end is not his married state, nor family relationships, but being a son.

INTERPRETATION

Recognizing the voice of a brother

The two commandments which deal with father and mother (5,19), appear contradictory. How can a man «honor» them by «leaving» them? Man is not called to leave his father and mother to remain alone, closed up in himself. He separates from them to «unite himself to his wife, to become one flesh» (5b); he honors them by «loving his neighbor as himself» (19), that is, by not doing him any harm, by not taking his life, his wife, his property, or the truth. In other words, by leaving his parents to go to the other, he honors them as a person who has become another in relation to them, free to live a truly new life, different from theirs. If a man remained «united» to his parents, making one flesh with them, he would not be an independent being, an individual, and could not «unite himself» to his wife; he would be unable of «loving his neighbor as himself». Living as a prisoner in the maternal bosom, not having «entered into life» (17), he would be incapable of «observing the commandments» (17). These, in fact, are not given to the child, but to the man, the «son of the commandment» (*bar mitzvah*), that is, to someone who is able to recognize the voice of the Father as the voice of another. In this condition man can also recognize the call of the «neighbor» (19b), and especially that of his own wife (5b), but also of each of his brothers.

Recognizing the voice of the Father

All men are invited to hear God's voice, «to enter the kingdom» (14.23.24) through the voice of their father and mother, the voice of their wife and neighbor, if they not only wish to «enter into life» (17), that is, be born, but also «be perfect» (*teleios*; 21), that is, reach the end (the *telos*), if they wish to «have treas-

72 See the commentary on the parallel passage in Luke in *Luc*, 768-771.

ure in heaven» (21). His father and mother point out his beginnings to him, while his wife and neighbor show him his end. It appears that this type of listening is out of reach for man; no one «can get it» if it is not «given» to him by God himself (11.12c): «for men this is impossible, but with God all things are possible» (26). However, those to whom this has been given—the person who «has made himself a eunuch for the kingdom of heaven» (12), the person who has cast away his property «to have treasure in heaven» (21), «to enter into the kingdom of God» (23.24)—are the prophets who hand down to all, those who have married and kept their property, the revelation received from God. Not all are called to eternal life; and at the end, no one is defined by his wealth, by his marriage, by the fact that he has children, but only by the fact that he is a child of God, of the only Father.

Recognizing the voice of the Son

When Jesus suggests to the rich young man that he leave behind the inheritance he received from his father and mother to follow him (21), he is inviting him to imitate his filial attitude. He had just left Galilee, his earthly family's region, to turn his steps to Judea, towards the end which had been appointed for him by his Father. Following Jesus thus means accompanying the person who has left his father and mother for the kingdom of God, the first one to be similar to children (14). To recognize the voice of the Son means listening to the person who blesses children in the name of the Lord, who «prays» to their Father and his Father[73]. It might appear strange that all the events reported by Matthew should be introduced by with the comment that, having «finished these words» (1a), «he healed them there» (2). After such an introduction, the reader might expect an account of a healing. We need to recognize that Jesus heals by the word, the word given to those who hear him, but particularly, perhaps, the word which he addresses to God in blessing and prayer (13), a word which the believing reader knows will be granted to him if he too agrees to become like a child.

73 Note that only Matthew uses the verb «to pray» in this context.

2. THE SUB-SEQUENCE IN MARK 10:1-27

In Mark, the passage about the rich man is integrated into a sub-sequence which is very similar to Matthew's, including, in addition to a short introduction, five passages focused around the scene with Jesus and the children.

Introduction	1
THE QUESTION ABOUT DIVORCE	2-9
To the disciples: The indissolubility of marriage	10-12
JESUS AND THE CHILDREN	13-16
THE RICH MAN	17-22
To the disciples: The danger of richness	23-27

2.1. *The question about divorce (Mark 10:2-9)*

INITIAL GLANCE AT THE SYNOPTICS

The first thing to note is that Matt 19:10-12 («Voluntary continence») has no parallel in the other synoptics; this passage begins with a question from the «disciples» (10a).

• In Mark, however, the «disciples'» question is anticipated (10) before Jesus' statement about the indissolubility of marriage (11-12). By changing the location («in the house») and those speaking with Jesus, Mark has made a passage out of these verses; in addition, he has developed Matthew's v.9 with the addition of the disciples' question at the start (10), and the addition of the repudiation by the woman at the end (12), while in Matthew v.9 is part of the controversy with the Pharisees.

- In Luke, there is no parallel of either the discussion about divorce or voluntary continence; only 16, 18 return to Matthew's v.9, while adding that a man who marries a woman who has been repudiated is also an adulterer (18ef)[74]. Finally, we should note that only Matthew (9d) gives an exception to the rule about the indissolubility of marriage.

The controversy with the Pharisees about divorce begins in a similar way in Matt 19:3 and Mark 10:2. Mark moves «to tempt» to the end. More importantly, only Matthew adds «for any reason» to the end (3e), which is matched by the Matthean exception at the end in 9d. The material in the rest of the passage is very similar, but organized in a very different way:

- Jesus' first reply in Matthew (4-6) is moved to the end of the passage by Mark (6-9).
- but the Pharisees' final question and the start of Jesus' reply in Matthew (7-8) is anticipated in Mark (3-5). However, this movement has led to significant differences —the Pharisees' question in Matthew (7) matches a question from Jesus in Mark (3), which is followed by the Pharisees' reply. These differences are made necessary by the inversion of the elements.

74 Luke 16:18 is the last verse of the central passage of the central sub-sequence (16:9-18) of sequence C5 (15:1-17:10). See *Luc*, 650.

The table which places the composition of the passages Matt 19:3-9 and Mark 10:2-9 in parallel (see p. 236) will be more clear than this initial synoptic presentation.

Matt 19:3-12	Mark 10:2-12	Luke 16:18
3 AND CAME NEAR to him SOME PHARISEES *TEMPTING HIM* and saying: «IS IT POSSIBLE FOR A man TO REPUDIATE his WIFE for whatever reason?». 4 NOW ANSWERING HE SAID: «Have you not read that the Creator *from the beginning* *male and female made them* 5 and he said: *For this* *man will leave (his) father and (his) mother* *and be joined to his wife and the two will be one* *flesh only?* 6 *So, they are no more two* *but one flesh only. Therefore what God has joined, let* *not man separate».* 7 They *SAID* to him: «Why then *MOSES COMMANDED* to give *A ROLL OF DIVORCE* *AND TO REPUDIATE HER*?». 8 *HE SAYS TO THEM*: «*MOSES BECAUSE* *OF THE HARDNESS OF YOUR HEART* allowed you to repudiate your wives but from the beginning it was not so.	2 AND CAME NEAR SOME PHARISEES who were asking him IS IT POSSIBLE FOR A husband TO REPUDIATE HIS WIFE *TEMPTING HIM.* 3 NOW ANSWERING HE SAID to them: «What did Moses command you?». 4 Now they *SAID*: «*MOSES PERMITTED* *A ROLL OF DIVORCE* to write *AND REPUDIATE HER*». 5 Now Jesus *SAID TO THEM*: «*BECAUSE OF THE HARDNESS OF* *YOUR HEART* he wrote for you this commandment. 6 Now *from the beginning* of the creation *male and female he made them.* 7 *For this man will leave his father and his mother* [*and be joined to his wife*] 8 *and the two will be one flesh only so they are no* *more two but one flesh only.* 9 *Therefore what God* *has joined, let not man separate».*	
9 Now I ***say*** to you that WHOEVER REPUDIATES HIS WIFE, except in case of immodesty, AND MARRIES ANOTHER COMMITS-ADULTERY».	10 And in the house again *THE DISCIPLES* on this were asking him. 11 And he ***said*** to them: «WHOEVER REPUDIATES HIS WIFE AND MARRIES ANOTHER COMMITS-ADULTERY against her; 12 and if she repudiates her husband, and marries another **she commits-adultery».**	18 «Every one WHO REPUDIATES HIS WIFE AND MARRIES ANOTHER, COMMITS-ADULTERY and one who marries a woman- repudiated by man **commits-adultery».**
10 To him say *THE DISCIPLES*: «If this is the condition of man with respect to his wife, it is not good to marry». 11 He said to them: «Not all understand this word, but only those to whom it is given. 12 For there are eunuchs who from the mother's womb are born so; and there are eunuchs who are made eunuchs by men; and there are eunuchs who are made themselves eunuchs for the kingdom of Heavens. Who can understand, let him understand!».		

+ [2] *And having come near some Pharisees*	*were asking him*:	
:: if is it lawful for a husband	to **REPUDIATE** a wife,	
+	*tempting*	*him*.

– [3] *And he answering*		*said to them*:	
: «What	did **Moses**	COMMAND	you?».
– [4] *And they*		*said*:	
: «**Moses**	permitted	a roll of divorce *TO WRITE* and **TO REPUDIATE**».	

+ [5] *And Jesus said to them*:			
= «For the hardness of your heart			*HE WROTE* for you this COMMAND;
:: [6] but from the beginning of the creation			"male and female he made them".
- [7] "For this	will leave [and be joined to his wife]	man	the father of him and the mother
- [8] and	will be	the two	for one flesh only".
:: So they are no more		two,	but one flesh only;
= [9] therefore what God has joined,			let not man **SEPARATE**!».

Mark's passage is organized into three parts: the last part (5-9) is the reply to the Pharisees' initial question (2); in the center (3-4), is Jesus' question about the law of Moses and the Pharisees' reply.— In the first part (2), Mark has inserted the question (2b) between the two syntagmas «asking him» (2a) and «tempting him» (2c), the second one interpreting the first.— The two segments of the second part (3 and 4) are parallel: «[what] did Moses command you» (end of 3b) is taken up by «Moses permitted» (start of 4b); the question at the start of 3b is matched by the end of 4b.— Jesus' reply to the last part (5-9) is much more developed than the initial question (2). It is justified by a literal reference to the start of Genesis (Gen 2:24), on which Jesus' statement is focused (7-8a). The first piece (5-6) places Moses' concession in opposition to «the beginning of creation»; the last piece (8b-9) has two bimember segments introduced by a balancing concluding conjunction, «and» and «so»; we might say that the four members are like matching mirrors, «two» being taken up by «separate» and «one» by «has joined». The last segment (9) refers to the start (5b): Jesus' commandment is opposed to Moses'.— The final verb, «separate» (9) refers back to «repudiate» in the first question (2b); «to repudiate» is taken up at the end of the central part (4b); «[did] command» in the central question (3b) is repeated at the start of the last part (5b).

Problems of textual criticism

—to begin with, some manuscripts have: «Now the Pharisees approaching...», and others have: «And some Pharisees approaching»; while the difference between the coordinations (*kai* or *de*) and the word order do not change the meaning, the definite article («the Pharisees», that is, all the Pharisees) is very different from the indefinite article («some Pharisees», that is, «some of the Pharisees»). However, the fundamental problem is the identification of those speaking with Jesus: the Beza (C) codex and some ancient versions do not mention the Pharisees, or only say: «And they questioned him...», without giving an explicit subject. The following commentary gives an idea of the way specialists reason:

> The chief problem posed by the variant readings involves the presence or absence of the words «having come near some Pharisees». Did the original text read merely «were asking», an impersonal plural [...] and has the reference to the Pharisees come into many [textual] witnesses by assimilation to the parallel passage in Matthew (19.3)? Despite the plausibility of such a possibility, the fact that the Matthean passage is not absolutely parallel [...] and the widespread and impressive support for the longer reading led a majority of the Commission to retain the words in the text[75].

—in 10:7 were the words in brackets added to a large number of manuscripts to harmonize Mark and Matthew, or were they omitted by haplology (when the eye jumps from one *kai* to another)? If they were not there, there would be some ambiguity, as «two» might refer to «father and mother»[76].

75 METZGER B., *A Textual Commentary on the Greek New Testament*, 103-104.

76 See METZGER B., *A Textual Commentary on the Greek New Testament*, 104; see VAGANAY L. - AMPHOUX C.B., *Initiation à la critique textuelle du Nouveau Testament.*

BIBLICAL CONTEXT

This is the same as it was for the parallel passage in Matthew (see pp. 193-195).

SYNOPTIC COMPARISON

See the following page.

INTERPRETATION

Jesus does not envisage any exception to the law of the indissolubility of marriage; here he makes no reference to the case of «immodesty» in Matthew. In addition, in their first question (2), the Pharisees did not add the Matthean «for any reason». For Mark, the law is absolute, as it is for Malachi 2 (see p. 194). We might thus conclude that Mark is older and that Matthew added this limitation to respond to problems which had arisen in his communities[77]. We might also note, in particular, that Matthew reflects the Jewish-Christian communities which followed the practice of the strict house of Shammai; in early days adultery was punished by death (Lev 20:10; Deut 22:22; see too John 8:4), and divorce for reasons of infidelity, even if it was obligatory, would have represented an alleviation of the punishment.

77 For a hypothesis on the history of the text, see for example BENOIT P. - BOISMARD M.-É., *Synopse*, II, 307-308.

SYNOPTIC COMPARISON (see pp. 192 and 233)

Matt 19:3-9	Mark 10:2-9
3 AND CAME NEAR **to him** SOME PHARISEES *TEMPTING HIM* and saying: «IS IT POSSIBLE FOR A man TO REPUDIATE **his** WIFE **for whatever motif?».**	2 AND HAVING COME NEAR SOME PHARISEES were asking him if IT IS POSSIBLE FOR A husband TO REPUDIATE HIS WIFE, *TEMPTING HIM.*
4 NOW ANSWERING HE SAID: **«Have you not read that** *the Creator* FROM THE BEGINNING "MALE AND FEMALE MADE THEM" 5 **and he said:** "*For this* MAN WILL LEAVE FATHER AND MOTHER AND BE JOINED TO HIS WIFE AND THE TWO WILL BE ONE FLESH ONLY?" 6 SO THEY ARE NO MORE TWO BUT ONE FLESH ONLY. THEREFORE, WHAT GOD HAS JOINED, LET NOT MAN SEPARATE».	3 NOW ANSWERING HE SAID ***to them***: «***What did*** *MOSES command* ***you***?». 4 ***Now they*** *SAID*: *«MOSES permitted* *TO WRITE A ROLL OF DIVORCE* *AND TO REPUDIATE».*
7 *THEY SAID* **to him:** **«Why then** *MOSES commanded* *to give* A ROLL OF DIVORCE *AND TO REPUDIATE* **her?».**	5 ***Now Jesus*** *SAID TO THEM*: *«BECAUSE OF THE HARDNESS OF YOUR HEART* ***he wrote for you this commandment.***
8 *HE SAYS TO THEM*: **«Moses** *BECAUSE OF THE HARDNESS OF YOUR HEART* **allowed you to repudiate your wives, but from the beginning it was not so.**	6 ***Now*** FROM THE BEGINNING *of the creation* "MALE AND FEMALE HE MADE THEM". 7 "*For this* MAN WILL LEAVE ***his*** FATHER AND (HIS) MOTHER [AND BE JOINED TO HIS WIFE] 8 AND THE TWO WILL BE FOR ONE FLESH ONLY"». SO THEY ARE NO MORE TWO BUT ONE FLESH ONLY. 9 THEREFORE WHAT GOD HAS JOINED, LET NOT MAN SEPARATE».
9 Now I SAY to you that WHOEVER REPUDIATES HIS WIFE, **except in the case of immodesty,** AND MARRIES ANOTHER COMMITS-ADULTERY».	10 ***And in the house again*** ***the disciples on this were interrogating him.*** 11 And HE SAYS to them: «WHOEVER REPUDIATES HIS WIFE AND MARRIES ANOTHER COMMITS-ADULTERY ***against her;*** 12 ***and if she, having repudiated her husband, marries another, commits-adultery».***

The composition of the two passages is very different, essentially because their boundaries do not match. The last verse in Matthew (9) is part of the passage, while its parallel in Mark (9-12) is part of another passage. The two passages have much material in common, but apart from the first verse (Mt: 3; Mc: 2), it is arranged in a very different manner. The biblical quotations are at the end of the first part in Matthew (4-6), while in mark they are at the end of the third part (6-9). However, the Pharisees' statement in the second part in Mark (4) has its match in Matthew, but as a question at the start of the second part (7). Finally, Jesus' reply on the «hardness of heart» is found in different places (Matt: 8; Mark: 5). In other words:

- Matthew starts by referring back to the accounts of the beginning of creation (in his first part, 4-6) in reply to the Pharisees' initial question. After this, in reply to their second question, he refers back to Moses' law (7), and explains the reason for this law.
- Mark reverses this order—in response to their initial question (first part, 2) Jesus leads the Pharisees, with another question, to recall the law of Moses (second part, 3-4). After this he gives a reason, before referring them to the first law (third part, 5-9).

In addition to minor differences, we should say again that neither the syntagma «for any reason» (Matt 3e) nor the Matthean exception which matches it (9c) has an equivalent in Mark.

2.2. *The indissolubility of marriage (Mark 10:10-12)*

COMPOSITION

+	10 And in the house again the disciples on this	*were asking*	*him.*
+	11 And	*he says to*	*them:*
–	«Whoever	*repudiates*	his wife
	: and	marries	***another***,
	=	COMMITS-ADULTERY	against her;
–	12 and if she,	*having repudiated*	her husband,
	:	marries	***another***,
	=	COMMITS-ADULTERY».	

The passage is the length of a part, made up of two pieces. The first piece has a single narrative bimember (10-11a).

In the second piece (11b-12), the two trimembers of Jesus' statement are clearly of parallel construction, with a slight abbreviation in the second one: «against her» in 11d has no equivalent at the end of the last segment.

SYNOPTIC COMPARISON (*see pp. 192 and 237*)

Matt 19:9	Mark 10:10-12
	10 ***And in the house again the disciples were asking him on this.***
9 Now I SAY to you **that**	11 And he SAYS to them:
«WHOEVER REPUDIATES HIS WIFE,	«WHOEVER REPUDIATES HIS WIFE
except in the case of immodesty,	
AND MARRIES ANOTHER COMMITS-ADULTERY».	AND MARRIES ANOTHER COMMITS-ADULTERY ***against her;***
	12 ***and if she, having repudiate her husband, marries another, commits-adultery».***

In addition to our earlier observations (pp. 230-232 and 236-237), Mark adds to Matthew the case of the woman who repudiates her husband (12).

BIBLICAL CONTEXT

Divorce pronounced by the woman

There is no case of this type of divorce in the Bible, and it does not exist in the Jewish world; however, it was a practice which was recognized in the Roman world.

INTERPRETATION

The fact that Mark considers the case of the woman who repudiates her husband (12) proves that his Gospel was written for communities which included many Christians of pagan, particularly Roman, origin. This trait would confirm the ancient tradition according to which Mark was Peter's translator, and wrote his Gospel in Rome[78].

2.3. *Jesus and the children (Mark 10:13-16)*

COMPOSITION

Two parts of the account (13.16), each of a single trimember only, frame a more developed part of discourse (14-15). The central member of the first segment (13b) expresses what is at stake in the opposition between those who brought their children to Jesus (13a) and the disciples who wish to prevent them from doing so (13c)[79]. The outer members of the last segment (16a.16c) match the cen-

78 See for example LÀCONI M. - *al.*, ed., *Vangeli sinottici e Atti degli Apostoli*, 136.

79 The pronoun «them» at the end of the verse is ambiguous. It could be considered to be masculine and to refer to the subject of the verb «brought» or a neuter describing «the children» (as it

ter of the first segment («kissing»/«laid his hands» and «touching»). The main verb of the last segment, «bless», at the center of the segment, indicates a significant difference between the parents' desire («that he might touch them») and Jesus' action, «blessing», that is, blessing God and invoking his blessing upon them.

+ [13] And they were bringing to him	CHILDREN,	
		that he might touch them;
+ but the disciples REBUKED	*them*.	

[14] Having seen, *JESUS* WAS INDIGNANT.	= *and he said to them*:			
	:: «Let			the CHILDREN
	. come		to	ME,
	:: do not prevent			*them*.
	For **to such as these**		is	THE KINGDOM OF GOD.
	= [15] *Truly I say to you*:			
	. Who	does not receive		THE KINGDOM OF GOD,
		:: like		a CHILD,
	.	shall not **enter**	into	IT».

+ [16] And KISSING	*them*,	
		He blessed,
+ laying his hands on	*them*.	

The central part, introduced by the narrative phrase in 14abc, is made up of three pieces. The outer pieces begin with a brief introductory member in which «say» (14d.15a) appears and continue with a trimember (14efg and 15bcd); «children» matched by «them» at the outsides of the first of the two segments (14e.14g) is repeated from one center to another (15c), «The kingdom of God», repeated by «it» at the outside of the last segment (15b.15d) seems to correspond to «me», that is, Jesus, at the center of the symmetrical segment (14f). In addition «to come» in 14f heralds «to welcome» and «to enter» in 15b.15d. At the center of the construction (end of 14), is a very short piece which summarizes the law of the «kingdom of God».

is twice in v.16). Textual variants (manuscript D among others), «the disciples threatened those who brought them» sought to remove the ambiguity; however, as this pronoun comes into the list of the four final terms of the outer members of the outer verses (13.16), we might imagine that the pronoun «them» in 13c refers to «children» like those in 16a and 16c.

SYNOPTIC COMPARISON (see pp. 200 and 239)

Matt 19:13-15	Mark 10:13-16
13 Then were presented TO HIM CHILDREN THAT he might lay the hands on THEM **and pray**.	13 And THEY were bringing TO HIM CHILDREN THAT he might touch THEM.
NOW THE DISCIPLES REBUKED THEM.	NOW THE DISCIPLES REBUKED THEM.
14 **Now** JESUS SAID:	14 ***Having seen,*** JESUS ***was indignant*** ***and*** SAID ***to them***:
«LET THE CHILDREN **and** DO NOT PREVENT THEM *to come TO ME*.	«LET THE CHILDREM *come TO ME*, DO NOT PREVENT THEM.
FOR TO SUCH AS THESE IS THE KINGDOM of Heaven».	FOR TO SUCH AS THESE IS THE KINGDOM of God.
	15 ***Truly I say to you,*** ***whoever does not receive the kingdom of God*** ***like a child shall not enter in it***».
15 And *HAVING LAID THE HANDS on THEM*, **he departed from there.**	16 And ***kissing them, he blessed***, *LAYING HIS HANDS on THEM*.

Mark's text is more developed. The main difference is the addition of v.15. This addition means that the composition of the two passages is different: although the last parts have the same boundaries (Mt 15; Mc 16), the first part of Mark includes 13c which in Matthew belongs to the second part (13d). According to Matthew's composition, the disciples (13d) are opposed to the children to whom the kingdom of heaven belongs (14de); in Mark, on the other hand, the disciples (13c) directly oppose those who bring their children to Jesus (13a), but in the central part, their behavior (14abc) is paralleled with the behavior of those who do not welcome the kingdom of God (15). The criticism of the disciples is therefore emphasized in Mark. «Laying on hands» in Matthew (13b, repetition in 15a) is more solemn than Mark's simple «touch» (13b); only Matthew uses the verb «to pray» at the start (13c), but «to bless» is its equivalent at the end of the passage in Mark (16a, to which «kiss» is added).

BIBLICAL CONTEXT

The theme of the child as the model of discipleship has already appeared in Mark 9:35-37:

[35B] «If anyone wants to be first, he will be last of all and servant of all». [36] He then took
a little child, set him in front of them, put his arms around him, and said to them,
[37] «Anyone who welcomes one of these little children in my name, welcomes me; and
anyone who welcomes me welcomes no me but the one who sent me».

INTERPRETATION

Jesus criticizes people's wishes

Jesus is a man who is out of the ordinary, so people want to see him and everyone wants to touch him, probably a bit like those people who are proud and happy to have had the opportunity to shake the Pope's hand. They want to be able to say that they have touched him, for a long time afterwards, and particularly after the great man's death; and if they manage to be touched, to have their small child kissed and blessed, they can talk about that for even longer! Jesus does not refuse this moving display of popular affection —he agrees to the contact, embraces the children brought to him, and lays his hands on them. But he does not stop there. He continues, and tries to continue the movement which brought those who have come to him. Through the blessing he addresses to the Lord, God of the universe, he invites them to look and think beyond himself, towards and about the One from whom those who listen to him, as well as he himself, come. It is towards Him that their desire should be extended, as towards the Father whose children they are.

Jesus criticizes the disciples' wish

With all the sensitivity of chimpanzees, the disciples seek to protect their teacher from the pressure of the crowd. Don't these people understand that he has better things to do than touch their kids? Just as for those who brought their children, the disciples' wish, while totally understandable, is also misplaced. Jesus, who is so patient with other people, is cross for good reason with those who have even given up their own families to follow him. It is because it is so important—this is about nothing more or less than the *sine qua non* of entry into the Kingdom of God. The Kingdom of God belongs to those who are like little children (14h). And, lest they have not understood, he repeats it, more strongly —no one will enter the Kingdom of God if he does not welcome him like a child (15). The juxtaposition of the two images, which appear different, if not quite opposed, is full of teaching. If the Lord God is presented as the King of the universe, and those who wish to enter into his Kingdom are called to be like children, it is because this King is their true Father. Not to behave like children would be a sort of blasphemy which would see God as a king like any other earthly king, a despot whose whole power is for no other reason than to crush his subjects to exploit them. To be like a child before the King is the opposite of idolatry, that perversion which consists of making oneself a god in the image of one's own poverty. Being like a child is to acknowledge joyfully the small children created in the image and likeness of the One who gives us life.

He is the path who leads to life

When he embraces the children who are brought to him and lays his hands on them, Jesus is behaving like a father. In the blessing which he addresses to God, Jesus states that, first and foremost, they are children of God; he thus acknowledges that he, too, is a child of the Father from whom he has received everything. It is those who come to Jesus like children who will enter the kingdom of God. To come to Jesus to follow the path which he walks is, like and with him, to go towards his Father and our Father (John 20:17), to enter his Kingdom. The disciples have not yet understood this, and so they treat Jesus like a king who needs to be protected from his subjects' fervor, just as earthly monarchs are guarded. By making a false image of Jesus for themselves, they make for themselves a caricature of God. As long as they are not like those children they are rejecting, they will not enter the kingdom of God.

2.4. *The danger of wealth (Mark 10:23-27)*

COMPOSITION

+ [23] And looking around,	*Jesus says*	to his disciples:	
: «WITH WHAT DIFFICULTY	***THOSE WHO HAVE WEALTH***	into the kingdom of **God**	will enter».
– [24] *The disciples*	*were amazed*	*at his words.*	

+ *Jesus* again answering	*says* to them:		
: «CHILDREN,	HOW HARD IT IS	into the kingdom of **God**	to enter!
[25] IT IS EASIER	for a camel	through the eye of a needle	to pass
: than	for ***A RICH-MAN***	in the kingdom of **God**	to enter!».

– [26] *They exceedingly*	*were astonished*	*saying to one another*:	
«And WHO	CAN	be saved?».	
+ [27] Looking at them,	*Jesus says*:		
: «For MEN	IS IMPOSSIBLE,	but not for	**God**;
: for all	IS POSSIBLE	to	**God**».

The outer parts (23-24a; 26-27) mirror one another. At the outsides (23.27), the narrative phrases begin with a participle verb of vision from the same family followed by «Jesus said». Jesus' first statement (23b) leads to the disciples' «amazement» (24a), and his last statement (27bc) answers their «astonishment» (26).

In the center, after the introductory phrase (24b), Jesus' second statement is an ABA'-type trimember, the first member of which (24c) refers to 23b.

«Those who have wealth» (23b) will be repeated by «a rich man» in the last member of the central part (25b), while «men» at the end (27b) are called «children» in the first member (24c). «God» is mentioned in 23b, 24c and 25b in the center, and twice more in the last part in 27b and 27c.

BIBLICAL CONTEXT

«Children»

This is the only time in the four Gospels that Jesus calls his disciples «(my) children» (*teknon*; from *tiktō*, «to give birth to»).

«Abba Father, for you everything is possible»

The last member of the passage (27c) recalls Jesus' prayer in Gethsemane: «Abba, Father, *for you everything is possible.* Take this cup away from me. But let it be as you, not I, would have it» (Mark 14:36). Only Mark uses the affectionate term «Abba»; «children» also, which is only in Mark, is a term of affection.

«Though he was rich ...»

The theme of wealth which Jesus has given up comes up several times in Paul's letters. «His state was divine, yet he did not cling to his equality with God, but emptied himself, to assume the condition of a slave, and became as men are» (Phil 2:6-7); «Remember how generous the Lord Jesus was; he was rich, but he became poor for your sake, to make you rich out of his poverty» (2Cor 8:9).

SYNOPTIC COMPARISON (*see pp. 224 and 242*)

Matt 19:23-26	Mark 10:23-27
[23] Now JESUS SAID TO HIS DISCIPLES : «**Truly I say to you** that a rich-man WITH DIFFICULTY SHALL ENTER IN THE KINGDOM of heavens!	[23] And ***looking around*** JESUS SAYS TO HIS DISCIPLES: «WITH ***what*** DIFFICULTY those who have wealth IN THE KINGDOM of God SHALL ENTER!». [24] ***Now the disciples were amazed at his words.***
[24] NOW AGAIN I SAY to you: IT IS EASIER FOR A CAMEL THROUGH THE EYE OF A NEEDLE TO PASS THAN FOR A RICH-MAN TO ENTER INTO THE KINGDOM OF GOD».	NOW ***Jesus*** AGAIN ***answering*** SAYS to them: «***Children, how it is difficult into the kingdom of God to enter***! [25] IT IS EASIER FOR A CAMEL THROUGH THE EYE OF A NEEDLE TO PASS THAN FOR A RICH-MAN INTO THE KINGDOM OF GOD TO ENTER».
[25] NOW **having heard** the disciples WERE ASTONISHED greatly SAYING: «WHO **then** CAN BE SAVED?».	[26] NOW they exceedingly WERE ASTONISHED SAYING ***to one another***: «AND WHO CAN BE SAVED?».
[26] **Now** LOOKING AT JESUS SAID TO **them**: «FOR MEN **this** IS IMPOSSIBLE; now FOR GOD ALL (is) POSSIBLE».	[27] LOOKING AT ***them*** JESUS SAYS: «FOR MEN IT IS IMPOSSIBLE, ***but not for God***; for ALL ***is*** POSSIBLE TO GOD».

Once again, Matthew is more concise than Mark. He suppresses Mark's «looking around» (23a), summarizes Mark 10:24 in four words (24ab), suppresses «them» (26c) and «but not for God» in Mark (27c) just as the verb «is» in 27d. On the other hand, he adds «having heard the disciples» (25a).

The differences between Mark (24) and Matthew (24a-d) are not only quantitative. In Mark, Jesus' first words in 23cde are interrupted by the narrative phrase in 24ab; this is why Mark introduces a second discourse into 24cd, with «he says» in the third person. Matthew, however, turns his first two verses into a single discourse: «Now again I say to you» in 24ab is in the first person and is part of Jesus' words.

It follows from this that the compositions are very different. In Matthew the it is the disciples' question (25) which joins Jesus' two declarations together; in mark, this question, at the start of the third part (26) is symmetrical with the disciples' first reaction at the end of the first part (24ab), and thus it is Jesus' second statement, introduced by «children» (24e) which constitutes the central part of his passage (24c-25).

INTERPRETATION

The temptation of wealth

Matthew twice repeats that it will be difficult «for a rich man» to enter the kingdom of God (19:23 and 24). However, when Mark repeats the first statement (23), after which the disciples are amazed (24ab), he is no longer only looking at «the rich»; his second statement might appear to be general, if it were not addressed to those whom he calls «my little children». This warning, therefore, is also for the disciples. One might interpret these words as Jesus' faith in his small children —for him, too, «how difficult it is to enter into the kingdom of God». At the decisive moment of entering his Passion, he asks his father to take the cup away from him, and it was «difficult» for him to accept his Father's will. Calling his disciples «little children», he invites them to enter into the kingdom of God with him, and, like him, to trust in his all-powerful grace (27d).

Wealth is a transparent idol, the more harmful because it does not look away. Elijah forbade the following of YHWH and Baal. In a more developed society, God is not rejected so that money can be chosen; God and money are confused. The rich man is not thrown out of the Kingdom, but «how hard it is» to go «through the eye of the needle» (Mark 10:25); a strong way of saying «be born».

Jesus says this twice: «How hard for the wealthy to enter...» and «How hard it is to enter...» (Mark 10:23f). This emphasis, and the disciples' horror, end the scene with such a strong emphasis that we cannot allow ourselves to attenuate it.

It is then that a comforting word comes: «For men, it is impossible, but not for God». The obvious meaning is that God can make us able to do what only the hero of the account can do.

Let us hazard another meaning—what is «possible for God», is to leave behind all wealth. And what wealth has God, but his divinity? God leaving his divinity? Saint Paul is not far from saying this. We hear it in two passages: «The Lord Jesus... he was rich, but he became poor for your sake, to make you rich out of his poverty...» (2Cor 8:9). However, Jesus did not have capital to share around. And again, «His state was divine, yet he did not cling to his equality with God, but emptied himself», becoming a servant and dying (Phil 2:6f).

So that the account goes deeper than the surface and further than the narcissistic areas of our generosity, we need to understand this: Jesus is not asking any more of the rich than what he himself has done. Without this, do we not risk believing that God asks us to abandon our property because he is insatiable? Such a divinity, which both wants our property and holds it as nothing, is lacking in nothing as an idol.

(BEAUCHAMP P., *D'une montagne à l'autre, la Loi de Dieu*, 27-28).

2.5. *The Sub-Sequence as a Whole (Mark 10:1-27)*

COMPOSITION

Let us leave the introduction (1) to one side for the time being.

• *The first two passages* (2-9 and 10-12) are closely linked, to the extent that most commentators consider them to be a single pericope on divorce[80]. The two occurrences of «interrogated him» (2.10) act as initial terms. «Wife» is used once in each passage (2b.11a); «to repudiate» is repeated twice in each of the two passages (2a.4 and 11a.12).

• *The last two passages* (17-22 and 23-27) are also closely linked, so that some consider them to form but a single pericope[81]. Jesus «looks» at the rich man (21a) and, twice, the disciples (23a.27b). «At this word» in 22b is repeated with «at his words» in 24a; this is how the disciples' amazement is related to the rich man's sadness. «To have» with synonymous objects («great wealth» in 22b and «wealth» in 23b) act as median terms, as do «at his word» (22b) and «at his words» (24a). «To inherit» in 17b must be linked not just to «father and mother» (19c), but also to «children» (24b); «to inherit» and «children» are only in Mark. In addition, «eternal life» (17b) and «treasure in heaven» (21b) in the penultimate passage correlate to «to be saved» (26) and «the kingdom of God» (23b.24b.25b) in the last passage.

The first two passages parallel the last two.

• *The first and penultimate passages* (2-9 and 17-22). The two occurrences of «was/were interrogating him» (2a.17b) act as initial terms. «Command» at the center of the first passage (3; and «commandment» in 5) is repeated in the plural in the penultimate passage (19b) and also in the center of the passage with

80 For example, the JB treats the first two passages as a single pericope, entitled «The question about divorce», as do most recent commenatires: Pesch (188), Ernst (460), Lamarche (240), Légasse (590), Mazzucco (111), Trochmé (255).

81 Trochmé (263) treats this as a single pericope. Others treat these two passages and the following one (28-31) as a single pericope: Pesch (210), Ernst (471), Lamarche (246), Légasse (608-609), Mazzucco (113).

[1] And rising from there, he comes into the territory of Judea [and] beyond the Jordan.
And the crowd departs together again **towards him**.
And as usual he **teaches** them again.

[2] Coming near, some Pharisees WERE ASKING HIM if it is possible for a husband to *repudiate* his *wife*,
in order to tempt him.

[3] But answering, he said to them: «What did Moses **COMMAND** you?».
[4] They said: «Moses permitted to write a roll of divorce and to *repudiate* her».

[5] Jesus said to them:
«Because of the hardness of your heart he had written for you this **COMMANDMENT**.
[6] But from the beginning of the creation "male and female he created them". [7] "For this man will
leave HIS FATHER AND MOTHER [and be joined to his wife] [8] and the two will become one flesh
ONLY". So they are no more two but one flesh **ONLY**. [9] Therefore what GOD has joined, let man not
separate».

[10] And in the house again the ***disciples*** WERE ASKING HIM on this.
[11] And he says to them: «Whoever *repudiates* his *wife* and marries another,
COMMITS-ADULTERY against her; [12] and if she *repudiates* her husband and marries another, she
too *COMMITS-ADULTERY*».

[13] They were bringing to him *CHILDREN* so that he might touch them, but the ***disciples***
rebuked them. [14] Having seen this, Jesus was indignant and said to them: «Let the *CHILDREN*
come to **me** and do not prevent them; for to such as these is the KINGDOM OF GOD.
[15] Truly I say to you, whoever does not receive the KINGDOM OF GOD like a *CHILD*, shall
not enter in it». [16] And kissing them, he blessed them laying his hands upon them.

[17] While he was going out on the way, someone, having run towards and knelt before him, WAS
ASKING HIM: «Good **Master**, what shall I do so that I might *INHERIT* ETERNAL LIFE?». [18] Jesus said to
him: «Why do you tell me good? No one is good, if not the **ONLY** GOD. [19] You know the
COMMANDMENTS: "Do not kill, do not *COMMIT-ADULTERY*, do not steal, do not testimony-
falsely", do not defraud, "honor YOUR FATHER AND MOTHER"».

[20] He declared to him:
«**Master**, **ALL THESE** I kept by myself from my youth».

[21] Jesus, **looking at him**, loved him and said to him: «**ONLY** one thing you lack: go, sell what you have
and give it to the poor and you will have TREASURE IN HEAVEN; then come, follow **me**». [22] But he,
gloomy *at this word*, went away afflicted; for *he was having great wealth*.

[23] And, **looking** around, Jesus says to his ***disciples***:
«With what difficulty those who *have wealth* will enter into the KINGDOM OF GOD!».
[24] The ***disciples*** were amazed *at his words*; but Jesus again answering says to them: «*CHILDREN*
how it is difficult to enter into the KINGDOM OF GOD! [25] It is easier for a camel to pass through
the eye of a needle, than for a rich-man to enter into the KINGDOM OF GOD». [26] They were
exceedingly astonished, saying to one another: «And who can BE SAVED?». [27] And **looking** at them
Jesus says: «For men it is impossible, but not for GOD! For all is possible to GOD».

the syntagma translated by «all these» (20b). The two occurrences of «only» in the first passage (twice in 8b) match «only» (21) in its symmetrical passage. «His father and mother» in 7b is repeated with «your father and mother» in 19c, to which the two occurrences of «God» (9a.18) should be added.

• The second and final passages (10-12 and 23-27) are both addressed by Jesus to the «disciples» (10 and 23a.24a), the first time after they have returned «to the house», therefore out of the presence of the Pharisees, and the second time after the rich man has left. The two passages do not have any other vocabulary in common, but their symmetry invites us to look for what they share. An attachment to wealth which prevents from entering into the kingdom of God (23-27) is probably connected in some way to adultery (10-12). Note, too, that «to commit adultery» in the second passage (11.12) is repeated in the last passage (19b).

• *The central passage* (13-16) is the pivot of the whole sub-sequence. Here we find the «disciples» (13) as in the second and the last passages (10a and 23a.24a); the three occurrences of «children» (13.14a.15b) are synonymous with «children» in the last passage (24b); «children», «father and mother» (7b.19c) and «to inherit» (17b) belong to the same semantic field.

• The introduction (1): the verb «to teach» (1c) has the same root as the two occurrences of «Master» (17b.20). What is more, «departs together towards him» (1b) is repeated with a very similar expression in the central passage, «come to me» (14).

SYNOPTIC COMPARISON

The major difference with Matthew is that the Matthean passage about eunuchs (19:10-12) is not taken up by Mark; in the place in the structure where this passage is, Mark has made the final verse of Matthew's passage on divorce (19:9) a passage on its own, about the indissolubility of marriage (10-12).

While in Matthew the two «approached him» act as initial terms for the first and penultimate passages (19:3a16a), Mark repeats «interrogate him», in the same role, at the start of the first and the penultimate passages (10:2a.17b), but also at the start of the second passage (10a). — While in Matthew the syntagma «father and mother» recurs at the center of these two passages (19:5b.19a), in Mark it is «commanded» which recurs in 10:5bc and «all these» in 20a (which refers back to «commandments» in 19a) which mark the centers of the two passages.

Another difference, surely significant, is that the final verb of the introduction is not «to heal» as in Matthew (19:2), but «to teach» (10:1d); we said that this verb heralds the two occurrences of «Master» (17c.20a; Matthew has only one «Master» in 16a). In addition, unlike Matt 19:1b, Mark does not say that Jesus «left from Galilee», but only that he «came into the territory of Judea» (1a); nor does he use the verb «to follow» for the crowds (Matt 19:2; recurrence in 21c for the rich young man), but «left together with him» (1b) which is echoed by «come to me» (14b).

The following general schema shows both the parallelism and the most important differences between the two sub-sequences.

Matt 19:1-26		Mark 10:1-27	
The question about divorce	3-9	**The question about divorce**	2-9
Eunuchs for the kingdom of God	10-12	***Avoiding adultery in marriage***	10-12
THE KINGDOM OF GOD FOR CHILDREN	13-15	THE KINGDOM OF GOD FOR CHILDREN	13-16
The call of the rich man	16-22	**The call of the rich man**	17-22
Poor for the kingdom of God	23-26	***Avoiding idolatry of riches***	23-27

Matt 19:1-26	Mark 10:1-27
1 It happened, when Jesus had finished his discourse, he departed ***from Galilee*** and came into the territory of Judea beyond the Jordan. 2 A large crowd ***followed him***, and there **HE HEALED THEM.**	1 Rising from there, he comes into the territory of Judea and beyond the Jordan, and the crowd ***departs together*** again ***towards him*** And, as usual, **HE TEACHES THEM** again.
3 *CAME NEAR TO HIM* some Pharisees and said to him, to tempt him: «Is it permitted for a man to repudiate his wife for any reason whatsoever?». 4 He answered: «Have you not read that the Creator, from the beginning, made them male and female, 5 and he said: Therefore man will leave **his father and his mother** to join to his wife, and the two will be one flesh only?». 6 So they are no more two, but one flesh only. Well then! What God has joined, man must not separate it». They said to him: 7 «Why then Moses commanded to give a roll of divorce and to repudiate her». He says to them: 8 «It is because of the hardness of your heart that Moses permitted you to repudiate your wives; but from the beginning it was not so. 9 *Now I say to you: whoever repudiates his wife, except in case of immodesty, and marries another, commits adultery».*	2 Coming near, some Pharisees WERE ASKING HIM if it is permitted for a husband to repudiate his wife. It was to put him to the test. 3 He answered them: «What did Moses **command** you?». They said: 4 «Moses permitted to write a roll of divorce and to repudiate her». 5 Then Jesus said to them: «It is because of the hardness of your heart that he had written for you this **commandment**. 6 But from the beginning of the creation He made them male and female. 7 Therefore man will leave his father and his mother, 8 and the two will become one flesh only. So they are no more two, but one flesh only. 9 Well then! What God has joined, man must not separate it».
10 The disciples say to him: ***«If this is the condition of man with respect to the wife, it is not good to marry». 11 He said to them: «Not all understand this language, but only those to whom it is given. 12 For there are eunuchs who from the mother's womb are born so, there are eunuchs who are made eunuchs by men, and there are eunuchs who have made themselves eunuchs for the Kingdom of Heavens. Whoever can understand, let him understand!».***	10 In the house again, the disciples WERE ASKING HIM again about that point. 11 *And he says to them: «Whoever repudiates his wife and marries another, commits adultery against her; 12 and if a wife repudiates her husband and marries another, she commits adultery».*
13 Then little children were brought to him, that he might lay the hands on them and pray; but the disciples rebuked them. 14 Jesus said then: «Let the little children and do not prevent them to come to me; for to such as these belongs the Kingdom of Heavens». 15 Then he laid the hands on them and departed from there.	13 People were bringing to him little children that he might touch them, but the disciples rebuked them. 14 Having seen this, Jesus was angry and said to them: «Let the little children ***come to me***; do not prevent them, for to such as these belongs the Kingdom of God. 15 Truly I say to you: whoever does not receive the Kingdom of God like a little child shall not enter in it». 16 Then he embraced them and blessed them laying his hands over them.
16 And behold a man *CAME TO HIM* and said: «Master, what good shall I do to obtain eternal life?». 17 He said to him: «Why do you interrogate me on good? Only one is good. If you want to enter into the life, observe the commandments». – 18 «Which?». He says to him. Jesus answered: «You shall not kill, you shall not commit adultery, you shall not steal, you shall not testimony falsely, 19 honor **your father and mother**, and you shall love your neighbor as your self». – 20 «All these», said to him the young man, «I have observed; of what still I lack?». 21 Jesus declared to him: «If you want to be perfect, go, sell what you have and give it to the poor and you will have treasure in heavens; then come, follow me». 22 Hearing this word, the young man went away afflicted; for he was having great wealth.	17 While he was going out on the way, a man running towards and, kneeling before him, WAS ASKING HIM: «Good **MASTER**, what shall I do to inherit the eternal life?». 18 Jesus said to him: «Why do you call me good? No one is good if not God only. 19 You know the **commandments**: Do not kill, do not commit adultery, do not steal, do not testimony falsely, do not defraud, honor your father and your mother». 20 «**MASTER**, he said to him, **all these**, I have observed from my youth». 21 Now, Jesus looked at him and loved him. He said to him: «Only one thing you lack: go, sell what you have, and give it to the poor and you will have treasure in heaven; then, come, follow me». 22 But he was gloomy and went away afflicted for this word, for he was having great wealth.
23 Jesus said to his disciples: «Truly, I say to you, that it is difficult for a rich person to enter into the kingdom of Heavens. 24 Yes, I repeat to you, it is easier for a camel to pass through the eye of a needle than for a rich person to enter into the kingdom of Heavens». 25 Hearing this, the disciples remained greatly astonished: «Who then can be saved?». They said. 26 Looking at, Jesus said to them: «For men this is impossible, but for God all is possible».	23 And then, looking around, Jesus says to his disciples: «How it shall be difficult for those who have riches to enter into the kingdom of God!». 24 The disciples remained amazed at these words. But answering again, Jesus says to them: «Children, how it is difficult to enter into the kingdom of God! 25 It is easier for a camel to pass through the eye of a needle than for a rich man to enter into the Kingdom of God!». 26 They remained exceedingly astonished and saying to one another: «And who can be saved?». 27 Looking at them, Jesus says: «For men it is impossible, but not for God: for all is possible to God».

INTERPRETATION

Adultery (the first two passages)

The question which the disciples ask Jesus (10-12) is clearly asked in relation to the controversy about divorce (2-9). However until this moment the question was only about whether divorce was licit, and Jesus had ended the discussion with the Pharisees with a clear condemnation of this practice. Now with the disciples, he goes further and examines the case of those people who, contract a new union after a divorce. Not only is divorce condemned (9), but also the remarriage of anyone who has repudiated his spouse, who is twice declared to be an «adulterer» (11-12). This only reinforces the invalid nature of divorce, or, in other words, the indissolubility of marriage. According to Mark, Jesus explains that adultery is committed «against» the spouse (11); it is, therefore, a sin which injures the neighbor, and the closest neighbor at that, the neighbor with whom the man or woman forms «one flesh». What is more, this same verb, «to commit adultery», which Mark uses twice (11-12), repeats the verb in the Decalogue: «You will not commit adultery» (Exod 20:14; Deut 5:18). This sin, therefore, means disobedience to the divine law, and is thus a sin against God himself. The formula «what God has joined, let no man separate» (9) already clearly stated that, by divorcing, man was in direct opposition to God's will, separating himself from him, repudiating him, and that adultery towards the spouse was also, in the final analysis, an adultery towards God.

Idolatry (the last two passages)

«No one can serve two masters: he will either hate the first and love the second, or treat the first with respect and the second with scorn. You cannot serve both God and Mammon» (Matt 6:24)[82]. Despite his desire for «eternal life» (17b), the rich man, presented with the choice between «what you have» and «a treasure in Heaven» by Jesus, finally decides to keep his «great wealth» (22). In this way Jesus sheds light on the fact that his perfect observance of God's commandments does not translate into a real respect for «the one [who is] good» (18): he «observes» (20) God's commandments as «wealth» rather than as God's word. The disciples are astonished (24), just as the young man is saddened on hearing Jesus' words (22). They do not understand that Jesus' warning, which empha-

82 It is significant that Matthew, like Luke, gives money a proper name, thus making it like an idol (see the commentary on Luke 16 in *Luc*, 646-658).

sizes the difficulty for humanity to enter into God's kingdom (23-24), in reality means that God alone can save (26). Jesus must explain this to them: «For men this is impossible, but not for God» (27). The disciples are astonished because, like the rich man, they think that their salvation is dependent on their «doing» 17b); they think they can count on their own strength, their wealth, to enter into God's kingdom. At the root of this shared attitude is hidden an insidious form of idolatry. For them, the Lord God is not the only one who is good, the only one able to bring them out of the land of Egypt, out of the house of slavery (Deut 5:6).

Adultery and idolatry

Not only are the two sins of idolatry and adultery brought together in the Decalogue, where the first is the essential sin against God and the second emblematic of an incorrect relationship with one's neighbor; but they are both images which are particularly present in the addresses of the prophets, where idolatry is often denounced as an «adultery». Going to other gods to serve them is an infidelity to God's love, which is also referred to as «prostitution» (Deut 31:16; Exod 34:15; Judg 2:17; 8:33; 2Kgs 9:22; Isa 57:3; Jer 3:1-13; and see especially Ezek 16 and 23).

Filiation (from the central passage)

The center of the composition acts as a keystone, the stone which, at the center and the high point of an arch, ensuring its structure. The central passage of the sub-sequence is the key to the reading of the whole.

Jesus indicates that children are models for the disciples. This model is not only possible and desirable, but indispensable. Only those who welcome the kingdom of God like children can enter into it (15). Reading this passage on its own, one would not understand exactly why the disciples sought to reject the children who were brought to Jesus (13); neither do we understand why their master is so «angry» (14a); nor do we understand what it might mean to say «be like children». We only notice this when Jesus calls his disciples «my children» (24b). Children are those who «are not wealthy» (23), who are unable to «do» anything (17), who have no other security than to be entirely trusting in the love and power of another person, which was already suggested by the fact that they «were brought» (13), not on their own initiative but on that of their parents.

The link between the central passage and the two previous passages is not as clear. It is not marked by any lexical repetition, apart from «God» (9a and 14b.15b), although this is not insignificant. A further link is constituted by the semantic link between «children» (13.14a.15b) and «father and mother» (7b). The fact that «father and mother» also returns on the other side of the central passage (19c) indicates an interpretative path which should not be ignored. What humanity is invited to «honor» (19c) in father and mother is not the father, on the one hand, and the mother, on the other, but the conjunction which unites them and makes them «one flesh» (8), this «and» through which he has been begotten. It is the single parental nature which the Decalogue had presented as the image *par excellence* of the single divine nature. To honor the single nature of one's parents, that is, to respect it, to emphasize it, means avoiding being joined to them, keeping one's distance and, eventually, «leaving» them (7a), to make another unit with a spouse with whom other children can be begotten. In the central passage, in a matching manner, we see parents honoring their children: they carry them, handing them to another person who takes them and lays his hands on them as though to adopt them. Jesus honors them in turn when he presents them with his blessing to the Other *par excellence*, their Father and his Father. This prayer addressed to God was the culmination of the teaching which Jesus offered to the crowds who had come towards him (1c).

3. THE SUB-SEQUENCE IN LUKE 18:15-30

In my analysis, the pericope of the call of the rich man (Luke 18:18-27) is the central passage of a sub-sequence made up of three passages (18:15-30). The JB, on the other hand, arranges these 16 verses into four pericopes, while the French *Traduction Œcuménique de la Bible* (TOB) divides them into only two pericopes[83]:

	JB (1966)	TOB (1972)	R. Meynet	
15-17	Jesus and the children	The example of the children	The kingdom of God	for the children
18-23	The Rich Aristocrat	Renouncing wealth to enter the Kingdom	The call	of the rich man
24-27	The danger of riches			
28-30	The reward of renunciation		Eternal life	for disciples

83 Note, however, that the second passage is sub-divided into three paragraphs which correspond to the division in the JB.

The JB, which distinguishes four pericopes in these verses, reflects the exegesis of its time[84], with the *form criticism* tendency to divide the Gospel text into almost independent small units, or «forms».

With the TOB, on the other hand, it is possible to see the influence of *redaction criticism*, which takes the work of re-arrangement which the editor has carried out into consideration, so it sees only two pericopes, the latter of which brings together the final three of the JB[85].

Finally, *biblical rhetorical analysis* offers truly scientific criteria to mark the edges of various units, at every level of the textual organization and to draw out the composition of each passage taken in itself as much as for groups of passages which form sequences and sub-sequences. At the level of the passage it emphasizes links between the different parts which make it up, so at the upper level it studies links between passages. Consequently, it chooses titles for passages which draw out their symmetry: here the titles of the outer passages match —«eternal life» in the third passage is the equivalent of «the kingdom of God» in the first; «the disciples» in the third passage are called to become like «children»; «children» and «disciples» are opposed to «rich man» in the central passage.

The passage of the call of the rich man in Luke (18:18-27) was analyzed in the first chapter (pp. 146-153). It remains to examine the other two passages which frame the central passage, and then the sub-sequence as a whole which is formed by these three passages.

84 An edition in 30 volumes published between 1948 and 1954 prepared the way for the first one-volume edition in 1956.

85 See pp. 54-56.

3.1. *The Kingdom of God belongs to children (Luke 18:15-17)*

COMPOSITION

+ 15 Now	THEY WERE BRINGING-UNTO	him also	INFANTS	
	.	that he may touch	them.	
– Now seeing,	*THE DISCIPLES*	***rebuked***	them.	

.. 16 Now Jesus	HAVING CALLED-UNTO	him	those	*saying*:
	+ «Let the		**CHILDREN**	
	:	*come to*	**me**,	
	+ and do not	prevent	them.	
	For to	such as these is	THE KINGDOM OF GOD.	
.. 17 Truly *I say*	to		*YOU* :	
	– Whoever	***does not receive***	THE KINGDOM OF GOD	
	:	like a	CHILD,	
	– *shall not*	*enter* in	IT!».	

The first part of the narrative (15) describes the scene, and the second part (16-17), which is more developed, reports Jesus' verbal reaction. In the first part, the disciples (15c) are opposed to those who carry their babies to Jesus (15a); in the center (15b), is the only member in which Jesus is the subject. The second part has three pieces. The outer pieces have an unimember (16a.17a) followed by a trimember (16bcd.17bcd). The first links «the children» with Jesus («me») in the center; the second links «the kingdom of God» with «a child» in the center. 16c and 17d use two similar movement verbs, «to come» and «to enter», which seems to put «me», that is, Jesus, at the same level as «the kingdom of God». At the center (16e), a piece made up of a single bimember expresses a general rule.

In the passage as a whole, «having called to» in 16a matches «were bringing to» in 15a and is opposed to «rebuked» in 15c, which «does not receive» in 17b is somehow synonymous with. In addition, while 16a-d seems to be addressed in particular to children in 15a, v.17 is mainly directed to the «disciples» («I say to you» in 17a).

BIBLICAL CONTEXT

Nothing in this passage indicates which quality it is of children which the disciples are to imitate; we need to go back to ch. 9 to learn more.

[46] An argument started between them about which of them was the greatest. [47] Jesus knew what thoughts were going through their minds, and he took a little child and set him by his side [48] and then said to them, «Anyone who welcomes this little child in my name welcomes me, and anyone who welcomes me welcomes the one who sent me. For the least among you all, that is the one who is great» (Luke 9:46-48).

SYNOPTIC COMPARISON *(see pp. 200, 239 and 255)*

Matt 19:13-15	Mark 10:13-16	Luke 18:15-17
[13] Then THEY presented TO HIM ***children*** SO THAT HE might lay the hands on them and pray.	[13] And THEY **brought** TO HIM ***children*** SO THAT HE **might touch them.**	[15] Now THEY **brought** TO HIM also some infants SO THAT HE **may touch them.**
NOW THE DISCIPLES REBUKED THEM.	NOW THE DISCIPLES REBUKED THEM.	NOW ***seeing*** THE DISCIPLES REBUKED THEM.
[14] ***Now*** JESUS SAID:	[14] ***Seeing*** JESUS was indignant and SAID to them:	[16] ***Now*** JESUS called them SAYING:
«LET THE CHILDREN ***and*** *DO NOT PREVENT THEM* *TO* come *TO ME*	«LET THE CHILDREN **come** *TO ME,* *DO NOT PREVENT THEM.*	«LET THE CHILDREN **come** *TO ME* ***and*** *DO NOT PREVENT THEM.*
FOR TO SUCH AS THESE IS THE KINGDOM of Heavens».	FOR TO SUCH AS THESE IS THE KINGDOM **of God.**	FOR TO SUCH AS THESE IS THE KINGDOM **of God.**
	[15] **Truly I say to you, whoever does not receive the kingdom of God like a child shall not enter in it».**	[17] **Truly I say to you, whoever does not receive the Kingdom of God like a child shall not enter in it».**
[15] ***And laying hands upon them,*** he departed from there.	[16] ***And*** kissing them, he blessed, ***laying his hands*** over ***them.***	

Mark's text is more developed than that of the others; the main difference is that he adds 15 (taken from Luke, 17). «Laying on hands» in Matthew (13c; repeated in 15a) is more solemn than the «touch» in Mark (13c) and Luke (15c). Only Matthew uses the verb «to pray» at the start (13d), but «to bless» is its equivalent at the end of Mark's passage (16a; to which is added «to kiss»). Rather than the «children» (*paidion*, «child under seven years») in Matthew (13b) and Mark (13b), Luke uses «infants» (*brephos*, which means «fetus», «new-born», «unweaned infant») at the start. Luke is very close to Mark, but does not have a conclusion which matches that of either Matthew (15) or Mark (16); strangely, the Evangelist who focuses most on Jesus' prayer does not mention it in this passage.

The composition of each passage is not the same. The differences between those of Matthew and Mark have already been described (see p. 240). Luke's composition is very similar to Mark's apart from the fact that he does not use the last part (Mark: 16). Luke has suppressed Jesus' anger (Mark: 14b), substituting «was indignant» by «called them» (Luke: 16b). He has also moved «seeing» (at the start of the second part in Mark: 14a, but at the end of the first part in Luke: 15d). The effect of these two small editorial changes is to considerably soften the conflict between Jesus and the disciples: even though the words which he says to them are exactly the same, they resonate less as a complaint than as a simple teaching which he seems to give them apart rather than in front of everyone.

INTERPRETATION

A strangeness

It must be said that Luke's passage, compared to those in Mark and Matthew, seems to have amputated an essential element. Luke does not repeat the final verse of the parallel passage in Mark: «And kissing them, he *blessed* (God), laying his hands over them» (Mark 10: 16). He has not even retained the mention of prayer which the parents asked from Jesus, as in Matthew: «so that he would lay hands on them and *pray*» (Matt 19:13). It seems strange that the Gospel of Luke, which emphasizes Jesus' prayer the most, has not mentioned it here, or has suppressed it if we accept that the Evangelist at least knew Mark. A possible explanation is that the whole of the previous sub-sequence, that is, the central sub-sequence of this sequence, three passages of which are unique to the third Gospel, is entirely given over to prayer, the prayer of the importunate widow, that of the Pharisee and the tax-collector, given as an example to the disciples and the Pharisees (see p. 338).

An enigma

Regardless of the question of prayer, this passage in Luke, like those of Matthew and Mark, is totally enigmatic. While Jesus twice insists that one has to be «such as» children (16e) and that it is indispensable to «receive the kingdom of God like a child» (17bc), or to be excluded from it, he says absolutely nothing about what it is that makes children a model for the disciples. The reader, like the disciples, has to wait for what comes next to learn which specific quality Jesus is recognizing in children.

3.2. *Eternal Life as a reward for the Disciples (Luke 18:28-30)*

COMPOSITION

+ 28 *Peter said:*			
– «Behold we,	HAVING	LEFT	what (was) ours
	:: have	followed	YOU!».

+ 29 *He said to them:*	*«Truly I say to you:*		
– there is no one	who has	LEFT	house, wife, brothers, parents, children
	:: for the sake of		THE KINGDOM OF GOD,
= 30	who would not *receive*		*MANY TIMES MORE at this moment*
	= and *in the age that comes*		*ETERNAL LIFE».*

Two parts follow one another, Peter's statement (28) and Jesus' reply (29-30). Peter's statement parallels the abandonment of «what (was) ours» and the attachment to Jesus («you»: 28c).

After the introductory narrative bimember (29a), the second part (29b-30) repeats both elements of the initial request in its first segment (29bc), filling in the «ours» in 28b in 29b, and then substituting «you» (28c) with «the kingdom of God» (29c); in the last segment, there is a double reward —the reward of «at this moment» (30a) and the reward of «the age to come» (30b). In this way a link is established between Jesus, on the one hand («you» in 28c), «the kingdom of God» (29c) and «eternal life» (30b), and, on the other, between «ours» (28b), «house, wife, brothers, parents, children» (29b) and «many times more» (30a).

Note about ta idia *and* oikia

In Peter's question, rather than Matthew and Mark's «everything» («We have left everything»), Luke uses *ta idia* («Behold we, having left *ta idia* have followed you»: 28). It is the only time that this nominalized adjective appears in the neuter plural in the synoptics; elsewhere, *eis ta idia* (John 16:32; 19:27; Acts 21:6) means «at home», «in his house». The translation with «our property» seems to come from Matthew and Mark (*ta panta*, neuter plural: «everything»), which, among all the things the disciples leave, also includes «the fields».

It is true that Luke, like Matthew and Mark, starts his list with *oikia* (29b: in the singular as in Mark, not the plural as in Matthew); *oikia*, however, does not only mean «house», in the sense of a material building, but also in the sense of «family», «household» (or, in the Hebrew, «the house of David» and «the house of Israel», whose equivalent is «the children of Israel»)[86]. In Luke «house» could be understood as a generic term (the family), then made more specific with «wife, brothers, parents and children». Luke's *ta idia* does not, therefore, only mean property, but also, and particularly, the members of the family.

BIBLICAL CONTEXT

Some[87] think that *ta idia* should be linked to Acts 4:32:

> 32 The whole group of believers was united, heart and soul; no one claimed *for his own use* (*idion*) anything that he had, as everything they owned was held in common [...]
> 34 None of their members was ever in want, as all those who owned land or houses would sell them, and bring the money from them 35 to present it to the apostles; it was then distributed to any members who might be in need.

In this case, Luke would be seeking to indicate fraternal communion *(koinōnia)* in his lexical choice.

INTERPRETATION

Jesus and the kingdom of God

Peter said to Jesus that, if they had left all that they had, including all the members of their family (28b), it was to «follow» him, him alone (28c). In his reply, Jesus does not parallel their homes and all their family members (29b) with himself, but with «the kingdom of God» (29c). Only God's love can justify separating from those who are closest to us, «wife, brothers, parents and children» (29b). Jesus does not agree to be «followed» as an absolute—he only called the Twelve, and only invites people to «accompany» him, to lead them to the Father, to make his disciples enter into the movement of his own and their own divine filiation.

What we have, much more, and eternal life

Whoever has «left what was his» (28b), «house, wife, brothers, parents, children» (29b) «will receive much more at this time» (30a). Such is the experience of anyone who has left what belongs to him to enter a community which holds property in common: what he receives goes far beyond what he has left behind, both

86 The same can be said in English: «the House of Savoy» does not describe a building, but rather a dynastic family.

87 See for example Rossé, 710.

material goods and, in particular, a much larger family than the one he has left. In addition, having left those who are his in flesh, he finds them increased, as it were, not in number but in quality, in their position of children of God, no longer destined to death but to «eternal life» (30b). As for «the time to come», this indicates what will follow death in the body, the disciple's as well as those close to him. The «eternal life» promised to the disciple is the only thing which really counts, because it is not transitory, it goes beyond the narrow limits of the pilgrimage of all humanity on this earth. Parents give life, but one day it ends in sorrow; only the life given by the Father in heaven has no end.

3.3. *The Sub-Sequence as a Whole (Luke 18:15-30)*

COMPOSITION OF THE SUB-SEQUENCE

The three passages are strongly linked to one another. We are not told that the leader comes to Jesus (as the rich man does in Matt 19:16 and in Mark 10:17), but only that he «questioned him» (18); one might therefore think that he was already there during the previous scene. At the end of the encounter, Luke does not say that he goes away (unlike in Matt 19:22 and Mark 10:22), as though he were still there in the scene which follows.

The outer passages match in that «the disciples» are mentioned at the start (15) and «Peter» at the end (28), who is also speaking on behalf of the others («we»). In the central passage, however, there is no mention of the disciples, but only of the rich leader. It is not said that the characters who intervene at the end are disciples—they are simply called «those who had heard» (26).

«The kingdom of God» appears in each of the three passages (16c.17a; 24b. 25b; 29c). «Come to me» at the start (16b) is matched by «we have followed you» at the end (28b); in the center, the same «to follow» (22d) reappears (preceded by the adverb *deuro*, a synonym of «to come»), followed by «me» which always describes Jesus. The same link between Jesus and «the kingdom of God» or «eternal life» is therefore made strongly in these three passages.

«Eternal life» at the start of the second passage (18b) reappears at the end of the third passage (30b). «Sell all that you have» (22c) heralds «we have left all that we had» (28b); Jesus adds people to this: «wife, brothers, parents, children» (29b). The emphatic formula, «Truly I say to you», is repeated in 17a and in 29a.

Finally, note the repetition of the same verb, «to leave» in the outer passages (16b and 28b.29b).

[15] People brought to him also some infants so that he may touch them. Seeing that, the
disciples rebuked them. [16] But Jesus CALLED them TO himself, saying:
«*Let the little children* COME TO ME and do not prevent them,
For to persons like them belongs the kingdom of GOD.
[17] ***Truly I say to you***: who does not **RECEIVE** the kingdom of GOD
like *a little child* shall not ENTER inside».

[18] A ruler asked him: «Good Master,
what must I do to ***INHERIT*** **ETERNAL LIFE**?».
[19] But Jesus said to him: «Why do you call me good?
No one is good, except GOD alone!
[20] You know the commandments : "Do not commit-adultery, do not kill, do not
steal, do not testimony falsely,
honor *your father and your mother*"».
[21] He said: «All these I have observed from my youth».
[22] Heard this, Jesus said to him:

«You still lack only one thing:
all that you have, sell it and **GIVE** it to the ***POOR***
and you will have a treasure in heavens;
then come, FOLLOW ME».

[23] Heard this, he became very sad for he was very rich.
[24] When Jesus saw this, he said: «How difficult it is for those who possess riches
to ENTER into the kingdom of GOD!
[25] It is easier for a camel to pass through the eye of a needle
than for a rich man to ENTER into the kingdom of GOD!».
[26] Those who heard said: «But who then can be saved?». [27] He said: «What
is impossible for men is possible for GOD».

[28] Peter said: «Behold we have
left *that was ours* and have FOLLOWED YOU!».
[29] He said to them: «***Truly I say to you***: there is no one who has
left *house or wife or brothers or parents or* ***CHILDREN***,
for the sake of the kingdom of GOD,
[30] who would not **RECEIVE** *many times more* at this time
present and in the age to come **ETERNAL LIFE**».

SYNOPTIC COMPARISON

Matt 19:3-26		Mark 10:2-27		Luke 18:15-30	
The Question about Divorce	3-9	The Question about Divorce	2-9		
Eunuchs for the Kingdom	10-12	*Avoiding adultery*	10-12		
The Kingdom for Children	13-15	The Kingdom for Children	13-16	The Kingdom for Children	15-17
The Call of the Rich Man	16-22	The Call of the Rich Man	17-22	**The Call of the Rich Man**	18-27
Poor for the Kingdom	23-26	*Avoiding idolatry*	23-27		
Eternal Life for the disciples	27-29	Eternal Life for the disciples	28-30	Eternal Life for the disciples	28-30

While the Matthean and Markan sub-sequences break up in very similar ways, Luke's is very different. The first two passages in Matthew (3-9 and 10-12) and Mark (2-9 and 10-12) have no parallel in Luke. In Matthew and Mark, «The call of the rich man» and the passage which follows (Matt: 16-22 and 23-26; Mark: 17-22 and 23-27) are parallel to the first two passages of the sub-sequence (Matt: 3-12; Mark: 2-12); in Luke, however, the parallel verses form a single passage (18-27) which makes up the center of the sub-sequence. The last passage of the sub-sequence in Luke (28-30) is symmetrical to the passage «the Kingdom for the children» (15-17), while in Matthew and Mark its parallel is part of the next sub-sequence, as we will see later (see pp. 273.301). Where the passage entitled «the kingdom for the children» is the first passage of the sub-sequence in Luke, it acts as the pivot in the sub-sequence in Matthew and in Mark.

INTERPRETATION

A tenacious leader

The rich man in Mark, like the young man in Matthew, is spontaneous. He arrives without warning, running, and goes as he came, without waiting for anything else. Luke's leader seems more mature and less impulsive. When he speaks (18), it seems as though he has been there for the whole of the previous scene; and when, in the center of the central passage, Jesus invites him to give all to the poor and to follow him (18), he does not reply, but it does not say that he goes away. It seems that he stays there, not only until the end of the central passage where he is named, but until the end of the sub-sequence. Like the reader, he would have heard the words addressed to Peter and to the others. In other words, one could have the impression that he is the main character of the whole sub-sequence. If he really wished «to inherit eternal life» (18), he would do as the Twelve did: he would leave what he had, imitating, like them, the Master (28). Sadness does not make him go away. Another path opens up before him —the path of the «kingdom of God» (16c.17; 24-25) that is, of «eternal life» (30).

Infants and the poor

While the first two gospels mention the «children» who are taken to Jesus, Luke uses the term «infants» (15). This word, placed right at the start, is the key to the reading of the whole sub-sequence, as long as it is linked to the central word, «the poor» (22c). The rich man is called to give all his property to the poor. If he does so, he himself will become as poor as the infant who has nothing and is unable to do anything. In reality, the new-born has a single choice, the life which he has just received. So we understand that wealth can prevent living. They do not allow us to reach «eternal life», that is, to be born into real life, unless they are given away. By distributing his wealth, the leader will allow the poor to live. In other words, it is not possible «to inherit eternal life», if one does not allow others to inherit life. To become a child, one has to become a parent.

To enter God's kingship

«The kingdom of God» is repeated in each of the three passages (16.17; 24.25; 29). One «enters» into such a reality. It is not something which one possesses, like wealth, nor is it something which one can pocket, box up, that is, «put in», which one shuts up into a strong-box. On the contrary, whoever agrees to enter into it is surrounded on all sides, enveloped, possessed, like a lover. The kingdom of God is not a place, like the kingdoms of this world, over which human dominion rules. It is the quality, the very essence of the Shepherd who feeds his sheep, who gives them life. To enter into God's kingdom means to share this quality with him, this essence of the Father who gives life to his children, who makes them inherit eternal life.

Chapter 3

The passage in its broader context
The sequence

The first chapter was given over to the study of only two «passages», although passages which are found in each of the three synoptics: the healing of one or two blind men in Jericho, and the calling of the rich man[1].

In Chapter 2, we placed each of the two passages in their immediate context. Both in the Gospel of Matthew and the Gospel of Mark, the healing at Jericho, together with the two passages which precede it —the request of Zebedee's sons and the discourse on service— forms a coherent whole; in Luke, on the other hand, it is paired with the passage which follows, Jesus' visit to Zacchaeus. In terms of the immediate context of Jesus' meeting with the rich man, in Luke this is formed by the previous passage, «Jesus and the children», and the passage which follows, «Jesus' reply to Peter's question»; in Matthew and Mark, this passage is part of a more developed whole made up of five passages.

We called these groups of passages «sub-sequences». As will be obvious, this term indicates that there is a level of textual organization above that of the «sub-sequence», which is the «sequence». This chapter will be dedicated to the study of four sequences:

- the Markan sequence, in which we find both the passage about the rich man and the passage about the blind man of Jericho: the two sub-sequences analyzed in the previous chapter frame a third, shorter, sequence;
- the parallel sequence in Matthew is very similar to that of Mark, but the center of the central sub-sequence is taken up by the parable of the laborers in the vineyard, which is unique to Matthew;
- in Luke, the passages about the rich man and the blind man belong to two different sequences.

A. THE SEQUENCE IN MARK 10:1-52

1. THE CENTRAL SUB-SEQUENCE (MARK 10:28-34)

This sub-sequence has three passages, two made up of three verses (28-30 and 32-34) framing a brief proverb (31).

1 It is possible to define the passage, or pericope, as the first unit of the «recitation». In fact, the pericope is what is read, or «recited», during the liturgy, except during the Easter celebrations, when the whole of the Passion is read. When the passage is an account, for example, an account of a healing, or a parable, it cannot be cut before the episode has reached its conclusion. In the account of the healing at Jericho, it is unthinkable that one might stop before the man is healed! Units which are less than a passage are units of «quotation», that is, they can be integrated in other texts, as we have seen for the quotations from the Decalogue in the accounts of the calling of the rich man. See *Traité*, 133.196.197.

1.1. *The fate of the twelve (Mark 10:28-30)*

COMPOSITION

+ 28 *Peter began to say to him:*			
:: «Behold we	have	LEFT	all
– and	have	followed	YOU».

+ 29 *Jesus declared: «Truly I say to you,*				
:: there is no one who has	LEFT			
	house	or brothers	or sisters	
	or mother	or FATHER	or children	or fields
– for the sake of		ME and for	THE GOSPEL,	
:: 30 who would not	receive	*A HUNDRED-FOLD*	*now, in this moment,*	
	house	and brothers	and sisters	
	and mother	and children	and fields with PERSECUTIONS,	
– and *in the age that comes*		*ETERNAL LIFE*».		

The passage has two parts, Peter's intervention (28), followed by Jesus' statement (29-30). After the introductory narrative phrase (29a), the first piece of Jesus' response (29b-e) repeats the two members of Peter's words, in the same order: «left» in 28b is repeated in 29b, «all» in 28b is given further detail by the list in 29cd, «me» in 29e refers to «you» in 28c, but Jesus adds «the Gospel» to it. The last piece (30) matches the previous piece: the reward is received in two time-periods, «now, in this time» (30a) and «in the age that comes» (30d); «a hundred times as much» (30a) is given detail in 30bc, where the terms in the list of 29cd are repeated; however, while the number of terms is the same (seven), «father» is not repeated the second time, and its absence is made up for by the addition of «persecutions».

BIBLICAL CONTEXT

The Gospel and the kingdom of God

In Mark, «the Gospel of God» is defined as the coming of the «kingdom of God»:

> Jesus went into Galilee. There he proclaimed the gospel from God,
> Saying, «The time is fulfilled, and the kingdom of God is close at hand.
> Repent, and believe the Gospel (Mark 1:14-15).

In Mark, the expression «for me and for the Gospel» is repeated in 8:35. In Matthew it is always used with «proclaim», once «this Gospel» (26:13), three times with «the Gospel of the kingdom of God» (4:23; 9:35), «the Gospel of the kingdom» (24:14). While Luke never uses the noun «gospel»[2], he does use the verb *evangelize*, «to evangelize», «to announce-the-good-news» ten times, and particularly twice «to the poor» (4:18; 7:22).

Persecution for eternal life

The second book of Maccabees tells the story of a mother of seven sons who did not fear the definitive separation of death which the ungodly king was inflicting on her sons, but encouraged them in their persecution with hope in «eternal life» (2Macc 7:9.36). To her last son she said, «Do not fear this executioner, but prove yourself worthy of your brothers and accept death, *so that I may receive you back with them in the day of mercy*» (2Macc 7:29).

Happy in persecution

When the apostles were persecuted and imprisoned (Acts 5:18), and then flogged before being released (40), «they left the presence of the Sanhedrin, glad to have had the honor of suffering humiliation for the sake of the Name» (41).

INTERPRETATION

Following Jesus for the Gospel

Jesus seeks to explain that whoever follows him (28c) has not been called to stop with him, but to listen to «the good news» of the kingdom of God, «the Gospel» (29e). Once again, Jesus does not intend the disciple to see him as the ultimate end of the *sequela*; he is not taking God's place; he is the Son who leads to the Father, the only God and the disciples' king just as his own king.

«One hundred times as much», but not exactly!

To the one who has «left everything» (28b), material goods and, especially, family members, «for Jesus and for the Gospel» (29e), «one hundred times as much» is promised (30a). However, what he will receive does not correspond precisely to what he has left. He will receive a «mother», but it is not said that he will find a «father», probably because, by following Jesus and thanks to the Gospel, he will

2 It is used twice in Luke's second volume (Acts 15:7; 20:24).

have found the one Father, the Father in heaven. On the other hand, he will also receive «persecutions» (30c). This addition, at the end of the list, unique to Mark, is surprising. Only the history of the Church, from the time of the first persecution of the apostles (Acts 5:41) enables us to understand that the persecutions represent the highest of the gifts received.

«Now, in this time»

Two time periods are distinguished: the present, and the future. Even though it is associated with persecutions which have not yet happened, the reward promised to the Twelve is not placed after death or at the end of time: it is «now, in this time» (30a); that is, it is at the very moment when they are living, when Jesus is speaking to them, that they have already received «one hundred times as much» as what they have left. It is, however, difficult to understand what this «hundredfold» is. It will be different «houses, brothers, sisters, mother and child, and fields» (30bc) to what they have left; these are what they will receive, multiplied, in their apostolate, the houses and fields of the Christian community, but, especially, their many disciples who will become their neighbors in Christ. We can also understand this as the same people and the same things which they will view differently, which they will receive anew, multiplied and now a gift from God[3].

«In the time to come»

As for future reward, the reward «in the time to come», it is called «eternal life»: it is what does not perish, which goes beyond the limits of mortal life. The day inevitably comes when parents, siblings, and even children die, leaving those who are left behind in deep sorrow. The person who has put their faith in Christ and in his good news knows that death will never have the final word; they believe that the resurrection of the Lord Jesus has opened to all the path to a life which goes beyond the horizons of this world. For them, eternal life is the supreme gift; the more so since they know that it they are not the only beneficiaries, but that their neighbors will inherit it with them.

3 Those who have abandoned their own family to dedicate themselves entirely to Christ and the Gospel often have the experience of having a different order of relationship, of a specifically spiritual order, with them.

1.2. *The fate of the son of man (Mark 10:32-34)*

COMPOSITION

+ 32 They were	on the way		
= GOING UP	TO JERUSALEM		
+ and was preceding them	Jesus.		
– And	*they were amazed;*		
– and those who followed	*were frightened.*		

+ And taking aside again	the Twelve,		
+ he began to say to them	what was about to happen to him:		
= 33 «Lo, WE ARE GOING UP	TO JERUSALEM		
– and the Son of man	*will be delivered*	to the high priests and to the scribes	
– and they ***will condemn***	him	***to death***	
– and they *will deliver*	him	to the gentiles;	
.. 34 and they will mock	him	and will spit	on him
.. and will flog	him	***and will kill***	(him)
:: and after three days		HE WILL RISE».	

The passage has two parts. The first part describes Jesus with the group of disciples and those who accompany him on the way (32a-e). In the second part, on the other hand, he has taken the Twelve to one side.

The first part is made up of two segments. The first segment, an ABA' type, describes the actions of the characters (32abc)[4], and the second describes the actions of those who are with Jesus (32de).

The second part (32f-34) has three trimember segments. The first describes the present, and the next two what will happen in the days to come. The second trimember, an ABA' type, announces what the Jews will do to Jesus: «delivered» to the leaders of the people (33b) Jesus will be «delivered» by them to the gentiles (33d); in the center (33c) is the condemnation to death. The third trimember (34), an AA'B type, announces what the gentiles will do to Jesus: after all the bad treatment which ends in his death (34ab), resurrection (34c).

«To go up to Jerusalem» refers to the first segments (32b.33a). In addition, the amazement and fear at the end of the first part (32de) are linked to what will happen to Jesus, which will be announced in the last two segments of the second part (33b-34).

4 Note the same periphrasis construction («to be» + participle) in the outer members.

BIBLICAL CONTEXT

The third and final prediction of the Passion and resurrection

Jesus had already foretold his fate twice, in 8:31-33 and in 9:30-32. Most exegetes are of the opinion that Peter's confession at Caesarea (8:27-30), followed by the first prediction of the Passion and resurrection (8:31-33), marks a decisive turning point in the arrangement of Mark's Gospel—from this point onwards everything is directed towards Jerusalem, where the Passion, which will end with the resurrection, will take place[5]. The three predictions of the Passion and resurrection have the function of preparing the disciples for what will happen. The triple occurrence of this announcement emphasizes its importance; we might think that these three passages take on a particular role in the composition of the Gospel, that is, that they occupy strategic positions. We will see this in this sequence. Finally, note that the third prediction is addressed, not to the disciples in general, like the first two, but only to the restricted circle of the Twelve.

The third day[6]

The Midrash on the psalms applies Ps 22 to Esther; referring to the fast observed by the Jews and the queen herself for three days and three nights (Esth 4:16; 5:1), it explains: «Why three days? Because the Holy One —blessed be he!— never leaves Israel in anguish for more than three days». And as examples it gives Gen 22:4; 42:17; Exod 15:22; 2Kgs 20:5.8; Josh 2:16; Jonah 2:1; Hos 6:2: «After two days, he makes us live again, the third day he will raise us up and we will live in his presence[7]».

INTERPRETATION

Amazement and fear

Only Mark reports the reaction of those who accompany Jesus on the road to Jerusalem (32de). It is difficult to know who precisely is the subject of the first verb, «were going up» (32ab) and whether we should distinguish two different groups: it could be, in fact, that it was the disciples who were «amazed» (32d) and the crowd of pilgrims accompanying them for the Passover pilgrimage who were «frightened» (32e)[8]. However, if Mark was not precise, the problem does

5 See, for example, the introduction to Mark in the JB (1966) 10; see too the TOB (1972), 126; and p. 409 n. 12.

6 See *Jésus passe*, 284-285.

7 *The Midrash on Psalms*, 301-302 (see BEAUCHAMP P., *Psaumes nuit et jour*, 236 ff).

8 See, for example, Pesch, 229-230.

not seem to be here. All those who went up to Jerusalem with Jesus would certainly have had good reason to be amazed and fearful.

Jesus' determination

Jesus, for his part, showed that he was aware of what was in store for him (33-34). Mark says absolutely nothing about his emotions; however, he depicts the master as totally determined, walking at the head of the procession (32c), like the shepherd leading his flock.

1.3. *The Sub-Sequence as a whole (Mark 10:28-34)*

COMPOSITION

[28] Peter began to say to him: «Behold, ***we*** have left all and have *FOLLOWED* you». [29] Jesus declared: «Truly I say to you, there is no one who has left house or brothers or sisters or mother or father or children or fields for my sake and for the sake of the gospel, [30] who would not receive hundred-fold more, now in this present time, house and brothers and sisters and mother and children and fields,

with	PERSECUTIONS,	*and*	*in the age to come*	ETERNAL LIFE.

[31] Many	FIRST	will be	LAST
and	the LAST		FIRST».

[32] They were on the way going up to Jerusalem, and Jesus was walking ahead of them. They were amazed and those who *FOLLOWED* were frightened. Taking aside again ***the Twelve***, he began to say to them what was about to happen to him: [33] «Behold we are going up to Jerusalem; and the Son of man will be delivered to the high priests and to the scribes and they will condemn him to death and they will deliver him to the gentiles; [34] and they will mock him and will spit on him and will flog him;

they will	KILL (him)	*and*	*after three days*	HE WILL RISE».

The outer passages (28-30 and 32-34) introduce «the Twelve» (32b), that is, «us», on whose behalf «Peter» intervenes (28). The verb «to follow» is repeated at the start of both passages (28b.32b). The final fate of the Twelve will be very similar to that of their master: in 30c and 34b, «they will kill» matches «persecutions», the temporal indications «after three days» matches «in the time to come» and «will rise» matches «eternal life». These repetitions act as final terms.

The statement which ends Jesus' words in the first passage (31) can be considered to be the center of the sub-sequence. This word of Jesus' is used almost identically in other contexts—it is a «mobile *logion*», as Form criticism would say (Matt 19:30; 20:16; Luke 13:30)— that is, a statement which has a certain independence. It is a proverb, that is, a text which is complete in itself, which can be independent. In this context, its meaning is applied both to the disciples (first passage) and to Jesus (last passage): the disciples, with the persecutions, will be «the last» like Jesus in his Passion and death; they will become «the first» with «eternal life» and resurrection[9].

[28] Peter began to say to him: «Behold, ***we*** have left all and have ***FOLLOWED*** you».
[29] Jesus declared: «Truly I say to you, there is no one who has left house or brothers or sisters or mother or father or children or fields for my sake and for the sake of the gospel, [30] who would not receive hundred-fold more, now in this present time, house and brothers and sisters and mother and children and fields,

with PERSECUTIONS, *and* *in the age to come* ETERNAL LIFE.

[31] Many	FIRST	will be	LAST
and	the LAST		FIRST».

[32] They were on the way going up to Jerusalem, and Jesus was walking ahead of them. They were amazed and those who ***FOLLOWED*** were frightened. Taking aside again ***the Twelve***, he began to say to them what was about to happen to him: [33] «Behold we are going up to Jerusalem; and the Son of man will be delivered to the high priests and to the scribes and they will condemn him to death and they will deliver him to the gentiles; [34] and they will mock him and will spit on him and will flog him;

they will KILL (him) *and* *after three days* HE WILL RISE».

At this higher level of the text's organization —the level of the sub-sequence— we can better understand the reason for Mark's «redactional interventions» (see the synoptic tables, pp. 287.297): the addition of «persecutions» in the first passage (30c), the addition of the verb «to follow» in the final passage (32b).

INTERPRETATION

To follow Jesus even unto death…

It is likely that Peter does not really see where following Jesus (28) will lead them. Of course his request looks to the future, but it is expressed in the past, as though they had already done «everything». In fact, the two verbs which he uses are in the «perfect»: «we have left», «we have followed you». It is true that, for some

9 See a similar composition in Luke 14:7-14, where the central proverb, «Everyone who exalts himself will be humbled, but the one who humbles himself will be exalted» applies to the guest as much as to the host (see *Luc*, 607).

time already, they had left their property and family to follow him. However, Jesus, by adding «persecutions» (30c), lets it be understood that they have not yet reached the end: on «the road» in fact «he went before them» (32a). Amazed by what they had just heard, they remained behind a little, as though they wished to slow down. And Jesus had to «take them aside again» (32b) to explain to them, for a third and final time, the aim of the journey, and how he would go before them on the path of persecution; probably a way of asking them if they were ready to continue going with him to the end.

...and to the resurrection

The amazement of those who followed Jesus was surely not caused by the promise of «eternal life» (30c). Their gaze stopped at the present moment, «now, in this time» (30a). They were not yet capable of seeing, beyond persecutions, the resurrection to eternal life, like the mother who encouraged her sons not to give in to fear of death (2Macc 7). They had to have the experience of Jesus' resurrection to overcome their amazement and to experience persecution as a joy, a prefiguration «now, in this time» of eternal life (Acts 5:41).

Many of the first will be last

While the second part of the central proverb «and the last will be first» (31b), resounds like an encouragement, the first part (31a) can be understood as a warning: «Many of those who are first will be last». We do not know exactly what Peter was expecting when, on behalf of the Twelve, he described their worthiness to Jesus. We might reasonably assume that he did not envisage persecutions, but the glory of the kingdom, in which they dreamed of occupying the first places. This is why, before promising them they would be the «first» Jesus had to warn them that this would not be possible unless they first of all agreed to be «the last». This, in fact, is the basic law of the kingdom of God.

2. THE SEQUENCE AS A WHOLE (MARK 10:1-52)

COMPOSITION

The three Markan sub-sequences examined up till now form a single sequence. The first verse indicates an important turning point in Jesus' journey: he is now definitively leaving Galilee to go to Judea. At the start of ch. 11, another stage begins—now Jesus is close to Jerusalem, preparing himself to enter the city.

The mention of the place at the start, «And rising up from there, he came into the territory of Judea, across the Jordan» (1) prepares us for the place in the center, «They were on the road going up to Jerusalem» (32); however, at the start of the last passage (46b), when they leave Jericho, they are still far from Jerusalem.

The centers of theSub-Sequences (Mark 10:13-16; 10:31; 10:41-46)

The passages on which the outer sub-sequences (13-16; 41-46a) are centered match:

- Jesus' address (14b-15 and 42b-45) responds to the reaction of the disciples, who «rebuke» those bringing their children to Jesus (13), who «were indignant» with James and John (41); note the repetition of «to be indignant» in 14a and 41b (only used one other time, at 14:4, when the disciples are indignant with the woman anointing Jesus at Bethany);
- in the first passage the disciples are invited to become like «children» (14b.15b) in order to be able to enter the kingdom of God; in the other passage they are invited to become «servants» (43b) and «slaves» (44b) if they wish to be «great» (43b) and «first» (44b).

With the opposition between «first» and «last», the proverb in the center of the central sub-sequence (31) summarizes the central passages of the outer sub-sequences; «first» in 31 is repeated in 44 and «last» refers back to «children» (14-15) and to «servant» and «slave» (43-44).

[13] They were bringing to him children so that he might touch them,
: but **the disciples** *rebuked* them.
–[14] Having seen (this), Jesus *was indignant* and **said to them:**

«Let the **CHILDREN** come to me and do not prevent them; for to such as these is the ***KINGDOM*** of God. [15] Truly I say to you, whoever does not receive the ***KINGDOM*** of God like a **CHILD**, shall not enter in it».

[16] And embracing them, he blessed them laying his hands over them.

[...]

[31] «Many ***FIRST*** will be **LAST** and the **LAST** ***FIRST***».

[...]

[41] Heard this,
: **the ten** *were indignant* at James and John.
–[42] And called them to him, Jesus **said to them:**

You know that those considered commanding the nations exercise lordship over them and the great ones among them exercise authority over them. [43] It is not to be so among you, but who wants to become ***GREAT*** among you shall be your **SERVANT** [44] and who wants to be ***FIRST*** among you shall be **SLAVE** of all. [45] For the Son of man did not come to be served but to serve and to give his life a ransom for many».

[46] And they come to Jericho.

Formal connections between the outer Sub-Sequences

[1] And **rising** from there, he comes to the territory of Judea [and] beyond the Jordan. And THE CROWD departs together again towards him. And, as usual, he teaches them again.

[2] And ***COMING-TOWARDS*** **him,** some Pharisees questioned him (to know) if it is permitted for a husband to repudiate his wife, to tempt him. [3] But answering he said to them: «What did Moses command you?». [4] They said: «Moses permitted to write a roll of divorce and repudiate her». [5] Jesus said to them: «It was because of the hardness of your heart that he had written for you this commandment. [6] But from the beginning of the creation "he created them male and female". [7] "For this, man will leave his father and his mother [and be joined to his wife] [8] and the two will be one flesh only". So they are no more two but one flesh only. [9] What therefore God has joined, let man not separate it».

[10] And in the house again the disciples questioned him on this matter. [11] And he said to them: «Whoever repudiates his wife and marries another, commits adultery against her; [12] and if she repudiates her husband and marries another, she commits adultery».

[13] They were bringing to him CHILDREN so that he might touch them, but the disciples ***rebuked*** them. [14] Having seen this, Jesus was indignant and said to them: «Let the CHILDREN come to me and do not prevent them; for to such as these is the kingdom of God. [15] Truly I say to you, who does not receive the kingdom of God like a CHILD, shall not enter in it». [16] And embracing them, he blessed them, laying his hands over them.

[17] *AND WHILE HE WAS GOING OUT* on the way, someone, running towards him and kneeling before him, asked him: «Good Master, what will I do to inherit eternal life?». [18] Jesus says to him: «Why do you tell me good? No one is good, if not God only. [19] You know the commandments: "Do not kill, do not commit adultery, do not steal, do not testimony falsely", do not defraud, "honor your father and your mother"». [20] He declared to him: «Master, all these I guarded by myself from my youth». [21] Jesus, looking at him, loved him and said to him: «Only one thing you lack: go, sell what you have and give it to the poor and you will have treasure in Heavens; then come, follow me». [22] But he, gloomy at this word, went away afflicted; for he was having great wealth.

[23] And, looking around, Jesus said to his disciples: «With what difficulty those who have riches will come in the kingdom of God!». [24] The disciples remained amazed for his words; now Jesus, answering again, said to them: «Children, how it is difficult to enter into the kingdom of God! [25] It is easier for a camel to pass through the eye of a needle, than a rich man to enter into the kingdom of God». [26] They were exceedingly astonished, saying to one another: «And who can be SAVED?». [27] And looking at them Jesus said: «For men it is impossible, but not for God! For all is possible to God».

We have already examined the links between the central passages (13-16; 41-46a, pp. 277-278).

After the introduction, the first passages begin with synonymous verbs, «come-towards» (*pros-erchomai*: 2), «leave-for» (*pros-poreuomai*: 35) which govern the same object, «him»; in the same way, the passages which follow the central passages begin with «And while he was going out» (17.46b)[10]. These four occurrences form a parallel system.

The two occurrences of the verb «to save» act as final terms (26.52).

«The crowds» appear in the introduction (1) and «a considerable crowd» at the start of the last passage (46bc); here they somehow act as outer terms.

35 And ***GOING-TOWARDS*** **him,** James and John, the sons of Zebedee, saying to him:
«Master, we want that what we will ask you, you may do for us». 36 He said to them: «What
do you want that I may do for you?». They said to him: 37 «Grant to us that we may be
seated in your glory one at your right and one at your left». 38 Jesus said to them: «You do not
know what you ask. Can you drink of the cup that I drink or be baptized with baptism in
which I am baptized?». 39 They said to him: «We can». Jesus said to them: «The cup of
which I drink you shall drink and the baptism with which I am baptized you shall be
baptized. 40 But to be seated at my right or at my left is not mine to grant it; it is for those to
whom it has been prepared».

41 Heard this, the other ten began to ***be indignant*** at James and John. 42 Having
summoned them, Jesus said to them: «You know that those considered commanding
the nations dominate them and the great-ones among them subdue them. 43 It is not
to be so among you, but who wants to be great among you shall be your **SERVANT**
44 and who wants to be the first among you shall be the **SLAVE** of all. 45 For the Son of
man did not come to be served, but to serve and to give his life a ransom for many».
46 And they come to Jericho.

AND WHILE GOING OUT from Jericho, he, his disciples and A CONSIDERABLE CROWD, the son
of Timaeus, Bartimaeus, a blind-man, was seated on the way, asking (alms). 47 This one
heard that it was Jesus the Nazarene, began to cry out and to say: «Son of David, Jesus,
have mercy on me!». 48 Many ***rebuked*** him so that he would be silent, but he cried out all
the more: «Son of David, have mercy on me!». 49 Stopped, Jesus said: «Call him». And they
called the blind-man, saying to him: «Have courage! **Rise,** he calls you!». 50 Throwing his
mantle, walking again, he came to Jesus. 51 Answering him, Jesus said: «What do you want
that I may do for you?». The blind-man said to him: «Rabbunì, that I may see again!».
52 Jesus said to him: «Go, your faith has **SAVED** you». And immediately he saw again and
he was following him on the way.

10 This expression, which is absent in Matthew and Luke, is only found in Mark 13:1.

The formal links between the central Sub-Sequence and the rest of the sequence[11]

---

1 And RISING from there, he came to the territory of Judea [and] beyond Jordan. And ***the crowd* were departing together again towards him**. And, as usual, he **was teaching** them again.

2 And came-towards him some Pharisees and questioned him to know if it is permitted for a husband to repudiate his wife, to tempt him. 3 But answering he said to them: «What did Moses command you?». 4 They said: «Moses permitted to write a roll of divorce and repudiate her». 5 Jesus said to them: «Because of the hardness of your heart that he had written for you this commandment. 6 But from the beginning of the creation "he created them male and female". 7 "For this, man will leave **HIS FATHER AND HIS MOTHER** [and be joined to his wife] 8 and the two will be one flesh only". So they are no more two but one flesh only. 9 What therefore God has joined, let man not separate it».

10 And in the house again the disciples questioned him on this matter. 11 And he said to them: «Whoever repudiates his wife and marries another, commits adultery against her; 12 and if she repudiates her husband and marries another, she commits adultery».

13 They were bringing to him children so that he might touch them, but the disciples rebuked them. 14 Having seen this, Jesus was indignant and said to them: «Let the children come to me and do not prevent them; for to such as these is the kingdom of God. 15 Truly I say to you, who does not receive the kingdom of God like a child, shall not enter in it». 16 And embracing them, he blessed them laying his hands over them.

17 While he went-out on the way, someone, running towards him and kneeling before him, asked him: «Good **Master**, what will I do to inherit ETERNAL LIFE?». 18 Jesus said to him: «Why do you tell me good? No one is good, if not God only. 19 You know the commandments: "Do not kill, do not commit adultery, do not steal, do not testimony falsely", do not defraud, "honor **YOUR FATHER AND YOUR MOTHER**"». 20 He declared to him: **Master**, all these I guarded by myself from my youth». 21 Jesus, looking at him, loved him and said to him: «Only one thing you lack: go, sell what you have and give to the poor and you will have treasure in Heavens; then come, FOLLOW ME». 22 But he, gloomy at this word went way afflicted; for he was having great wealth.

23 And, looking around, Jesus said to his disciples: «With what difficulty those who have wealth will enter into the kingdom of God!». 24 The disciples remained AMAZED for his words; but Jesus answering again, said to them: «***Children***, how it is difficult to enter into the kingdom of God! 25 It is easier for a camel to pass through the eye of a needle, than a rich-man to enter into the kingdom of God». 26 They were exceedingly astonished, saying to one another: «And who can be saved?». 27 And looking at them Jesus said: «For men it is impossible, but not for God! For all is possible to God».

With the first sub-sequence: «eternal life» promised to the Twelve (30) was what the rich young man asked for (17); the disciples were «amazed» (32) as in the last passage of the first sub-sequence (24); «father or mother» in 29 echoes the quotation in the first passage of the first sub-sequence («will leave his father and mother»: 7) and in its symmetrical passage («honor your father and mother»: 19); and we should add that «son» in 29 and 30 repeats «my children» in the last passage of the first sub-sequence (the same *tekna* in 24).

11 In addition to the links already indicated between the central passages of the three sub-sequences (see pp. 276-277).

With the last sub-sequence: «the Son of man» in 33 is repeated at the center of the last sub-sequence (45).

With the whole: the two occurrences of «to follow» (28.32) recall, on the one hand, the occurrence in the story of the rich man (21) and, on the other, the occurrence in the story of the blind man (52); the first verb of the sequence, «having risen» (*anastas*: 1), is repeated at the end of the central sub-sequence, translated by «will rise again» (*anastēsetai*: 34) and with its usual synonym at the center of the last passage of the last sub-sequence, when they tell the blind man to «get up» (*egeire*: 49).

28 Peter began to say to him: «Behold, we have left all and have FOLLOWED You». 29 Jesus declared: «Truly I say to you, there is no one who has left house of brothers or sisters or **MOTHER OR FATHER** or ***children*** or fields, for my sake and for the sake of the gospel, 30 who would not receive a hundred-fold more, now in this present time, house and brothers and sisters and mother and ***children*** and field, with persecutions, and in the age to come ETERNAL LIFE.

31 **Many of the first will be last and the last first».**

32 They were on the way going up to Jerusalem, and Jesus was walking ahead of them. They were AMAZED and those who FOLLOWED were frightened. Taking aside again the Twelve, he began to say to them what was about to happen to him: 33 «Behold, we are going up to Jerusalem; ***the Son of man*** will be delivered to the high priests and to the scribes and they will condemn him to death and they will deliver him to the gentiles; 34 they will mock him and spit on him, and flog him; they will kill him and after three days he will *RISE*».

35 And went-towards him James and John, the sons of Zebedee, saying to him: «**Master**, we want that what we will ask you, you may do for us». 36 He said to them: «What do you want that I may do for you?». They said to him: 37 «Grant to us that we may be seated in your glory one at your right and one at your left». 38 Jesus said to them: «You do not know what you ask. Can you drink of the cup that I drink or be baptized with baptism in which I am baptized?». 39 They said to him: «We can». Jesus said to them: «The cup of which I drink, you shall drink and the baptism with which I am baptized you shall be baptized. 40 But to be seated at my right or at my left is not mine to grant it; it is for those to whom it has been prepared».

41 Heard this, the other ten began to be indignant at James and John. 42 Calling them to him, Jesus said to them: «You know that those considered commanding the nations dominate them and the great-ones among them subdue them. 43 It is not to be so among you, but who wants to be great among you will be your servant 44 and who wants to be the first among you will be the slave of all. 45 For *the Son of man* did not come to be served, but to serve and to give his life a ransom for many». 46 And they come to Jericho.

And while (they) went out from Jericho, he, his disciples and ***a considerable crowd***, the sons of Timaeus, Bartimaeus, a blind-man, was seated on the way, asking (alms). 47 This one heard that it was Jesus the Nazarene, began to cry out and to say: «Son of David, Jesus, have mercy on me!». 48 Many rebuked him to be silent, but he all the more cried: «Son of David, have mercy on me!». 49 Stopped, Jesus said: «Call him». And they called the blind-man, saying to him: «Have courage! *RISE*, he calls you!». 50 Throwing his mantle and walking again, he came to Jesus. 51 Answering him, Jesus said to him: «What do you want that I may do for you?». The blind man said to him: «Rabbunì, that I may see again!». 52 Jesus said to him: «Go, your faith has saved you». And immediately he regained his sight and began to FOLLOW him on the way.

In the following lay-out the titles given to the different passages of the sequence aim to bring out the links which are between them; in some way, then, these titles already represent a kind of interpretation.

Jesus departs towards Judea		and teaches the crowd	1
Jesus reveals	to the Pharisees	the hardness of their heart	2-9
and invites	the disciples	*to fidelity*	10-12
The disciples	are called to be	like *children*	13-16
Jesus reveals	to a rich man	what makes him sad	17-22
and invites	the disciples	*to faith*	23-27
The Twelve	will be persecuted	and will receive eternal life	28-30
«Many first	will be last	and the *last* first"	31
Jesus	will be killed	and will be raised	32-34
Jesus opens the eyes and invites	of the sons of Zebedee them	*to faith*	35-41
The Twelve	are called to be	like *servants*	42-46a
Jesus opens the eyes and recognizes	of the son of Timaeus	*his faith*	46b-52

INTERPRETATION

This is a linear-type interpretation, following the text of the sequence, passage by passage, trying to draw out the logic of the successive encounters of Jesus. The presupposition of our reading, as we have said several times, is that these different passages are not simply juxtaposed, but that they are linked to each other in a tight composition and they therefore form a true discourse.

Jesus reveals the hardness of their hearts to the Pharisees and invites the disciples to faithfulness

After the introduction (1), the sequence begins with a discussion between Jesus and the Pharisees on the question of whether divorce is permitted (2-9). Jesus takes a very clear position: going beyond Moses' concession (4), which demonstrates the hardness of their hearts (5), he means to be faithful to God's original words (6-9). In the house, the disciples return to the subject (10) and Jesus again insists on the indissolubility of marriage (11-12), giving them to understand that those who remain faithful to their spouse, and thus to the Law of God, *avoid being adulterous towards them.*

The disciples are called to be like children

At first sight, the episode with the children (13-16) seems to have nothing to do with the previous episode. The child is still joined to his father and mother, still far from the time of marriage and the temptation of divorce. Of course Jesus' surprising statement does not mean that the kingdom of God is reserved for those who have not reached sexual maturity. The child is someone who allows himself to be carried by his parents, who sinks into Jesus' arms, and agrees to be blessed and thus given over to God's care. The child is one who trusts. The child is the image and model of those who welcome «the kingdom of God», that is, who accept that the Lord reigns totally, without division, over them, *who therefore are not adulterous towards him.*

Jesus reveals to a rich man what makes him sad and invites the disciples to faith

Then there comes a man whose attachment to the commandments Jesus will put to the test. He will show him his infidelity, the idolatry hidden behind his preference for wealth, and will shed light on how this has frozen his heart (22). In fact, he had invited him to follow him (21) in his fidelity to the first commandment, and in his desire for the only «treasure» which lasts, that which is «in heaven». After this, he invites his disciples to be wary of wealth (23.25) but rather to put his trust only in God (27), the only one who is able to save them (26). Mark does not say whether the rich man was a Pharisee; however, his constant fidelity to the commandments makes us think of those whom the Gospel presents as the most faithful practitioners of the Law, but also those who are more tempted by idolatry of the Law, which makes them unfaithful to God, *adulterous towards him.*

The Twelve will be persecuted and will receive eternal life

After the warning which Jesus has just given to all the disciples, Peter, on behalf of the Twelve, asks what will happen to those who have left everything, wealth and relatives, who have «followed» him (28). With «persecutions», they will receive what the rich man wished to «inherit» (17), «*eternal life*» (30).

«Many of the first will be last and the last first»!

At the center of the central sub-sequence, a succinct formula, like a proverb, sums up the fundamental law of the kingdom of God (31). This could be used as the title for the whole sequence. It applies, in fact, not just to Jesus and his disciples, who made themselves last when they left everything for the kingdom of God and will become the first when they rise again into eternal life (28-34); it also applies to the rich, who are invited to abandon their wealth to obtain the one true good (17-27); to those invited to become last, like children (13-16); to the Pharisees and to the disciples, invited to give up the hardness of heart which is typical of those who believe themselves to be first, to listen, as children, to the first word of God (2-12). The same formula is also applied to Zebedee's sons, who are called to drink Jesus' cup to gain the glory of the kingdom (35-40); to the son of Timaeus (46b-52), called to abandon everything, even his mantle, to follow Jesus on the path to the Passion, into the light of the *resurrection.*

Jesus will be killed and will rise

The law of the kingdom which Jesus has just expressed must now be applied: the master leads the column of his disciples towards Jerusalem. To the Twelve who, despite the «horror» provoked by the prospect of persecution, continue on the road to Jerusalem (32), he predicts all that he must suffer before reaching the «resurrection», thus going before them into «*eternal life*» (33-34).

Jesus opens the eyes of Zebedee's sons and invites them to faith

Hardly had James and John heard this prediction than, with the spontaneity of «sons of thunder»[12], they only saw the throne of promised «glory» (37); they were probably still looking for the ultimate success for their master, whom they wished to see accede to the earthly throne over the people of Israel. They had trusted in Jesus, to obtain from him the places of honor, at his right and left; they then trusted in their own strength to share their master's cup and baptism (38). Inviting them to leave their final fate in the hands of the one who grants places in his kingdom, Jesus opens their eyes and calls them to *trust in the one God.*

12 «James and John the brother of James, to whom he gave the name of Boanerges, or 'Sons of Thunder'» (Mark 3:17).

The Twelve called to be like servants

The request of Zebedee's sons unleashes the anger of the other ten (41) and Jesus has to open the eyes of all the Twelve and explain to them what the conditions of reaching the kingdom are. He invites them to abandon the wisdom of this world (42) and to follow him when he gives his life for others (45), *trusting in the one who will give them the first place and true greatness.*

Jesus opens the eyes of the son of Timaeus and recognizes his faith

At the start of the road which leads from Jericho to Jerusalem (46b), a blind man calls insistently for Jesus' «mercy» (47-48); in this man, the son of David, a king according to the heart of God, recognizes the faith in the one who alone can «save» him (52). The Pharisees' hearts were hardened, and that of the rich man remained frozen; Jesus did not succeed in changing it. The eyes of the son of Timaeus were closed, like those of Zebedee's sons, and of the ten other apostles; Jesus tries to open the eyes of the Twelve, without the reader knowing their response. The blind man, on the other hand, abandons the false security of his place at the side of the road (46c) and the mantle in which he collected the offerings which people threw to him, rose up (50) and «followed» Jesus (52). And so the sequence ends with the image of this poor man who —the antithesis of the rich man and model for the disciples— follows «the road» with Jesus (52) which, as we all know, will lead them both to Jerusalem; which will, in the end, lead those who, like the son of Timaeus, *will have trusted in Jesus and, through him, in God himself*, to resurrection

B. THE SEQUENCE IN MATTHEW 19-20

The Matthean sequence is made up of three sub-sequences. At the outsides, the two sequences which we examined in the previous chapter are very similar to those in Mark. Matthew's central sub-sequence, on the other hand, is much more developed than Mark's; Matthew here is adding a parable which is unique to his Gospel (see p. 303).

1. THE CENTRAL SUB-SEQUENCE (MATT 19:27-20:19)

This sub-sequence has five passages. The outer passages each have three verses (19:27-29 and 20:17-19); the central passage is a lengthy parable of fifteen verses (20:1-15), which is framed by two almost identical proverbs (19:30 and 20:16); see p. 301.

1.1. *The disciples' fate (Matt 19:27-29)*

COMPOSITION

. [27] *Then answering Peter said to him:*					
– «Behold,	WE	have *LEFT*	all		
+ and		have FOLLOWED	YOU;		
= WHAT		then *WILL BE*	for us?».		

. [28] *And*	*Jesus said to them:*		*«Truly I say to you,*		
+	YOU who	have FOLLOWED	ME	in the NEW BIRTH,	
: when the Son of man		*will sit*	on the ***throne***	of his glory,	
=	you also	*will sit*	on *twelve*	***thrones***	
= judging			the *twelve*	tribes of Israel.	
– [29] And WHOEVER		has *LEFT*	houses	or brothers	or sisters
			or FATHER		
			or mother	or children	or fields
+ for the sake of			MY NAME,		
= *HUNDRED TIMES MORE*		*HE WILL RECEIVE*			
= *AND ETERNAL LIFE*		HE WILL INHERIT».			

The passage has two parts: Peter's question (27) and Jesus' reply (28-29). The first part is made up of a narrative unimember (27a) and a trimember of words (27bcd) of AA'B type. In the second part, Jesus replies to Peter's question by reversing it: he begins with the *sequela* (27c.28b), and then comes to the leaving of everything (27b.29abc). He distinguishes between two groups, the Twelve («you» in 28b), and «anyone» (29a). Because they have followed Jesus (28b) the Twelve will share in their master's kingdom (28cde); the person who leaves things for Jesus' name (29a-d) will receive a double reward, «a hundred times as much» (29e) and «eternal life» (29f).

At the start of the last piece, Jesus explicates the «everything» in 27b; the list (29abc) has seven terms: things («houses» and «fields») are at the outside, «father» is in a strategic position at the center. «Father» needs to be linked to «inherit» (29f), because an inheritance is received from the father, with «new birth», for the father passes on life, and also to «son» (29c.28c).

SYNOPTIC COMPARISON (see pp. 286, 268 and 258)

Matthew adds 27f and, especially, the sharing of the kingdom with Jesus (28c-i). Luke replaces the «everything» in Matthew and Mark with «what (was) ours» (28d); he adds «woman» (29e), suppresses «fields» and his «brothers» includes the «brothers or sisters» in Matthew and Mark. «For me» in Mark 29g corresponds to «for my name» in Matthew (29f); «for the kingdom of God» in Luke (29h) corresponds to «for the Gospel» in Mark (29i). Matthew's distinction between «you» (28c) and «whoever» (29a) is unique to him. Matthew suppresses Mark's 10:30c-f; Luke only suppresses Mark's «now» (30c) and Mark Mc 10:30def.

Matt 19:27-29	Mark 10:28-30	Luke 18:28-30
27 Then answering *PETER* *SAID* ***to him***: «BEHOLD, WE HAVE LEFT ***all*** ***and*** HAVE FOLLOWED YOU. What then will be for us?».	28 *PETER* began *TO SAY* ***to him***: «BEHOLD, WE HAVE LEFT ***all*** ***and*** HAVE FOLLOWED YOU».	28 Now *SAID* *PETER*: «BEHOLD, WE, HAVING LEFT what (was) ours HAVE FOLLOWED YOU».
28 ***Now*** *Jesus* ***said to them***: «TRULY I SAY TO YOU that you who have followed me in the new birth, when the Son of Man will sit on his throne of glory, you will also sit on twelve thrones, judging the twelve tribes of Israel.	29 *Jesus* declared: «TRULY I SAY TO YOU,	29 ***Now*** he ***said to them***: «TRULY I SAY TO YOU:
29 And whoever HAS LEFT HOUSES OR BROTHERS ***or sisters*** ***or father or mother*** OR CHILDREN ***or fields*** ***for the sake of*** my name	**there is no one who** HAS LEFT HOUSES OR BROTHERS ***or sisters*** ***or father or mother*** OR CHILDREN ***or fields*** ***for the sake of*** me and **for the** gospel,	**there is no one who** HAS LEFT HOUSE or wife OR BROTHERS or parents OR CHILDREN **for the** kingdom of God,
hundred TIMES MORE WILL *RECEIVE* AND ETERNAL LIFE he will inherit».	30 **who would not** *RECEIVE* ***hundred*** TIMES MORE now **in this moment** houses and brothers and sisters and mothers and children and fields with persecutions AND **in the age that comes** ETERNAL LIFE».	30 **who would not** *RECEIVE* many TIMES MORE **in this moment** AND **in the age that comes** ETERNAL LIFE».

The composition of each passage resembles the others in that Peter's request makes up the first part, and Jesus' reply the second part. Mark's and Luke's second parts are very similar; in Matthew and in Mark they are subdivided into two pieces, but, where Matthew distinguishes the case of the «Twelve» (28) and that of «whoever» (29), Mark and Luke, who only keep the latter, subdivide it into «giving up» (Mark: 29; Luke: 29) and reward (Mark: 30; Luke: 30).

«Regeneration» or «new birth»

The word *palin-genesia* (28b) only appears here in the Gospels; it is only used one other time in the New Testament, in Titus 3:5, where it describes baptism:

> [3] There was a time when we too were ignorant, disobedient and misled and enslaved by different passions and dissipations; we lived then in wickedness and malice, hating each other and hateful ourselves. [4] But when the kindness and love of God our Savior for mankind were revealed [5] it was not because of any upright actions we had done ourselves; it was for no reason except his own faithful love that he saved us, but means of the *cleansing water of rebirth* and renewal in the Holy Spirit [6] which he has so generously poured over us through Jesus Christ our Savior, [7] so that, justified by his grace, we should become heirs in hope of eternal life [NJB].

Many English translations translate *palin-genesia* in Matthew and Titus as «regeneration». Modern commentaries interpret this word of Mark as the regeneration of the cosmos after its destruction at the end of the world[13], but literally this word means «new genesis», «new birth».

In addition to the lexicographical problem, that is, determining the meaning of the word, there is a grammatical problem. «In the *palingenesia*» is generally considered to be the temporal object of the verb «you will sit», which is then amplified by the temporal clause, «when the Son of man will sit on the throne of his glory»[14]. It is, however, possible to analyze this syntagma as an adverbial phrase attached to the preceding verb: «you who have followed me in the new birth, when...»[15]. This is how Hilary of Poitiers understood it in the fourth century[16]:

13 For example, see Hagner II, 565. See too SIM D.C., «The Meaning of paliggenesi,a in Matthew 19:28»; he begins his article, «The text of Matthew 19:28 reads: Truly I say to you, in the re-creation (paliggenesi,a), when the Son of Man shall sit...»; but in fact Matthew's text is quite different!

14 And all the translations and commentaries we have consulted.

15 The verb *akolouthein* can govern an object introduced by the preposition *en*, for example, at the end of the account of the healing of the blind man Bartimaeus at Mark 10:52, which completes the Markan sequence: «and he followed him on the way».

16 *Sur Matthieu*, II, 105-106. In the same line see ORIGEN, *On Matthew*, cap. XV, 23; Origen distinguishes two phases in the rebirth: «In *regeneration by bathing* we were therefore buried with Christ: *In baptism we were buried with Christ* (as the Apostle says). In regeneration by bathing in the fire and the Holy Spirit, on the other hand, we will be made like the *glorious body* of Christ, which sits on the *throne of his glory*, and we will be seated on twelve thrones, if we will have left *everything* [...] to *follow* Christ (244-245).

You who have followed me in the rebirth, you will judge the twelve tribes of Israel. They followed him in rebirth, in baptismal purification, in sanctification through faith, in the adoption of inheritance, in the resurrection of the dead. This is the rebirth which the apostles followed, which the Law was not able to give, which, at the time of the judgment of the twelve tribes of Israel brought them together on the twelve thrones, so that they would reach the glory of the twelve patriarchs. To all the others who followed them in scorning this world, he promises the abundance of a hundred-fold reward.

This is the new birth which Jesus talked about with Nicodemus: «Truly I say to you, no one can see the Kingdom of God without being born from above» (John 3:3). We know that the adverb *anōthen* has a double meaning: «from on high» or «again». New life is the life which man receives from God.

INTERPRETATION

Peter's request is direct: he addresses Jesus directly, without the slightest explanation. They have left «everything» and have followed «him». Jesus will tell him what the reward of the Twelve and of all disciples will be, but first of all he will indicate what «following him» means, then he will explain what is included in «everything».

«You have left everything»

Peter does not give a detailed list of what has been left behind; he simply says that they have left «everything» (27b); or, better, we can understand that what they have left was «everything» for them. We know that, when Jesus had called him, with his brother Andrew, to follow him, they had «left the nets» (Matt 4:19) and that soon afterwards, the two brothers James and John had left «the boat and their father» (Matt 4:22). So they had abandoned not only their property and their livelihood as fishermen, but also their relatives. They had separated themselves from their work tools which enabled them to subsist and to feed their families. They had separated themselves from their father, from whom they had received life, and from whom they had learned the work which helped them live.

«You have followed me into the new birth»

What does it mean «to follow Jesus»? The question is certainly important, since Jesus answers it. There are so many ways of following someone, some of which are wrong, even damaging, leading to death: enough to think about the various kinds of fascism and totalitarianism[17]. For Jesus, following him means entering, like him, into «the new birth», birth from on high, that is, from God. Jesus calls himself «Son of man» (28c); everyone is born naturally as a «son of man»[18]. But the vocation of every human person is to reach true filiation, to become a child of God. To follow Jesus as the absolute end of the way could become idolatry; he is «the way» (John 14:6) who leads to the Father, his Father, and the Father of whose who follow him.

The divine inheritance

Anyone who remains simply a child of man will of course inherit his earthly father's «houses» and «fields», but his life will end in death. However, the person who is born again, from the life of his heavenly Father, will receive «a hundredfold»: in place of a house or a field, or of the members of his family, Peter and his companions will share the «throne of glory» (28c) which Jesus will receive from his Father and they will judge the whole land of Israel; «whoever» has followed them on the same path will also «inherit eternal life» (29f).

The name of Jesus

When Peter describes what they have left to follow Jesus as «everything» (27b), this means, indirectly, that Jesus had become «everything» for them, and even more, since they preferred him to everything they had previously had. One keeps one's eye on the ball. Now Jesus reveals to them what his Name is. Of course, he continues to call himself «the Son of man», but he is destined to become king, and each of them will have a share in his kingship. In Israel, the king was in fact considered to be the «son of God» (Ps 2:7). This is the ultimate identity of Jesus and of each of his disciples.

17 On this see M. BALMARY's reflections in *La Divine Origine*, 291-319.

18 In Hebrew the syntagma «son of man» is synonymous with «man» (for example, Ps 8:5: «What is man that you think of him, mortal man that you keep him in mind?»; see too Ps 80:18; 144:3).

1.2. *The parable of the workers in the vineyard (Matt 20:1-15)*

COMPOSITION

The passage is framed by two almost identical proverbs (19:30 and 20:16), whose terms «first» and «last» mirror one another.

---

30 «Many FIRST will be *LAST* and the *LAST* FIRST!

+ 1 For it is similar the kingdom of heavens to a man, MASTER OF THE HOUSE
+ who WENT OUT *early in the morning*
. to TAKE-TO-WAGE *workers* for his vineyard.
- 2 **Agreed** with the *workers* for *A DENARIUS* a *DAY*,
: **he sent them in his vineyard.**

+ 3 And, GOING OUT *about the third hour*,
. he saw OTHERS STANDING on the marketplace without *work*.
: 4 He said to them: **"Go also you in my vineyard;**
- and what is **JUST** I will **GIVE** you". And they went away.

+ 5 Again GOING OUT *about the sixth* then *about the ninth hour*,
: he did the same.

= 6 And *about the eleventh hour* GOING OUT,
. he found OTHERS STANDING around.
- He says to them: "Why are you standing here all the *DAY* without *work*?».
- 7 They say to him: "Because no one TOOK-TO-WAGE us".
: He said to them: **"Go also you in my vineyard".**

8 Evening came,
the LORD OF THE VINEYARD says
to his steward:
"Call the *workers* and **GIVE** them the WAGE,
Beginning from the *LAST* up to the FIRST".

= 9 *And, having come* those of the *eleventh* hour, RECEIVED *each one A DENARIUS.*
+ 10 *And, having come* those FIRST, they thought that they would RECEIVE more;
AND RECEIVED *each one A DENARIUS* even them.

– 11 But HAVING RECEIVED IT, they were murmuring against the MASTER OF THE HOUSE saying:
. 12 "These *LAST* **only one hour** *they did*
. and equal to us for them *you did*,
. we who bore **the burden of the *DAY* and the heat".**

– 13 But he, answering one of them, said:
- "Friend, I am not being **UNJUST** with you;
- not for *A DENARIUS* **did you agree** with me?
- 14 **TAKE** what is yours and go away.
: I wish to this *LAST* **TO GIVE** as much as to you.
: 15 Is it not permitted for me *to do* what I wish with my own?
: Or is your eye evil because I am good?".

16 So the *LAST* will be FIRST and the FIRST *LAST*!».

---

30 «Many FIRST will be *LAST* and the *LAST* FIRST!

+ 1 For it is similar the kingdom of heavens to a man, MASTER OF THE HOUSE
+ who WENT OUT early in the morning

. to TAKE-TO-WAGE *workers* for his vineyard.
- 2 **Agreed** with the *workers* for *A DENARIUS* a *DAY*,
: **he sent them in his vineyard.**

+ 3 And, GOING OUT about the third hour,
. he saw OTHERS STANDING on the marketplace without *work*.
: 4 He said to them: **"Go also you in my vineyard;**
- and what is JUST I will **GIVE** you". And they went away.

+ 5 Again GOING OUT about the sixth then about the ninth hour,
: he did the same.

= 6 And about the eleventh hour GOING OUT,
. he found OTHERS STANDING around.

- He says to them: "Why are you standing here all the *DAY* without *work*?».
- 7 They say to him: "Because no one TOOK-TO-WAGE us".
: He said to them: **"Go also you in my vineyard".**

8 Evening came,
the LORD OF THE VINEYARD says
to his steward:

"Call the *workers* and **GIVE** them the WAGE,
Beginning from the *LAST* up to the FIRST".

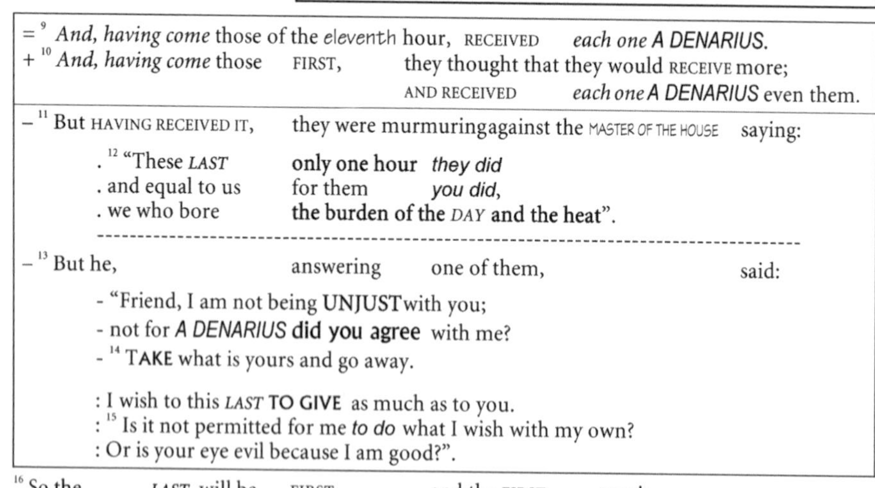

= 9 *And, having come* those of the eleventh hour, RECEIVED *each one A DENARIUS.*
+ 10 *And, having come* those FIRST, they thought that they would RECEIVE more;
AND RECEIVED *each one A DENARIUS* even them.

– 11 But HAVING RECEIVED IT, they were murmuringagainst the MASTER OF THE HOUSE saying:

. 12 "These *LAST* **only one hour** *they did*
. and equal to us for them *you did*,
. we who bore **the burden of the** *DAY* **and the heat".**

– 13 But he, answering one of them, said:

- "Friend, I am not being **UNJUST**with you;
- not for *A DENARIUS* **did you agree** with me?
- 14 **TAKE** what is yours and go away.

: I wish to this *LAST* **TO GIVE** as much as to you.
: 15 Is it not permitted for me *to do* what I wish with my own?
: Or is your eye evil because I am good?".

16 So the *LAST* will be FIRST and the FIRST *LAST*!».

The parable has three parts. The first part (20:1-7) narrates what happened during «the day»[19]. The first three pieces (1-2; 3-4 and 5) can be regrouped into one sub-part which is distinguished from the second (6-7): in fact, with the first group, the landowner agrees payment («one denarius») as he does with the second group («a fair wage») and even with those at the sixth and ninth hours («he did the same»); he does not mention a wage, however, to those at the eleventh hour.—The last part (9-15) is organized into two sub-parts. The two segments of the first sub-part (9-10), narrative, parallel the first and the last groups. The second sub-part (11-15) reports the dialogue between the first group (11-12) and the landowner (13-15); the two pieces are introduced by two phrases of parallel narrative (11; 13a).

In the center (8) is the order given by the landowner to his bailiff: the first member echoes «master of the house» at the start of the first sub-part of the first part (1a) and at the start of the second sub-part of the last part (11); the second member repeats three words of the previous part («workers» as in 1c.2a; «give» as in 4b; «wage» from the same root as «take for wage» in 1c.7a); «last» and «first» are repeated in the next part («first» in 10a, «last» in 12a and 14b)[20]. This concentration of lexical repetitions in the center is very common in biblical texts.

Note certain lexical repetitions between the first and last parts: «eleventh» (6a; 9), «agree(d)» (2a; 13c), «a denarius» (2a; 9.10b.13c), «give» (4b; 14b), «day» (2a.6c; 12c), «master of the house» (1a; 11) and, in particular, the opposition between «just» (4b) and «unjust» (13b).

BIBLICAL CONTEXT

The wage to be paid each day

In Deut 24:14-15 (see too Lev 19:13), the wage of the poor hired servant is to be paid punctually:

19 «Day» has two meanings: 1) the nictemeral period, that is, the whole of «a day and a night»; 2) the time of light (as opposed to «the night»). In the modern world, the day is divided into 24 hours. In the Hebrew world, «the day» as opposed to «the night», was divided into twelve hours; the diurnal hours were only 60 minutes at the equinox, when the time of light is equal to the night (21 March and 23 September); the hours were longer in summer, shorter in winter. The translation of the «third hour» by «nine a.m.», of the «sixth» by «midday», the «ninth» by «3 p.m.» is thus entirely approximate—this would only be the case at the equinox. «At dawn» means before the first hour; «the evening» means the time which followed the twelfth hour, that is, the end of the «day». If one wished to translate with our hours, we would have to explain that the workers at 5 p.m. were taken on only an hour before the end of the working day.

20 They also appear twice in the proverbs which frame the parable (19:30 and 20:16), which are considered to be passages in their own right.

[14] You are not to exploit the hired servant who is poor and destitute, whether he is one of your brothers or a stranger who lives in your towns. [15] You must pay him his wage each day, not allowing the sun to set before you do, for he is poor and is anxious for it; otherwise he may appeal to Yhwh against you, and it would be a sin for you.

«Give us today our daily bread»

«A denarius» was the wage for a day's work; it was also what was needed for a worker's daily subsistence. The landowner, the king of heaven, is thus giving each man his daily bread, without taking his worthiness into account, as the father of a family gives each of his children the food they need.

The Gentiles come before the Jews

Just as the freedom of divine election had already led the younger Jacob to take precedence over the elder Esau, God is free in his gifts and is not unjust when he justifies the pagans who come before the children of Israel: they, in fact, count on their own works rather than come to God only through faith (see Rom 9-10).

Admiration for the landowner's goodness (part one)

The reader cannot but be impressed by the care with which the landowner goes about seeking workers for his vineyard (1-7). It is not enough that he hires those whom he needs from among those waiting in the square early in the morning (1-2); he comes out four more times, every three hours, to invite the others, who had remained «without work» to work (3b.6c); and does so right up until the eleventh hour (6), when the day is almost over. If he had not hired this last group, they would have remained in the square «for the whole day» and would not have had anything to feed their family with. It seems obvious that he does not act in his own interest, but in the interest of the workers who move him, as though he were more interested in the workers than in his vineyard. The reader can guess that the vineyard in fact represents the workers themselves.

Irritation with the master's injustice

However, the reader's admiration is soon completely overturned. Who would expect that the payment of wages would begin with the last to arrive (8)? The first, who have «done a heavy day's work in the heat» (12c), are obviously anxious to return to their homes; now they have to wait, and to accept that the others go before them! This is already an injustice. The reader then shares the anger of those who have tired themselves out for twelve long hours and who see themselves paid the same salary as those who have only worked for one short hour (9-10). Their reaction (12) is not only understandable, but completely justified. But it is not over yet. The landowner's reply is not really convincing, at least, not for the modern reader. It is true that he has respected the initial contract—the first group receives the money agreed in the contract (2a) and in this sense the landowner «is not unjust» (13b). But when he sends away the worker unceremoniously, «Take your wage and go» (14a), and adds that he has the right to do what he wants to with what is his (15a), this is what seems to be the height of injustice and scorn.

The evil eye of jealousy

Only the landowner's final question, «Or is your eye evil because I am good?» (15b) enables us to understand where the problem is, where the injustice is hidden. The evil is in the eye of the first group, the eldest—it is jealousy towards the youngest, the last group. It is Cain's jealousy of Abel, Jacob's sons' jealousy of Joseph. The jealous person is blind to the good he has received, seeing only what the other has, and considering it to be something which has been taken from him. Rather than rejoicing that the other has received the denarius which will enable him to live like he does, he wishes to deprive him of the gift which he has received, thus preventing him from living. Cain kills his brother (Gen 4) and, while Joseph escapes death he is sold, and his brothers tell their father that a wild animal killed him (Gen 37). They are not lying—the wild animal is their jealousy, like Cain's. In denying the gift they deny the donor. The workers from the first hour do not want to acknowledge that having been hired was a gift. Of course they have worked for twelve hours, but only thanks to the landowner's invitation. The work which we do is a gift; like life itself, given by the Father, without any merit on the part of the person who receives it.

Healing

The landowner does not address all the workers from the first hour, but only «one of them». In this way, each scandalized reader can better recognize himself in the mirror held out to him, as though he was called to reply in the first person to the final question, to open his eyes to his own wrong-doing[21], and, in partic-

21 The primary meaning of *ponēros*, translated as «evil», is «sick».

ular, to the goodness of the One who cares for the life of al his children. Jesus gives the man in the parable the title of the «master of the house» (*oiko-despotēs*); this is certainly not the «despot» the hasty reader might be tempted to think, the one who does whatever he pleases, but a «master of the house», the head of a family, a father who feeds all his children, the Lord, the king of heaven, good, and fair:

9 *Good* is Lord to all,	and his tenderness for all his creatures.
10 All your works praise you, Lord	and your faithful bless you.
11 They tell the glory of *your kingdom*	and speak of your power,
12 to manifest to men your mighty deeds	and glorious splendor of *your kingdom.*
13 *Your kingdom* is a kingdom of all ages,	your dominion for every generation.
15 *The eyes of all look to you in hope*	*and you provide them food in its season.*
16 *You open your hand*	*and satisfy the hunger of all living thing.*
17 *Just* is the Lord in all his ways,	holy in all his works (Ps 145).

1.3. *The fate of the son of man (Matt 20:17-19)*

COMPOSITION

+ 17 And Jesus GOING UP	TO JERUSALEM,	
. took aside the Twelve	by themselves	
. and on the way	he said to them:	

+ 18 «Behold we are GOING UP	TO JERUSALEM	
– and the Son of man	**will be delivered**	to the high priests and scribes,
: and they will condemn	him	*to death*
– 19 and **they will deliver**	him	to the gentiles
: to be mocked	and flogged	*and crucified;*
= but the third	day	*he will rise».*

The two parts are marked by very similar initial terms (17a.18a) with different subjects, first of all «Jesus» alone, then a second person plural which associates the Twelve with Jesus' going up to Jerusalem.

The second part parallels the leaders of the Jewish people, the «high priests and scribes», two of the groups which made up the Sanhedrin (the elders are missing), and the Gentiles: the responsibility for Jesus' «death» (18c) is attributed to the Jews just as much as to the Gentiles who will carry out the sentence «by crucifying him» (19b). Everything leads to the resurrection (19c).

SYNOPTIC COMPARISON *(see pp. 296 and 271)*

Matt 20:17-19	Mark 10:32-34
[17] NOW being on the point of GOING UP *JESUS* *TO JERUSALEM*,	[32] NOW they were *ON THE WAY* GOING UP *TO JERUSALEM* ***and* JESUS *was preceding them.*** ***And they were amazed;*** ***and those who followed were frightened.***
HE TOOK ASIDE **by themselves** THE TWELVE [disciples] **and** *ON THE WAY* HE SAID TO THEM:	***And*** TAKING ASIDE ***again*** THE TWELVE, ***he began to*** SAY TO THEM ***what was about to happen to him that***
[18] «BEHOLD WE ARE GOING UP TO JERUSALEM AND THE SON OF MAN WILL BE DELIVERED TO THE HIGH PRIESTS AND SCRIBES AND THEY WILL CONDEMN HIM [TO DEATH]; [19] AND THEY WILL DELIVER HIM TO NATIONS to BE MOCKED AND BE FLOGGED AND be crucified AND THE THIRD DAY HE WILL RISE».	[33] «BEHOLD WE ARE GOING UP TO JERUSALEM AND THE SON OF MAN WILL BE DELIVERED TO THE HIGHT PRIESTS AND ***to the*** SCRIBES AND THEY WILL CONDEMN HIM TO DEATH AND THEY WILL DELIVER HIM TO NATIONS; [34] and THEY WILL MOCK ***him*** ***and they will spit on him*** AND THEY WILL FLOG ***him*** AND they will kill, AND AFTER THREE DAYS HE WILL RISE».

The accounts of the prediction of the Passion and resurrection are very similar, particularly at the start (Matt: 18-19a; Mark: 33). However, with the use of «for» (Matt: 19b) rather than Mark's simple coordination (34a), Matthew organizes the two stages of the trial in a different way. The fact that Jesus is delivered up to the Gentiles is linked to what follows (19), while in Mark it concludes what has preceded it (33b-e). Matthew adds the detail that Jesus will be «crucified» (19d) rather than Mark's simple «they will kill» (34d); Mark adds spitting (34b); finally, in the final members, the temporal object is slightly different (Matt: 19e; Mark: 34e).

At the start of the passages, the differences are more marked. In Matthew the narrative introduction is made up of a single phrase which is the first part (17). In Mark, on the other hand, the division is different: the second part, in which Jesus predicts his Passion and resurrection (33-34) is linked by «behold» in the narrative segment which directly introduces it (32fgh); this second part thus responds to the «amazement» and «fear» in the first part, which are unique to Mark. In describing the apprehension of those who accompany Jesus, Mark's account is more dramatic; Matthew's, on the other hand, as usual, is more hieratic.

BIBLICAL CONTEXT

«He will be delivered»

In 18b, Matthew uses a passive and thus does not say by whom Jesus «will be delivered» to the high priests and scribes; however, the reader already knows, from the election of the Twelve (Matt 10:1-4), that it will be Judas Iscariot, «one of the Twelve» (Matt 26:14.47).

Paul uses the same verb to say that Jesus delivered himself up: «The life I now live in this body I live in faith: faith in the Son of God who loved me and who *sacrificed himself* for my sake» (Gal 2:20; see too Eph 5:2.25). In Rom 8:32 God is the subject of the verb: «He who did not spare his own Son, but *handed him over* for us all, how will he not also give us everything else along with him?». The first Passover sequence (26:1-56) of course presents Judas as the one who «hands over» Jesus (15-16.20-25.47-56); but at the center of the sequence, it is Jesus who delivers himself up when he «gives» the cup of his blood (27) and when, in the prayer at Gethsemane, he agrees to drink the cup of the Passion and death, because this is the will of the Father.

«High priests and scribes»

These are two of the groups which made up the Sanhedrin[22]. The elders are not mentioned in this passage, but they were mentioned, along with the high priests and scribes, at the time of the first prediction of the Passion and resurrection (Matt 16:21) and they are also mentioned under the cross, when they mock Jesus (Matt 27:41).

The two phases of Jesus' trial

In Matthew, Jesus' trial has two phases, the Jewish and the Roman phases[23]. These two phases are predicted in this passage of the third prediction of the Passion and resurrection (18bc and 19ab). We find the same two phrases in the parallel passage in Mark. However, in his account of the Passion, Jesus' trial takes place in three phases —the scene of Peter's denial is not, as it is in Matthew, in the Jewish phase of the trial, but is an intermediary phase, between the Jewish and Roman phases[24]. For Matthew, the evangelist to the Jewish-Christian com-

22 For example, see LÉON-DUFOUR X., *Dictionary of the New Testament*, 228-229.363; see too *Lire la Bible*, 47.

23 See *Jésus passe*, 200-201.

24 See *Jésus passe*, 230-232.

munities in the Middle East, the world was divided into two —Jews and Gentiles; for Mark, on the other hand, whom tradition places in Rome, in a community made up of Christians of Jewish and of Gentile origin, the world seems to be organized into three groups: Jews, pagans and Christians. Matthew's point of view resembles that of the ancient prophets —while the Gentiles' sin is serious, the Jews' sin is greater still. The same development is found in Mark, but this time in three terms: while the Romans are responsible for Jesus' death, the Jews' sin is greater, but the Christians, represented by their leader, Peter, cannot claim to accuse others, for the person they have betrayed is not anyone, but their own master[25].

«The third day»

This is traditionally the day of salvation (see p. 272).

INTERPRETATION

The invitation to the Twelve

Unlike in Mark, Matthew begins by saying that Jesus is going up to Jerusalem (17a) as though he was going towards his Passion alone. However, he quickly adds that he «took the Twelve to one side», which suggests that the others were going up to the holy city with him. It seems that then, very discreetly, Jesus wished to share with the small group of the Twelve what he was preparing to accomplish: «Behold, we are going up to Jerusalem». This first person plural is inclusive and resounds like an invitation to follow him on the road which leads him to his Passion and to his resurrection.

Jesus «will be delivered up»

The first thing which Jesus announces is that he «will be delivered up to the high priests and scribes» (18b). Of course Jesus does not speak the name of the one who will «deliver» him to the Jewish authorities; but the reader has known for a long time that it would be «one of the Twelve» who would betray him, one of those whom Jesus takes to one side and to whom he predicts his Passion. We do not know whether Judas had already thought about betraying his master. The reader notes a little further on that, although only one of them delivered Jesus up in exchange for money, they all abandoned him. It is, of course, up to him to

25 See *Jésus passe*, 268-270.

find his own place in this story which is not only in the past—is he on the side of the disciples, who betray, or on the side of Jesus and God.

An encouragement for everyone

The pericope is often called the «Third prophecy of the Passion»[26]. One commentator calls it: «Third Prediction of Jesus' Suffering and Death»[27]. One can of course understand that the title should be brief; but the risk is that the text is betrayed. Jesus does not limit himself to announcing his Passion and death. The events of Easter lead to the resurrection (19c), which should be a decisive encouragement for the Twelve, and for every reader.

1.4. *The Sub-Sequence as a whole (Matt 19:27-20:19)*

COMPOSITION

The outer passages

These passages (19:27-29; 20:17-19) match. Note, first of all, some lexical repetitions: «Behold, we» which Peter's (19:27b) and Jesus' (20:18a) words begin with[28], «the Son of man» (19:28b. 20:18a), «twelve» (19:28c; 20:17), the verbs «judging» (19:28c) and «will condemn» (20:18c), which have the same root (*krinō* and *katakrinō*). The two passages end with a similar prediction, «will inherit eternal life» (19:29c) and «will rise on the third day» (20:19bc) which act as final terms. The two occurrences of «to follow» (19:27b.28a) match the two occurrences of «to go up» (20:17.18a), since the Twelve are following Jesus as he goes up to Jerusalem.

The two proverbs

The proverb in 20:16 is the end of the parable: the «so» which it begins clearly indicates this. The proverb in 19:30 is usually considered to be the conclusion of the first passage (this is how the traditional chapter division interpreted it); however, the «now» (*gar*) with which the parable begins (20:1) indicates that the parable is an illustration of the proverb. The two proverbs can thus be considered to be passages in themselves, which ensure the transition between the three other passages. They are the hinges which join the three panels of this triptych together[29].

26 See the JB; Gnilka II, 274. The French 1997 edition of the BJ has «Third prediction of the death and resurrection».

27 Hagner, II, 573.

28 The first time the pronoun *hēmeis* is used; the second time, however, this pronoun is not used but the verb «we go up» is in the first person plural, as is «have left».

29 Luke 6:27-38 is a further case of a triptych composition joined with two formulas (see *Luc*, 288).

Across the whole Sub-Sequence

[27] Then answering Peter said to him:
«**Behold,** *WE* have left all and have *followed* you; what then WILL BE for us?». [28] And
Jesus said to them: «Truly I say to you, you who have *followed* me in the new birth,
when THE SON OF MAN will sit on the *THRONE* of his glory, you also will sit on
TWELVE *THRONES* ***judging*** the twelve tribes of Israel. [29] And whoever has left houses,
or brothers or sisters, or father or mother or children, or fields for the sake of my
name, will RECEIVE hundred times more and he will inherit eternal life.

[30] Many FIRST will be *LAST*
and the *LAST* FIRST!

20: [1] For the *KINGDOM* of Heavens is similar to a man, a master of house, who
went out early in the morning to hire workers for his vineyard. [2] Agreed with the
workers for a denarius a day, he sent them in his vineyard. [3] And, going out about
nine o'clock, he saw others standing on the marketplace without work [4] and he
said to them: «*Go* you also in my vineyard, and what is just I will give you». And
they went away. [5] Again going out about noon and about three o'clock, he did the
same. [6] And going out about five o'clock, he found others standing around and
he says to them: «Why are you standing here all the day without work?». [7] They
say to him: «Because no one hired us». He said to them: «*Go* you also in my
vineyard».

[8] Evening came, the Lord of the vineyard says to his steward:
«Call the workers and GIVE them the wage,
Beginning from the *LAST* up to the FIRST».

[9] And when those of the five o'clock came, each one RECEIVED a denarius. [10] And
when those first came, they thought that they would RECEIVE more; but each one
RECEIVED a denarius even them. [11] But while RECEIVING it, they murmured against
the master of the house, saying: [12] «These last only one hour they did and for
them you did equal to us, we who bore the burden of the day and the heat!» [13] But
he, answering one of them, said: «Friend, I am not being unjust with you; did not
for a denarius you agree with me? [14] Take what is yours and go away. I wish to
give this last also as much as to you; [15] is it not possible for me to do what I wish
with my own, or is your eye evil because I am good?».

[16] So the *LAST* will be FIRST
and the FIRST *LAST*!».

[17] And Jesus *going up* to Jerusalem, took aside the **TWELVE** by themselves and on the
way he said to them:
[18] «**Behold,** *WE are going up* to Jerusalem and THE SON OF MAN will be delivered
to the high priests and scribes, and they ***will condemn*** him to death; [19] and they will
deliver him to the pagans to be mocked and flogged and crucified but the third day
he will rise».

«Throne» in the first passage (28b.28c) belongs to the same semantic field as «kingdom» at the start of the parable (20:1); «to receive» in 19:29c (which matches «will be» in 27b) is repeated four times in the second part of the parable (20:9-11).

The two instances of «go» to the vineyard (20:4a.7b) match the two instances of «follow» in the first passage (19:27b.28a) and of «go up» in the last passage (20:17.18a).

The opposition between «the first» and «the last» expressed at the center of the parable (20:8c) and in the two proverbs which frame the parable (19:30 and 20:16) are reflected in the outer passages. In the first passage, Jesus states, in reply to Peter's question, that, from the last that they are because they have left everything to follow him, they will become the first, seated on twelve thrones and inheritors of eternal life; in the last passage Jesus predicts his Passion, when he will be last, and his resurrection, when he will become the first.

SYNOPTIC COMPARISON

Matthew's sub-sequence has five passages, while Mark's only has three. In fact, Mark's central proverb (31) is doubled by Matthew: its first occurrence, after the first passage (19:30) corresponds to a second occurrence before the last passage (20:16). The two proverbs in Matthew are in mirror image framing the central parable (20:1-15) which is unique to the first Gospel.

The parable is a parable about «the kingdom of Heaven» (20:1); this theme has already appeared in the first passage with the «thrones» on which the Son of Man and the Twelve «will sit» (19:28); the theme of the kingdom is absent from Mark. The end of Peter's petition (Matt: 27c; absent from Mark) raises the question of the wages of the *sequela*; the central problem of the central parable is the «denarius». What is more, the distinction which Matthew makes in the first passage between «the Twelve» (28) and «whoever» (29), also unique to Matthew, is repeated in the central parable between the workers of the first hour, as are the Twelve, and those who have come or will come after them, that is, «the last».

Matt 19:27–20:19	Mark 10:28-34
27 Then answering Peter said to him: «Behold, we have left all and followed you; **what then will be for us?».** 28 And Jesus said to them: «Truly I say to you, **that you who have followed me in the rebirth, when** **the Son of man *WILL SIT* on the *THRONE* of his glory,** **you also *WILL SIT* on twelve *THRONES*, judging the** **twelve tribes of Israel**. 29 And whoever has left houses, or brothers or sisters, or father or mother or children, or fields for the sake of my name, will receive a hundred times more and will inherit eternal life.	28 Peter began to say to him: «Behold, we have left all and followed you!». 29 Jesus declared: «Truly I say to you: there is no one who has left house or brothers or sisters or mother or father or children or fields, for me and for the Gospel, 30 who would not receive a hundred times more, now in this present time, houses and brothers and sisters and mother and children and fields with persecution, and in the ages to come eternal life.
30 Many of the first will be last and (the) last first!	31 Many of the first will be last And ***the*** last first».
20: 1 **The *KINGDOM* of Heavens is like a master of house** **who went out early in the morning to hire workers for his** **vineyard.** 2 **Agreed with the workers for denarius a day, he** **sent them in his vineyard.** 3 **And, going out about nine** **o'clock, he saw others standing on the marketplace** **without work** 4 **and he said to them: "Go you also in my** **vineyard; and what is just I will give you". And they went** **away.** 5 **Going out again about noon then about three** **o'clock he did the same.** 6 **Going out about five o'clock he** **found others standing around and he says to them: "Why** **are you standing here all the day without work?".** 7 **They** **say to him: "Because no one hired us". He says to them:** **«Go you also in my vineyard».** 8 **In the evening, the Lord** **of the vineyard says to his steward: "Call the workers and** **give them the wage, beginning from the last up to the** **first".** 9 **Coming, those of the five o'clock received a** **denarius each.** 10 **Coming, those first thought that they** **would receive more, but they also received a denarius** **each.** 11 **And on receiving it, they murmured against the** **master of the house saying:** 12 **"These last did only one** **hour but you did for them like us who bore the burden of** **the day and the heat!".** 13 **But he, answering one of them,** **said: "Friend, I am not being unjust with you; did you not** **agree with me for a denarius?** 14 **Take yours and go away.** **I wish to give to this last also as much as to you;** 15 **is it** **not possible for me to do what I wish with my own, or is** **your eyes evil because I am good?".**	
16 **So the last will be first** **and the first last!».**	
17 Jesus on the point of going up to Jerusalem, took aside the Twelve by themselves and on the way he said to them: 18 «Behold, we are going up to Jerusalem and the Son man will be delivered to the high priests and scribes, and they will condemn him to death; 19 and they will deliver him to the pagans to be mocked and to be flogged and to be crucified but the third day he will rise».	32 Now they were on the way, going up to Jerusalem, and Jesus was preceding them. And they were amazed; and those who followed were frightened. Taking aside again the Twelve, he began to say to them what was about to happen to him, 33 «Behold, we are going up to Jerusalem and the Son of man will be delivered to the high priests and to the scribes, and they will condemn him to death and they will deliver him to the pagans; 34 and they will mock him, spit on him, flog him and will kill him, and after three days he will rise».

INTERPRETATION

Jesus' reward

From the start, Peter's request asks a question about action and its reward, work and its wage, giving up and reward (19:27). It might be scandalous to see Peter so interested in a reward which he seems to consider to be his due. However, we should be astonished that, on the one hand, he does not do it for himself alone, but for all the others, and, most of all, that he has waited for so long to ask this question. Like his companions he had left everything and had gone to follow the master without asking what was in it for him. Jesus does not reproach him at all before answering him, which certainly indicates that the question is not inappropriate. Jesus willingly acknowledges the sacrifice that the Twelve have made, and does not refuse to describe the reward which is theirs, when they will share in the reign of the Son of man (28). He even widens the narrow circle of the Twelve to «whoever» will follow their example (29).

However, in the symmetrical passage (20:17-19), Jesus calls the disciples to take a further step, a decisive step, in fact. Of course, the Twelve have left everything to follow him: «Behold, we have left everything and followed you» (19:27b). But they have not yet fully followed the road which is to lead them to the «throne of glory» (19:28), to «eternal life» (19:29c). So Jesus invites them, discreetly, to go all the way: «Behold, we are going up to Jerusalem» (18a). He does not —yet— say that they will have to suffer and be put to death; he limits himself to predicting that he will have to suffer. The reader, however, understands that they too will be called to follow him to death. The title the JB gives to the last passage, «Third prophecy of the Passion», could be misleading. Jesus, in fact, is not only prophesying his Passion, but also his resurrection: «on the third day he will rise again» (20:19b), just as he had already announced that whoever had left everything to follow him «will inherit eternal life» (19:29c).

The Lord's denarius

The proverb which precedes the parable, «Many of the first shall be last, and the last first» (19:30), is usually considered to be the end of the first passage. It sums up the reversal of the current situation of the disciples' voluntary poverty and what they will receive in return, «thrones» of «glory» (28), «a hundred times as much» (29b) and «eternal life» (29c): they have made themselves «last», and they will become «first». However, it is only the second member of the proverb which is applied to the first passage: «the last will be first», while the parable, on the other hand, illustrates the two members: not only will the last workers to come be the first to receive the denarius, but the first group will also be paid last. The fact that the same proverb is repeated at the conclusion of the parable, but in reverse order, further emphasizes the idea of the double reversal of the situation between the first and the last.

«The kingdom of Heaven» is God's country, with its own laws, like any other country. His justice[30] is different from the justice in human kingdoms. It is the reign of goodness, as the last word of the parable says («because I am good»: 14c). The landowner does not look at the work which has been done, but at the workers' needs. He seems to be more concerned with the fate of the workers than with the fate of his vineyard—he wants everyone to have the denarius he needs so that he and his household can live. It is true that, with the first group, he agrees a contract for work which includes the precise sum of the wage; however, for the last, there is no question of this, as though it were not this, but only the work, which were important. It seems that, more than money, what really counts is the collaboration with the employer, participating in his plans. In reality, this «lord of the vineyard» (8a) is a «landowner» (1a.11a), a father of a family who treats the workers as he would his own children: he makes them all inherit life, whether they are the eldest or the youngest in the family, whether they are the children of Israel, the first to be called, or the Gentiles who arrive at the last minute; whether they are «the Twelve», the disciples called at the first hour (19:28) or «whoever» joined them later to work in the vineyard of the Lord (19:29). All will equally inherit «eternal life» (19:29c), the free gift of his goodness (20:14c).

The first group of workers did not understand that the gift was not the denarius received at the end of the day, as much as having been able to work in the vineyard: this, without any doubt, the first and greatest reward.

New birth

In predicting what he is preparing to accomplish in Jerusalem, Jesus clearly distinguishes between two times, the time of the Passion and the time of the resurrection, which will happen «on the third day» (20:18-19). When he prophesies the fate of the Twelve, he also distinguishes between the time of the *sequela* and the sacrifices, and that of the glorification, «when the Son of man will sit on his throne of his glory» (19:28). However, when he adds that this will happen to

30 «I will give you what is just» in 4 matches «I have not been unjust with you» in 13.

«anyone who has left» everything «because of his name», he does not seem to be differentiating between the past and the future; Matthew here is far from Mark's redaction, in which Jesus promises a hundred-fold for «now, in this time» and eternal life for «the world to come» (Mark 10:30). It is certainly possible to read Matthew in the light of Mark and to say that Matthew thought that it was useless to emphasize the difference between the two times, the present and the future; however, it is not impossible to interpret the reward as not being placed even partially in the future, but as being concomitant with the giving up and following it even in this world. «Eternal life» is not what comes after death, but is already present in the here and now.

In the same way, the *palingenesia* in 28, which many interpret as being the «regeneration» of the cosmos following the eschatological destruction, can also be understood as the «new birth» which all those who have left everything to follow the Lord have already entered into, who have stripped off the old man to «put on the new self that has been created in God's way, in the goodness and holiness of truth» (Eph 4:24). The new life is also new wisdom: what the central parable illustrates and the double proverb which frames it summarizes: «the last will be first and the first last».

2. THE SEQUENCE AS A WHOLE (MATTHEW 19-20)

COMPOSITION

Links between the outerSub-Sequences

- The end of the introduction matches the start of the last passage, with the repetition of an almost identical syntagma: «numerous crowds followed him» (19:2) and «a numerous crowd followed him» (20:29). Also, the sequence ends with «they followed him», still in the plural, because the subject of the verb is the two blind men who have been healed (20:34); the verb «to follow» is repeated in the third passage of the first sub-sequence (19:21), and we can also add «to come», in the center of that sub-sequence (14), because they have the same objective.
- The first passage in each sub-sequence begins with an almost identical syntagma: «And approached him» (19:3) and «Then approached to him» (20:20), which act as initial terms. The third passage in the first sub-sequence begins in an analogous way, with the same verb: «And behold someone approaching him» (19:16).
- «Father» and «mother», which are repeated together in the first and third passages of the first sub-sequence (19:5.19) are also at the outsides of the first passage of the last sub-sequence, but this time separated (20:20.23); «my Father»,

19:1 And it happened that, when Jesus had finished these words, he left from Galilee and went to the territory of Judea beyond the Jordan. 2 And **numerous crowds** FOLLOWED HIM, and he healed them there.

3 And *approached him* some Pharisees, to put him to a trial: «Is it permitted for a man to repudiate his wife for any condition?». 4 He answered: «Have you not read that the Creator, from the beginning, "*MADE* them male and female", 5 and that he said: "Therefore man will **LEAVE HIS FATHER AND HIS MOTHER** to join to his wife, and the two will be one flesh only?". 6 So they are no more two, but one flesh only. Well then! What God has joined, man must not separate it». 7 They said to him: «Why then Moses commanded to give a roll of divorce when one repudiates?». 8 He said to them: «It is because of the hardness of your hearts that Moses permitted you to repudiate your wives; but from the beginning it was not so. 9 Now I say to you: whoever repudiates his wife, except in case of immodesty and marries another, commits adultery».

10 The disciples say to him: «If this is the condition of man with respect to the wife, it is not good to marry». 11 He said to them: «Not all understand this language, but only those to whom *it is given*. 12 For there are eunuchs who are born so from the womb of their **MOTHER**, there are eunuchs who are made eunuchs by **MEN**, and there are eunuchs who are made themselves eunuchs for the sake of the KINGDOM OF HEAVENS. Who can understand, let him understand!».

13 Then children were presented to him, that he might lay the hands on them and pray; but the disciples ***rebuked them***. 14 Jesus however said: «Let the **children** and do not prevent them TO COME TO ME; for to such as these belongs the KINGDOM OF HEAVENS». 15 Then he laid his hands on them and departed from there.

16 And behold, someone, *approached him*, saying to him: «Master, what good shall I *DO* to obtain ETERNAL LIFE?». 17 He said to him: «Why do you ask me on good? One only is good. If you WANT to enter INTO THE LIFE, observe the commandments». 18 He said to him: «Which ones?». Jesus answered: «"You shall not kill, you shall not commit adultery, you shall not steal, you shall not testimony falsely", 19 "honor **YOUR FATHER AND YOUR MOTHER**, and love your neighbor as yourself"». 20 The young man said to him: «All these I have observed; of what still I lack?». 21 Jesus declared to him: «If you WANT to be perfect, go, sell what you possess and *give* it to the poor, and you will have A TREASURE IN HEAVENS; then come, FOLLOW ME». 22 Hearing this word, the young man went away afflicted, for he was having great wealth.

23 Jesus said then to his disciples: «Truly I say to you, it shall be difficult for a rich man to enter INTO THE KINGDOM OF HEAVENS. 24 Yes, I repeat to you, it is easier for a camel to pass through the eye of a needle than for a rich man to enter INTO THE KINGDOM OF GOD». 25 Hearing this, the disciples remained greatly astonished: «Who then can be saved?». They said. 26 Looking at them, Jesus said to them: «For men this is impossible, but for God all is possible».

[...]

20: 20 Then *approached to him* **THE MOTHER** of the sons of Zebedee, with her sons, and she prostrated before him and asking something. 21 «What do you WANT?», he said. She said to him: «Say that these my two sons may sit, one at your right and one at you left, in YOUR KINGDOM». 22 Jesus answered: «You do not know what you ask. Can you drink of the cup that I am about to drink?». They said to him: «We can». 23 He said to them: «My cup you shall drink of; but to sit at my right or at my left, is not mine to *give*, but it is for those to whom it has been prepared by **MY FATHER**».

24 The other ten, having heard, were indignant at the two brothers. 25 Having called them to him, Jesus said: «You know that the rulers of the nations exercise lordship over them and the great ones exercise power over them. 26 It shall not to be so among you: in the contrary, who WANTS to become great among you, shall be your **servant**, 27 and who WANTS to be the first among you, shall be your **slave**. 28 As the Son of man did not come to be served, but to serve and to *give* HIS LIFE a ransom for many».

29 And while they were leaving from Jericho, **a numerous crowd** FOLLOWED HIM. 30 And behold two blind men were seated along the way; when they heard that Jesus was passing by, they cried out: «Have mercy on us, Lord, SON OF DAVID!». 31 The crowd ***rebuked them*** so that they would be silent; but the more they cried out, saying: Have mercy on us, Lord, SON OF DAVID!». 32 Jesus, stopping, called them and said: «What DO YOU WANT that *I DO* for you?». They said to him: 33 «Lord, that our eyes may be opened!». 34 Moved with pity, Jesus touched their eyes and immediately they regained the sight. And they FOLLOWED HIM.

that is, God, is, to some extent, opposed to the «mother» of Zebedee's sons; note, too, that «mother» also appears paralleled to «men» in 19:12.

- The verb «to want», which occurrences mark each of the three passages of the last sub-sequence (20:21.26.27.32), appears twice in the last passage of the first sub-sequence: «If you want to enter into the life» (19:17) and «If you want to be perfect» (19:21).
- The verb «to give» appears twice in the first sub-sequence (19:11.21) and twice in the last sub-sequence (20:23.28).
- «Kingdom of Heavens» or «of God» often reappears in the first sub-sequence (19:12.14.23.24), and is matched at the start of the last sub-sequence by «your reign» (20:21); we should also add the royal title given to Jesus by the two blind men, «son of David» (20:30.31); this reign is in opposition to the reign of the «leaders of the nations» and the «great ones» (20:25).
- In the first sub-sequence, «eternal life» (19:16), an equivalent to «kingdom of heaven», is repeated in 17 with «in the life», and then with «treasure in heaven» in 21; in the last sub-sequence, at the end of the central passage, the Son of man is to «give his life» (20:28).
- The central passage of the last sub-sequence seems to shed light upon the meaning of «children» in the central passage of the first sub-sequence (19:14), with «servant» and «slave» (20:26.27); only those who will be like children will enter into the kingdom of heaven, and only those who make themselves servants and slaves will be able to become great and first.
- «To do» appears once in each sub-sequence (19:16; 20:32).

Links between the central and first Sub-Sequences (Matt 19-20)

- «The kingdom of heavens», which appears three times in the first sub-sequence (19:12.14.23; and we should add «kingdom of God» in 24 and also «treasure in Heavens» in 21) appears at the start of the central parable of the central sub-sequence (20:1; we should also add the two occurrences of «throne(s)» in 28 which belong to the same semantic field).
- «Eternal life» in 19:16 (repeated by «life» in 17) is also in 19:29b in the second sub-sequence; the last words, «will rise again» in 20:19, match this.
- The two occurrences of the couplet «father» and «mother» in 19:5 and 19 (repeated in 12 with «mother» and «men») also appear in 19:29 in the first passage of the second sub-sequence; «new birth» in 28 also belongs to the same semantic field.

19: 1 And it happened that, when Jesus had finished these words, he left from Galilee and went to the territory
of Judea beyond the Jordan. 2 And numerous crowds FOLLOWED HIM, and he healed them there.

3 Some Pharisees approached him, to put him to a trial: «Is it permitted for a man to repudiate his wife for any
condition?». 4 He answered: «Have you not read that the Creator, from the beginning, "*MADE* them male and
female", 5 and that he said: "Therefore man *WILL LEAVE* **HIS FATHER AND HIS MOTHER** to join to his
wife, and the two will be one flesh only?". 6 So they are no more two, but one flesh only. Well then! What God
has joined, man must not separate it». 7 They said to him: «Why then Moses commanded to give a roll of
divorce when one repudiates?». 8 He said to them: It is because of the hardness of your hearts that Moses
permitted you to repudiate your wives; but from the beginning it was not so. 9 Now I say to you: whoever
repudiates his wife, except in case of immodesty, and marries another, commits adultery».

10 The disciples say to him: «If this is the condition of man with respect to the wife, it is good not to
marry». 11 He said to them: «Not all understand this language, but only those to whom *it is given*. 12 For
there are eunuchs who are born so from the womb of their **MOTHER**, and there are eunuchs who are
made eunuchs by **MEN**, and there are eunuchs who are made themselves eunuchs for the KINGDOM OF
HEAVENS. Who can understand, let him understand!».

13 Then children were presented to him, that he might lay the hands on them and pray; but the
disciples rebuked them. 14 Jesus however said: «*LEAVE* the **children** and do not prevent them TO
COME TO ME; for to such as these belongs the KINGDOM OF HEAVENS». 15 Then he laid his hands on
them and departed from there.

16 And behold someone approached him and said to him: «Master, what good shall I *DO* to HAVE *ETERNAL
LIFE*?». 17 He said to him: «Why do you ask me on good? **One only is Good**. If you want to enter *INTO THE
LIFE*, observe the commandments». 18 He asked him: «Which ones?». Jesus replied: «"You shall not kill, you
shall not commit adultery, you shall not steal, you shall not testimony falsely, 19 *HONOUR* **YOUR FATHER
AND YOUR MOTHER**", and "love your neighbor as your self"». 20 The young man said to him: «All
these, I have observed; of what still I lack?». 21 Jesus declared to him: «If you want to be perfect, go, sell what
you possess and *give*-it to the poor, and you WILL HAVE TREASURE IN HEAVENS; then come, FOLLOW ME».
22 Hearing this word, the young man went away afflicted, for he was having great wealth.

23 Jesus said then to his disciples: «Truly I say to you that it shall be difficult for a rich man to enter INTO
THE KINGDOM OF HEAVENS. 24 Yes, I repeat to you, it is easier for a camel to pass through the eye of a needle
than for a rich man to enter INTO THE KINGDOM OF GOD». 25 Hearing this, the disciples remained greatly
astonished: «Who can then be saved?». They said. 26 Looking at them, Jesus said to them: «For men this
is impossible, but for God all is possible».

27 Then, answering Peter said to him: «Behold, we have *LEFT* all and WE HAVE FOLLOWED YOU, what then WILL
BE for us?». 28 Jesus said to them: «Truly I say to you, to you who HAVE FOLLOWED ME in the *NEW BIRTH*,
when the Son of man will sit on his THRONE of glory, you also will sit on twelve THRONES, to judge the twelve
tribes of Israel. 29 And whoever has *LEFT* houses, brothers or sisters, **FATHER OR MOTHER**, children or
fields, for the sake of my name, *will receive* hundred times more and *HE WILL INHERIT ETERNAL LIFE*.

30 Many of the first will be **last**, and the **last** will be first.

20: 1 For THE KINGDOM OF HEAVENS is like a landowner who went out early in the morning to hire
workers for his vineyard. 2 Agreed with the workers for denarius a day, he sent them in his
vineyard. 3 Going out around the third hour, he saw others standing, without work, on the
marketplace, 4 and to these he said: Go, you also, to the vineyard, and I *will give* you a fair wage.
5 And they went there. Going out again around the sixth hour, then around the ninth hour, he
DID the same. 6 Around the eleventh hour, he went out again, founding others standing there he
said to them: Why are you staying here all the day without work? They say to him: 7 Because no
one hired us. He says to them: Go, you also, to the vineyard. 8 Evening came, the lord of the
vineyard says to his steward: Call the workers and *give* to each one his wage, beginning from the
last up to the first. 9 Those of the eleventh hour came then and *received* each one a denarius.
10 Those first, coming at their turn, thought that they would *receive* more; but it is a denarius that
each one *receive*, even them. 11 While *receiving* it, they murmured against the landowner: 12 These
last-comers *HAVE DONE* only one hour, and you *HAVE DONE* for them as for us, who bore the
burden of the day, with its heat. 13 But he replied, saying to one of them: My friend, I did
nothing wrong to you: have we not agreed for denarius a day? 14 Take what is yours and go
away. I wish to *give* to this **last**-comer as much as to you: 15 do I not have right *TO DO* of my
own as I wish? Or is your eye evil because **I am good**?

16 Thus, the **last** will be first, and the first will be **last**».

17 As about to go up to Jerusalem, Jesus took aside the Twelve by themselves and said to them on the way:
18 «Behold, WE ARE GOING UP to Jerusalem, and the Son of man *will be given* to the high priests and scribes;
they will condemn him to death 19 and they *will give* him to the pagans to be mocked, flogged and crucified;
and the third day, he *WILL RISE*».

• The two coordinating verbs «will inherit» and «will receive» in 19:29 are linked to «father and mother»; «to receive» is repeated four times in 20:9-11; the correlative verb «to give» reappears in 19:11.21; 20:4.8.14.18.19; «to have» is used twice in 19:16 and 21 and «to be for» once, at the start of the second sub-sequence (19:27).

• «To leave» reappears twice in the first sub-sequence (19:5.14; «honor» in 19 matches this to a certain extent) and twice in the second sub-sequence (19:27.29).

• «Last» (19:30; 20:8.12.14.16) matches «children» (19:14).

• «To do», which appears twice in the first sub-sequence (19:4.16) reappears four times in the second sub-sequence (20:5.12 -x2- and 15).

• The verb «to follow» in the introduction (19:2) is repeated in 19:21 and in 19:27.28, and to this we can add «come to me» in 19:14 and «to go up» in the last passage (20:18).

• «Good» is an attribute of God in 19:17 and of the landowner at the end of the parable in 20:15.

Links between the central and last Sub-Sequences (Matt 19-20)

• The theme of the kingdom is present in both sub-sequences, with «kingdom of Heavens» (20:1) and «in your kingdom» (20:21) and also with «the throne of your glory» and «thrones» (19:28), with «son of David» (20:30.31); in addition, Jesus is called «Lord» (20:30.31.33) like the landowner in the parable (20:8).

• The syntagma «eternal life» (19:29), which «will rise again» matches (20:19), is repeated with «give his life» in 20:28.

• The verbs «to give» and «-give» (*didōōmi* and *paradidōōmi*) recur in 20:4.8. 14.18.19.28; the verbs «to inherit» in 19:29 and «to receive» in 20:9.10 -x2- and 11 are related to them.

• The verb «to be seated» recurs twice in the first passage of the central sub-sequence (19:28 -x2-) and in the outer passages of the last sub-sequence (20:21.23 and 30).

• The four occurrences of the verb «to follow» act as outer terms (19:27.28 and 20:29.34).

• «Father» and «mother» in the first passage of the central sub-sequence (19:29) are matched by «the mother» and «my father» at the outer edges of the first passage of the last sub-sequence (20:20.23); «son» (19:28.29; 20:18.20 -x2- and 21.28. 30.31) belongs to the same semantic field, as does «new birth» in 19:28. «Son of man» recurs at the outsides of the central sub-sequence (19:28; 20:18) and in the center of the last sub-sequence (20:28).

27 Then, answering Peter said to him: «Behold, we have left all and WE HAVE FOLLOWED YOU, what then WILL BE for us?». 28 Jesus said to them: «Truly I say to you, you who HAVE FOLLOWED ME in the *NEW BIRTH*, when *the Son of man will sit* on HIS THRONE OF GLORY, you also *will sit* on twelve THRONES, to judge the twelve tribes of Israel. 29 And whoever has *LEFT* houses, brothers or sisters, FATHER OR MOTHER, CHILDREN or fields, for the sake of my name, *will receive* hundred times more and *HE WILL INHERIT ETERNAL LIFE*.

30 Many of the ***first*** will be last, and the **last** will be ***first***.

20: 1 For the KINGDOM OF HEAVENS is like a landowner who went out early in the morning to hire workers for his vineyard. 2 Agreed with the workers for denarius a day, he sent them in his vineyard. 3 Going out around the third hour, he saw others standing, without work, on the marketplace, 4 and he said to them: Go, you also, to the vineyard, and I *will give* you a just wage. 5 And they went there. Going out again around the sixth hour, then around the ninth hour, he *DID* the same. 6 About the eleventh hour, he went out again, founding others standing there and he said to hem: Why are you staying here all the day without work? They say to him: 7 Because no one hired us; he said to them: Go, you also, to the vineyard. 8 Evening came, the Lord of the vineyard says to his steward: Call the workers and *give* to each one his wage, beginning from the **last** up to the ***first***. 9 Those of the eleventh hour came then and *received* each one a denarius. 10 Those ***first***, coming at their turn, thought that they would *receive* more; but it is a denarius that each one received, even them. 11 While *receiving* it, they murmured against the landowner: 12 These last- comers *HAVE DONE* only one hour, and you *HAVE DONE* for them as for us, who bore the burden of the day, with its heat. 13 But he replied, saying to one of them: My friend, I did nothing wrong to you: have not we agreed for denarius a day? 14 Take what is yours and go away. I wish to *give* to this last-comer as much as to you: 15 do I not have right to *DO* of my own as I wish? Or is your *EYE* evil because I am good?

16 Thus, the **last** will be ***first***, and the ***first*** will be last».

17 And about to go up to Jerusalem, Jesus took aside the Twelve by themselves and said to them on the way: 18 «Behold, WE ARE GOING UP to Jerusalem, and *the Son of man will be given* to the high priests and scribes; they will condemn him to death 19 and *they will give* him to the pagans to be mocked, flogged and crucified; and the third day, he WILL RISE».

20: 20 Then approached to him THE MOTHER of the SONS of Zebedee, with HER SONS, and she prostrated to him asking some thing. 21 «What do you WANT?». He said. She said to him: «Say that these MY TWO SONS *may be seated*, one at your right and the other at your left, in YOUR KINGDOM». 22 Jesus replied: «You do not know what you ask. Can you drink of the cup that I am about to drink?». They said to him: «We can». 23 He said to them: «My cup you shall drink of; but to *be seated* at my right and at my left, it is not mine to *give*, but it is for those to whom it has been prepared by MY FATHER».

24 The other ten, having heard, were indignant at the two brothers. 25 Having called them to him, Jesus said: «You know that the rulers of the nations exercise lordship over them and the ***great ones*** exercise power over them. 26 It shall not to be so among you: on the contrary, who wants to be great among you, shall be your **servant**, 27 and who wants to be the ***first*** among you, shall be your **slave**. 28 For *the Son of man* did not come to be served, but to serve and to *give* HIS LIFE a ransom for many».

29 While they were leaving from Jericho, a numerous crowd FOLLOWED HIM. 30 And behold two blind men *were seated* along the way; when they heard that Jesus was passing by, they cried out: «Have mercy on us, Lord, SON OF DAVID!». 31 The crowd rebuked them so that they would be silent; but the more they cried out: «Have mercy on us, Lord, SON OF DAVID!». 32 Jesus, stopping, called them and said: What do you want that *I DO* for you?». They said: 33 Lord, that our *EYES* be opened! 34 Moved with pity, Jesus touched their *EYES* and immediately they regained the sight. And they FOLLOWED HIM.

- The opposition between «last» and «first» in the center of the central sub-sequence (20:8; repeated in 19:30 and 20:16) is also in the center of the last sub-sequence, between «great» and «servant» and between «first» and «slave» (20:26-27); note the six recurrences of «first» (19:30 -x2-; 20:8.10.16 -x2- and 27).

• «Eye» at the end of the parable (20:15) is repeated at the end of the last sub-sequence (20:33); a synonym (in Greek) is also used in the last verse (34). Note that only Matthew uses «eye» in his account of the blind men (see p. 85; Matt: 33-34 compared to Mark: 51-52 and Luke: 41-42).

The following schema attempts to visualize the composition of the sequence; the titles given to the different passages seek to emphasize the links which are between them.

Jesus leaves Galilee		and heals the crowds		19:1-2
Jesus reveals	to the Pharisees	the hardness of their hearts		3-9
and invites	the disciples	*to celibacy*	for the kingdom of God	10-12
The	disciples	called to be	like *children*	13-15
Jesus reveals	to a rich man	what makes him sad		16-22
And invites	the disciples	*to poverty*	for the kingdom of God	23-26

The Twelve	who left all		will receive eternal life	27-29
«Many of the first		will be last	and the *last* first»	30
THE PARABLE		OF THE LAST	AND THE FIRST	20,1-15
«So the *last*		will be first	and the first last»	16
Jesus	who will be killed		will be raised	17-19

Jesus opens the eyes And calls them	of the two sons of Zebedee	*to faith*	in the Father	20-23
The	Twelve	called to be	like *servants*	24-28
Jesus opens the eyes and recognizes	of the two blind men at Jericho	*the faith*	that saved them	29-34

SYNOPTIC COMPARISON

The three sub-sequences of Matthew and Mark have already been compared (pp. 177, 249, 302). The two sequences are very similar. The major difference is that Matthew has inserted the parable of the laborers in the vineyard in the very middle of the sequence, doubling Mark's (10:31) central proverb to frame the parable. In addition, the passage on celibacy is unique to Matthew (19:10-12).

The sequence in Mark 10:1-52

In addition, while at the start of the introduction Mark notes merely that Jesus leaves for Judea (10:1), Matthew adds that he leaves his homeland («he left Galilee»: 19:1). While at the end of the introduction Mark presents the sequence

Jesus departs towards Judea		and teaches the crowds		1
Jesus reveals	o the Pharisees	the hardness of their hearts		2-9
and invites	the disciples	*to fidelity*		10-12
The	disciples	called to be	like *children*	13-16
Jesus reveals	to a rich man	what makes him sad		17-22
and invites	the disciples	*to faith*		23-27

The Twelve	will be persecuted	and will receive eternal life	28-30
«Many of the first will be last		and the *last* first»	31
Jesus	will be killed	and will be raised	32-34

Jesus opens the eyes and invites them	of the sons of Zebedee	*to faith*		35-41
The	Twelve	called to be	like *servants*	42-46a
Jesus opens the eyes and recognizes	of the son of Timaeus	*his faith*		46b-52

as teaching (10:1), Matthew gives his sequence a different dimension, with «and he healed them there» (19:2).

INTERPRETATION

«And he healed them there»

It is surprising that, at the end of the introduction of the whole of his sequence, Matthew announces that Jesus «healed them there» (19:2). There then follow different encounters: with the Pharisees (19:3-9), with a rich young man (19:16-22), with the mother of Zebedee's sons (20:20-21), which alternate with conversations between Jesus and his disciples (19:10-12; 13-15; 23-26; 27-30; 20:17-19; 22-23; 24-28), to whom he tells a long parable (20:1-15), and the reader has to wait until the last passage to finally get an account of healing (20:29-34)! With this finale for the introduction, Matthew as it were gives a title to the sequence, a title designed to draw the reader's attention, and make them reflect. What if all eleven passages of the sequence were healings of one sort or another? We have already seen that Jesus not only opens the eyes of the blind men of Jericho (20:29-34), but also those of Zebedee's sons (20:20-23) and of the ten other apostles (24-28).

In the central sub-sequence, he pursues the same aim when he replies to Peter to say what their reward will be (19:27-29), when he predicts the fate which is awaiting him in Jerusalem (20:17-19); with the parable of the laborers in the vineyard (20:1-15), he opens their eyes to the inversion in divine wisdom and reveals to his interlocutor the illness affecting him: «or is it that your eye is evil because I am good?» (20:15).

The first word which he addresses to the Pharisees who question him about divorce again concerns eyes: «Have you not read?». (19:4). They have eyes and they cannot read. Jesus gives them a reading lesson and tries to open their eyes to the illness they are suffering from, literally «hardness of the heart» (*sklērokardia*: 19:8). Apparently, he sheds light on the sadness which overshadows the heart of the rich young man (19:22). Finally, he reveals to the disciples God's power which is at work in those who have made themselves poor (19:23-26) and eunuchs (19:10-12) for «the kingdom of Heaven» (19:17. 23-24).

From the start of the end of the sequence, Jesus offers healing to all, trying to heal them in their blindness. He only succeeds with the two blind men from Jericho. Matthew does not say whether the Pharisees were convinced by Jesus' lesson in reading; nor do we know what becomes of the rich young man, after he left with his sorrow; we do not know, either, whether the disciples understood the revelation about celibacy and poverty for the kingdom of God, whether they accepted the call to become like little children (19:14); Matthew says absolutely nothing about Peter's reaction, nor the reaction of Zebedee's two sons, nor of the other apostles on their master's teaching. It is up to the reader, like them, to make his own response to the invitation given to him.

New birth

The healing which Jesus offers to all is not limited to simply correcting sight. He does not suggest that those he is speaking to put on glasses. He opens the eyes which were shut, dead, of the two beggars in Jericho; by making them walk, as a father teaches his children (Hos 11:3), he helps them to enter into new life, makes them be born again. He offers the Pharisees a return «to the beginning», to the first chapters of Genesis; he does not only intend to heal their eyes so that they may read, he wishes to heal their hardened hearts, the source of their life. He explains to the disciples that they must become like «children» (19:14), like the new-born baby who has no wealth (23-26), and is incapable of begetting (12), defined only by being a son, who knows nothing except that for him everything is a free «gift»: «the money» which he receives like a present which the master of the house gives him and which enables him to live from day to day (20:1-15), the place in the «kingdom» which his Father «will give» him (20:23), the intelligence which will be «given» him to «understand» (19:11-12), the «eternal life» which is not won through works (19:16) but which is received as an «inheritance» (19:29). This is the «new birth» into which the disciples have entered (19:28), without even being aware of it, just as the new-born baby does not know what is happening to him and where this will lead him: «What then will there be for us?» (19:27). Jesus reveals to Peter and to the other apostles both that they will be born again when they have followed him and that the path that they have taken will bring them to «inherit eternal life» (19:29). In the same way, he invites the rich young man to «enter into life» (19:17), that is, to be born into a new life, giving up the inheritance received from his father and his mother to the poor; thus, «perfection», true «maturity» (19:21), paradoxically, consists in becoming a child again, in order to begin a new life in following Jesus. Zebedee's sons, too, have remained linked to their mother, who speaks «on their behalf». It is certainly not accidental that their proper names are not mentioned by the narrator: they are not mature, as thought they had not yet been born. By addressing himself to them, by making them speak, by allowing them to express their own wish, and even their own «power» (20:22), he brings them out of the maternal care, bringing them into the light of life. This is what he had already indicated to the Pharisees when he quoted to them the first words of the «Creator», «in the beginning»:

«This is why a man leaves his father and mother» (19:4-5). Birth is the first step on the path to being open to the other, whether that other is known as «spouse» (19:5), «neighbor» (19:19), or, particularly, «the poor» (21), the Lord Jesus, for whom one leaves everything and «follows», because he leads to a very different Other, «his Father» (20:23), to whom his prayer rises (19:13). The introduction gives the tone to the whole sequence, when it shows Jesus definitively leaving Galilee, his native land, the country of his father and mother, to return a second, and final, time the «Jordan», in whose waters he was born to new life (3:13), like all those who were baptized by John (3:5-6)[31].

«Giving life»

«Giving life» means «to bring to birth» just as much as «to die», to die one-self to be reborn into a new life, without accepting or integrating death as an essential part of one's life. Death is not only the limit which closes the final horizon of one's life, but, for humanity, it is also the limit drawn at the edge of our existence. The Son of man must «be given up» to «death» to «rise again» to new life (20:18-20); he «will give his own life in ransom for many» (20:28). In the same way, everyone is invited to get their hands on what is supposed to give life, if he wishes to gain the true life, the life which is only life if it is received from another and given to another: the rich young man must give up the wealth inherited from his parents, and make the poor his heirs in order to «enter into eternal life». The first workers are invited to give the first place to those who arrived last, and not to consider the gift received as the fruit of their own work, but as a gift from the Lord of the vineyard. The sons of Zebedee must leave the security of maternal care and leave it to someone else, the Father, to grant them their place in the kingdom. The disciples must give up not only their wealth, but also begetting in the flesh, for the kingdom of Heaven, at least, those to whom it will be given from on high. The Pharisees must give up the security of the Law and its concessions to listen to the original voice of the Creator and to rediscover the meaning of the covenant between man and woman, a symbol of the covenant with God, despite the death which represents the acceptance of the limits of the other and of oneself. Jesus' path leads him to leave the heights of Nazareth in Galilee and to go down to the Jericho, close to the Dead Sea, the lowest point of the earth, then to go back up to Jerusalem. This geographical peregrination is not only

31 The introduction to the sequence is the only passage after the baptism in which the Jordan is mentioned.

historic, but also symbolic: the «great crowd» which «follows» him (19:2), like the Twelve have «followed» him (19:27-28), like the rich young man was invited to «follow» him (19:21), all are to go down with him into the total obscurity of the pit where they will join the two blind men to receive light and to decide, with them, to «follow» him (20:34) towards Jerusalem, to the mount of Calvary and the resurrection.

Initiation

The first time I gave a course on the Synoptic Gospels, one of my African students pointed out that many of themes in this sequence are also found in traditional initiation ceremonies, like the one he had undergone in his own country[32]. One of the most important dimensions of initiation is the opening of the eyes; and, in fact, a young person who is initiated is called «four eyes». Now, as we have already seen, Jesus opens the eyes of the two blind men of Jericho at the end of the sequence; at the end of the central parable he tries to do the same with the first workers who complain to him: «Or is your eye evil because I am good?» (20:15); in the first account, he calls the Pharisees to open their eyes to read the Scriptures: «Have you not read… ?» (19:4).

Here we are not making a systematic comparison between Matthew's sequence and initiation rites, which would require skills which I do not have. We must limit ourselves to some observations which can shed light on the Gospel text, by helping us to glimpse its anthropological value.

Initiation rites always include a separation from the mother, passing through renunciation, suffering and death, in order to reach new birth[33]. Often the person being initiated is led to return to the state of being a child, even a fetus, to be able to be born again[34]. These themes are found in Matthew's sequence: leaving father and mother (19:5; 19:29; repeated, as we have seen, for James and John, whom Jesus symbolically separates from their mother, who speaks for them: 20:20-23); giving up property (19:21; 19:27.29); accepting suffering and death to rise again (20:17-19; and earlier in 19:29); becoming like children again (19:13-15).

32 I am very grateful to Ghislain TSHIKENDWA MATADI SJ, for having opened my eyes to this anthropological dimension of Matthew's sequence, and for having introduced me to NANGE KUDITA WA SESEMBA's doctoral thesis, *L'homme et la femme dans la société et la culture Cokwe*.

33 ÉLIADE M., *Rites and symbols of initiation: the mysteries of birth and rebirth*, 7-10. Note that the title of this work, written by one of the greatest scholars in this area, emphasizes the central concept of initiation.

34 ÉLIADE M., *Rites and symbols of initiation*, 30 ff.

At the point of initiation, one of the essential rites is circumcision (in some areas the removal of a tooth), and an equivalent for young women, as an obligatory step towards reaching sexual maturity and marriage. This ritual clearly has something to do with giving up, with suffering and with symbolic death. In Matthew's sequence there is no question of circumcision; however, it is not by chance that his sequence begins with a discussion on marriage, followed by a passage on those who are eunuchs for the kingdom of God. This represents a symbolic castration for the person who gives up owning the phallus, that is, all power, which is acknowledged to belong to an other, an Other; in doing this, man agrees not to be his own origin and acknowledges this in the only one who is worthy that everything should be sacrificed to him, for in Him alone is the source of eternal life. Being open to this is one of the essential components of initiation rites.

c. THE SEQUENCE IN LUKE 17:11-18:30

In Matthew and in Mark, the two passages about «the healing at Jericho» and «the call of the rich man» belong to the same sequence (Matthew 19-20; Mark 10): the first concluding the last sub-sequence, the latter being the penultimate passage of the first sub-sequence.

In Luke, on the other hand, both passages are part of a different sequence: the passage of the «call of the rich man» is integrated into an initial sequence (Luke 17:11-18:30), while the passage about the «healing at Jericho» belongs to the sequence which follows (Luke 18:31-19:46).

The first of these two sequence is the sixth in the third section of Luke's Gospel, often called «The going up to Jerusalem»[35] (see p. 405). This sequence is made up of three sub-sequences.

The central sub-sequence (18:1-14) is distinguished from the other two by the fact that it is the only one which includes two parallel parables which frame a question (18:8b).

The last sub-sequence (18:15-30) includes three passages: the central passage, «The calling of the rich man» (18:18-23) was examined in the first chapter (see pp. 146-153); the outer passages, «The kingdom of God belongs to children» (15-17) and «Eternal life as a reward for the disciples» (28-30), and the sub-sequence as a whole, were analyzed in the second chapter (see pp. 253-264). It remains, therefore, to examine the first sub-sequences, and then the sequence as a whole[36].

35 This is why this sequence is called «C6», «C» for «section C» and «6» for the «sixth» sequence.
36 This analysis repeats *Luc*, 673-706.

Not only are the two parables of the central sub-sequence (18:1-14) unique to Luke, but so too are the first two passages of the first sub-sequence («The cleansing of ten lepers»: 17:11-19 and «The Pharisees' request»: 20-21); on the other hand Luke 17:23-37 has scattered parallels to Matt 24:

Luke 17:23-24	//	Matt 24:26-27;
Luke 17:26-27.30	//	Matt 24:37-39;
Luke 17,31	//	Mt 24:17-18 [and Mark 13:15-16];
Luke 17:34	//	Matt 24:40;
Luke 17:37b	//	Matt 24:28).

The limitations of this introduction do not allow us to pursue the synoptic comparison systematically.

The Samaritan leper recognizes in Jesus	**the work of God**	17:11-19
WHEN comes	the kingdom of God?	17:20-21
The day of the Son of man is	**the day of God**	17:22-36
WHERE,	LORD?	17:37

The parable of the unjust judge	and the widow	18:1-8a
WHEN THE SON OF MAN COMES, WILL HE FIND FAITH?		18:8b
The parable of the Pharisee	and the publican	18:9-14

Accepting like a child	the kingdom of God	18:15-17
Wealth hinders following	Jesus	18:18-27
Leaving all to inherit	**eternal life**	18:28-30

1. THE FIRST SUB-SEQUENCE (LUKE 17:11-37)

This sub-sequence has four passages, organized in parallel: the purification of the ten lepers, (11-19) followed by a brief dialogue, the Pharisees' question and Jesus' reply (20-21), then Jesus' address to the disciples (22-35) followed by a short dialogue, the disciples' question and Jesus' reply (37).

1.1. *The Faith of the Samaritan Leper (Luke 17:11-19)*

COMPOSITION

This passage is made up of three parts. The first part (11-14) has three pieces. The outer pieces are parallel (11-12 and 14). The two segments of the first piece have the subordinate clause in the first member (11a and 12a) followed by the main clause in the second member (11b and 12b; this is followed by a relative clause in 12c). The same construction is found in the final piece (14b-e). The outer segments begin with the syntagmas «It happened while» which act as inclusios (11a and 14d); «leaving» is repeated at the start of the outer pieces (11a and 14b); «were purified» (14e) is opposed to «lepers» (12b). The part is focused on the lepers' request (13). The last two pieces begin with a narrative phrase (13a and 14a).

The third part (17-19) includes two words of Jesus (17bc.19bc) at the outside, introduced by a narrative phrase (17a.19a), in which the two verbs relating to healing, «purify» and «save», match one another. At the center (18), is the aim of the return, «to give praise to God».

At the outside of the central part (15-16), «one of them», is identified as being «Samaritan». Between the two parts are his actions («returned» and «fell»), then his words («praising» and «giving thanks»). So Jesus («he» in 16a) is united to «God» (15b) in the same praise and thanksgiving.

The play at the centers: the two characters united at the center of the passage are also at the center of the outer parts: «Jesus» invoked by the lepers at the start (13b) and God at the end, to whom Jesus wanted all ten to «give praise» (18). Note the repetition of «voice» at the center of the first part (13a) and at the center of the central part (15b); each time the voice is strong. In the same way, note the repetition of «return» at the center of the central part (15b) and at the center of the third part (18a).

All are cleansed

Leprosy, and the sin it indicated, had brought these ten men together, removing all, without distinction, from the community (12c) and from worship (Lev 13:45-46). They may not approach men or God. However, their cry strikes Jesus (14a). His compassion does not differentiate between men. All those who beg for his mercy will be purified together (14e), because all have obeyed his invitation (14d). All can show their healing to the priests, according to the prescriptions of the Law (14c).

+ 11 IT HAPPENED WHILE		he	DEPARTED	towards Jerusalem,
	–	he	was passing	between Samaria and Galilee.
+ 12 And as		he	was entering	into a village,
	–		came to meet	*TEN LEPERS*
	–	who	stood	at a distance.
	. 13 They lifted up		the VOICE saying:	
	«JESUS, MASTER,			*HAVE MERCY ON US!*».
	. 14 Seeing (this),		Jesus said:	
+		«Having	DEPARTED,	
	–		show yourselves	to the priests».
+ AND IT HAPPENED WHILE		they	were going away,	
	–			*THEY WERE PURIFIED.*

15 One of them,	seeing that	*HE WAS HEALED,*	
: RETURNED,	with a loud VOICE	GLORIFYING	GOD,
: 16 and fell	upon face at feet of Jesus	THANKING	HIM;
and he was a Samaritan.			

+ 17 Answering, Jesus	said:		
– «Were not	the ten	*PURIFIED?*	
.. Where are	the (other) nine?		
: 18 Are they not found to RETURN			
		to GIVE GLORY	TO GOD,
: except this foreigner?».			
+ 19 And he said to him:			
.. «Rise up	and DEPART,		
– your faith		*HAS SAVED YOU*».	

The faith of the Samaritan

All ten believe Jesus on his word, and even before having been healed (14e), they set out to show themselves to the priests (14d), according to the prescriptions of the Law (Lev 14:1-32). On the way, they are purified (14de). On seeing this, one of them returns immediately (15), thus apparently disobeying the order received (14bc). But Jesus, far from reproaching him for not having done what he had ordered him, is astonished that the other nine have not done the same (17). And the Samaritan is the only one whose faith Jesus praises (19c), as though the other nine had not believed in him, and as though they, too, had not been saved. Is the narrative incoherent? Is Jesus incoherent? Or is it that faith does not only consist in obeying orders (14d), but also in speaking, proclaiming the good news of salvation (15b), acknowledging the grace received before the one who has given it (16a), in as strong a voice as one cried out to ask for it (15b.13a)? Praise is inseparable from supplication. For the Samaritan, and for Jesus, it happens even before the ritual of purification is accomplished.

Praise God and give thanks to Jesus

The healed Samaritan unites God and Jesus in the same praise and thanksgiving (15b-16a). He acknowledges before all that the salvation which he has just received is the work of God in Jesus. His faith makes no distinction between them and he prostrates himself before the one by whom he has been purified as one prostrates oneself before the Lord.

He was a Samaritan

So the only one to proclaim his faith in this way, who goes to the end of the road in returning to Jesus and to God, is «a Samaritan» (16b); he was not Jewish, he was a heretic, even more despised than a foreigner. Once again, it is the worst of everything, a healed leper but still acknowledged as such, a shameful Samaritan, whose faith is greater than that of the Jews.

1.2. *The day of the son of man (Luke 17:22-35)*

COMPOSITION

A short narrative phrase (22a) introduces two pieces of discourse.

The first part of the discourse (22-30)

The first part has three sub-parts.—In the first sub-part (22b-24), which has three pieces, «one of the days of the Son of Man» and «the Son in his day» make an inclusio.—The third sub-part (26-30), bordered by a similar inclusio (26b.30), has three pieces: the first two (26-27.28-29) are parallel (water and fire are two of the usual means of judgment; see Isa 30:27-30).—The central sub-part (25) has a single bimember which is opposed to the rest of the part: «first» indicates the difference between the time of suffering and death of the Son of man and «his day», the day of judgment.—In addition to the double inclusio of «day(s)» and «Son of man» (22d. 24c; 26b.30), «will be revealed» (30b) refers to «shines» (24b); «lightening» (24a) like «the flood» (27c) and «fire and sulfur» (29b) are related phenomena; «heaven» is repeated in 24b and 29b; «day(s)» is repeated nine

---

+ [22b] «Are coming *the days*
: when you will desire

+ to see **one of the days** OF THE SON OF MAN
: and you will not see it.

- - -

:: [23] And they will say to you:
.. "Look, it is there!",
.. "Look, it is here!".

– Do not go away,
– or pursue them.

- - -

+ [24] For as the lightning enlightening,
+ from one side of *THE SKY* to other side of *THE SKY* *IT SHINES*,
= so *will be* THE SON OF MAN **in his day**.

---

[25] BUT FIRST HE MUST SUFFER MUCH
AND BE REJECTED BY THIS GENERATION.

+ [26] And as it happened ***in the days*** of Noah,
= so it *will be* ***in the days*** OF THE SON OF MAN:

- [27] they were eating, they were drinking,
- *they were marrying, they were giving in marriage,*

: till **the day** in which Noah entered into the ark
= and came the flood
= and destroyed all.

- - -

+ [28] And as it happened ***in the days*** of Lot:

- they were eating, they were drinking,
- *they were buying, they were selling,*
- *they were planting, they were building,*

: [29] and, **the day** in which Lot came out of Sodom,
= rained fire and sulfur from *THE SKY*
= and destroyed all.

- - -

= [30] *According to these things it will be* **the day**
= in which THE SON OF MAN *WILL BE REVEALED*.

---

times (22bd.24c.26ab.27c.28a.29a.30a). The opposition in number between «days» and «day» should be emphasized: for Noah and Lot, the days in which life followed its normal course, marked by the list of man's different activities, were in the plural[37], opposed by the singular of the day of catastrophe, judgment and death. 26b is in the plural because is linked to Noah's «days»; 30a is in the singular because it is linked to the «day» when Lot left Sodom. «One of the days[38]» at the start is in the singular and announces «during his day» (24c); the day of the Son of man is opposed to the «days» at the start (22b).

The second part of the discourse (31-35)

– [31] **In that day,**	he who will be		*on the terrace*		
– and	*his goods* are		in the house,		
::	let him not come down		to TAKE them		
– and	who *in the field*		likewise		
::	let him not turn		backward.		
	= [32] Remember	**you**	of the wife of Lot!		
	[33] Whoever seeks to	PRESERVE	*one's own life*	*WILL LOSE*	it
	And whoever	*LOSES*	(it)	WILL SAVE	it.
	= [34] I say	to **you**,			
– **in that night,**	there will be	two men	*on one bed,*		
:: one	WILL BE TAKEN				
:: and the other	*WILL BE LEFT*;				
– [35]	there will be	two women	*grinding together,*		
:: one	WILL BE TAKEN				
:: and the other	*WILL BE LEFT*».				

The second part has three sub-parts the size of a piece, two of which are more developed (31-32; 34-35) around another, much shorter, one (33). The first two segments (31) are parallel (with abbreviation the second time), as are the last two (34b-35); their initial terms, «In that day» (31a) and «that night» (34b), match.

37 Both lists begin with «they were eating, they were drinking»; «they were marrying, they were giving in marriage» is not repeated for the inhabitants of Sodom, probably an allusion to their behavior (Genesis 19).

38 Not «only one day» as is often translated; see Blass - Debrunner, par. 247.

The first sub-part ends with a unimember (32) and the last sub-part begins in the same way (34a); these are the only ones addressed to «you». In the center, the formula in 33 is in two bimembers. The same opposition, between, on the one hand, «take» (31c), «preserve»/«save» (33), «taken» (34c.35b) and, on the other, «lose» (33a.33b), «left» (34d.35c). «His life» (33a) refers back to «his goods» (31b).

Links between the parts

22 He said to the disciples:

. «Are coming *the days* in which you will desire
. to see **one of the days** of the Son of man
: and you will not see it.

- 23 They will say: "Look, it is there!", "Look it is here".
- Do not go or pursue them.

. 24 For as the lightning, enlightening,
. from one side to other of the sky, it shines
: so will be the Son of man **in his day**.

25 BUT FIRST HE MUST SUFFER MUCH
AND BE REJECTED BY THIS GENERATION.

- 26 As it happened *in the days* of Noah,
- so will it be *in the days* of the Son of man:
. 27 they were eating and drinking, they were marrying and giving in marriage,
: till **the day** in which Noah entered into the ark
= and the flood came and destroyed them all.

- 28 As it happened also *in the days* of Lot:
. they were eating and drinking, they were buying and selling, they were planting and building,
: 29 and, **the day** in which Lot came out of Sodom,
= fire and sulfur rained from the sky and destroyed them all;
- 30 So will it be **the day** in which the Son of man will be revealed.

- 31 *In that day*, he who will be on the terrace and his goods are in the house,
: let him not come down to take them
- and who will be in the field likewise
: let him not turn backward.

= 32 Remember the wife of Lot!

33 WHOEVER SEEKS TO PRESERVE HIS LIFE WILL LOSE IT
AND WHOEVER LOSES IT WILL SAVE IT.

= 34 I say to you,

- **in that night**, there will be two men on a same bed,
: one will be taken and the other will be left;
- 35 there will be two women grinding together,
: one will be taken and the other will be left».

[22] He said to the disciples:

. «Are coming *the days* in which you will desire
. to see **one of the days** of the Son of man
: and you will not see it.

- [23] They will say: "Look, it is there!", "Look it is here".
- Do not go or pursue them.

. [24] For as the lightning, enlightening,
. from one side to other of the sky, it shines
: so will be the Son of man **in his day**.

[25] BUT FIRST HE MUST SUFFER MUCH
AND BE REJECTED BY THIS GENERATION.

- [26] As it happened *in the days* of Noah,
- so will it be *in the days* of the Son of man:
. [27] they were eating and drinking, they were marrying and giving in marriage,
: till **the day** in which Noah entered into the ark
= and the flood came and destroyed them all.

- [28] As it happened also *in the days* of Lot:
. they were eating and drinking, they were buying and selling, they were planting and building,
: [29] and, **the day** in which Lot came out of Sodom,
= fire and sulfur rained from the sky and destroyed them all;
- [30] So will it be **the day** in which the Son of man will be revealed.

- [31] *In that day*, he who will be on the terrace and his goods are in the house,
: let him not come down to take them
- and who will be in the field likewise
: let him not turn backward.

= [32] Remember the wife of Lot!

[33] WHOEVER SEEKS TO PRESERVE HIS LIFE WILL LOSE IT
AND WHOEVER LOSES IT WILL SAVE IT.

= [34] I say to you,

- **in that night**, there will be two men on a same bed,
: one will be taken and the other will be left;
- [35] there will be two women grinding together,
: one will be taken and the other will be left».

The same alternating between «the days» (22b.26a.26b.28a) and «the day» (22c.24c.27b.29a.30), still «of the Son of man» (22c.24c.26b.30) which the first part is organized around, is found in the second part: while «that day» (31a) in the singular is the day in which man is given the time to flee leaving everything behind, just before «the night» (34b) of judgment comes. «Lot»'s name at the end of the first part (28a.29a) is repeated at the start of the second part (32a). The two centers (25.33) match: one announces Jesus' Passion, the other the suffering of the disciple who, like his master, must lose his life in order to save it.

Days of patience and suffering

On the one hand there are many «days» when everyone goes about his business, day after day, eating, drinking, buying, selling, planting, building, marrying or being given in marriage (27a.28b), in which every day-to-day activity prepares for future life. These are days in which the righteous are mixed up with the unrighteous; just as in the time of Lot the righteous one (28) who lived among sinners in Sodom, and in the days of Noah (26-27a), «a righteous man, a man of integrity», among those whose heart «fashioned thoughts of wickedness all day long» (Gen 6:5). For the righteous these days are days of suffering. Jesus' «days» are no different from Noah's and Lot's; nor are those of the disciples. Like Jesus, they will have to suffer much and be rejected by their generation (25 and 33). For them there will be lengthy days of persecution and patience —the patience of God who, with time, gives the wicked the possibility of repentance before it is too late.

The disciples' impatience and the suddenness of judgment

Like Noah and Lot (26-29), the disciples see little more than heedlessness and injustice around them, of which they will be the victims every day. Persecution and suffering will become so intense that they will cry out in their anguish and impatience; and so they will long to see «the day of the Son of man» (22bc) come, the day of God's judgment, who, in crushing their enemies (27c.29b), will free them from persecution. They will be told that here and there false prophets have been able to eliminate injustice by eliminating the evil-doers (23). How mistaken! During the days of mortal life, it will always be the same story of the oppression of the righteous and man's domination of man. Freedom is not of this world, and the persecuted righteous one will not have the time to «see» the day of judgment (22d). The revelation of the Son of man (30) will be as sudden as un-forecast lightening (24).

The judge

Judgment is reserved to God. It was he who brought the flood to the earth and made the wicked perish, saving only the one who was faithful to him (27bc). It was he who rained down fire and sulfur on Sodom and made all those who committed evil perish, having set Lot aside to save him (29). Jesus will be both judge and victim of evil, taking the punishment for sin upon himself (25); and the day of his suffering and death will be at the same time the day of his «revelation» (30). That day the mercy of God, who has not refused to give up his son for sinners, will be revealed. That day, Jesus, judged and executed by men, will be the instrument of their judgment. The disciples who wish to see the destruction of their enemies will not see it (22bcd). It is only later, after the lightening has flashed (24), that they will understand all that has happened.

How to prepare for the night of judgment

Judgment will surprise everyone at the moment they least expect it, during the day (31a), or in the middle of the night (34b). Men and women will be working or sleeping next to one another (34-35), when in the darkness God will make light to separate those who will be «taken» with him from those who will be «left» (34c.35b) in the outer darkness. God's judgment will only repeat, upside-down, what each person has themselves done (33) during the day when they were visited and warned that punishment was imminent. They will be judged according to what they have done: whoever who slows down because they want to take goods they are so attached to (31b), whoever thinks about «saving their life» in this way (33a), will be left by God to the vanity of their «perdition»; however, whoever leaves everything to listen to God's voice will be «taken» into the kingdom of the One in whom he has placed his trust.

1.3. *When and where? (Luke 17:20-21; 17:37)*

These are two brief dialogues, the first with the Pharisees (20-21), the second with the disciples (37) to whom Jesus has just spoken. Each time there is a question, the first one about time («when»: 20), the second about place («where»: 37). To the Pharisees' question, Jesus answers that the kingdom of God is not for later; it is present now, «among you» (21b). Jesus replies to the disciples' question with an enigmatic proverb. Does he mean himself and the enemies who will surround him at his death? Their question's symmetry with the Pharisees' question rather invites us to seek a solution to the enigma in the first answer. If the response to the question «when?» is «always» or «now», the answer to the matching question «where?» must be «everywhere» or «here». Everywhere where there is a corpse, vultures come to take it; this is why the future «will gather» can be interpreted as a gnomic future and, therefore, translated with the present.

+ [20] *Questioned by the Pharisees*:

- «*WHEN* comes THE KINGDOM OF GOD?».

+ *He answered them:*

- «THE KINGDOM OF GOD does not come with observation.

- [21] No one will say: «Look, it is here!», or «It is there!»

: For behold, THE KINGDOM OF GOD **IS IN THE MIDST OF YOU**».

[...]

+ [37] *Answering, (the disciples) said to him*:

- «*WHERE*, Lord?».

+ *He said to them:*

- «WHERE the corpse is, THERE are gathered the vultures».

These two short pieces will be considered as passages, for they are not directly part of the composition of the other two. It is possible to understand them as forming one single passage with Jesus' discourse (22-35), in which case they would be the outer terms[39]. In fact, the start of 21, «No one will say, "It is here, or there!"», is repeated at v.23: «They will say, "It is here, or there!"». However, it seems that it would be more correct to hold that, just as the disciples' question in 37 is clearly the reaction of those listening to the discourse which they have just heard (22-35), in the same way the Pharisees' question is the reaction to what they have just seen, the healing of the ten lepers and the Samaritan's profession of faith. The three occurrences of the «kingdom of God» in 20-21 have no later echo, while they seem to be prepared for by the double occurrence of «praise God»/«give praise to God» in 15 and 18.

A final reason for preferring this arrangement is the symmetry with the matching sub-sequence, as we will see below.

39 This is J. TOPEL's opinion in «What Kind of a Sign are Vultures? Luke 17:37b».

1.4. *The kingdom of god is here and now (Luke 17:11-37)*

COMPOSITION

The four passages of this sub-sequence are therefore held to be arranged in parallel. The relationship established by the Samaritan at the center of the first passage (15b-16), between «God» whom he «praises» and Jesus to whom he «gives thanks» is repeated in the third passage: «the day of the Son of man» is paralleled with God's actions in the past when he sent the flood (27b) and rained fire and sulfur from heaven (29b, where the name of «God» is used; furthermore, the passives in 34 and 35 are divine passives).

The central segments, 25 and 33, which both predict the Passion, seem to be prepared for at the start of the first passage by the reminder that Jesus «left for Jerusalem» (11), the place of his Passion and revelation[40].

BIBLICAL CONTEXT

The opposition between the faith of the foreigner and the Pharisees' lack of faith is also found between the faith of Naaman the Syrian, healed of his leprosy, and the bad behavior of Gehazi, Elisha's Hebrew servant (2Kgs 5).

The purification of the lepers is one of the signs given by Jesus in response to John the Baptist's question, «Are you he who is to come?» (Luke 7:22). The one who is to come to «save» (as in 17:19), is the one whom Isa 35 foretells, 4-5.

40 Verse 36 —«Two will be in a field: one will be taken, the other left»— acknowledged by textual criticism to be a harmonizing addition (see Matt 24:40), is not repeated here.

[11] IT HAPPENED THAT, WHILE HE DEPARTED TOWARDS JERUSALEM, he was passing between Samaria and
Galilee. [12] When he was entering in a village, arrived ten lepers who stood at a distance. [13] They lifted up the
voice saying: «*JESUS, MASTER, HAVE MERCY ON US!*». [14] Seeing (this), Jesus said: «Go and present yourselves
to the priests». And while they were going away, they were purified. [15] One of them, seeing himself healed,

returned, with a loud voice	GLORIFYING	GOD
[16] and he fell on his face at Jesus' feet	*THANKING* to	*HIM*.

And he was a Samaritan. [17] Answering, Jesus said: «Were not the ten purified? Where are the other nine?
[18] Are they not found to *return* to GIVE GLORY TO GOD, except this foreigner?». [19] And he said to him: «Rise
up and depart, your faith has saved you».

\+ [20] *The Pharisees questioned him:*
«WHEN does THE KINGDOM OF GOD come?».
= *He answered them:*
«THE KINGDOM OF GOD does not come with things to be observed.
[21] No one will say: «Look, it is here!», or «It is there!»
For behold, THE KINGDOM OF GOD is in the midst of you».

[22] *He said to his disciples:* «The days are coming in which you will desire to see ONE OF THE DAYS OF THE SON
OF MAN and you will not see it. [23] They will say to you: "Look it is there", "look it is here!". Do not go or
pursue them. [24] For as the lightning, enlightening, it shines from one side to other of the sky, so will be THE
SON OF MAN IN HIS DAY.

[25] BUT FIRST IT IS NECESSARY THAT HE SUFFER MUCH
AND IS REJECTED BY THIS GENERATION.

[26] As it happened in the days of Noah, so will it be in THE DAYS OF THE SON OF MAN: [27] they were eating and
drinking, they were marrying and giving in marriage, till the day in which Noah entered into the ark and
the flood came and destroyed them all. [28] As it happened also in the days of Lot: they were eating and
drinking, they were buying and selling, they were planting and building, [29] and, the day in which Lot came
out of Sodom, GOD made fire and sulfur to rain from the sky and destroyed them all;
[30] So will be THE DAY IN WHICH THE SON OF MAN will be revealed.

[31] In that day, he who will be on the terrace, if his goods are in the house, let him not come down to take
them and who is in the field likewise, let him not turn backward. [32] Remember the wife of Lot!

[33] WHOEVER SEEKS TO PRESERVE HIS LIFE WILL LOSE IT
AND WHOEVER LOSES IT WILL SAVE IT.

[34] I tell you, in that night, there will be two men in the same bed, one will be taken and the other will be left;
[35] there will be two women grinding together, one will be taken and the other will be left».

\+ [37] *Answering, they said:*
«WHERE, Lord?».
= *He said to them:*
«Where the corpse is, there THE VULTURES are gathered».

INTERPRETATION

Here and now with Jesus

The kingdom of God is here (21) and now (37) present in Jesus himself. The Samaritan who is healed at Jesus' word recognizes that the kingdom of God has arrived in this Jesus who has told him to go and show himself to the priests (15b-16). This is why he returns immediately—if the kingdom of God is now, there is not a moment to lose, if it is with Jesus, there is no hesitation about which direction to follow.

Knowing how to recognize the signs

Just as they have been shown the kingdom of God by the healing of the ten lepers, the Pharisees ask Jesus when it will come (20). They could not find a better moment to ask him such a question! Their lack of faith cannot show itself in a more shocking way just after the Samaritan has demonstrated his own faith (15b-16). The kingdom of God certainly does not impose itself as evidence which no one can fail to observe (21). The Samaritan was able to recognize the sign of God's kingdom in Jesus in his healing. Like the nine lepers who were also healed, the Pharisees remain blind: they see the signs, but do not know how to read them. Their question is a way of rejecting the Son of man who could bring them salvation, just as he freely offered it to the lepers.

«Will those who are saved be few?»

For having believed in God's word, Noah, alone of all, found salvation by going into the ark (27). Alone of all the inhabitants of Sodom, Lot escaped extermination by fire and sulfur, for having obeyed the warning of God's angels (29). The Samaritan alone of all the ten lepers who were healed is said by Jesus to be saved because of his faith (19). However, the nine lepers are also healed, and Jesus does not call down fire from heaven on them because they did not come back to praise God. This is because the day of judgment has not yet come (24.30) and there is still time for nine lepers to convert, just as there is for the Pharisees. Will they take advantage of it to return to the only one who is able to save them?

A question of time

The time of salvation and deliverance may seem long for those who suffer (22). For the wicked the time of God's judgment seems a long way off. For the righteous and for sinners it seems as though it will never come; and yet the day of judgment comes, inexorably, just as does the day of death (24.27.29.31.34-35). It is already at work, just as death, without us wanting to be aware of it, does its work day after day and can complete it suddenly at any time. Anyone who is wise enough to have his end always in mind will not leave himself to go and act as though the future were in his own hands. In truth, conversion is the most urgent thing, and the kingdom of God (21) or of the vultures (37d) is not for tomorrow; it is to be sought nowhere but in the here and now.

A question of attitude

Whether one can eat and drink, buy and sell, plant and build, marry or be married (27.28), or whether persecution stops one from doing all of this, the disciple will see, at the very moment and in the very place where he is, the kingdom of God presently at work (21). Whether he has to fight against the injustice which he is always tempted to commit, or against the injustice which he suffers, the disciple will also be in the joy of the permanent presence of God, whose reign he seeks to extend in him and around him, today and all the days of life given to him, knowing that it is in abandoning himself and his life that he will receive life for ever (33).

A question of life and death

The Pharisees expect the kingdom of God (20). Their only problem is to know «when» it will come, so that they can benefit from it. They do not ask the question to know whether they will be admitted, as they are so sure that they will be. The disciples, too, would like to see the day of judgment and freedom from their enemies (22). All envisage condemnation and death as being only for others. Now, if one will be taken and one left (34-35), the threat of being abandoned to the vultures (37d) concerns them, just as it concerns everyone else. Jesus clearly announces the law which will govern the judgment at the end of which one will be taken into the kingdom of God for eternal life (21) and one left without life, a corpse which the carrion crows will feast on (37d): whoever wishes to save his life will lose it and whoever loses his life will save it (33). Jesus' paradox, the path he shows in accepting death (25), means that everything is now turned upside-down for Christ's faithful: it is not the death of others which will save us from our foes, but our accepted death which will save us, and with those, those who persecute us.

2. THE SECOND SUB-SEQUENCE (LUKE 18:1-14)

This sub-sequence has two parables, «the parable of the unscrupulous judge and the importunate widow» (1-8) and «the parable of the Pharisee and the tax-collector» (9-14), which frame the question at 18:8b (see p. 338).

2.1. *The unscrupulous Judge and the importunate widow (Luke 18:1-8)*

COMPOSITION

+ [1] *He said a parable to them*
    - on the necessity for them to *PRAY* *always*
    - and not to become tired.
+ [2] *saying:*

. «**There was a judge** *in a city*
   : WHO DID NOT FEAR GOD AND HAD NO REGARD FOR MEN.
. [3] **There was a widow** *in that city*
   : who kept coming to him *SAYING*:
      – «DO ME JUSTICE against whom that is unjust to me».
      = [4] But he did not want ***for a long time.***

. After that he said to himself:
   : «EVEN IF I DO NOT FEAR GOD AND HAVE NO REGARD FOR MEN,
   : [5] because **this widow** *IMPORTUNES* me,
      – I WILL DO HER JUSTICE
      = lest ***till the end*** she comes to *TROUBLE* me»».

+ [6] *The Lord said:*
   :: «Hear what the unjust judge said.
   - [7] And WILL NOT God DO JUSTICE to his elected
   - who *CRY ALOUD* to him ***night and day***,
      . even if he **delays long** over them!

+ [8] *I say to you*
   - that HE WILL DO JUSTICE to them **speedily**.

This passage is made up of three parts: a parable in the center (2b-5), framed by two lessons (1 and 6-8).—The parable (2b-5) is sub-divided into two parallel sub-parts (2b-4a and 4b-5). The second sub-part brings together 2b and 3a along with the end of 3c; «saying» at 3b is interpreted in the judge's mouth by «importunes me» at 5a and «troubles me» at 5c; «for a long time» at 4a heralds «until the end» at 5c.—The first part (1) expresses first positively (1b) and then negatively (1c) the lesson of the parable which will follow.—The last part (6-8) gives the parable's application, not by saying what the disciples must do, but what God does. In the first piece, an *a fortiori* reasoning links the judge's behavior (6b) to God's (7). The first segment expresses the idea negatively (7), the second positively (8)[41]; the statement in the second piece (8), parallel to the first, corrects v.7.

Note the repetition of «do justice» (3c.5b.7a.8b), the list of asking verbs; «pray» (1b), «say» (3b), «importune» (5a), «trouble» (5c) and «cry» (7b), and of words which mark time: «always» (1b), «for a long time» (4a), «till the end» (5c), «night and day» (7b), «delay» (7c) and finally «suddenly» (8c) which is opposed to all the others.

INTERPRETATION

Persecution

Just like the widow, deprived of any support and in the grip of every injustice (3), the disciples will be persecuted and delivered, with no defense, into the hands of their enemies (7b). Just like the people oppressed in Egypt, like Israel deported to Babylon, lacking her spouse and reduced to the loss of widowhood, the Church of Jesus' disciples will only keep their «cry» (7b). The cry is a word which no longer has the strength to articulate itself. It is the word of the person who has plumbed the depths of agony. The disciples will experience this agony, the agony of those who know that they are «elect» (7a) but still see themselves attacked on all sides by men, abandoned by God himself, a God who seems to be deaf to their cry (7c).

The time of testing and the moment of judgment

The time of persecution and testing seems to be desperately long (4a), as indeed it is. It seems never-ending (7c). Injustice and oppression never stop ruling with those who «do not fear God and have no regard for me» (2c.4c). The just person and the little person will always be crushed. And, scandalously, God remains dumb, not listening to the cry which calls on him for help night and day (7b). Jesus, however, announces that justice will be as quick and sudden (8) as the time of persecution and testing will have been long (7bc). It will be vain to expect a time of justice after the time of injustice, tomorrows of song after today's crying out. Injustice and oppression will always be the disciples' daily bread. The moment for re-establishing justice will nonetheless come (7-8) for the person who fears God and has regard for men, just as it will for all those who are unjust. Each will receive his reward at a time he does not know, but which cannot but swoop down on him.

41 Many scholars consider 7 to be a question; it can also be interpreted, as in the French *Bible de Jérusalem*, as an exclamation.

2.2. *The Pharisee and the tax-collector (Luke 18:9-14)*

COMPOSITION

. [9] He said also to some — who were convinced in themselves of being JUST
. and despised *others* — this parable:

- [10] «Two men	WENT UP to the Temple	*to pray*,
- one was a Pharisee,	and the other *a tax-collector*.	

+ [11] THE PHARISEE, *standing*, *prayed* to himself:

: «O God, I thank you
– that I am not like *the other men*
. thieves, *UNJUST*, adulterers,
– or even like *this tax-collector*:
. [12] I fast twice a week,
. I give a tenth of all that I possess».

+ [13] *THE TAX-COLLECTOR* *standing at a distance*,

– would not even lift up *his eyes* to heaven
– but he was beating *his breast* saying:

: «My God, have mercy on me SINNER».

- [14] I tell you	RETURNED	*this man*	JUSTIFIED	to his house,
-	rather than	that one.		

. For who — exalts himself — *WILL BE HUMBLED*
. and — *who humbles himself* — WILL BE EXALTED».

Like the previous passage, this one has three parts, two very short parts (9 and 14cd) framing a parable.

The two bimember segments in the introduction (9) are constructed in a chiasmus: the central members are relative clauses, which describe the attitude of the interlocutors towards themselves and others.

The two segments in the conclusion (14cd) are parallel and opposed term by term.

The central part (10-14b) is the parable proper, organized in three sub-parts. The first part introduces the two men who are doing the same thing (10); in the last sub-part (14ab) Jesus' judgment makes the different between the opposing results of their prayer (note the chiasmus: «Pharisee»/«tax-collector» in 10 and «this man»/«that man» in 14). The central sub-part is made up of two pieces (11-12 and 13) which place «the Pharisee» (11a) in opposition to «the tax-collector» (13a). The thanksgiving of one (11b) is opposed to the prayer of the other (13d), introduced with the same «My God». The Pharisee justifies his thanksgiving at length with a comparison with «the other men» and with the «tax-collector»: his good acts (12) are opposed to theirs, which are bad (11d). The tax collector, on the other hand, makes no comparison, and his prayer is very short; however, it is his gestures which oppose «heaven», (13b) to which he dare not «raise his eyes» and he himself, «beating his breast» (13c).

Across the passage as a whole, «just»/«justified» (9a.14a) are opposed to «unjust» at 11d, synonymous with «sinner» at 13d.

INTERPRETATION

The Pharisee's sin

The Pharisee fulfils the Law, and even more: he is not lying when he states that he fasts twice a week, following the practice, which was common at the time, among the pious, nor when he says he pays a tithe on all his income, according to the strictest observance of the commandment (12). He does not steal or commit adultery, and is not unjust (11d). He behaves like a just man; and yet, he will not return to his house justified (14b). His injustice, the sin which corrupts even the best actions, is in the fact that he despises and judges other men (11c), particularly the tax collector (11e) who has gone up to the Temple with him to pray (10). He blasphemes, because he puts himself in God's place to deal out justice, granting it to himself and refusing it to others.

Justice belongs to God alone

The tax collector does not compare himself to others, whether to the Pharisee who observes the Law or those who, more sinful than him, have not come to the Temple to pray. He knows, and says, that he is a «sinner» (13d), without even listing his failings, and his request recognizes and confesses God's kindness and «mercy». Justice belongs only to God. He alone can judge, forgive, or condemn (14), as he alone has given the Law. The tax collector knows that the Law is good and that it is a sin not to fulfill it. The Pharisee knows this too; but while one leaves justice to the mercy of the one who can forgive failing the Law, the other one, by judging in God's place and in refusing mercy to God just as he does to men, despises both God and men. By rejecting his brother, he rejects his Father.

2.3. *The judgment of the son of man (Luke 18:1-14)*

COMPOSITION

[1] He told them a PARABLE on the necessity for them to **PRAY** always and not to become tired. [2] He said:

«There was in a city a judge who did not fear **GOD**
and had no regard for men. [3] There was in that city a widow, who kept coming to him to say: «Do me *JUSTICE* against one who is *UNJUST* with me».
[4] For a long time he did not want. But then he said to himself:
«Even if I do not fear **GOD**
and have no regard for men, [5] because this widow importunes me, I will do her *JUSTICE*, lest till the end she comes to trouble me».

[6] The Lord said: «You heard what the *UNJUST* judge said. [7] And will not God do *JUSTICE* to his elected who cry aloud to him night and day, and will he make them to wait long? I SAY TO YOU that he will do them *JUSTICE* speedily.

BUT THE SON OF MAN, WHILE COMING, WILL HE FIND FAITH ON THE EARTH?».

[9] He told also for some who were convinced in themselves of being *JUST*
and despised others this PARABLE:

[10] «Two men went up to the Temple to **PRAY**; one was a Pharisee, the other a tax collector. [11] The Pharisee standing **PRAYED** to himself:
«**GOD**, I thank you that
I am not like other men, thieves, *UNJUST*, adulterers, or even like this tax collector.
[12] I fast twice a week, I give a tenth of all that I posses». [13] The tax collector standing at a distance, would not even lift up his eyes to heaven, but was beating his breast saying:
«**GOD**, have mercy on me sinner».

[14] I SAY TO YOU that this man returned home *JUSTIFIED*, rather than that one. For who exalts himself will be humbled and who humbles himself will be exalted».

This sub-sequence has two parables which frame the only question in the whole text (8b). The two parables are introduced by narrative pieces (1-2a and 9); the noun «parable» is used in both cases (1a.9b) as is the verb «to say» (1a.2a.9a).

The two parables are followed by a commentary from Jesus (6-8; 14); the emphasizing formula, «I tell you [that]», is repeated at the start of the last member in the first case (8a) and at the start of the first member in the second case (14a).

In both cases, it is a question of «praying» (1a; 10a.11a) and «God»'s name recurs twice in each parable (2b.4b; 11b.13c). Words from the «justice» family abound (3b - x2- and 5b.6.7b.8a; 9a.11c.14a); note that «unjust» first of all (3b) describes the person who oppresses the widow, while the second time (11c) it is used by the Pharisee to describe the other men and, in particular, the tax collector. The judge «has no regard for men» (twice: 2c.4c) just as the Pharisee «despises other men» (twice: 9b.11c). The widow's prayer begins with an imperative (3b) as does that of the tax collector (13c); the Pharisee's, on the other hand, is, from beginning to end in the first person singular (11b-12b). In both cases, God finally gives justice (8a.14a).

BIBLICAL CONTEXT

«The Son of man» (see p. 167): applied to Jesus, this expression first of all describes the person who is to suffer (see 9:22.44.58; 18:31; 22:22; 24:7), but also the one who, having passed the test, will be glorified at the right hand of the Father (22:69) as judge (9:26; 12:8.40); when the expression is the subject of «to come» (as it is here in 18:8b), it describes the one who will come to judge (21:27.36); at the start of the sequence itself, the Son of man is also presented «in his day», that is, the day of judgment (17:22-37).

INTERPRETATION

The widow and the tax collector

The two characters resemble one another: both are defenseless and ask for justice (3b.13c); neither puts their faith in themselves, but they expect their salvation from the only one who can give justice. It is in «God» that the tax collector puts his faith, and, if the character whom the widow begs is an «unjust judge» (6), he is only there to bring out, *a fortiori*, God's justice (7-8). However, while the widow demands justice against someone else, the tax collector asks God's «mercy» on himself (13c): in fact, as the Pharisee says, he is «unjust» (11c), and is well aware of it himself.

The Pharisee and the judge

They too resemble one another: one «has no regard for men» (2c.4c), while the other «despises» all of them (9b.11c). In their relationship with God, however, they seem to be totally opposed: the former «does not fear God» (2b.4b), while the other one, a faithful observer of the divine Law (12), goes up to the Temple to pray (10). But refusing to give justice to the others (4), and not accepting that they can be justified by God (11), could well be sins with the same root: the person who does not fear God, like the unjust judge, cannot respect men; and the person who despises God makes themselves a false image of God. One behaves as though God did not exist, and the other worships a false god, an idol made in his own image. Neither one nor the other has «faith» (8b).

3. **WHEN THE SON OF MAN COMES, WILL HE FIND FAITH? (LUKE 17:11-18:30)**

COMPOSITION

The Samaritan leper recognizes in Jesus	the work of God		17:11-19
WHEN comes	the kingdom of God?	Pharisees	17:20-21
The day of the Son of man is	the day of God		17:22-36
WHERE,	Lord?	DISCIPLES	17:37

The parable of the unjust judge	and the widow	DISCIPLES	18:1-8a
WHEN THE SON OF MAN COMES, WILL HE FIND FAITH?			18:8b
The parable of the Pharisee	and the tax collector	Pharisees	18:9-14

Receiving like a child	the kingdom of God	DISCIPLES	18:15-17
Wealth hinders from following Jesus	a ruler		18:18-27
Leaving all to inherit	eternal life	DISCIPLES	18:28-30

Jesus' interlocutors

This sequence is constructed by alternating the disciples and the Pharisees. In the central sub-sequence, the first parable (18:1-8a) is addressed to the disciples, while the second has the Pharisees in sight (18:9-14); the first sub-sequence first of all introduces the Pharisees (17:20-21) on the occasion of the purification of the ten lepers (17:11-19), and then the «disciples» (17:22.37), while the last sub-sequence places the disciples at the outsides (18:15-17 and 28-30) and «a leader», who strongly resembles a Pharisee, in the center (18:18-27)m even if Luke does not say this.

The first Sub-Sequence and the first parable

From the start of the sequence (17:11) until the end of the parable of the unjust judge and the widow (18:8a), the question is about judgment, of a judgment which is to be expected: the disciples wish to see the day where justice will be given them (17:22), like the widow. Judgment, like lightening (17:24) will arrive «suddenly» (18:8a).

The second parable and the last Sub-Sequence (18:9-30)

The Pharisee thinks he is being faithful to the Law: he is not «a thief, unjust, an adulterer» (11). The leader observes the commandments (20); «adulterer» is again at the start of the list («You shall not commit adultery, you shall not kill,…»), as at the end of 11. The Pharisee «gives» «a tenth of all his income» (12), but Jesus asks the leader to «give» «everything which he has» (22), which the disciples did when they «left what was theirs» (28).

The central question (8b)

This goes back to the *first panel* of the sequence by the repetition of «the Son of man» as in 17:22.24.26.30; «coming»[42] repeats the verb of the Pharisees' first question: «When will the kingdom of God come?» (17:20) and describes judgment, like the judgment of the flood: «and the flood came» (17:27). The word «faith» only appears at the end of the first passage, in the words addressed by Jesus to the Samaritan: «Your faith has saved you» (17:19), but it is the only question in the whole of the rest of the sequence: the faith of Noah and of Lot, who listened to God's word and were saved (17:26-29), the faith which will enable the person who has given up taking his property to be saved as Lot was (17:31), the faith of the widow who did not stop praying and who saw the day justice was given to her (18:2-6), the faith of Jesus and the disciples who will agree to lose their lives (17:25 and 33).

In the *second panel* of the sequence, faith is opposed to Law, in whose observance the Pharisee (18:11) and the leader (18:20-21) have placed their trust. It is faith which enables the disciple to give everything up (18:28) and like a little child (18:16-17) and the tax collector (18:13) to abandon himself to God's mercy.

This faith is addressed to Jesus: his day is the day of God's kingdom (17:20-30); to follow him is to enter into «the kingdom of God» and to inherit eternal life (18:15-30).

42 The translation of the participle «coming» by a temporal («When the Son of man will come») is not very precise, since the conjunction «when» does not exist in the Greek text, but it gives the sense well.

The first passages of the two panels of the sequence

> 17: [11] It happened that while he departed towards Jerusalem, he was passing between Samaria and Galilee. [12] And entering in a village, arrived ten lepers who *STOOD AT A DISTANCE*. [13] They lifted up the voice saying: «Jesus, Master, **have mercy on us!**». [14] Seeing this, Jesus said: «Go and present yourselves to the priests». And while they were going away, they were purified. [15] One of them, seeing himself healed, returned, with a loud voice glorifying God [16] and he fell on his face at Jesus' feet to THANK HIM. And he was a Samaritan. [17] Answering, Jesus said: «Were not all the ten purified? Where are the other nine? [18] Are they not found to return to give glory to God, except this foreigner?». [19] And he said to him: «Rise up and depart, your faith has saved you».

[...]

> 18: [9] He said also to some who were convinced in themselves of being just and despised others this parable: [10] «Two men went up to the Temple to pray; one was a Pharisee, the other a tax-collector. [11] The Pharisee standing prayed to himself: «My God, I THANK YOU that I am not like other men, thieves, unjust, adulterers, or even like this tax-collector. [12] I fast twice a week. I give a tenth of all that I possess». [13] The tax collector *STANDING AT A DISTANCE*, would not even lift up his eyes to heaven, but was beating his breast saying: «My God, **have mercy on me** a sinner». [14] I say to you that this man returned home justified, rather than that one. For who exalts himself will be humbled and who humbles himself will be exalted».

The first passage (17:11-19) and the passage which follows the central question (18: 9-14) share several lexical repetitions: «to stand at a distance» (17:12; 18:13), «to give thanks» (17:16; 18:11), «have pity on us (me)» (synonyms in Greek: 17:13; 18:13). In addition, the Samaritan falls at Jesus' feet (17:16) and the tax collector does not dare lift up his eyes (18:13); Jesus tells one to get up (17:19) and says of the other that the one who humbles himself will be exalted (18:14). The despised tax collector therefore resembles the Samaritan and the nine Jewish lepers resemble the Pharisee.

The outer Sub-Sequences (17:11-37; 18:15-30)

In the second and fourth passages of the first sub-sequence (17:20-21; 17:37), Jesus answers a question; the central passage of the last sub-sequence (18:18-27) is framed by two questions which Jesus answers. In the first case, the questions relate to the kingdom of God («when» at 17:20; «where» at 17:37) and in the second case they have the same object in mind with synonymous expressions: «eternal life» at 18:18 and «to be saved» at 18:26 («saved» like the lepers: 17:19); but the questions are now personalized: they relate to the subject of salvation («who»: 18:26) and what must be done («what»: 18:18).—«The kingdom of God» (three times in 17:20-21) is assimilated to the «day(s) of the Son of man» in the first sub-sequence; and in the last sub-sequence this same «kingdom of God» (18:16. 17.24.25.29) —«eternal life» (18:18.30) or salvation (18:26)— is linked to Jesus. Note, too, the recurrence of «to leave» (17:34.35; 18:28-29) and, above all that «not to take» «one's things» (17:31) is symmetrical with «leave what we had» (18:28).

17:[11] It happened that while he departed towards Jerusalem, he was passing between Samaria and Galilee. [12] Entering in a village, arrived ten lepers who stood at a distance. [13] They lifted up the voice saying: «Jesus, Master, have mercy on us!». [14] Seeing this, Jesus said: «Go and present yourselves to the priests». And while they were going away, they were purified. [15] One of them, seeing himself healed, returned, with a loud voice glorifying God [16] and he fell on his face at Jesus' feet to thank him. And he was a Samaritan. [17] Answering, Jesus said: «Were not all the ten purified? Where are the other nine? [18] Are they not found to return to give glory to God, except this foreigner?». [19] And he said to him: «Rise up and depart, your faith ***has saved*** you».

[20] THE PHARISEES QUESTIONED HIM: «WHEN will **the kingdom of God** come?».
HE ANSWERED THEM: «**The kingdom of God** does not come in way of attracting the attention. [21] No one will say: «Look, it is here!», or «It is there!» For behold, **the kingdom of God** is in the midst of you».

[22] He said to the disciples: «The days are coming in which you will desire to see ***one of the days of the Son of man*** and you will not see it. [23] They will say to you: "Look it is there!", "Look it is here!". Do not go, do not pursue them. [24] For as the lightning, enlightening, it shines from one side to other of the sky, so will be ***the Son of man in his days***. [25] But first it is necessary that he suffers much and is rejected by this generation. [26] As it happened in the days of Noah, so will it be in ***the days of the Son of man***: [27] they were eating and drinking, they were marrying and giving in marriage, till the day in which Noah entered into the ark and flood came and destroyed them all. [28] Likewise as it happened in the days of Lot: they were eating and drinking, they were buying and selling, they were planting and building, [29] and, the day in which Lot came out of Sodom, God made fire and sulfur rain from the sky and destroyed them all; [30] So will be in ***the day in which the Son of man will be revealed***. [31] In that day, who will be on the terrace with his goods in the house, let him not come down to take them and who will be in the field likewise, let him not turn backward. [32] Remember the wife of Lot! [33] Whoever seeks to preserve his life will lose it, whoever instead loses, will save it. [34] I tell you, in that night, there will be two men in a bed, one will be taken and the other will be LEFT; [35] there will be two women grinding together, one will be taken and the other will be LEFT».

[37] ANSWERING, THEY SAID: «WHERE, Lord?».
HE SAID TO THEM: «Where the corpse is, there the vultures will be gathered».

[...]

18:[15] They brought to him also infants so that he might touch them. Seeing this, the disciples rebuked them. [16] But Jesus called them to himself, saying: «Let the children come to me and do not prevent them, for to such as these is **the kingdom of God**. [17] Truly I say to you: who does not receive **the kingdom of God** like a small child shall not enter into it».

[18] A RULER QUESTIONED HIM: «Good Master, WHAT must I do to inherit **eternal life**?». [19] *BUT JESUS SAID TO HIM*: «Why do you call me good? No one is good except God alone!

[20] You know the commandments: "Do not commit adultery, do not kill, do not steal, do not testimony falsely, honor your father and your mother"». [21] He said: «All this, I have observed from my youth». [22] Hearing this, Jesus said to him: «You still lack only one thing: all that you have, sell it and give it to the poor and you will have treasure in heaven; then come, follow me». [23] Hearing this word, he became very sad because he was very rich. [24] Seeing it, Jesus said: «How difficult it is for those who have riches to enter into **the kingdom of God**! [25] It is easier for a camel to pass through the eye of a needle than for a rich man to enter into **the kingdom of God**!».

[26] THOSE WHO HEARD SAID: «But WHO then can ***be saved***?».
[27] *HE SAID*: «What is impossible for men is possible for God».

[28] Peter said: «Behold, having LEFT what was ours, we have followed you!». [29] He said to them: «Truly I say to you, there is no one who had LEFT house, wife, brothers, parents, children, for the sake of **the kingdom of God**, [30] who would not receive many times more in the present time and in the age to come **eternal life**».

INTERPRETATION

Asking the right question

Of course, one can have good in view, as do the Pharisees for whom nothing but the kingdom of God, which they are expecting intently, counts: «When will the kingdom of God come?» (17:20). However, their question initially receives an entirely negative response, which will certainly have disappointed them: «The kingdom of God will not come... And no one will say...». Jesus' conclusion: «the kingdom of God is among you», will have surprised them and doubtless left them incredulous. The fact is that their question was badly framed, just as the disciples' question, «Where, Lord?» (17:37a) was, which receives a totally enigmatic answer. It is not for man to know either «when» or «where» the kingdom of God will come. That is not the problem or, if we wish to put it in these terms, the answer would be that the kingdom of God is everywhere and always, here and now. What is really at stake for man is to enter into it, in order not to fall into the clutches of vultures (37b). The problem is one of faith (18:8b). What matters is not so much what God will do, as what man must do. In this sense, the ruler asks the question which counts: «What shall I do to inherit eternal life?» (18:18).

Giving the right answer

With the expression «to inherit eternal life», the ruler's question already implies an initial answer. If he had thought that total observation of the Law could guarantee him eternal life, he would certainly not have framed his question in this way. However, preferring his own inheritance (18:23) to God's, he contradicts what he had stated at the beginning. Those who seem to have given the right answer are the disciples, since they have left everything (18:28). On the Son of man's invitation, they did not look back and, without taking their things from their homes (17:31), they followed him (18:28). If they had really realized what this meant, would they have asked the question, «Where, Lord?» (17:37a). And would Peter have intervened (18:28) to emphasize their worthiness, almost behaving like the Pharisee in the parable? To observe the whole of the Law is not bad, on the contrary (18:21); but to leave everything to follow Jesus (18:28) is even better. However, «who can be saved?» (18:26). The only right answer is the one Jesus gives: «What is impossible for men is possible for God» (18:27). Only God justifies. Man cannot save himself—it is totally out of his power.

Welcoming the kingdom of God with faith

Humanity's many activities are not condemned. It was not because, in Noah's and Lot's time, people «ate and drank, married, bought and sold, planted and built» (17:27-28), that they were given up to punishment (17:27.29). It is not because he has observed the Law, and even more (18:12) that the Pharisee was not justified (18:14). It is not even because they have left everything that was theirs behind (18:28) that the disciples will enter the kingdom of God (18:16) and will inherit eternal life (18:30). Human activities, observing the Law, giving up wealth, only find their meaning and their justification through «faith» (18:8b): the faith of the leper who knows that God alone can save him (17:15); the faith of the small child (18:15-17) who receives everything from his parent's hands, starting with life; the faith of the person who, as a child, receives from the father the good works which it is given to him to carry out, as the wealthy leader should also have understood (18:18-27) just as much as Peter and the Twelve (18:28-30); whoever receives forgiveness of his sins, like the tax collector (18:13-14). The faith of the person who goes as far as losing his life so that God can save it for him (17:33), as the Son of man accepts the prospect of «suffering much and being rejected by this generation» (17:25); he knows that it is thus that he will reach the kingdom of God and eternal life.

Prayer, an expression of faith

The disciple knows that his salvation is in no way dependent on himself (18:26-27). He believes that God can give him everything and will refuse him nothing (18:7-8). He prays in all circumstances (18:1). He prays to ask that justice be done: like the widow who cries out before the injustice she suffers (18:3), like the tax collector who asks for mercy for the injustice he has committed (18:13). These two forms of prayer express the same «faith» (18:8b): justice belongs only to God (18:27), he alone can re-establish it, just as he alone can heal from leprosy (17:15) and from sin (18:13). The only way to obtain it is to ask for it (17:13; 18:13). There is no faith without prayer.

D. THE SEQUENCE IN LUKE 18:31-19:46

All translations agree on the limits of the first three passages in the sequence: «The third prediction of the Passion» (18:31-34), «The healing of the blind man at Jericho» (18:35-43), and «Zacchaeus the tax-collector» (19:1-10). The agreement ends for the following pericope, «The parable of the pounds[43]»: while everyone makes it start at 19:11, the same does not go for the end: the JB ends at v. 27, where the French TOB includes v. 28. As for what follows, the TOB distinguishes three pericopes (up until v. 48) where the JB has four, but others only have two.

43 Translator's note: Greek *mina* has been translated by «pound» throughout.

Geographical notations form a system whose regularity predicts the organization of the sequence: it is enough to note all the place names with the movement verb which precedes them.

we are going up	to		JERUSALEM	18:31
he came near	to		Jericho	18:35
he passed			Jericho	19:1
he was near	to		JERUSALEM	19:11
going up	to		JERUSALEM	19:28
he came near	to	[...]	the Mount of Olives	19:29
he came near	to	[...]	the Mount of Olives	19:37
he came near		[...]	THE CITY	19:41

«The City» at the start of the conclusion (19:41) matches «Jerusalem» at the start of the introduction (18:31); «Jerusalem» is also at the outsides of the central parable (19:11 and 28). The verbs which precede the four names match in a parallel way: «to go up» at 18:31 and 19:28, «was near» and «came near» at 19:11 and 41. Between the introduction and the central parable, «Jericho» recurs at the start of the two passages which form a sub-sequence; between the central parable and the conclusion, «came near to» followed by «the Mount of Olives» (19:29 and 37) mark the start of two passages which also form a sub-sequence.

The symmetry of the two panels of the sequence is quite strict. The movement of approaching Jerusalem is accentuated: from Jericho, Jesus goes up towards Jerusalem, comes near to the city, and finally «enters the Temple» (46)[44].

The seven passages are marked in this way (see the schema of the sequence, p. 102). Only the passage which is numerically central includes two mentions of the same place, at the start (19:11) and the end (19:28). This passage is framed by two pairs of narratives which begin with the mention of the same place, «Jericho» before the central parable, and «the Mount of Olives» afterwards; these pairs of passages form two sub-sequences. Finally, the first and last passages of the sequence begin with the mention of Jerusalem, called «the City» at the end. Examining the links between the passages will confirm this construction which, for now, is merely hypothetical.

44 All the verbs of movement have Jesus as their subject, except the first (18:31), where the Twelve are associated with their master's going up to Jerusalem.

1. **THE PREDICTION OF JESUS' FATE (LUKE 18:31-34)**

COMPOSITION

The passage, the size of a part, is made up of three pieces. The first piece (31) introduces the prophecy (32-33), and the third (34) reports the disciples' reaction to what they have heard.

+ [31] Taking aside the Twelve,	he SAID	to them:
: «Behold, we are going up	to Jerusalem,	
- and will be accomplished	all that	*IS WRITTEN*
- by the prophets about	the Son of man.	
. [32] For he will be given	to the nations,	
. he will be mocked,	he will be insulted,	he will be spat upon
. [33] and having flogged,	they will kill	him
— and the third	day	he will rise».
= [34] But they none of these	*understood*;	
– and this SAYING	was *hidden*	for them
= and they *did not understand*	what	WAS SAID.

The first piece has two segment, a narrative unimember which introduces a trimember of speech; the outer members of the trimember end with a proper name, «Jerusalem» and «the Son of man». What Jesus «says» (31a) is «all that is written» (31c).

The second piece (32-33) has a trimember which predicts the Passion (32-33a) and a unimember (33b) predicting the resurrection.

The third piece (34) has a single trimember segment: the outer members are synonymous, the central member gives the reason for the other two; the passive «was hidden» can be interpreted as a divine passive.

In this last piece, «saying» (34b) and «was said» (34c) match «said» (31a) and «is written» (31c) in the first piece.

BIBLICAL CONTEXT

The third and final prediction of the Passion and the resurrection

The first two predictions of Jesus' fate are in the last sequence of the second section (sequence B8). The first (Luke 9:22) is very close in its formulas to the central piece of the third section (18:32-33); in the second one (Luke 9:43b-45), only the Passion is predicted, very briefly, but the disciples' incomprehension is strongly emphasized.

The fourth Song of the Servant of the Lord

This is the first time, in these predictions, that Jesus refers to «all that is written in the prophets». The main text where the suffering, death and resurrection are prophesied is Isa 52:13-53:12[45].

SYNOPTIC COMPARISON (see pp. 296, 271 and 347)

Matt 20:17-19	Mark 10:32-34	Luke 18:31-34
17 *Now* being on the point of *going up to Jerusalem Jesus,*	32 *Now* they were *on the way* *going up to Jerusalem* and *Jesus* was preceding them. And they were amazed; and those who followed were frightened.	
TOOK ASIDE by themselves THE TWELVE [disciples] and *on the way* HE SAID TO THEM:	And TAKING ASIDE again THE TWELVE, he began to SAY TO THEM What was to happen to him, that	31 Now TAKING ASIDE THE TWELVE, HE SAID TO THEM:
18 «BEHOLD, WE ARE GOING UP TO JERUSALEM AND THE SON OF MAN *will be delivered* *to the high priests and scribes* *and they will condemn him* *[to death].* 19 ***AND*** THEY WILL DELIVER HIM TO THE NATIONS to BE MOCKED AND TO BE FLOGGED AND to be crucified AND ***the third*** DAY HE WIL RISE».	33 «BEHOLD, WE ARE GOING UP TO JERUSALEM AND THE SON OF MAN *will be delivered* *to the high priests and* to the *scribes* *and they will condemn him* *to death* ***and*** THEY WILL DELIVER HIM TO THE NATIONS. 34 And they will MOCK him and **they will spit on** him AND THEY WILL FLOG *him* AND **they will kill** AND after three DAYS HE WILL RISE».	«BEHOLD, WE ARE GOING UP TO JERUSALEM, and will be fulfilled all that is written by the prophets about THE SON OF MAN. ------------------------------ 32 For he will be DELIVERED TO THE NATIONS, he will be MOCKED, he will be insulted, he will be **spat on** 33 AND, HAVING FLOGGED, THEY **will kill** *him* AND ***the third*** DAY HE WILL RISE». ------------------------------
		34 But they understood nothing of these; and this saying was hidden for them and they did not understand what was said.

While the passages in Matthew and Mark each have two parts, Luke's, the length of a single part, is composed concentrically. Luke clearly distinguishes himself from the other two: he has no parallel to Mark's first part, nor to Matthew's first part; he adds the fulfillment of the Scriptures (31fg); he omits the Jewish phase of the trial (Matt: 18def; Mark: 33def); he adds insults (32d) and, in particular, his third piece on the disciples' incomprehension (34; which partly corresponds to the amazement and fear in the first part of Mark: 32def).

45 See MEYNET R., «Le quatrième chant du serviteur».

INTERPRETATION

The revelation to the Twelve

Jesus predicts to his closest disciples what is about to happen. He does not seem to be saying anything new—he is happy to refer to the words of Scripture (31cd). The novelty is not, in fact, in the contents of the prophecy, but in its reading, in the interpretation which Jesus gives of all the prophetic books, in the choice of a particular prophecy in which the totality of Israel's prophecy is concentrated and summarized. The novelty is also in the fact that Jesus clarifies where the prophecy will be realized, «Jerusalem», and, above all—and this really is new—he indicates that it will be fulfilled in his person, «the Son of God». The novelty is also to be found in the fact that the prophecy announces the imminence of the fulfillment of the Scriptures of the prophets and, in addition, that the Twelve will be implicated in what will happen to the Son of man. Jesus does not, in fact, say that he is going up to Jerusalem, but that he is going up there with the Twelve: «Behold, we are going up» (31b). This is not an invitation, but a statement which, very clearly, does not only have to do with the present time-frame of the journey, but which is looking towards its end—the Passion and the resurrection— in which the Twelve will also be actors.

The incomprehension of the Twelve

In opposition to the wisdom of Jesus, who has been able to discover the Lord's will for him in the Scriptures (31), the incomprehension of the Twelve (34) takes on a singular emphasis. They do not grasp what their master was saying, and do not understand anything of what is written in the Prophets. They are in exactly the same situation as the characters in the Fourth Song of the Servant: it is only after the glorification of the Servant that they are able to recognize what they did not understand, nor what the Lord had accomplished through the hand of his servant, nor what they had done to him: «For they shall see something never told, and witness something never heard before» (Isa 52:15). The incomprehension of Twelve is an integral part of the prophecy. But anyone who knows Isaiah's oracle also knows that the incomprehension was overcome after the resurrection.

2. IN JERICHO (LUKE 18:35-19:10)

We examined the passage about the blind man in the first chapter (see pp. 82-91), and that of Zacchaeus along with the sub-sequence which forms these two passages in the second chapter (see pp. 183-190).

3. THE CENTRAL PARABLE

The Lukan parable has a parallel in Matt 25: the «parable of the talents». Compared to Matthew's version, Luke's appears to be more complex, composite, even. Luke seems to have added to his account a theme which is totally absent from Matthew's, the theme of the main character's kingship which he receives from afar, having distributed his money among his servants. To better understand Luke's originality, it will be helpful to begin with a brief commentary on Matthew's parable, broadly inspired by Marie Balmary's analysis, which profoundly renews—and fortunately corrects— the usual reading of this parable[46].

3.1. *The parable of the talents (Matt 25:14-30)*

The re-writing on the opposite page should be enough to emphasize the text's composition, without more explanation being required.

One observation must be made about the translation of 19b. The JB, NJB, Catholic Study Bible have: «He went through» or «settled» «his accounts with them». This interpretation is widespread (the same expression, with the same meaning, is used at Matt 18:23-24). Another interpretation is at least possible: that the master did not ask for «financial accounts», but for «an account», or, even better, «the tale»: he invites them to «give an account» of what they have done with the money he has given them. A further comment: «immediately» (at the end of v. 15) can refer either to the preceding verb (traditional punctuation) or to the verb which follows (modern punctuation).

Sovereignty

Rather than simply «his servants», the text says «his own servants» (14a); these are the servants for whom the master assumes total responsibility, for whom he is ready to answer to others. In the same way, he gives them not only property, not only *his* property, but his possessions, things he rules over (*hyparchonta* in Greek). «The servants who are his own and the property which he rules over ... I am surprised at this emphasis in the Greek text signifying *how much this man has what he has*[47]». He is sovereign of his property and rules sovereignty over his own servants. What he hands over to his servants is not just property, but full authority over things, that is, the ability to exercise their own sovereignty. Only

46 See BALMARY M., *Abel, ou la traversée de l'Éden*, 64-109. My commentary is too short in its summary of the forty wonderful pages in which the author *gives an account* of her reading.

47 BALMARY M., *Abel*, 66.

: 14 For as a man leaving the country		called his **own** servants		
and distributed to them his possessions:	15 to one he gave five talents, to other two, to other one,			
: to each according to his **own** ability,		and he left the country immediately.		

+ 16 Going out	one who	received	five talents	
.	worked with them	and gained	other five.	
+ 17 Likewise	that (of the)	two		
.		he gained	other two.	
+ 18 But	he who	received	one,	
. went away,	dug the earth	and hid	the money	of his master.

: 19 After a long time,	comes	the master	of those servants
:	and raises	the word	with them.

+ 20 And coming forward	one who	received	five talents	
+ presented other five	talents	saying:		
: «Master, five talents	you gave me;	behold,	five other talents	I gained».
= 21 His master declared	to him:			
- «Well, good and faithful servant,		you were faithful on little,	I will set you on greater;	
- Enter into the joy of your master».				

+ 22 And coming forward also	that of the		two talents,	
+	said:			
: «Master, two talents	you gave me;	behold,	two other talents	I gained».
= 23 His master declared	to him:			
- «Well, good and faithful servant,		you were faithful on little,	I will set you on greater;	
- Enter into the joy of your master».				

– 24 And coming forward also he who		received	one talent said:
- «Master,		I know you	that you are a hard man
- reaping where you did not sow		and gathering	where you did not scatter.
: 25 And being afraid, having left I hid		your talent	in the earth;
: behold,	you have		what is yours».

– 26 Answering	his master		said to him:
- «Wicked servant and slothful,		you know	that
- I reap where I did not sow		and gather	where I did not distribute.
: 27 Then you should have	cast	my money	to the bankers
: and coming	I would have	received	what is mine with interest.

– 28 Take therefore from him	the talent
+ and give (it) to one who has	ten talents.

29 For to one who has	will be given	and he will have more than enough	
but one who does not have	even what he has	will be taken from him.	

– 30 And throw the worthless servant into the darkness outside;
– there will be weeping and gnashing of teeth».

the one who is sovereign can hand over sovereignty; only the one who is really a proprietor can grant authentic property. The text does not say that the master «lends» or that he «grants» his goods; the text says: «and to this one he *gave* five talents, to this one two, to this one» (15a); in the previous phrase, «he *distributed* his possessions to them» (14b), the verb has the same root. This is not a loan, but a gift, which has no conditions attached. No imperative tells them what they are to do. Hardly has he handed over his property and possessions than the master goes; even, according to the traditional punctuation, leaving the country «immediately». Now the talents no longer belong to the master, but to the servants; they are fully sovereign over them.

An equal gift for all

Some will probably be surprised or even scandalized to see that the master does not give the same number of talents to each of his three servants. However, the first thing to note is that the gift is huge: a «talent» is a silver ingot weighing 34.272 kg, that is, 6,000 denarii. Since the denarius represents the salary for one day's work, a talent is equivalent to sixteen and a half years' salary! So even the one who «only» received one talent received an enormous sum. What is more, the text explains why the gift is not equal for all of them: «each according to his ability» (15b). They all, therefore, received to the maximum of their own ability; no one received more than he could bear. In this way, all were treated equally.

The leveling of the gift

The first two servants «immediately» (according to modern punctuation) begin work, to make their talents bear fruit. One might think that their work accentuated their inequality, for, in effect, at the end the difference between the number of each of their talents has increased: when the first one received five talents and the second two, the difference was three talents; now that the first has ten talents and the second four, the difference has doubled to six talents. This is one possible reading. It could also be understood in a different, or totally opposite way, which is the master's reading, on his return. The two servants have done exactly the same thing: each has earned exactly the same number of talents as he received. The strict parallelism in the text emphasizes their equality. It matters little that one received more and the other less, because both have doubled the number of their own talents; and they receive the same praise, word for word, from their master. In the divine arithmetic, three equals five. Not only are they equal to one another, according to their master's logic, but they have become equals of the master: each has earned the same number of talents as the master gave them. If this is true, how could they still be considered to be «servants»? This is why the master invites them to «enter into the joy of their master», that is, the joy of the masters. Like Adam, they have received «the image»; having appropriated it, they have shown themselves able to attain «likeness» (see p. 105). God gave half, and they have produced the other half.

They have accomplished their human vocation, which is nothing else than to be deified.

«The one who has not»

One often hears preachers or reads commentaries explaining that talents have been «granted» or «loaned» to us, and that we must make them productive for the Lord, for they belong to him alone[48]. When he returns at the day of our death, he will ask us for them and we will have to return them all, with those which we have earned[49]. This interpretation is precisely that of the third servant. He does not consider the talent received to be his own personal property, saying, «I hid *your* talent» (25a). And, unlike the other two, he brings it back to restore it to his master: «See, you have *what is yours*» (25b). He received the talent, not as a gift, but as something entrusted to him, which is why he hid it in the ground. The law of the time required that someone who held something in trust and who was robbed was held to be responsible and was to reimburse it from his own pocket, while the one who had buried it was not responsible in case of theft.

Take from him what he does not have

The master does not say, «Take his talent from him», but «Take the talent from him», without the possessive (28a)[50], precisely because it is not «his», because he has not appropriated it. It is taken from him to point out his inability to him. One might say that in reality nothing is taken from him, because it did not belong to him. To a certain extent it takes the weight he was unable to carry from him. It only does what the servant wanted, which is to restore the talent which

48 For example, Gnilka writes: «A slave could make the money which his master had given him be productive. In this case he represented his master, *except that the benefits would not come to him, but would go to his master*» (II, 525).

49 «The two who worked successfully show their winnings. *As a result, their owner receives fourteen talents in total from them*» (Gnilka, II, 526); my emphasis. The French Bible Bayard (Paris 2001) gives this interpretation. Not only does it say that the man «*entrusts* his property to them. To one he *hands over* five talents…», but it goes as far as «translating» the words of the first two servants as follows: «Master, he said, you *entrusted* me with five talents. *I hand over to you* the other five talents I drew from them» (20c.22c), where the «see» in the Greek text becomes «I hand over to you!» At v.28 «Take from him *the* talent» of course becomes «*his* talent»: «Let his talent be taken from him and given to the one who has ten». The contradiction with the words of the first servant does not seem to have bothered the translator: how can one «give [the talent] to the one who has ten», while he had «handed over» the very five talents to the master which he had won from the five which had been «entrusted» to him?

50 The French BJ (even the 1998 edition) translates: «So take from him *his* talent»; as does the French TOB. Osty, on the other hand, does not have the possessive.

was hindering him; thus fear is also taken away from him. Note, too —confirming our interpretation— that the talent which the master takes away from the third servant he does not take for himself, but adds it to the ten which the first one possesses. The fact that the master says, «to the one who has ten talents» (28b) is a proof that these talents are the property of that man, and not his.

Weeping and grinding of teeth

Because the third servant, being afraid of both, cannot tolerate either the gift or the giver, the master has him thrown out into the outer darkness, that is, outside a presence which is intolerable to him. What might be read as a punishment, a sort of vengeance —if our eye is bad, like the third servant's— is in fact a remedy. Far from the master, the servant will be able fit himself to at least one thing: weeping and grinding of teeth. If he is able to live this suffering in the first person, and this rage against himself and probably, initially at least, against the master, his soul can force itself to open up to reflection and conversion. So many other texts, particularly in the First Testament, teach us that God's anger and punishment are always ordained for the conversion of the sinner: «Would I take pleasure in the death of the wicked man —declares the Lord Yhwh— and not prefer to see him renounce his wickedness and live?» (Ezek 18:23)[51].

3.2. *The parable of the gold coins (Luke 19:11-28)*

COMPOSITION

The outer parts (11-12a; 28) introduce and conclude the parable: «Having said these» (28) matches «hearing these things» (11a); «was near to Jerusalem» (11b) is parallel to «going up to Jerusalem» (28).

The outer parts of the parable (12b-15 and 27) match one another. The first part introduces two kinds of characters linked to the king (12b.15a): «ten of his servants» in the outer pieces (13.15bc) and «citizens» in the center (14a). The two outer pieces (12b-13 and 15) parallel what the «nobleman» does before he «left» to «receive the kingdom» and what he did after his return, «when» he had received the kingdom: he «calls» his servants before going and «convokes» them on his return. The last part (27) no longer mentions the servants (to whom the rest of the parable, from 16 to 26, is given over), but only the king's «enemies» (those who «hate» him in 14a) who did not want him to reign over them (14b and 27b). «Bring them» (27c) matches «call» and «convoke» (13a and 15b).

51 See too *Amos*, 182-185 (particularly section 6.3.3); 274-276; 393-405.

. [11] (They) *hearing these things*, he said again a parable
- because he was near to JERUSALEM
- and they thought that immediately was about to appear **THE KINGDOM OF GOD;**
. [12] he said therefore:

+ «A nobleman left for a far country to *receive* **THE KINGDOM** and to return.
– [13] *CALLING* ten of his servants, *he gave them* *ten pounds*,
= and he said to them: "*Do business* while I go".

: [14] But his citizens *HATED* him
: and sent an embassy after him saying: "WE DO NOT WANT that he **REIGN** over us".

+ [15] It happened that, when he returned, *having received* **THE KINGDOM,**
– he asked to *CONVOKE* the servants to whom *he had given* the money,
= to know what they *had gained* *in business.*

+ [16] Came near (to him) the first saying:
"Lord, *your pound* *has produced* *TEN POUNDS*".
. [17] He said to him: "Well done, good servant; because in little you were faithful,
YOU SHALL **have** **POWER** OVER TEN CITIES".
+ [18] And came the second saying:
"*Your pound*, Lord, *has made* *FIVE POUNDS*".
. [19] He said also to him: "Even you, be (chief) over FIVE CITIES".

+ [20] Another came saying:
: "Lord, behold *your pound*, that **I have** stored in a napkin.

- [21] For I was afraid of you *that you are* *a hard man*
- *who* **takes** *what you did not lay down* *and reaps what you did not sow*".

[22] He said: "OUT OF YOUR MOUTH **I JUDGE YOU,** WICKED SERVANT!

- You knew *that I am* *a hard man,*
- *who* **takes** *what I did not lay down* *and reaps what I did not sow.*

: [23] Why then *did you* *not give* *my money* to the bank?
+ And I, coming, with interests could have required it".

+ [24] Then he said to those standing by:
- "**Take** from him *the pound*
- and *give it* to one who **has** *TEN POUNDS*".
[25] They said: "LORD, he **has** *TEN POUNDS!*".
+ [26] «I say to you:
- to every one who **has** *will be given*
- and to one who **has not,** even what he **has** **will be taken.**

: [27] And these my *ENEMIES*
: who DID NOT WANT that I **REIGN** over them,

– *BRING THEM* here
= and slay them before me"».

[28] *And having said these,* he went on ahead, going up to JERUSALEM.

The parts which frame the center oppose the treatment meted out by the king to the good servants (16-19) to that inflicted on the bad servant (24-26).

The first part (16-19) narrates the dialogue between the king and two of his servants in parallel: «ten pounds» (16b) are counted as «little» (17a), and, in parallel «five pounds» (18b) are worth «five cities» to the second servant (19). This leaves «Have power over ten cities» (17b) at the center. The other part (24-26) is centered on v.25: «take» and «give» match, at the start of Jesus' first speech (24bc) and at the end of his second speech (26bc); v.25 is distinguished from the rest of the part, for here are only the words of the characters. The centers of the two parts match: the «ten pounds» in 25 recall the «ten cities» in 17b, which emphasizes the opposition between what happens to, respectively, the good and the bad servants: the bad servant not only does not receive a city, but sees even the pounds which was given to him taken away, while the good servant receives ten cities and makes a total of eleven pounds: the ten which the pound he received have made (16b) and that of the third servant (24).

The central part (20-23) is a concentric construction. The outer segments mirror one another: the two occurrences of «come» form an inclusio (20a.23b); in 20b the servants explains what he has done with the pound he received: (he «stored it in a napkin»); in 23a the master tells him what he should have done at the very least («given it to the bank»). In 22bc the king repeats exactly what the servant has just said to him (21). At the center of this part, and therefore at the center of the whole parable, is the judgment: «From your own mouth I judge you, wicked servant» (22a).

Words from the same family as «king» are found throughout the passage (11c.12b.14b.15a.27b; and we should add «power» in 17b). «To give» (13a.15b.23a. 24c.26b), «to receive» (12b.15a), «to take away» (21b.22c.24b. 26c) and «to have» (17b.20b.24c.25.26bc) belong to the same semantic field.

BIBLICAL CONTEXT

The judgment of Solomon (1Kgs 3:16-28)

The central statement of the parable (22a) recalls the judgment of Solomon[52]: the threat of the sword made the two prostitutes respond in different ways, and the king gave his judgment according to the words of their mouths.

52 See the rhetorical analysis of this text, in French, in MEYNET R., *Initiation*, 113-118 and tables 17 and 18.

The fate of King Solomon's enemies (1Kgs 2:12-46)

After David's death, Solomon «established» his power (1Kgs 2:12 and 46) by executing his enemies, Adonijah, Joab and Shimei; the first two, like the priest Abiathar, did not want him to be king. Abiathar was stripped of the priesthood and exiled, but his life was spared, since he had carried the ark of the covenant and shared in David's trials (26-27). As for Adonijah and Joab, with Shimei who had cursed David, all three were judged on the «words» of their own mouth. —Adonijah (12-25) asks for his father's concubine, Abishag of Shunem, in marriage; in this way he makes a claim on the kingdom, making Solomon say, «May God bring unnamable ills on me, and worse ills too, if Adonijah does not pay for these *words* with his life» (23). — When the news about Abiathar's stripping and exile reached Joab (28-35), like him a supporter of Adonijah against Solomon, Joab went to seek refuge by the Altar. To the king's messenger, who asked him to come out, he said, «No, I will die here». So the king tells his messenger, «Do *as he says*: strike him down and bury him» —Finally, Shimei (36-46) accepts the punishment of house arrest under pain of death, given to him by King Solomon, saying, «That is a fair *word*. As my lord the king has said it, so will your servant do». He would be put to death for not having held to the word he gave to the king.

INTERPRETATION

Compared to the very regular structure of Matthew's parable of the talents, Luke's construction seems to be composite, like those churches which are remodeled down the centuries, in which later additions and modifications make it almost impossible to find the original plan. Effectively, Luke has inserted the theme of kingship from the introduction —which is also an addition (12b)— and into the parable itself (14 and 27). The theme of the cities given to the good servants is derived from this theme of kingship, received and contested by the king's enemies[53].

A deceptive king?

Luke's king is very different from Matthew's man. First of all, he seems much less generous. Of course, the «pound», which was 571 grams of silver, is not insignificant; but the «talent», with its 34.272 kilograms, is worth sixty times more. In

53 The son of Herod the Great, Archelaus, was in this situation after his father's death (see, for instance, Fitzmyer, 1235; Bovon, III, 258).

addition, while Matthew's master «distributes his possessions» (eight talents, that is, four hundred and eighty pounds), Luke's, giving out only ten pounds, has surely not distributed all that he has. But this is not all. In Matthew, only the third servant mentions the talent he has received in the second person possessive: «your talent», while in Luke, all three say «your pound» (16b.18b.20b), as though it had not really been «given», but only lent. It is true that the first two do not return the pound they received, as the third one does (20b), but they give their accounts in the first person. Unlike those in Matthew, they do not say, «I have earned», but rather that it is «the pound» which «has produced ten pounds» (16b), which «has made five pounds» (18b). The Lord seems to confirm the fact that the pound which each received was not really given, but only «entrusted», lent; so, when he says, «give it to the one who has ten pounds» (24c), it might be thought that he has only left him the pounds he has earned and not the original pound, which was lent to him. However, this interpretation does not seem to respect the text. First of all, the pounds were «given»; this is the word which appears twice at the start (13a.15b); when the first two servants then arrive and recount what has happened, we can understand, not that the pound has produced ten or five «other» pounds, as some translators say[54] —adding a word which is not found in the Greek text—, but simply that the pound has become ten or five pounds. Finally, note that the king does not take the pound from the bad servant, but «gives» (24c) it to the first, who is more capable. So how can he recover the nine other pounds which he gave out at the start? And when we see him giving power over ten cities to the first and over five cities to the second, we cannot reasonably think that he intends to recover the pounds, either those which his servants have earned, or, even less, the pounds which he gave them before leaving. He is not content to give his money to his servants, but then shares with them the kingship which has been given to him —ten or five cities are worth far more than ten or five pounds.

The deceptive servant

Luke's first two servants are quite different from Matthew's. They do not emphasize their work, but seem to give all the credit to their master and to the gift they have received: it is his pound which «has produced» (16b) and «made» (18b), as though they counted for nothing. The third, «bad servant», on the other hand,

54 Like the official Italian translation, even in the revised 1997 edition; this is also how Fitzmyer, II, 1235; Rossé, 733; Ernst, II, 733 understand it.

is very like Matthew's. He states that he «had» the pound (20b) —the same verb will then be used by his master: «he who has» (24c), «everyone who has» (26b)— but his way of «having» is very different from the other two. It is the «having» of someone who does not believe in the gift, who thinks about keeping a deposit which he will have to return. He says this clearly: «Here is your pound» (20b). And, clearly, he projects the hardness of his own heart onto his master: «you are a hard man». Not only does he not believe in the gift, but he even denies the deposit: «you did not deposit» (21b); and, what is more, he accuses the master of taking what is not his, «you reap where you did not sow». So we can understand Jesus' statement which at first sight can appear odd: «From the one who has not, even what he has will be taken from him» (26c). «Even what he has» means what he does not consider to be his property.

The slain enemies

The master's behavior towards the bad servant is, therefore, perfectly admissible —it is right that he takes the pound away from him, thus freeing him from a gift which he did not believe in and which weighed on him. The final fate of his enemies, on the other hand, slain in his presence, on his explicit orders, is scandalous. This practice was, of course, common at the time —just as it was in Solomon's day— and his enemies knew the punishment they risked if their maneuvers failed. So should we be scandalized, when they would not have been in the least surprised that the law then in force was applied? Still, it is no less true that the king's judgment is in total contradiction to Jesus' attitude and all his teaching. There is really something disconcerting in what seems to be a cruel and merciless vengeance, the more so since it is at the end of a parable narrative, and we know that the last image marks the reader the most. In fact, if this final verse in the parable causes a problem, that it means that it is the most important; its enigmatic nature has the function of provoking reflection. The first thing to note, probably, is that the whole story is no joke —what is at stake is entirely serious: everyone must commit himself before this king. This is a capital question —in the way that we talk about capital punishment— a question of life and death. Neither should we forget that it is the conclusion of a «parable»; of course, the king represents Jesus, but that does not mean that there cannot be a distance, a significant difference, between the parable and the reality. A parable does not always present a model to be followed —we need only think of the dishonest steward (Luke 16:1-8), who is certainly not to be imitated in his injustice. Finally, and above all, a parable *must be read in its context*, here, in the sequence as a whole. It is only at this level that the enigma can be solved and the message decoded.

4. AT THE MOUNT OF OLIVES (LUKE 19:29-40)

This sub-sequence includes two passages: «The enthronement of the king» (29-36) and «The acclamation of the king» (37-40).

4.1. *The enthronement of the king (Luke 19:29-36)*

COMPOSITION

+ [29] And it happened that, when he came near to Bethphage and Bethany,		
+ at the mount called of the Olives,		
+ HE SENT two of the disciples	*SAYING*:	
. [30] «*Go* into the village in front		
. in which, entering,	YOU WILL FIND a COLT tied,	
----- **ON WHICH NO MAN HAS EVER YET SAT.** -----		
= And *HAVING UNTIED IT*, bring it (here).		
- [31] And if anyone	*ask you*:	"*Why DO YOU UNTIE* it?",
- so you	*shall say*:	"Because its Lord has need of it"».

+ [32] *Having gone*, those SENT	FOUND	
. as he had	*SAID*	to them.
= [33] While *THEY WERE UNTYING* the colt,		
- its lords	*said* to them:	«*Why DO YOU UNTIE* THE COLT?».
- [34] They	*said*:	«Because its Lord has need of it».

: [35] And they brought it to Jesus,	and throwing	their garments	ON THE COLT,
----- **THEY MADE JESUS TO MOUNT.** -----			
: [36] And as he was going,	they spread	their garments	*on the way*.

This passage has two parts: the finding of the colt (29-34) and Jesus' enthronement (35-36). The first part is made up of two sub-parts: the order given by Jesus to two of his disciples (29-31) and its carrying out (32-34). The last pieces (30d-31b and 33-34) are completely parallel. The parallelism between the first pieces (29-30b and 32) is less strict: Jesus' words (30) are not reproduced in 32, but 32b summarizes them; note, however, the lexical recurrences: «sent»/«sent» (29c.32a), «you will find»/«they found» (30b.32a), «saying»/«said» (29c.32b), as well as «go»/«having gone» (30a.32a, which are synonymous in Greek). The relative in

30c, which is not repeated between the two pieces of the second sub-part, is thus at the center of the first sub-part.

The translation of the final answer at 31b, repeating in an identical way that at the end of 34, is not the traditional translation, but was chosen to draw attention to the ambiguity of the Greek text. It can in fact be understood in two different ways: «the Lord needs it» or «his Lord needs it»; the second possibility might seem more likely given that «his lord» is opposed to «its lords» (33b; proper to Luke), and because, in Luke, Jesus never calls himself «the Lord».

The second part (35-36) has two parallel segments (35a and 36), which frame «they made Jesus to mount [it]»; this brief central clause is the counterpart of the member, emphasized by being at the center of the sub-part 29-31: Jesus is thus the first man to sit on this colt.

BIBLICAL CONTEXT

«A colt on which no man has yet sat»

Jesus will be buried in a tomb «in which no one had yet been laid» (Luke 23:53).

Zech 9:9-10

9 Rejoice greatly, daughter of Zion!	shout, daughter of Jerusalem!
Behold, your king comes to you: humble and RIDING on a donkey,	he is righteous and victorious, on a COLT son of a she-ass.
10 He will cut off the CHARIOTS from Ephraim, the bow of war will be cut off,	and the HORSES from Jerusalem ; he will announce peace to the nations.
His dominion will be from sea to sea,	and from river to the ends of earth.

This short poem presents the king of Jerusalem who will come at the end-time, king of all the earth. Force or violence will not bring about his empire, but justice and humility: he will prefer the peaceful mount of the first of Israel's shepherds, «the donkey»[55], in opposition to the «horses» of war (see too Deut 17:16ff).

55 Luke has re-used the word in the LXX, *pōlon*; «to make mount» (Luke 19:35b) is also in Zech 9:9c (LXX).

INTERPRETATION

The prophet

Everything happens exactly «as he had said» (32b), word for word: the disciples «find» the donkey (32a), as predicted (30b); the owners ask the precise question (33b) which Jesus had foreseen (31a) and the answer will be «as» (31b) he had predicted (34). Jesus' word is carried out to the letter. This is the work of prophets, and the sign that they are indeed God's messengers.

The king

This prophet is also a king. He is «lord» of the donkey which he sends people to look for (31b.34). He is seated on the garments of his attentive servants (35a); a carpet of garments is laid on the road before the hooves of his mount (36). Like every king, he needs a mount which has never been used by anyone else (30c): he must be the first to mount it, for it is inappropriate for the king not to be the first in all things.

The prince of peace

Jesus does not mount a horse, but is seated on «a donkey». He is the king prophesied by Zecharaiah; he is not a war-lord. His empire does not depend on arms; he will suppress the war chariots and war horses. He will call the nations to peace. This king is the just one whose humility will win over the peoples. He will even be the humiliated servant who is prepared to suffer the violence he rejects. He will soon be the first king whose throne is a cross. This is how he will become the prince of peace.

4.2. *The acclamation of the king (Luke 19:37-40)*

COMPOSITION

The passage, the size of a part, is made up of three pieces. The first (37) has two bimember segments. The first (37ab) introduces the place (37a) and then the characters (37b). The second piece (37cd) narrates what they do: the second member is the cause of the first; the «sight» of «mighty works» provokes «praise» of «God», recognized as their origin, from the disciples. The second members both begin with «all». — The symmetrical piece (39-40) recounts the Pharisees' demand (39) and Jesus' reply (40): «be silent» matches «rebuke» and «stones» is opposed to «disciples». — Between one piece and the other, «some Pharisees» in 39a is opposed to «all the multitude of disciples» in 37b, whose cries of praise

+ [37] As he was approaching at the descent of the Mount of Olives,				
+ ALL the *multitude* of the ***disciples*** began,				
: rejoicing,	to	PRAISE	God	*WITH A LOUD VOICE*
: for ALL that they had		SEEN	of mighty works,	[38] saying:
«"**Blessed be**	**one who comes**",	THE KING,	"**in the name**	**of the Lord**".
In the heaven	peace		and glory	in the highest!».
+ [39] SOME ***Pharisees***,	among the *crowd*,	said to him:		
– «Master,		REBUKE	your disciples».	
+ [40] Answering,		he said:		
– «I say to you	if these	BE SILENT,	the stones	*WOULD CRY OUT*».

they wish to prevent. The last word of the last segment, «would cry out» (40b), refers back to the end of 37c («with a loud voice»).

The passage centers on a double acclamation (38bc). The first acclamation is in a concentric construction. This is the traditional formula, still used today, to welcome someone; in the center, Luke adds «the king», to qualify «one who comes»; this word often indicates the Lord God, who comes to judge as king (e.g., Isa 35:4). The second acclamation (38c) is in mirror construction. It matches the first, being no longer situated on earth, but «in heaven», «in the heights»; «glory» and «peace» belong to the royal, divine vocabulary, the glory of the king being to bring peace to his people (see Zech 9:9-10).

BIBLICAL CONTEXT

The acclamation in Ps 118

At the center of the passage, the first acclamation repeats the one in Ps 118:26: «Blessed in the name of the Lord is he who comes». The second acclamation recalls that of the angels at Jesus' birth: «Glory to God in the highest and on the earth peace to men in his favor» (Luke 2:14).

Solomon

In this narrative, as in the previous one, several details unique to Luke recall the account of Solomon's enthronement (1Kgs 1:28-48)[56]:

56 See the rhetorical analysis of this text in MEYNET R., *Initiation*, 101-106 and table 15.

«they made mount[57] Jesus»,

rather than «he sat» in Mark and Matthew (see 1Kgs 1:33.38.44: «they made mount» Solomon on his father, King David's mule[58]);

«the descent» (from the Mount of Olives)

absent in Mark and Matthew (see 1Kgs 1:33);

«rejoicing»

absent in Mark and Matthew (see 1Kgs 1:40.45);

«the king»

absent in Mark and Matthew (see 1Kgs 1:34...);

39-40 (with the opposition between Pharisees/disciples)

absent in Mark and Matthew (see 1Kgs 1:41-43).

These are merely indications, which will be corroborated later at the level of the whole sequence, particularly in the central parable of the man who invests himself with kingship.

INTERPRETATION

To believe or to murmur

The disciples, worthy sons of Abraham, father of believers, proclaim their faith: in Jesus' «manifestations of mighty works» which they «had seen» (37d), they recognize the work of «God» (37c), in Jesus they see the active presence of the «king» of heaven (38b). The Pharisees oppose the disciples at every point (39.37). As passive unbelievers, they could be silent, restricting themselves to a discreet refusal to participate in the general acclamation. As militant unbelievers, however, they wish to silence the disciples (39), as the faith of others is unbearable to them. They could also shout at the disciples, or try to cry louder than them. But no, they want Jesus himself to impose silence on them (39), they demand that «the king» (38b) abdicates, that he gives up his titles of «glory» (38c); they are not attacking the believers, but directly attacking the person who is the object of their faith (39b), just like modern atheists who are not content to shut believers up, but fight so fiercely to try to destroy the very idea of God. God cannot stop being God, nor can Jesus stop being king. «God can raise children of Abraham from these stones» (Luke 3:8). The only thing which he cannot do is to impose faith on those who refuse it.

57 This verb, used for Solomon (LXX), only appears here in the Gospels.

58 «The mule», a cross between a donkey and a mare is a peaceful animal, like the donkey.

The king who judges

Jesus says nothing, and yet, those who see him take sides for or against him. Just as on the *tympana* of cathedrals, believers and unbelievers line up on the right and left of Christ in glory. Both are judged before him. On one side are acclamations and praise (37), and on the other complaints (39). All are turned towards Jesus and address him, some making a profession of faith in his kingship (38), others charging him to find against them by silencing them (39). Paradoxically, he will deal with them, too, as a judge! The sentence which is demanded will be passed, but Jesus will impose silence on them: not only will he let the disciples say what they have to say, but he will find against the Pharisees who appeal to him for the judgment which they deserve: their heart is harder than the stones (40).

4.3. *Enthronement and the royal procession (Luke 19:29-40)*

COMPOSITION

29 It happened, WHEN HE CAME NEAR, towards Bethphage and Bethany,
at the **Mount** called **of Olives,** he sent two of the DISCIPLES saying:
30 «Go into the village in front in which, entering,
you will find a colt tied,

ON WHICH NO ONE HAS EVER YET SAT.

Untie it and bring it here. 31 And if anyone will ask you: "Why do you untie the colt?", you shall say so: "Because the LORD has need of it"». 32 Having gone, those sent, found as it was said to them. 33 While they were untying the colt, its LORDS said to them: «Why do you untie the colt?». 34 They said: «Because the LORD has need of it».

35 And they brought it to Jesus, and throwing their garments on the colt,

THEY MADE JESUS TO MOUNT.

36 And as he was going, they spread their garments on the way.

---

37 WHEN HE CAME NEAR to the descent
at the **Mount** **of Olives,** all the multitude of the DISCIPLES,
rejoicing, began to praise God with a loud voice, for all that they saw of manifestation of power, 38 saying:

«Blessed is the one who comes, **THE KING,** in the name of the Lord.
In the heaven peace and glory in the highest!».

39 But some Pharisees, among the crowd, said to him: «MASTER, rebuke your DISCIPLES».
40 Answering, he said to them: «I say to you, if they were silent, the stones would cry out».

These two scenes begin with a similar note of location: «he came near [...] the Mount the Olives» (19:29 and 37). The mention of the «disciples» follows (29 and 37, also 39).

The first account reports what they do, the second what they say, but in both cases Jesus is treated as a king: they «make him mount» (35b) on a donkey, «on which no one had yet sat» (30c) and they acclaim him as «the king» (38b).

«Lord» is repeated in 31b and, in Jesus' mouth, in 34a, in the plural in 33a to describe the donkey's owners, in 38b to name God; the Pharisees call Jesus «master» (*didaskalos*, «one who teaches»).

INTERPRETATION

The king

Acclaiming Jesus as «the king» (38b), the disciples seem to have interpreted their master's intentions correctly. Until now, he has never been seen astride any mount, but went everywhere on foot. If, at this particularly crucial moment, he asks his disciples to go to find a donkey for him, and a donkey on which no one has ever sat, this indicates that he has come to accept what he had always refused, kingship over Israel. Now Jesus is finally responding to their expectations: he is going to present himself before his city as the king predicted by Zecharaiah. And the disciples do not even feel the need to ask him the —final— question which they will ask him during the final meeting, before the Ascension: «Lord, has the time come? Are you going to restore the kingdom to Israel?» (Acts 1:6).

The Lord

During his ministry, many people addressed Jesus by calling him «Lord». Luke, too, in his narrative, often gives him this title. Jesus did not refuse it —we need only think of his words: «Why do you call me 'Lord, Lord', and not do what I say?» (6:46). But this is the first time that, according to the normal translation, Jesus attributes this title to himself: «so you will say, "Because *the Lord* needs it"» (31b). It is so surprising that we would be right to think that he is not speaking about himself, but about the «Lord» God, in whose name the disciples will give the blessing: «Blessed is he who comes, the king, in the name of the *Lord!*» (38b). According to this interpretation, it is God himself who sought Jesus' enthronement.

The master

If the disciples exult and are glad in this moment of joy, as the summit of their own path following their master, a shadow is growing and threatening the end of the narrative. In the crowd around the king, a group of Pharisees come up to Jesus. They do not call him «king» or «Lord», but only «master», a title which seems out of place in such circumstances. They are clearly distinct from the group of disciples. They probably fear that this demonstration will end badly, possibly with intervention by the Romans, always on the look-out to nip in the bud the slightest nationalist claim which might challenge the emperor's authority. More likely, their intervention is a kind of anticipation of what will happen during the Passion. The evangelist has not lost sight of the fact that the king who is coming close to the city to enter it in triumph will, at the end, be seated on the throne of the cross.

5. THE PREDICTION OF JERUSALEM'S FATE (LUKE 19:41-46)

COMPOSITION

+ [41] As he came near,	seeing	THE CITY,	
+	he wept	over it,	
. [42] SAYING that:			

– «*If you had understood,*	in this day,	even you,	the things for ***peace***!
– But now	*it is hidden*	*FROM YOUR EYES*	
:: [43] that *the days*	will come	upon you	
. in which your enemies	will cast ramparts	around you,	
. and will surround you	and hem you in	on every side,	
. [44] and dash you	and your children	within you	
. and they will not leave	stone upon stone	within you,	
– because *you did not understand*	the moment	of	***your visitation***».

+ [45] And, entering		IN THE TEMPLE,
+ he began to	drive out	the sellers,
. [46] SAYING		to them:

. «*IT IS WRITTEN*:			
: "My house	will be	a house	of prayer";
: but you	made it	«a den	of robbers!"».

The passage has two parts (41-44; 45-46); each includes a narrative sub-part (41-42a; 45-46a), which introduces Jesus' words (42b-44; 46bcd).

The narrative sub-parts are made up of a single trimember segment, which ends with «saying» (42a.46a); at the end of the first members «the Temple» (45a), which is at the heart of Jerusalem, and «the City» (41a) are mentioned.

Jesus' final words (46bcd), a single trimember of ABB' type, quote (46cd) the Scriptures (46b); his first words (42b-44) are more developed. At the outsides, are two segments, one a bimember (42bc) and one a unimember (44c), in which «on that day», «now» and «the moment» are synonymous; «peace» and «your visitation», at the end of the outer members, form an inclusio, as do «you have not understood» and «if you had understood», matched by «has been hidden» in the second member. At the center (43-44a) is a piece made up of three segments: after the introductory unimember (43a), the first bimember describes the siege of the city (43), the second predicts its destruction (44ab); «the days» to come (43a) are opposed to «on that day» (42b), «now» (42c), that is, «the moment of your visitation» (44c).

Note in particular that the matching couplet «saying» and «is written», which pin the two sub-parts of the last part together, appear to be matched by a similar couplet in the first part: «saying» (42a) and «from your eyes» (42c).

BIBLICAL CONTEXT

The prophecy of the destruction of Jerusalem

Even though it does not quote a particular prophetical text, the description of the siege and fall of the city (43-44b) weaves together biblical expressions (Isa 29:3; 37:33; Jer 52:4-5; Ezek 4:1-3; Hos 10:14; 14:1, etc.), and therefore refers back to the body of prophetical writings.

The funerary lament

Predicting Jerusalem's destruction, and therefore the end of Israel, Jesus «weeps» over the City. The whole central sequence of the book of Amos is a long *qînâ*, a long funerary lament for the «virgin of Israel» (Amos 5:1-17); these words which God addresses to his people through the prophet Amos are not words of vengeance, but are the final call to conversion «so that they may live» (Amos 5:4.6.14)[59].

Jesus' quotation in the Temple

Jesus' quotation (46cd) is composite: the first member takes up Isa 56:7, and the end of the second member (46d) comes from Jer 7:11. The whole of Jeremiah 7 is an oracle against the Temple in Jerusalem: because of the people's sins, the Temple will be destroyed, as has already happened to the temple at Shiloh. —Jesus' gesture, in chasing out the sellers from the Temple, recalls the end of the final chapter of Zechariah (14:21): «There will be no more traders in the Temple of

59 See *Amos*, Séquence B4, 159-185.

the Lord of Hosts on that Day». Zech 14 first predicts the capture of Jerusalem and the deportation, and then the restoration of the city and its new consecration.

• Jesus' entry into the Temple also recalls the person who will enter the sanctuary to purify it (Mal 3:1f).

INTERPRETATION

Tears and anger

It is surprising that Jesus goes so quickly from lamentation (41b) to anger (45b). He weeps over the city: he foresees, as a prophet, that its buildings, including the Temple, are destined for destruction (43) and that the whole population will be exterminated by the enemy (44ab). When he then starts to chase the sellers from the Temple (45b), his gesture is typically prophetical. It is surely not that he is angry with the people, whose commercial activity was, after all, necessary to the good organization of religious worship[60]. One might think that Jesus was angry because all these activities had invaded the Temple itself, when they should have been kept outside the sacred space. One might also imagine that he meant to criticize the more or less illicit, or at any rate exaggerated, gains of the shopkeepers profiting from the faith of pilgrims, who he calls «thieves», whose job is to rob. The context of the episode leads us to go beyond these simple reasons. The prophet is the person who sees what others are unable to see, who cries out to invite them to open their eyes; Jesus' words, his tears and his anger only have this aim, in each of the two episodes in this passage. The blindness of the salesmen, who look for their subsistence from the people they rob, rather than turning in prayer to the one who alone is able to give life, refers back to the blindness of the whole city and all the people who did not see in Jesus the «visitation» of the God who sought to bring them true «peace». Jesus weeps and becomes angry because the true enemy is not the external enemy, but is rather found inside the city, and inside the Temple itself. Jerusalem is the true architect of its own ruin, «for it has not understood the moment of its visitation» (44c).

60 Those who came to the Temple from far away were surely happy to find money-changers and merchants who sold them the animals for the sacrifices, and flour and oil for the offering.

Jesus interprets the Scriptures

Jerusalem is blind: both the present of the visitation of God in Jesus and the future unhappiness which flow from it «have been hidden from its eyes» (42c). However, Jesus shows that he has understood, he has been able to see, that is, he knows how to read the Scriptures. In the words which he speaks, the hearer can hear expressions which come from what «is written» (46), but also the fact that he takes them on personally, as a summary of various prophecies (43-44). Jesus is not content to read or repeat the biblical text in an automatic way; he interprets it, making it is own, creating a text which is proper to him. This is extremely clear in his description of the fall of Jerusalem (43-44), but it can also be seen in his final words (46cd), where he does not quote literally, but refers to two different passages, in an expression and composition which are quite personal to him. This can only be attributed to the fact that he would be quoting from memory, that is, without the precision required from a professional scribe. Rather, we should consider the fact that Jesus was able to discover God's design, his will for him and his people, in the Scriptures.

Jerusalem's blindness

Jesus was able to recognize his own vocation in the Scriptures, that of being sent by the Lord to bring «peace» (42b) and to be the instrument of God's «visitation» (44c). At the same time, he was able to see that he would be rejected by this generation, and that the divine punishment would hammer the city inexorably. His unshakeable faith pushed him to interpret this rejection as mysteriously willed by God himself: «It is hidden from your eyes» (42c). However, he does not say, in his case, what the aim of such blindness might be.

6. JESUS, CONTESTED KING, EXERCISES JUDGEMENT (LUKE 18:31-19:46)

COMPOSITION

The seven passages in the sequence are organized concentrically around the only parable. The second and third passages, on the one hand, and the fifth and sixth passages on the other, form the sub-sequences which have already been analyzed and commented on. It therefore remains to examine the links between the symmetrical passages and to draw out the axes which bear the load of the sequence as a whole.

ANNOUNCEMENT OF JESUS' FATE		*we are going up to* JERUSALEM 18:31-34
THE BLIND MAN	HEALED	**he came near to** *JERICHO* 18:35-43
THE TAX-COLLECTOR	JUSTIFIED	he passed through *JERICHO* 19:1-10
THE PARABLE	OF THE KING	**he was near to** JERUSALEM 19:11-28 *going up to* JERUSALEM
THE ENTHRONEMENT	OF THE KING	**he came near to**... *THE MOUNT OF OLIVES* 19:29-36
THE ACCLAMATION	OF THE KING	**he came near to**... *THE MOUNT OF OLIVES* 19:37-40
PREDICTION OF THE FATE OF JERUSALEM		**he came near to**... THE CITY 19:41-46 entering into THE TEMPLE

Links between passages in pairs

The outer passages (18:31-34 and 19:41-46)

18:[31] Taking aside the Twelve, he **SAID** to them:
«Behold, we are GOING UP to JERUSALEM, and will be accomplished all that
Is written by the prophets regarding the Son of man:

[32] *He will be given* to the nations, *he will be mocked, he will be insulted, he will be spat upon*
[33] *and, having flogged him, they will kill him, and the third* DAY *he will rise».*

– [34] But they UNDERSTOOD nothing of these;
– and this **SAYING** for them *WAS HIDDEN*
– and they did NOT UNDERSTAND what was **SAID.**

[...]

19:[41] As he CAME NEAR, seeing THE CITY, he wept over it, **SAYING:**

– [42] «IF YOU HAD UNDERSTOOD, in this day, even you, what makes for peace!
– But now this *WAS HIDDEN* **to your eyes:**

[43] DAYS *will come for you in which* your enemies *will cast ramparts around you, and they will surround you, and hem you in on every side;* [44] *and they will dash you and your children within you and they will not leave stone upon stone within you,*

– because YOU DID NOT UNDERSTAND the moment of your visitation».

[45] And, ENTERING in the TEMPLE, he began to drive out the traders, [46] **SAYING:**
It is written: "My house will be a house of prayer", but you made it "a den of robbers"»!

The first passage begins with a movement verb and a place-name: «we are going up to Jerusalem» (18:31b); just as both parts of the last passage begin with «he came near [...] the City» (19:41) and «entering in[to] the Temple» (45). — The pair «word»/«Scripture» is found: at the start, Jesus «says» (31a) «all that is written» (31b); in the same way, in the last passage, «saying: "It is written..."» (46a); «to say» is also repeated in 34a and 41, matched by the synonymous «word» (*rhēma*) in 34b. —At the center of the first passage (32-33), Jesus predicts his Passion and resurrection; in the last passage, at the center of his first address (43-44b), he predicts the suffering of Jerusalem. Each of the two prophecies is a long list of six verbs in the future tense. «Your enemies» in 43a matches «the nations» in 32; «day» at the end of the first list (33) matches «days» at the start of the other list (43a). — The three members which, in the last passage, frame the prophecy of the destruction of Jerusalem (42.44c) are matched by the three members of last segment of the first passage: «understood nothing» (34a) and «did not understand» (34c) are repeated with «if you had understood» (42a) and «you did not understand» (44c); the same verb «to be hidden» recurs in 34b and 42b. While it is «the Twelve» who do not understand in the first passage, in the last passage it is «the City» of Jerusalem.

«The blind man of Jericho» and «The proclamation of the king» (18:35-43 and 19:37-40)

18:35 It happened that, when HE CAME NEAR TO *Jericho*,
a blind-man was sitting along the way, begging alms. 36 Hearing a crowd passing by, he
inquired what it was. 37 They announced to him: «Jesus the Nazorean **COMES** in this way!».
38 He exclaimed saying: «Jesus, **SON OF DAVID**, have mercy on me!». 39 Those who were
walking before **rebuked** him, so that **he might be silent**; but he **was crying out** all the more:

«**SON OF DAVID**, have mercy on me!».

40 Jesus, stopping, ordered that he might be brought to him. As he came near, he asked
him: 41 «What do you want that I may do for you?». He said: «Lord, that I may see again!».
42 Jesus said to him: «See again! Your faith has saved you». 43 And instantly he saw again
and followed him **praising GOD**. And ALL THE PEOPLE, *seeing*, gave ***glory to GOD***.

[...]

19:37 As HE CAME NEAR TO *the descent of the Mount of Olives*,
ALL THE MULTITUDE OF THE DISCIPLES, rejoicing, began to **praise GOD** with a loud
voice, for all that *they had seen* of manifestation of power, 38 saying:

«Blessed is the One who **COMES**, **THE KING**, in the name of the Lord.
In the heaven peace and ***glory IN THE HIGHEST***!».

39 But some Pharisees, among the crowd, said to him: «Master, **rebuke** your disciples!».
40 Responding, he said to them: «I say to you, if these **were silent**, the stones **would cry out**».

The first passage ends with the «glorification of God» by «*all* the people» who «saw» (18:43); the other passage begins in the same way: «*all* the multitude of disciples» «praise God» for what they have «seen» (19:37). — The centers match, for the «son of David» (18:39) is «the king» (19:38)[61]. — At the end of the second passage (19:39-40), the Pharisees wish to «silence» the disciples who «cry-out», asking Jesus to «rebuke» them. In symmetrical position, before the center of the first passage (18:39), the same words are found when the blind man who «cries-out» is «rebuked» so that he «is silent». This gives:

a	they rebuke– be silent	– he was crying-out			18:39
b	SON OF DAVID				39
c	ALL the people		SEEING	*glory to God*	43
c'	ALL the multitude of the disciples	*praising God*	HAVING SEEN		19:37
b'	THE KING				38
a'	rebuke – be silent	– they will cry-out			39-40

61 Luke is the only synoptic author to use the word «king» (see Matt 21:9 and Mark 11:9), although John 12:13 also uses it.

The pair «praise»/«glory» is found on both sides (18:43 and 19:37.38); joy motivates the disciples (19:37) like Zacchaeus (19:6). Jesus is still «the one who comes» (18:37 [19:10] and 19:38).

Zacchaeus and the colt (19:1-10 and 29-36)

19:[1] *Having entered, he was passing by Jericho.* [2] And behold a man **called** by name Zacchaeus, and he was the chief of the tax-collectors and he was rich. [3] He was seeking to see who Jesus was. But he could not because of the crowd, for he was short in stature. [4] And running forward before, he climbed upon a sycamore to see him because he was about to pass there.

[5] When he arrived at that place, looking up, Jesus said to him: «Zacchaeus, come down quickly! BECAUSE TODAY I MUST STAY IN YOUR HOUSE». [6] And in haste, he came down and received him with great joy. [7] Seeing this, all murmured saying: «It is with a sinner he has gone to ***LODGE***!». [8] Stood up, Zacchaeus said to the Lord:

«Behold, ***half of my goods***, Lord,	to the poor I GIVE them;
and if I have defrauded any one,	I will GIVE BACK to him ***four times***».

[9] Jesus said to him: «TODAY SALVATION HAS COME INTO THIS HOUSE, because he is also a son of Abraham; [10] for the Son of man has come to seek and to save what was lost».

[...]

19:[29] It happened that, ***when he came near,*** *towards Bethphage and Bethany, at the Mount* **called** *of Olives,* he sent two of the disciples saying: [30] «Go in the village in front in which, entering, you will find a colt tied, on which no one has ever yet sat. ***UNTIE IT*** and bring it here. [31] And if anyone will ask you: "Why ***DO YOU UNTIE*** the colt?", you shall say so: "BECAUSE THE LORD HAS NEED OF IT"».
[32] Having gone, those sent, found as he had said to them.
[33] While they were ***UNTYING*** the colt, his lords said to them: «Why ***DO YOU UNTIE*** the colt?». [34] They said: «BECAUSE THE LORD HAS NEED OF IT».

[35] And they brought it to Jesus, they made Jesus to mount.	AND THROWING	***their garments***	on the colt,
[36] And as he was going,	THEY SPREAD	***their garments***	on the way.

Just as the symmetries between «The blind man of Jericho» and «The proclamation of the king» are evident, so they are not obvious, not at first sight, at least, between «Zacchaeus» and «The enthronement of the king». However, «Lord» is repeated twice in each passage, to describe Jesus (19:8a.8b; 31b.34); «called» recurs in 19:2a and 29a; in addition, «to lodge» (*kata-lyō*)[62] at 7b has the same root as «to untie» (*lyō*: 30c.31a.33 (x2)).

62 «To untie» the horses during a journey, to rest or overnight.

Where the second and penultimate passages are centered on the acclamation of the «king», the «son of David», in the accounts of «Zacchaeus» and «The enthronement of the king», there is apparently no question of the king, not acclaimed, at least; however Jesus asks for something, first of all Zacchaeus' «house», then «the colt» in a neighboring village. Thus he demonstrates his regal behavior: he does not ask permission, as an inferior would, but expresses his royal wish: «I must stay» (19:5b), «the Lord has need of it» (19:31b and 34). In response, while some murmur or question (19:7 and 31), others, Zacchaeus and the disciples, even give what they have not been asked for —Zacchaeus, half his goods to the poor, and four-fold for those he has defrauded (19:8), the disciples, their garments not only on the colt, but also on the road (19:35.36). In each case the gift is doubled, which is normal for a king, as the honor of being able to give to him is so great.

THE MAIN AXES OF THE SEQUENCE AS A WHOLE

Jesus is king

Invoked as «son of (king) David» by the blind man of Jericho (18:39), acclaimed as «king» by the disciples in 19:38, in the central parable he presents himself as someone who is leaving «to receive kingship» (19:12); he exercises it by «judging» (19:22) both the bad servant and his «enemies», those who «did not wish» him to «reign over them» (19:14 and 27).

Throughout the whole of the sequence this king is presented with Solomon's characteristics: like Solomon he is the «son of David» (18:38.39); like Solomon he is «made to mount» a royal mount and led into his city to cries of joy (19:35-40; see p. 365); like Solomon he judges his servants on the words of their own mouths (19:22; see p. 355) and has them put to death (19:27; see p. 355); like Solomon, whose name means «man of peace», this king «comes» (18:37; 19:10. 23.38; and in 44 «visits»), for «salvation» in the first side of the sequence (three times: 18:42 and 19:9.10), for «peace» in the second side (twice: 19:38 and 42)[63]; finally, like Solomon, he describes the Temple as the «house of prayer» (19:45)[64].

63 The humble king mounted on a colt in the prophecy in Zech 9:9-10 (see p. 361) also «comes» to «announce peace».

64 More than one-third of the pages which narrate Solomon's reign (1Kgs 1-11) are given to the Temple, to its building and inauguration (1Kgs 5:15-9:9). In the long prayer of dedication and in the blessing which follows (1Kgs 8:22-53), the Temple is called «house» (nine times) of «prayer» (twelve times) and of «supplication» (eleven times).

Two contrary attitudes before the king

We noted above in discussing the passages about «the blind man» and «the acclamation of the king» (see the table on p. 373), that the attitude of the blind man and «all the people», as well as «all the multitude of disciples» who «having seen» «praise God» and «give [him] glory» (18:43 and 19:37-38) is opposed to the attitude of those who «rebuke» the blind man and the disciples who «cry-out» «to be silent». This opposition occurs throughout the sequence.

In the passage about Zacchaeus, while the leader of the tax-collectors, who wished «to see» Jesus, welcomes him into his house and converts, «all» those who «see» «murmur» against Jesus' behavior (19:7); this last verb is directly opposed to «to praise»[65]. In the symmetrical passage, «The enthronement of Jesus», the opposition between «the Lord» and «the lords» of the colt seems to demonstrate their resistance to lending out the animal.

The same opposition is repeated in the central parable. The first two servants are opposed to the third; the third one, unlike Zacchaeus who promised «to give» his money, did not know how to make the pound which he received bear fruit; he did not even «give» it to a bank (19:23). The king's «enemies» who «did not want him to reign over them» (19:14.27) recall all Jesus' adversaries, particularly those who wished to prevent others —the blind man, and following him, all the people, and the disciples who gave their cloaks and acclaimed him— from treating Jesus like a king. These enemies of Jesus are those who, in the first passage, «will give» him (18:32) to the nations so that he will be killed. The final fate of the king's enemies in the parable (19:27) predicts Jerusalem's fate, as it was not able to recognize in Jesus the king of peace (19:43-44).

These opposing attitudes towards Jesus could, in the light of the parable, be summarized by the binomial *to say/to do*: to say, to confess Jesus' kingship; to do, to produce gifts for the king. In other words, this is about faith and works. «Faith», and consequently «salvation», are recognized by Jesus not only in the person who seems him as the «son of David» (18:42), but also in the person who «gives the half of his goods to the poor...» (19:9), and in the person who makes fruitful, who is called «reliable» or «faithful» (19:17).

65 Cultural opposition: «to murmur» does not just mean to criticize, but to revolt against (see Exod 15:24).

Son of man and son of David

«Son of man» (18:31 and 19:10) forms an inclusio for the first side of the sequence; this title is opposed to the title «son of David» (twice: 18:38.39) which is matched by «the king» in the second side (19:38): Son of man in fact indicates the one who will be glorified, after having gone through the Passion. These are Jesus' two matching faces—the king, but the king crucified.

To see and to understand

It is not only the blind man of Jericho and Zacchaeus who cannot see, but also Jerusalem at the end of the sequence which cannot see «the one who is for peace», because «this has been hidden from its eyes» (19:42); the disciples, too, in the first passage, do not understand, for Jesus' word «was hidden for them» (18:34). If those who «see» Jesus entering Zacchaeus' house «murmur» against him (19:7), it is because they have not «understood» that the moment of salvation has arrived. However, the blind man of Jericho «sees again» (18:43), while «all the people» (18:43), and «all the multitude of disciples» «praise God» for what they «have seen» (19:37).

The «house»

The two occurrences of «house» (*oikos*), at the end of the first side (19:5.9) and at the end of the second side (19:46), act as final terms; the first time, it is Zacchaeus' house, and the second time the Temple, God's house; Jesus «enters» both houses (6.45). Thieves are found in both houses.

BIBLICAL CONTEXT

Throat-cutting

In the whole of the New Testament, Luke alone uses, at the end of the parable of the pounds, the verb «to cut the throat», *kata-sphazō*, with the prefix which emphasizes the fact that the operation must be completed, that is, until the last enemy is dead[66]. However, the simple verb without the prefix is found elsewhere, mainly in Revelation, applied four times to Jesus, «the Lamb slain[67]» (Rev 5:6.9.12; 13:8) and also to the martyrs (Rev 6:9; 18:24). In the Septuagint a word from the same root (*sphagē*) indicates the place where animals' throats are cut: the servant of the Lord «was like a lamb going to the *slaughter-house*» (Isa 53:7).

66 This is the verb used in 2Macc 5:12.24; 6:9 for the massacres.

67 Translations which use «the sacrificed Lamb» soften the image.

INTERPRETATION

«He went ahead, going up to Jerusalem» (19:28)

From the surroundings of Jericho near the Jordan, where, with the Baptism and the temptations, everything had started for him (Luke 3:21-4:13), going up via Bethphage and Bethany (19:29) to the Mount of Olives (19:37), Jesus walks; he proceeds towards «what is written» (18:31), he goes up to Jerusalem, he approaches his end. The end is predicted from the beginning: «The Son of man will be given up to the nations...» (18:32).

On this path which leads to the cross and the resurrection, Jesus meets many people. He is accompanied by «a crowd» (18:36); «all the people» (18:43), «all the multitude of disciples» (19:37) follow him, expanded by those whom he «saves» (18:42; 19:9-10). Finally, acclaimed by this immense procession, he approaches the descent from the Mount of Olives (19:37-40).

But, having reached the end of his journey, when Jesus finds himself facing the city which he gazes on from the heights of the Mount of Olives (19:41), neither the crowd nor the disciples are mentioned, as though now he finds himself alone. It seems that all have disappeared, to leave him face to face with the City and his fate, their shared fate.

The Twelve had been invited to accompany him to the end: «Behold, we are going up to Jerusalem» (18:31). If Jesus seems to go ahead on the road alone, while they are so close to the end, it is probably because they understood nothing of what he said to them (18:34); and from Jerusalem —which represents all the people of Israel— Jesus is confronted with the same incomprehension and blindness (19:42). Only he sees clearly what will be not only his own end (18:32-33), but also that of his City (19:43-44), and tears spring into his eyes, the same eyes which were able to decipher the Scriptures (18:31): «he wept» (19:41).

A long history of blind people

With the exception of the Twelve, the first person which whom Jesus dealt personally is the blind man of Jericho (18:35-43). This man is emblematic of so many others whom he met all along the path taking Jesus to Jerusalem. «All the people» who, «seeing, glorified God» (18:43): like the blind men, they, too, were healed of their blindness[68].

68 See p. 88, first paragraph.

Immediately Zacchaeus comes, the leader of the tax-collectors, who «wished to see who Jesus was, but could not» (19:3); not only did he see Jesus and welcome him into his house, but his eyes were opened to himself and his savior: he recognized himself as a sinner and, like the blind man, he was «saved» (18:42; 19:9-10). «All» the others «see» (19:7) what takes place, but they do not understand, they are blind; however, with his final statement (19:9-10)[69], Jesus tries to open their eyes both to Zacchaeus, who has become a «son of Abraham», and to «the Son of man come to save».

The third servant of the parable seems to be blind, too: when he says to the master that he «even takes what he has not laid down and reap what he has not sown», he shows himself to be blinded by «fear», as though he were incapable of seeing that the Lord has given him a coin like the other nine (19:21). If the master takes the coin from him (19:24) to give it to the one who has ten, it is possible to understand that «the person who has come to find and save what was lost» (19:10) is not punishing him, but offering him a further possibility to open his eyes both to his own wickedness and to the goodness of the giver. One could probably also interpret the word addressed to the «lords» of the colt in the same way: «Because the Lord needs it» (19:34), and also the reply to the Pharisees: «If they were silent, the stones would cry out» (19:40).

In all this long history of blindness, we should not forget the characters who match one another, at the start and the end of the sequence: the Twelve and the City, who «do not understand», because «this has been hidden», «hidden *from their eyes*» (18:34; 19:42.44b); they, too, therefore, are blind. What Jerusalem «has not understood» and «does not understand», is that «he is for peace» (19:42) and «the time of his visitation» (19:44); what the Twelve «do not understand» and «have not understood» (18:34), is the prediction of Jesus' Passion and resurrection (18:32-33). All of this, which Jesus tries to make them understand, and tries to open their eyes to, is what he has been able to see in reading «what was written by the Prophets about the Son of man» (18:31). From the first verse the key to reading the whole sequence is provided: with his words and deeds, Jesus «accomplishes the Scriptures».

69 These words, in the third person, seem to be addressed to those witnessing the scene rather than to Zacchaeus himself; the sentence which introduces them could even be translated as: «Jesus said about him»; see Fitzmyer, 1225.

Jesus, Christ

Having seen Jesus cure the blind man and save the leader of the tax-collectors in Jericho, all «thought that the kingdom of God was about to appear» (19:11). With his parable, Jesus does not contradict them, even though, at the start he talks about a man who «left to receive kingship and to return» (19:12). The kingdom of God is close, and all understand that the man who receives royal anointing is none other than Jesus himself; however, before this, «he will leave for a distant country»: as he had predicted to the Twelve, he has to confront the leaving which is death (18:33) and he will only be consecrated with the resurrection. But it is not only in the parable that Jesus assumes the title of king. When, at the start of the road to Jerusalem, the blind man twice calls him «son of David» (18:38-39), Jesus does not reprimand or silence him; on the contrary, he silences those who wish to reduce the sick man to silence, he has him called (40) and, at the end, he praises his faith (42). The same happens after the parable, when «all the multitude of disciples» treat him and acclaim him as «the king» (19:35-40). Jesus does not refuse this title; he even snubs the Pharisees who wish to silence the disciples (39-40).

Not only does he agree to be called king, but he even behaves in a regal manner. The fact that, hardly is the parable ended, than Jesus sends two disciples to find a colt, describing himself as «the Lord» (19:31), gives us to understand that he wished to enter into his City astride a royal mount. He orders and is immediately obeyed, as is appropriate for a king: he «orders» that the blind man be brought to him, and it is done without discussion (18:40); his order, «See again» is «immediately» carried out (18:42). With Zacchaeus, he uses the imperative: «Come down quickly» (19:5) and «he came down quickly» (6); he invites himself to the home of the leader of the tax-collectors where he is «welcomed with great joy» (6). With his disciples he uses three imperatives: «Go [...], untie it and bring it here» (31); he replies regally to the Pharisees who demand that he «reprimand his disciples». Looking at the City, he denounces its blindness (19:42-44) and predicts its punishment; and, finally, in the Temple, he behaves as though he is the master of the house (45-46).

He is the king in the parable, the one who «calls» his servants to give them, along with pounds, his orders: «Make it bear fruit» (19:13); it is he who, on his return, has them «called» (15), who is appreciative: «Well done, good servant», and orders: «Have authority over ten cities» (17); it is he who, like King Solomon, «judges» the bad servant «from his own mouth» (22), who orders those who surround him: «Take the coin from him and give it…» (24); and, finally, he who condemns his enemies: «Take them away and slay them before me!» (27).

All that blood!

One cannot understand the parable's ending without placing it in context, that is, in the sequence as a whole. The surprise —the scandal— which leads to all these cut throats probably acts to draw attention and ask questions. As it happens, it is an important question. Right up till the last verse, the parable proceeds calmly; but at the end, like a thunder-clap, is a totally unexpected enigma.

One might think that this final scene predicts the final passage in the sequence, where Jerusalem's punishment is predicted, Jerusalem which did not wish to welcome Jesus as its king: «for you did not understand the time of your visitation» (19:44). However, we should note that is not Jesus who punishes the city, but the Romans, led by Titus, son of the Emperor; the king of Israel, on the other hand, predicting the disaster, weeps over the city (19:41).

Such a reading is possible, and is the reading given in many commentaries. However, it does not resolve the enigma in a truly satisfactory way. There is absolutely no doubt that the king in the parable represents Jesus, from the start and throughout this fictitious account. The order given by the king to cut the throats of his enemies remains unacceptable and scandalous. For, in the closer reality—not forty years hence, but in a few days—who is it who will be «slain»? It is Jesus who says so, at the start of the sequence: «the Son of man will be given up to the nations, he will be mocked, maltreated, spat on, and having scourged him, *they will kill him*» (18:31-33). Rather than acting as any other king of this world would have done, to establish his power, without risking a later revolt, this king, who has come to establish «the kingdom of God» (19:11), agrees to be the victim of his enemies. Luke could not have set up a stronger contrast between the wisdom of the world, and that of the Gospel.

Blood and tears

Jesus will not shed the blood of his enemies, those who «did not want him to become their king» (19:27). Predicting his Passion from the outset (18:32-33), going ahead to go up to Jerusalem after the parable (19:28), he accepts that his own blood will be shed (18:33). Arriving before the City, «he weeps», shedding tears of bitter sadness (19:41). He knows that Jerusalem will be destroyed, and its children killed by a foreign enemy; he knows, and he says so clearly, that this is the punishment for the blindness of its people, who have rejected his kingship (42.44). Like God, he does not rejoice in evil, but suffers from it: «Would I take pleasure in the death of a wicked man —it is the Lord Yhwh who speaks— and not prefer to see him renounce his wickedness and live?» (Ezek 18:23). Tears and blood which are shed together indicate Jesus' compassion. He does not weep for himself, but for the death of those who will give him up to the nations so that he may be killed. His tears are a funerary lament.

And yet more violence to end!

The last passage, and the final passage of the whole sequence, ends —we should probably say «opens»— with an event which could appear superfluous. The reader may well ask how the scene in which Jesus chases the traders out of the Temple (19:45-46) fits into the logic of the whole. Perhaps the narrator simply wishes to lead Jesus to the end of his journey? He could have simply said that, in the Temple, Jesus «taught the people», as in the verses which frame the following sequence (19:47; 21:37-38). He perhaps intends to end the sequence by referring back to the Scriptures, as he had started with the prediction of the Passion and the resurrection, so that «everything which had been written by the prophets about the Son of man» (18:31) should be accomplished. So why finish with an act of violence, which somehow recalls and revives the end of the parable (19:27)?

One could probably interpret Jesus' behavior by accusing him, as the third servant in the parable does the king who had given him a coin to make it bear fruit: «I know that you are a hard man» (19:21). But one can also explore another path and place one's trust in the coherence of Luke's account. Prior to the parable, Jesus had already «entered» (19:6.45) into another «house», the house of Zacchaeus, the leader of the tax-collectors, who was considered by all to be «a sinner» (19:7), and, more precisely, a thief. In fact, when Zacchaeus himself promises to reimburse four-fold all those he has «extorted from» (8), this indicates that he is confessing to having stolen, and that he repents. He «has understood the moment of his visitation» (19:44). Jesus' final declaration, «The Son of man has come to find and to save what was lost» (10) gives us to understand that, when he enters into the other «house» (19:45-46), God's house, Jesus has no intention apart from «salvation». Like the prophet Jeremiah, whose expression «a den of thieves» (Jer 7:11) he repeats, his attack does not aim at destruction; it is a final invitation to repentance, the desperate effort of one who is trying the impossible, even though he knows full well that he will not be listened to and that destruction is now inevitable.

The true ending—the resurrection in sight!

The sequence ends in a dramatic, almost desperate way, with the prediction of the destruction of Jerusalem and its Temple. However, we should not forget that it had begun, not just with the prediction of Jesus' Passion and death, but also with the prediction of his resurrection. «Salvation» was accepted by the leader of the tax-collectors and the blind man of Jericho, followed by «all the people» who «gave glory to God» (18:43). In the parable, while the third servant was judged to be «wicked» (19:22), the other two were «good servants». Where later «some Pharisees» opposed Jesus (19:39), «all the multitude of his disciples» served him and acclaimed him as they would their king (37-38). The relationship, so strongly emphasized, between the outer passages—the prediction of Jesus' Passion and resurrection (18:31-34) and the prediction of the destruction of Jerusalem (19:41-46)—is, however, unsymmetrical, for it is not said that Jerusalem will rise again. Does this mean that its destruction is definitive, without the slightest hope of restoration? In the following sequence, Jesus will announce that «Jerusalem will be trampled underfoot by the nations, until the time of the nations is fulfilled» (21:24), which gives us to understand that the condemnation is not for ever. How are we to understand this «fulfillment of the time of the nations»? By returning to «what is written» at the end of the sequence under discussion (19:46), the reader who is familiar with prophetical oracles cannot but notice, in Jesus' incomplete quotation, «My house will be a house of prayer», the words of the prophet Isaiah: «My Temple shall be called a house of prayer *for all the peoples*» (Isa 56:7). It is probably this universality of salvation which will accomplish Jerusalem's resurrection.

E. SYNOPTIC COMPARISON OF THE SEQUENCES

Matt	Mark	Luke
—	—	The ten lepers 17:11-19
—	—	When? 20-21
24:26-27; 37-39; 17-18; 40	13:15-16	The day of Jesus 22-36
24:28	—	Where? 37
—	—	The judge and the widow 18:1-8a
—	—	Question 8b
—	—	The Pharisee & the tax-collector 9-14
Introduction 19:1-2	Introduction 10:1	
Question on divorce 3-9	Question on divorce 2-9	—
	Against adultery 10-12	(16:18)
Eunuchs for the kingdom 10-12	—	—
Jesus and the children 13-15	Jesus and the children 13-16	Jesus and the children 15-17
The call of the rich man 16-22	The call of the rich man 17-22	The call of the rich man 18-27
Poor for the kingdom 23-26	Against idolatry 23-27	
Fate of the Twelve 27-29	Fate of the Twelve 28-30	Fate of the Twelve 28-30
The last becomes first 30	The last becomes first 31	(13:30)
Parable of the workers 20:1-15	—	—
The first becomes last 16	—	—
Jesus' Fate 17-19	Jesus' Fate 32-34	Jesus' Fate 18:31-34
The two sons 20-23	The sons of Zebedee 35-41	—
Discourse on service 24-28	Discourse on service 42-46a	(22:25-27)
The two blind men 29-34	The son of Timaeus 46b-52	Healing of the blind man 35-43
—	—	Healing of Zacchaeus 19:1-10
25:14-30 (parable of the talents)	—	Parable of the pounds 11-28
21:1-8	11:1-8	Enthronement of Jesus 29-36
21:9	11:9-10	Acclamation of Jesus 37-40
21:12-13 (merchants driven out)	11:15-17 (merchants driven out)	Jerusalem's fate 41-46

1. MATTHEW AND MARK

The sequences of Matthew 19-20 and Mark 10 are very similar; their general construction is the same. However, some differences mean that the meaning of some passages take on, in their links to one another, a very different emphasis.

In the first sub-sequences, the passage on «Eunuchs for the kingdom of God» is proper to Matthew; Mark gives it a compositional parallel, removing the last verse from Matthew's passage «On divorce» (19:9) to make this a freestanding passage, «Against adultery» (10:10-12); this is why the titles do not match between one sub-sequence and another, to emphasize the links between the symmetrical passages (see p. 249). In the second sub-sequences, Matthew adds the «Parables of the laborers in the vineyard» (20:1-15), repeating the proverb in Mark 10:31 after the parable (20:16); the parable allows Mark to explicate the significance, not only of the first passage, but also of the whole (see p. 302).

The last sub-sequences show the same assembly of three passages, even though it is carried out with different means, as the titles of this scene aim to recall (see p. 177).

2. MATTHEW, MARK, LUKE

What is called the Lukan «great addition» ends at Luke 18:14. Luke had started his third section at 9:51 (the great journey towards Jerusalem), by inserting material which is, for the most part, unique to him; from this point onwards his account is separate from Mark's. Now he returns to the thread at 18:15, with the passage where Jesus welcomes the children (Luke 18:15-17). In fact, most of the seven previous passages —from «The cleansing of ten lepers» (17:11-19) until «The parable of the Pharisee and the tax-collector» (18:9-14)— do not have parallels in Matthew and Mark; only the third passage in Luke, «The Coming of the Son of man» (17:22-36), has some pieces in common with Matt 24, but in a very different order. Mark shares only two verses with the same Lucan passage (Mark 13:15-16).

However, Luke has no parallel with the controversy on divorce (Mattt 19:3-9; Mark 10:2-9 and 10-12), nor with the passage on the eunuchs in Matthew; only Luke 16:18 repeats, but in a different context, Matt 19:9 (and 5:52) and Mark 10:12, with a very different expression. Clearly, Luke has not parallel to the introductory sequences in Matthew (19:1-2) and Mark (10:1). It is Luke 17:11 which introduces the first sequence: «It happened, as he left for Jerusalem, that he passed between Samaria and Galilee». In fact, a new stage in the journey begins with this new mention of the departure towards Jerusalem, noted by all the commentators.

Luke has organized the material which he shares with Matthew and Mark into two very different sequences. His account of the calling of the rich man (18:18-27) matches two passages in Matt 19:16,22 and 23-26 and Mark 10:17-22 and 23-27; his last sub-sequence of sequence C6 also integrates, in addition to the coming to the children (15-17) the passage of the «Fate of the Twelve» (28-30) whose parallels are in fact the first passage of the central sub-sequence in Matthew and Mark. In sequence C7, the organization is totally different: it begins with «Jesus' Fate» paralleled with the «Fate of Jerusalem» which is for the most part unique to Luke.

With this example we see clearly how, from the material received from the tradition, each Evangelist has composed a specific discourse. While very similar, Matthew and Mark each have their uniqueness; and the third Gospel is clearly distinguished from the first two.

Chapter 4

The passage in the global context
The section and the book

The two passages, «The healing at Jericho» and «The call of the rich man», analyzed by themselves in the first chapter, were then situated in the immediate context of the sub-sequence to which they belonged, and then in the wider context of the sequence. But the sequence, to which the previous chapter was given over, is not the highest level of organization of Gospel texts. Sequences, in fact, form sections —which might be organized into several sub-sections— and the sections as a whole make up the book.

We therefore need to go to the end of the path which has led us from the simple passage, ending with the whole work. We will do so systematically, but also partially. It is not so much that the place matters as that, primarily, for the time being, only one of the three Synoptic Gospels has been analyzed at every level of its organization following the rigorous procedures of biblical rhetorical analysis. The two Lukan passages examined at the end of the third chapter (c6 and c7) are part of a sub-sequence of three passages. We therefore first of all need to systematically present sequence c8; then the main links which hold the three sequences together in a coherent whole will be shown[1]. This sub-section will then be situated in the third section of the Gospel of Luke. Finally, after a schematic presentation of the other three sections, it will be possible to examine the architecture of the third Gospel as a whole.

A. SEQUENCE C8 (LUKE 19:47-21:38)

COMPOSITION

This sequence has two long sub-sequences, the controversies (20:1-40) and the apocalyptic discourse (20:45-21:36), which frame a short enigmatic passage (20:41-44). The whole is introduced and concluded by two short passages (19:47-48 and 21:37-38) which situate the whole of the sequence in the Temple. These two outer passages parallel one another, as the following re-writing demonstrates:

+ 19:[47] **He was** TEACHING *every day* IN THE TEMPLE.
: The chief priests and the scribes were seeking to kill him, also the chiefs of the people;
: [48] but they were not able to find what they should do.
= For ALL THE PEOPLE hung upon (his words) *TO LISTEN TO HIM*

+ 21:[37] **He was** *during the day* IN THE TEMPLE TEACHING.
: But during the night, going out, he was lodging on the Mount called of Olives.
= [38] And ALL THE PEOPLE early in the morning came to him in the Temple *TO LISTEN TO HIM.*

1 In my commentary on Luke, I did not analyze the composition of each of the sub-sections in themselves, merely examining the whole of the section; the pages which follow therefore complement my earlier work.

The first two passages of the sub-sequence on the controversies (1-8; 9-19) share many points. The outer verses (1.19) form an inclusio, with the repetition of «the chief priests and the scribes» and «people». The answer which Jesus refuses to the authorities in the first passage is given to the people in the second passage: the one who «has given him the power» (2) is the one whose «beloved son» he is (13). «To teach the people» (1) and «began to say this parable to the people» (9) act as initial terms; «to reason», in the center of the first (5) and second (14) passages act as central terms. In the center of the first passage his enemies do not dare to speak, from fear of being stoned by «the people» (6), and at the end of the second passage (19) they do not dare to lay a hand on Jesus because they are afraid of the «people». In both cases, it is life which is at stake, Jesus' life in the second passage (14.15.19), but also their own (6; 16.18).

«To question» (21.27), «work» and «said» (20.27; same root) are the initial terms of the last two passages (20-26; 27-40). «Were silent» and «they did not dare to question him any more» (26.40), «word» and «you have spoken» (26.39) are final terms. The outer terms are «question» (21.40). The enemies' interventions begin with «Master» (21.28). «God» recurs three times in the first passage (21.25 -x2-), and five times in the second passage (36.37 -x2- and 37.38). In the first passage, humanity's relationship with God is opposed to humanity's relationship with Cesar; in the second passage, humanity's relationship with their descendents is opposed to humanity's relationship with their forebears, that is, with God.

Over the sub-sequence as a whole, the three occurrences of «to teach» (1.21b. 21c) act as initial terms for the two pairs of passages. The two occurrences of «scribes» (1.39) act as outer terms; this term is also found in the center (19).—The end of the second passage and the start of the third passage (19.20) ensure both a kind of pause and a transition between the two pairs of controversies; «give him to the authority and power of the governor» matches «put a hand on him». The sub-sequence is thus focused on the only place where Jesus' enemies' intentions are expressed.—At the start (1) Jesus «teaches», at the end (40) his enemies are silent; the same happens at the end of the first passage (7-8) and the symmetrical passage (26). The first passages of each side raise the problem of «power» (2.8; 20.22).—The second and fourth passages, longer than the earlier ones, are marked by the theme of death («to kill»: 14.15, «to make perish»: 16, «to die»: 28.29.31.32.36) and by the theme of divine filiation (Jesus' at 13, humanity's at 36). They finish with a citation from the Old Testament (17 and 37).

1 It happened on one of these days, when he WAS TEACHING the *people* in the Temple and proclaiming the good news, came up the *CHIEF PRIESTS* and the *SCRIBES* with the elders.

2 They spoke to him, saying: «Tell us, by what ***power*** you do these things or who is the one who gave you this *power*?». 3 Answering, he said to them: «I will also ask you a question and tell me: 4 the baptism of John, was it from heaven or from men?». 5 They were reasoning among them saying: «If we say "From heaven", he will say "Why did you not believe in him?". 6 But if we say "From men", all the *people* will stone us for it has been convinced that John was a prophet».

7 They answered that THEY DID NOT KNOW FROM WHERE it was.
8 Jesus said to them: «Neither will I tell you by what *power* I do these things».

9 He began to SAY to the *people* this parable:

«A man planted a vineyard, he gave it out to vine-growers and went on a journey for a long time. 10 At the season he sent unto the vine-growers a servant so that they might give him some of the fruit of the vineyard. But the vine-growers, having beaten him, sent him away empty. 11 He went on to send another servant. But they, having beaten and even dishonored him, sent him away empty. 12 He proceeded to send a third. But they, having wounded, cast him out. 13 The lord of the vineyard said: "What shall I do? I will send MY SON, the beloved; perhaps they will respect him". 14 But seeing him, the vine-growers reasoned among themselves saying: "This is the heir; **let us kill him** so that the inheritance may become ours". 15 Having cast him out of the vineyard, **they killed him.** What therefore will do to them the lord of the vineyard? 16 He will come and **destroy** these vine-growers and he will give the vineyard to others». Hearing, they said: «Let it not be!». 17 Looking at them, he said: «What then is this Scripture:

* "THE STONE WHICH THE BUILDERS REJECTED HAS BECOME THE CORNER STONE".
** 18 Everyone who falls on that stone will be broken to pieces; on whom it falls, it will scatter him».

19 At this same hour the *SCRIBES* and the *CHIEF PRIESTS* were seeking to lay hands on him
but they were afraid of the *people* for they knew that it was against them he had said this parable.

20 Having watched him closely, they sent forth spies who were pretending to be righteous
that they might TAKE HOLD OF HIS WORD, to deliver him to the authority and to the *power* of the governor.

21 They INTERROGATED him *saying*:

«MASTER, we know that you SAY and TEACH *in right manner* and do not consider the appearance but you TEACH the way of God according to the truth. 22 ***Is it possible*** for us to give tribute to Caesar?». 23 Perceiving their craftiness, he said to them: 24 «Show me a denarius. Whose image and inscription does it have?». They said: «Caesar's». 25 He said to them: «Well then, give to Caesar what belongs to Caesar and to God what belongs to God».

26 And THEY COULD NOT TAKE HOLD ON HIS SAYING before the *people*
and, amazed at his answer, ***THEY BECAME SILENT.***

27 Came near some Sadducees who were saying that there is no resurrection, ASKED him:

28 «MASTER, Moses wrote for us: "If any one's brother **dies,** having a wife and being without children, his brother should take the woman and raise up a descendant for his brother". 29 There were seven brothers; the first having taken a wife **died** without children. 30 So also the second. 31 The third took her and likewise all the seven left no children and **died.** 32 At last the woman also **died.** 33 The woman in the resurrection, whose wife will she be for the seven had her as wife?». 34 Jesus said to them: «The children of this age marry and are given in marriage. 35 But those who are judged worthy to have part of that age and the resurrection from the death neither marry nor are given in marriage. 36 For they can no longer **die** for they are like angels, and they are the CHILDREN OF GOD being sons of the resurrection. 37 And that the dead are resurrected, even Moses showed at the bush when he said:

* "THE LORD, *GOD* OF ABRAHAM, *GOD* OF ISAAC, *GOD* OF JACOB".
** 38 He is not God of the **dead** but of the living for all live to him».

39 Answering, some *SCRIBES* said: «MASTER, you have SAID well!».
40 And **THEY NO LONGER DARED TO ASK HIM ANYTHING.**

The final Sub-Sequence is made up of five passages (Luke 20:45-21:36)

[45] While all the people were listening, he said to his disciples: [46] «BE ON GUARD against the scribes who wish to walk around in long robes and love greetings on the marketplaces and the best seats in the SYNAGOGUES and the best places at the banquets; [47] and they devour the houses of widows and for a pretence they make long prayers. These will receive more abundant condemnation». 21:[1] Having looked up, he saw some rich people casting their offerings in the Treasury. [2] And he saw a poor widow casting in two small coins. [3] He said: «**Truly I say to you that** this poor widow has cast in more than all. [4] For all of these, out of their abundance, they cast into the offerings, but she, out of her need, cast in all the living that she had».

[5] While certain people were saying about the Temple that was adorned with beautiful stones and votive offerings, he said: [6] «These things that you are staring at, will come the days in which there will not be left stone upon stone that shall not be destroyed». [7] They asked him saying: «Master, when therefore will these things be and what will be the sign when these things are about to happen?». [8] He said: «See that you not be deceived, since many will come *IN MY NAME* saying: "I am he!" or "The time has come near!". Do not go after them. [9] When you hear of wars and uprisings, do not be terrified for it is necessary that these happen first, but it will not immediately be the end». [10] Then he said to them: «Nation will rise against nation and **KINGDOM** against **KINGDOM**. [11] There will be great earthquakes and from place to place famines and plagues, there will be fearful things and great signs from the sky.

[12] Before all these, they will lay upon you their hands and persecute you, delivering you to the SYNAGOGUES and to the *prisons*, bringing you before **KINGS** and governors *FOR THE SAKE OF MY NAME*. [13] This will lead you to bear testimony. [14] Set up therefore in your **hearts**, not to prepare beforehand your defense.

[15] For I myself will give you a **mouth** and wisdom,
which none will be able to resist or to contradict, of your adversaries.

[16] You will be delivered even by parents, brothers, relatives, friends; they will put to death some of you [17] and you will be hated by all *BECAUSE OF MY NAME*. [18] But not a hair of your HEAD will perish: [19] by your perseverance you will secure your lives.

[20] When you see Jerusalem surrounded by armies, then know that has come near its desolation. [21] Then those who are in Judea let them flee to the mountains, and those who are in the midst of it let them depart, and those are in the fields let them not enter into it. [22] For these will be the days of vengeance to fulfill the Scriptures. [23] Woe to those who are pregnant and who suckle in those days, for there will be great distress upon the earth and wrath against these people: [24] they will fall by the **mouth** of the sword and be *led captive* unto all the nations. And Jerusalem will be trodden down by nations, till be fulfilled the times of nations. [25] And there will be signs in sun, moon and stars and upon the earth distress of nations within the perplexity at the roaring of the sea and waves, [26] men fainting away because of fear in the expectation of the things which are coming upon the world, for the powers of heavens will be shaken. [27] Then they will see *THE SON OF MAN* coming in a cloud with great power and glory. [28] When these things begin to happen, straighten yourselves up and lift up your HEAD because **has come near** your deliverance». [29] He said to them a parable: «Look at the fig tree and all the trees; [30] when they already burst forward, watching it, you know for yourselves that summer is already near. [31] So you also, when you see these things happening, you know that **is near** the **KINGDOM OF GOD**.

[32] **Truly I say to you that** this generation would not pass away until all may have happened; [33] the sky and the earth will pass away, my words will not pass away. [34] BE ON GUARD to yourselves lest your **hearts** may be weighed down with dissipation, and drunkenness, and anxieties of life and will come upon you suddenly that day [35] as a snare. For, it will come upon all those who are dwelling on the face of all the earth. [36] Be vigilant, praying at every moment, that you may have strength to escape all these that are about to happen and to stand before *THE SON OF MAN*».

A similar warning is introduced in the outer passages with «Be on guard» (20:46; 21:34). The disciples are asked not to let themselves be weighed down with the «anxieties of life» (21:34) like the conceited scribes (20:46) and those who love money (20:47). Like the widow who gives everything on which she has «to live» (21:4), they have to abandon «the anxieties of life» (21:34). The continual prayer to which they are called, therefore, (21:36) will not be put on like that of the scribes (20:47). In the last passage, the end («what is about to happen»: 21:36) is closely linked to the present («this generation will not pass»: 32, «suddenly»: 34, «at every moment»: 36); in the first passage, only the present is mentioned and judgment is brought to bear immediately by Jesus on the attitudes of the wealthy and the widow (21:3). «Truly I say to you» (32) refers back to «Truly I say to you» (3); this syntagma does not appear anywhere else in the sequence.

The second and penultimate passages begin with the prediction of the destruction of the «Temple» (5) and «Jerusalem» (20). The catastrophe will strike the people and the nations (10-11; 23-26) and will take on the same cosmic nature (with the same «signs» in «heaven» 10-11; 25-26). While one warns about the «coming» of the Son of man (27), the other warns about those who «will come» in his name, claiming to announce the moment of the catastrophe (8).

At the start of the central passage, «before all this» (21:12) indicates that the persecution of the disciples will occur before all the events predicted in the rest of the sub-sequence, the destruction of Jerusalem and its Temple and the agony of the nations. This is the only passage in the sub-sequence in which the persecution of the disciples is predicted. Note the lexical repetitions: «king» (21:12) and «kingdom(s)» (10.31), «synagogues» (21:12; 20:46), «mouth» (15.24), «hearts» (14.34), «head» (18.28); «prisons» (12) and «led captive» (24) are synonymous. The two occurrences of «my name» (12.17) refer back to «my name» in 8 and to the two occurrence of «the Son of man» (27.36).

In between the two major sub-sequences, and therefore at the heart of the sequence, a brief passage (20:41-44) has two questions framing a quotation from Ps 110:

---

[41] He said to them:

+ «HOW do they say that Christ is SON OF DAVID?
: [42] For *DAVID* himself *says* in the Book of Psalms:

- «The Lord said to my LORD:
. sit at my right hand,
. [43] till I make your enemies a stool for your feet».

: [44] *DAVID* therefore *calls* him LORD.
+ HOW can he be HIS SON?».

Thus once again, one, and even two, of the great laws of biblical and Semitic rhetoric are proven: on the one hand, the central passage asks questions, and on the other hand is it focused on a quotation. As often happens, it is enigmatic, as shown by the many interpretations which have been made of it. It acts as the key to reading the sequence as a whole.

Jesus, threatened with death, *teaches all the people in the Temple*		19:47-48
Jesus refuses to say to the members of the Sanhedrin who is **the One** who **gave** him his power		20:1-8
Jesus reveals to the people who is **Son of God**		20:9-18
THE MEMBERS OF THE SANHEDRIN SEEK TO *LAY HANDS UPON* JESUS TO **give** him TO THE POWER OF THE *GOVERNOR*		20:19-20
Jesus invites the spies of the members of the Sanhedrin to **give** to **God** what is belongs to God		20:21-26
Jesus answers the Sadducees that man is **son of God**		20:27-40
IS THE CHRIST THE SON OR **THE LORD** OF DAVID?		20:41-44
Jesus *warns* his disciples against the anxieties of *life* and asks them not to imitate the conduct of the scribes		20:45–21:4
Jesus announces to his disciples the destruction of the Temple and the coming of false messiahs		21:5-11
JESUS ANNOUNCES TO HIS DISCIPLES THAT THEY WILL *LAY HANDS UPON* THEM AND THAT THEY WILL BE **given** TO THE SYNAGOGUES AND TO THE *GOVERNORS*		21:12-19
Jesus announces to his disciples the devastation of Jerusalem and the coming in glory of the **Son of man**		21:20-31
Jesus *puts on guard* his disciples against the preoccupations of *life* and ask them to be ready for the day of the **Son of man**		21:32-36
Jesus, threatened with death, *teaches all the people in the Temple*		21:37-38

This outline of sequence C8 not only shows its architecture, but the summaries of each passage allow us to see the links between the passages, without there being a need for lengthy commentaries here.

The whole of the first sub-sequence (20:1-40) is marked by the active presence of adversaries: «chief priests and Scribes» (1.19), the spies whom they have sent (20), the Sadducees (27), and, in the end, «some Scribes» congratulate Jesus for his answer to their enemies (39). Note that the «chief priests and Scribes» have already been mentioned in the introduction to the sequence (19:47). The whole of the second sub-sequence, on the other hand, (20:45-21:36) is addressed to the disciples. Only «the Scribes» are mentioned in Jesus' words at the start (20:46), but they are not present. In the conclusion (21:37-38), the enemies are not named, while they were in the introduction.

In the first sub-sequence, Jesus presents himself as Son of God, via the detour of the parable («I will send my beloved son»: 20:13) and says that those who are judged worthy of the other world are «children of God» (20:36). In the second sub-sequence, Jesus twice presents himself as «the Son of man» (21:27.36).

The two sub-sequences are focused on persecution. In the first sub-sequence, enemies «will lay their hands on» Jesus (20:19), and in the second one, on the disciples (21:12). Jesus and his disciples will be persecuted both by the Jews («Scribes and Pharisees»: 20:19; «the synagogues»: 21:12) as by the pagans («the governor»: 20:20; «the governors»: 21:12).

The central passage provides the transition between the two sides of the sequence. On the one hand, it is addressed to «those», that is, the enemies in the first sub-sequence; on the other hand, the Christ, the son and lord of David, predicts that «the Son of man» will come like a powerful and glorious king (21:27). Ps 110, quoted in the central passage, is closely linked to the Son of man in Daniel, because, like him, he will vanquish his enemies (Dan 7).

The central passage is the only one in which the name of «Christ» appears (20:41) as does the name «David». Jesus is «son of David» but he is greater than David his father: in the first sub-sequence, Jesus presents himself as Son of God, «the beloved son» of the «lord» of the vine (20:13). He may be the last to be sent, but is the first in rank, because all his predecessors were only «servants», while he is the «heir». In the second sub-sequence, Jesus presents himself as «the Son of man» (21:27.36): in the Gospel, the Son of man describes the person who suffers and is put to death, but also the person who, for this, receives eternal kingship and on whom the divine attributes, such as the «cloud» (21:27) and judgment, are conferred. So Jesus is not only the «son of David», he is also «his Lord[2]».

2 Fitzmyer is of the opinion that «the title "Son of God" has nothing to do with this episode» and that «the importation of the title "Son of Man" into this passage is as arbitrary as that of Son of God» (Fitzmyer, 1313). If the passage is taken in isolation, this could be true; but the context of the sequence as a whole clearly shows that the opposite is true.

The quotation from Ps 110, in the center of the passage, links the king's enthronement at the Lord's right hand to dominion over his «enemies». David's enemies were not only the nations round about, but also internal. So the whole sequence is marked by the presence of Jesus' enemies. These are the leaders of the people, in particular, the «scribes and the chief priests», from the start of the first sub-sequence (20:1); like the vine-dressers, they wish «to kill» him, «laying their hands on him» to «give him to the authority and power of the governor», at the center of the first sub-sequence (20:19-20); the enemies are also those who will lay Jerusalem waste (21:20-24) and destroy the Temple (21:5-11), and those who will persecute the disciples, at the center of the second sub-sequence (21:12-19). In a very coherent way, therefore, the centers of the two sub-sequences match the center of the sequence.

Throughout the whole sequence, Jesus is presented as the one who reigns over «the people»: not only in the introduction and in the conclusion, but also in the whole of the first sub-sequence (20:1.6.9.19.26) and the start of the second (20:45); the first verses of the two sub-sequences clearly act as initial terms:

20:1	while he WAS TEACHING	**the people**	in the Temple and proclaiming the Gospel.
20:45	While **all the people**	WERE LISTENING,	he said to his disciples.

Although all the words in the second sub-sequence are addressed «to the disciples», «all the people were listening». The whole sequence unfolds in the presence of the people who are listening.

INTERPRETATION

A question without an answer

In the sequence's central passage, Jesus asks two questions about the Christ, David's son or lord (20:41-44), and these questions remain unanswered. His adversaries, «the chief priests and scribes» (20:1-19), the spies that the scribes have sent to him (20-26), and even the Sadducees (27-40), are all reduced to silence, one after the other (20:7-8; 26; 40). After this, none of them dares enter into a discussion on the identity of the Christ, which Jesus, now taking the initiative, asks them; and Jesus himself does not answer the questions he has asked. No-one even has the courage to ask him what he means, and what his own opinion is about the Christ, not even those scribes who had congratulated him on his answer to their enemies, the Sadducees: «Master, you have spoken well!»

(20:39). If the double question remains in suspense, this surely means that it is crucial. It seems to be an exegetical question, which raises a contradiction between the general opinion on the Davidic origin of the Christ, and a verse from a psalm. The Scribes, the acknowledged specialists of the Scriptures, would no doubt have their answer; and yet, they say absolutely nothing: they have probably understood that the decisive point in the argument has been reached. Since no one, not even Jesus, answers the sequence's central question, it is up to the reader to find the solution, taking the context into account, and, in particular, to give their own response. Of course, such is not limited to an intellectual understanding. Just as for the disciples, it must end with belonging to Christ himself.

«God's beloved Son»

The Sanhedrin judges questioned Jesus while he was «teaching all the people in the Temple and announcing the good news» (20:1). They do not give him any title, not even the title of «Master», as their spies (21) and some Sadducees (28)[3] would later do. Jesus refuses to answer their questions (8), because they refused to give a judgment on John the Baptist (7). However, just after this initial scene, with the parable of the murderous vine-dressers, he gives an answer «to the people», which is indirect, but clear, to the chief priests' and scribes' question —he himself is the «beloved Son» and «heir» of «the Lord of the vineyard» (13-14). So it is God himself who «has given to him the power of doing these things» (2): he has received this power like the son receives his father's inheritance, and he makes use of it regally. Jesus lets the spies, sent by the scribes and chief priests «to catch him out in his words and hand him over to the governor's authority and power» (20), understand that he belongs not to Cesar, but to God, being his «image and inscription» (24-25). One could probably read in all this an allusion to the son of David who, like his father, «was begotten» by God (LXX: Ps 109:3c). In this reading, Jesus would present himself as a king, the «Christ», or anointed one of God, expected by all.

«The Son of man»

The title which Jesus uses in the second sub-sequence, «the Son of man» (21:27. 36), might, at first sight, appear to be less glorious and, in particular, less explicit than those which he used in the first sub-sequence, «Son of God» and his «heir»

3 However, at the very end of the sub-sequence (20:39), some Scribes acknowledge that Jesus «has spoken well», after he replied to the Sadducees, their enemies.

(20:13-14), «his image and inscription» (20:24-25). And yet, «the Son of man», as presented here, goes far beyond the royal figure of whom one might legitimately think. The Son of man, in fact, is no king like David, like «the son of David», whom so many people expected, a political sovereign who would chase out the invaders and occupiers of the land of Israel and restore «the kingdom of God», which was understood as an earthly kingdom. The Son of man is the eschatological king who «will come on a cloud with great power and glory» (21:27); he is the one before whom all men are to appear when he returns to judge all nations (36). He is the person described by the prophet Daniel, who will reign over all people, not only Israel; he is the universal king, whose kingdom will have no end. In addition, at the center of the central passage of the sub-sequence, Jesus presents himself as the one who exercises the power of God himself: «I shall give you a mouth and wisdom that none of your opponents will be able to resist or contradict» (21:15). Luke's expression here is unusual: in the parallel passage (Luke 12:11-12), he had said that it would be «the Holy Spirit» who would teach the disciples what they were to say. Jesus' power goes beyond that of all his enemies, because it is a divine power. It is even greater than David's. Jesus is the son of David, but he is also his Lord.

Like his master, the disciple is the son of God

Jesus reveals himself in this last sequence of the third section of the Gospel of Luke, perhaps more than he had done up until now[4]. But this revelation is not limited to his personal identity: it also concerns the identity of the disciple, of all humanity, even. The disciples will share their master's fate: just as Jesus is persecuted, at the center of the first sub-sequence (20:19-20), so, at the center of the second sub-sequence, will they be persecuted (21:12-19): «they will lay their hands on them», «they will be dragged before governors», «hated by all» «because of the name» of the Son of man. But, like Jesus throughout all his arguments with his enemies, they will receive «a mouth and a wisdom that no one can resist» (21:15). Some of them will be killed (21:16) like the master. But, «being judged worthy of the other world and the resurrection [...] they will no longer die, because they are children of God» (20:35-36). Jesus' disciple shares divine filiation with him.

4 See MEYNET R., «Jésus fils de David dans l'Évangile de Luc».

B. SUB-SECTION C6-8 (LUKE 17:11-21:38)

In this introduction there is no question of carrying out a detailed study of the links between the three sequences; it will be enough to emphasize the most marked, which demonstrate the coherence of the whole.

THE THEME OF KINGSHIP

The titles which I have been led to give to the three sequences of the sub-section give an initial idea of their content. The theme of kingship recurs there in an insistent fashion.

C6: Leaving all for the *kingdom*

C7: Jesus, *the* contested *king*, exercises **judgment**

C8: *Christ* **judges** at the end.

Recall that sequence C6 is marked from beginning to end by «the kingdom of God»; this expression recurs seven times, seven being the number of totality (17:20 -x2- and 21; 18:16.24.25.29). First of all, it is the question which the Pharisees ask having participated in the purification of the ten lepers, an unequivocal sign of the work of God: «When will the kingdom of God come?». (17:20); this coming coincides with the coming of the Son of man (22-37; see p. 331). In the last sub-sequence of this same sequence, C6, this is the only subject—only children will enter into the kingdom of God (18:15-17), the rich man will not be brave enough to do what he has to do to enter it (18-27), unlike Peter and his companions, who have left all «for the kingdom of God» (28-30; see p. 260). As for the central sub-sequence (18:1-14), if «the kingdom of God» is only mentioned there once, it is still focused on the mention of the coming of the Son of man: «But, when the Son of man comes, will he find faith on earth?». And so, at the very heart of the sequence, Jesus introduces himself as the one who judges the faith of men, which is the role of the eschatological king.

Sequence C7, even more than the previous sequence, if this is possible, also plays out Jesus' kingship. The central parable, often called the parable of the pounds, or pounds, is told «because he was close to Jerusalem and they thought that the kingdom of God was going to appear» (19:11); unlike the parable of the talents in Matthew, Jesus' parable is a parable of kingship, since the main character «left for a distant region to receive kingship» and, once returned, exercises it by judging his servants as well as his enemies. Arriving near to the Mount of

Olives, Jesus is first of all enthroned on a mule, and then led in procession towards the city, acclaimed as a king by the crowd of his disciples (see p. 365). Finally entering the Temple, he behaves as the master of the house, in a sovereign fashion, as he had already done when he entered Zacheaus' house, having been twice called «son of David» by the blind man of Jericho (see p. 188). We should add that it is not only Jesus who is presented as a king—the faithful servants of this king are closely associated with his kingship, since, in the parable, they receive governance over ten or five cities.

At the center of the last sequence of the sub-section, too, Jesus appears as the Christ, seated at the right hand of the Lord, ruling over his enemies reduced to act as a footstool for his feet. His kingship is manifest all through the controversies with his enemies, whom he reduces to silence, in which he presents himself as the Son of God. In the apocalyptic discourse he depicts himself as the «Son of man coming on clouds with great power and glory», but also, at the center of the sub-sequence, as the one who will defend his disciples at the time of persecution by giving them royal wisdom, that wisdom which, in biblical tradition is the prerogative of the king.

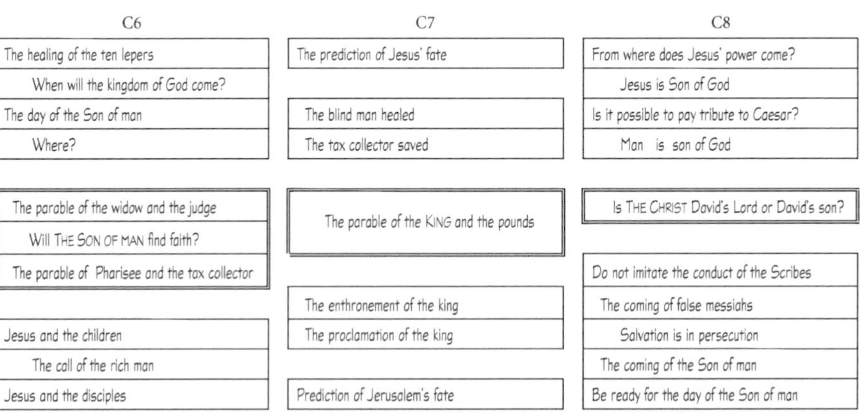

We shall now examine only two things —the links between the outer sub-sequences, and those between the centers of the sequences.

17:[11] IT HAPPENED THAT, WHILE HE DEPARTED TOWARDS JERUSALEM, he was passing between Samaria and Galilee. [12] And when he was entering in a village, arrived ten lepers who stood at a distance. [13] They lifted up the voice saying: «*LORD JESUS, HAVE MERCY ON US*!». [14] Seeing this, Jesus said: «Go and present yourselves to the priests». And while they were going away, they were purified. [15] One of them, seeing himself healed,
returned, with a loud voice glorifying **GOD**
[16] and he fell on his face at Jesus' feet, thanking *HIM*.
And he was a Samaritan. [17] Answering, Jesus said: «Were not the ten purified? Where are the other nine? [18] Are they not found to return to give glory to **GOD**, except this foreigner?». [19] And he said to him: «Rise up and depart, your faith has saved you».

[20] The Pharisees asked him: «**WHEN** does **THE KINGDOM OF GOD** come?».
He answered them: «**THE KINGDOM OF GOD** does not come with things that can be observed.
[21] No one will say: "Look it is here!", or "It is there!". For Behold, **THE KINGDOM OF GOD** is in the midst of you».

[22] He said to his disciples: «***The days are coming*** in which you will desire to see *ONE OF THE DAYS OF THE SON OF MAN* and you will not see it. [23] They will say to you: "Look it is there, look it is here!". **Do not go or pursue them.** [24] For as lightning while enlightening, it shines from one side to other of the sky, so will be *THE SON OF MAN IN HIS DAY*.

[25] BUT FIRST IT IS NECESSARY THAT HE SUFFER MUCH AND IS REJECTED BY THIS GENERATION.

[26] As it happened in the days of Noah, so will it be in the days of the Son of man: [27] they were eating and drinking, they were marrying and giving in marriage, till the day in which Noah entered into the ark and the flood came and destroyed them all. [28] Likewise as it happened in the days of Lot: they were eating and drinking, they were buying and selling, they were planting and building, [29] and, the day in which Lot came out of Sodom, **GOD** made fire and sulfur to rain from the sky and destroyed them all; [30] So will be on *THE DAY IN WHICH THE SON OF MAN* will be revealed.

[31] *On that day, he who will be on the terrace, if his goods are in the house, let him not come down to take them and who is in the field likewise, let him not turn backwards.* [32] Remember the wife of Lot!

[33] WHOEVER SEEKS TO KEEP HIS LIFE WILL LOSE IT, AND WHOEVER LOSES IT, WILL SAVE IT.

[34] **I tell you**, in that night, there will be two in the same bed, one will be taken and the other will be left; [35] There will be two women grinding together, one will be taken and the other will be left».

[37] Answering, they said: «WHERE, Lord?».
He said to them: «Where the corpse is, there are gathered ***THE VULTURES***».

The days of destruction and persecution are predicted. The same expression, «the days will come» recurs in 17:22 and in 21:6. These are the days when the disciples, isolated among sinners, as Noah and Lot were, (17:26-29), will have to be patient and cope with this testing; they are the days in which not only will the Temple be destroyed (21:6) and the city (20-24), but when wars will put nations against one another, and evil will reach cosmic dimensions (21:9-11.25-26), as at the time of the flood and the destruction of Sodom (17:26-29).

In those days, the disciples, in the image of the master who has been rejected by this generation (17:25), are to agree to lose their life to save it (33); these two predictions are at the center of the two sub-parts of the third passage. At the heart of the final sub-sequence (21:12-19) the future suffering of the disciples is predicted; they will be supported by their master, who by then will have gone through his own Passion.

17:[11] IT HAPPENED THAT, WHILE HE DEPARTED TOWARDS JERUSALEM, he was passing between Samaria and Galilee. [12] And when he was entering in a village, arrived ten lepers who stood at a distance. [13] They lifted up the voice saying: «*LORD JESUS, HAVE MERCY ON US!*». [14] Seeing this, Jesus said: «Go and present yourselves to the priests». And while they were going away, they were purified. [15] One of them, seeing himself healed,
returned, with a loud voice glorifying GOD
[16] and he fell on his face at Jesus' feet, thanking *HIM*.
And he was a Samaritan. [17] Answering, Jesus said: «Were not the ten purified? Where are the other nine? [18] Are they not found to return to give glory to GOD, except this foreigner?». [19] And he said to him: «Rise up and depart, your faith has saved you».

[20] The Pharisees asked him: «**WHEN** does THE KINGDOM OF GOD come?».
He answered them: «THE KINGDOM OF GOD does not come with things that can be observed.
[21] No one will say: "Look it is here!", or "It is there!". For Behold, THE KINGDOM OF GOD is in the midst of you».

[22] He said to his disciples: «***The days are coming*** in which you will desire to see *ONE OF THE DAYS OF THE SON OF MAN* and you will not see it. [23] They will say to you: "Look it is there, look it is here!". **Do not go or pursue them.** [24] For as lightning while enlightening, it shines from one side to other of the sky, so will be *THE SON OF MAN IN HIS DAY*.

[25] BUT FIRST IT IS NECESSARY THAT HE SUFFER MUCH AND IS REJECTED BY THIS GENERATION.

[26] As it happened in the days of Noah, so will it be in the days of the Son of man: [27] they were eating and drinking, they were marrying and giving in marriage, till the day in which Noah entered into the ark and the flood came and destroyed them all. [28] Likewise as it happened in the days of Lot: they were eating and drinking, they were buying and selling, they were planting and building, [29] and, the day in which Lot came out of Sodom, GOD made fire and sulfur to rain from the sky and destroyed them all; [30] So will be on *THE DAY IN WHICH THE SON OF MAN* will be revealed.

[31] *On that day, he who will be on the terrace, if his goods are in the house, let him not come down to take them and who is in the field likewise, let him not turn backwards.* [32] Remember the wife of Lot!

[33] WHOEVER SEEKS TO KEEP HIS LIFE WILL LOSE IT, AND WHOEVER LOSES IT, WILL SAVE IT.

[34] **I tell you**, in that night, there will be two in the same bed, one will be taken and the other will be left; [35] There will be two women grinding together, one will be taken and the other will be left».

[37] Answering, they said: «WHERE, Lord?».
He said to them: «Where the corpse is, there are gathered ***THE VULTURES***».

During those days of persecution, the disciples are to avoid being taken advantage of by those who will foretell the coming of false messiahs (17:21.23; 21:8). They must rather wait until they have plumbed the depths of agony and destruction after which, finally, «the day of the Son of man», the day of judgment, will come (17:24.26.30; 21:27).

The question «when?» is asked at the outsides of the sub-section. First of all the Pharisees want to know «when the kingdom of God» will come (17:20); and at the end, the disciples want to know «when» the Temple will be destroyed (21:7).

20:45 While all the people were listening, he said to his disciples: 46 «Be on guard against the Scribes who wish to walk around in long robes and love greetings on the marketplaces and first seats in the synagogues and first places in the banquets; 47 and they devour the houses of widows and for a pretence they make long prayers. These will receive more abundant condemnation». 21:1 Having looked up, he saw some rich people casting their offerings in the Treasury. 2 And he saw a poor widow casting in two small coins. 3 He said: «**Truly I say to you that** this poor widow has cast in more than all. 4 For all of these, out of their abundance, they cast into the offerings, but she, out her need, cast in all the living that she had».

5 While certain people were saying about the Temple that was adorned with beautiful stones and votive offerings, he said: 6 «These things that you are staring at, ***will come the days*** in which there will not be left stone upon a stone that shall not be destroyed». 7 They asked him saying: «Master, **WHEN** will therefore these things be and what will be the sign when these things are about to happen?». 8 He said: «See that you not be deceived, since many will come *IN MY NAME* saying: "I am he!" or "The time has come near!". **Do not go after them.** 9 When you hear of wars and uprisings, do not be terrified for it is necessary that these happen first, but it will not immediately be the end». 10 Then he said to them: «Nation will rise against nation, and KINGDOM against KINGDOM. 11 There will be great earthquakes and from place to place famines and plagues, there will be fearful things and great signs from the sky.

12 Before all these, THEY WILL LAY UPON YOU THEIR HANDS AND PERSECUTE YOU, DELIVERING YOU TO THE SYNAGOGUES AND TO THE PRISONS, BRINGING YOU BEFORE KINGS AND GOVERNORS *FOR THE SAKE OF MY NAME.* 13 This will lead you to bear testimony. 14 Set up therefore in your hearts not to prepare beforehand your defense.

15 For I myself will give you a mouth and wisdom,
which none of your adversaries will be able to resist or to contradict.

16 YOU WILL BE DELIVERED EVEN BY PARENTS, BROTHERS, RELATIVES, FRIENDS; THEY WILL PUT SOME OF YOU TO DEATH. 17 AND YOU WILL BE HATED BY ALL *BECAUSE OF MY NAME.* 18 But not a hair of your head will perish: 19 by your perseverance you will secure your lives.

20 When you see Jerusalem surrounded by armies, then you know that has come near its desolation. 21 Then those who are in Judea let them flee to the mountains, and those who are in the midst of it let them depart, and those are in the fields let them not enter into it. 22 For these will be the days of vengeance to fulfill the Scriptures. 23 Woe to those who are pregnant and those who give suck in those days, for there will be great distress upon the earth and wrath against these people: 24 they will fall by the edge of the sword and be led captive among all the nations. And Jerusalem will be trodden down by nations, till be fulfilled the times of nations. 25 And there will be signs in sun, moon and stars and upon the earth distress of nations within the perplexity at the roaring of the sea and waves, 26 men fainting away because of fear in the expectation of the things which are coming upon the world, for the powers of heavens will be shaken. 27 Then they will see *THE SON OF MAN* coming in a cloud with great power and glory. 28 When these things begin to happen, straighten yourselves up and lift up your heads because your deliverance has come near». 29 He said to them a parable: «Look at the fig tree and all the trees; 30 when they already burst forward, watching it, you know for yourselves that summer is already near. 31 So you also, when you see these things happening, you know that is near the KINGDOM OF GOD.

32 **Truly I say to you that** this generation would not pass away until all may have happened; 33 the sky and the earth will pass away, but my words will not pass away. 34 Be on guard to yourselves lest your hearts may be weighed down with dissipation, and drunkenness, and anxieties of life and will come upon you suddenly that day 35 as a snare. For, it will come upon all those who are dwelling on the face of all the earth. 36 Be vigilant, praying always, that you may have strength to escape all these that are about to happen and to stand before *THE SON OF MAN*».

At the end of the sub-section, the coming of the «day of the Son of man» is equally the day of «deliverance» and of the «kingdom of God» (21:27-31); the disciples will know that he is close when the time of persecution, «the time of the nations» (24) is accomplished. This day is therefore far from close. And yet, at the start of the sub-section —when «the day of the Son of man» is already assimilated to the «kingdom of God» (17:20-24)— Jesus states that it has already come: «For the kingdom of God is among you» (17:21).

When the day of the Son of man comes, the disciples are to flee, leaving behind «their business» and are «not to turn back» (17:31-32); the same advice is given for the day when the devastation of Jerusalem comes (21:21). But since the kingdom of God is already present, the disciples are called not to wait, so that they are not distracted by «the cares of life» (21:34) as the Scribes are (20:45-21,4), summarized in the formula at 17:33.

THE CENTERS OF THE SEQUENCES

The central sub-sequence of sequence C6 has two parables, the parable of the unscrupulous judge and the widow, and the parable of the Pharisee and the tax-collector, which frame one question: «When the Son of man comes, will he find faith on the earth?» (18:1-14). The center of sequence C7 is occupied by a lengthy parable about the king and the pounds (19:11-28). Sequence C8 is focused on a short passage which includes two questions tightly framing a quotation from Ps 110 (20:41-44). In this way, three laws of biblical and Semitic rhetoric are fulfilled: at the center of a concentric construction are often a question, a parable, and a quotation[5].

These three units, sub-sequences or passages, act as «central terms» to the extent that their content is remarkably similar. The two parables in the central sub-sequence of sequence C6 both indicate divine judgment: the judgment made by the unscrupulous judge serves to emphasize God's judgment, for he «will give justice to his elect who cry to him night and day» (18:6), and the judgment which «justifies» the tax collector, but not the Pharisee («this man went home justified, the other did not»: 18:14). Between these two parables, the question: «But when the Son of man comes, will he find faith on earth?» presents Jesus as the one who will come to judge, separating those who, like the widow and the tax collector, will have demonstrated their faith in God and those who, like the unscrupulous judge and the Pharisee, have not.

In the parable which is the focus of sequence C7, the man of high birth, representing Jesus, goes to a far-off land «to receive kingship» (19:12). On his return, invested with kingship, he now not only exercises judgment by judging the servants to whom he had given the pounds, but also by condemning his «enemies» (19:27). Jesus, who was invested with royalty by another, then shares it with his servants, who receive the governance of his cities from him.

5 See *Traité*, 417-469.

At the heart of sequence c8, the quotation of Ps 110 shows Christ enthroned at the Lord's right hand (20:42), ruling over his «enemies» whom he places underfoot (43). Of course, these enemies recall the parable of the king and the pounds at the center of the previous sequence.

As can be seen, these three centers depict Jesus as the Son who inherits kingship from his father and who exercises it regally: the central parable of the central sequence is distinguished from the others by the fact that Christ hands on as an inheritance to his disciples the authority which he holds from God. This might be said to be the point of the sub-section.

c. SECTION C (LUKE 9:51-21:38)

The third section of the Gospel of Luke consists of eight sequences organized in three subsections:

C1 : Departure	for mission		9:51–10:42
C2 : Jesus,	disputed sign,	judges	11:1-54
C3 : *The disciple*	*judges according to the end*		12:1–13:21

C4 : «Anyone raises himself will be made lowly, and anyone makes himself lowly will be raised»	13:22–14,35
C5 : «Whatever is raised for men is an abomination to God»	15:1–17:10

C6 : Giving up	for the kingdom		17:11–18:30
C7 : Jesus,	disputed king,	judges	18:31–19:46
C8 : *Christ*	*judges according to the end*		19:47–21:38

The outer sub-sections each have three sequences which parallel one another. The central sub-section only has two sequences (c4 and c5) which are distinct from the other two because they bring together many parables. The titles which we have given them repeat similar formulas which are found at the center of each of the two sequences (14:11 and 16:15). So, once again, at the level, not of the sequence, but of the section, the law which sees parables at the center of the composition is proven. We cannot discuss this further in this work, but we can refer the reader to the chapter of my commentary on the Third Gospel in which section C is analyzed in detail[6].

6 See *Luc*, 803-827.

D. THE BOOK (1:1-24:53)

After a brief Prologue, Luke's Gospel has four sections. Section A has eight sequences, paired as follows:

Prologue		1:1-4
First sub-sequence:	TWO ANNUNCIATIONS	
Sequence A1:	*The annunciation of the birth of John*	1:5-25
Sequence A 2 :	The annunciation of the birth of Jesus	1:26-56
Second sub-section:	TWO BIRTHS	
Sequence A3 :	*John's birth*	1:57-80
Sequence A4 :	Jesus' birth	2:1-20
Third sub-section:	TWO DEDICATIONS OF JESUS IN THE TEMPLE	
Sequence A5:	Jesus is dedicated to the Lord	2:21-40
Sequence A6:	Jesus dedicates himself to his Father	2:41-52
Fourth sub-section:	TWO PREPARATIONS FOR JESUS' COMING	
Sequence A7:	*John prepares for the coming of the Christ*	3:1-20
Sequence A8 :	Jesus prepares for his coming	3:21– 4:13

The first two sub-sections give the accounts of the coming into the world of John the Baptist and Jesus: these are the annunciations, to Zecharaiah and to Mary (completed by the Visitation and the Magnificat), then Jesus' birth in Bethlehem followed by the account of John's birth and his circumcision.

The two sequences of the last sub-section, on the other hand, take place when the two protagonists are adults. Sequence A7 describes John the Baptist's ministry up until his imprisonment, while sequence B8 narrates Jesus' baptism, his genealogy and his temptations in the desert.

The third sub-section is the transition between these two periods. In sequence A5, Jesus is taken to the Temple for his mother's purification and to be dedicated to the Lord; and, once again in the Temple, in sequence A6, he dedicates himself to his Father when he goes there at the Passover pilgrimage at the age of twelve, that is, when he reaches adulthood. This is why this sub-section can be considered to be the center of the section.

The Gospel's final section (22-24) has four sequences which, take place on the three days of the Lord's Passover, Holy Thursday, Good Friday and the Sunday of the resurrection. The second and the third sequences, which take place on the same day form a pair and are, therefore, considered as a sub-section.

First sub-section:	THURSDAY DAY OF PREPARATION	
Sequence D1 :	**Christ leaves instructions for his disciples who abandon him**	22:1-53

Second sub-section:	FRIDAY DAY OF THE PASSION	
Sequence D2 : King of the Jews,	the Christ of God, is condemned	22:54–23:25
Sequence D3 : King of the Jews,	the Christ of God, is executed	23:26-56

Third sub-section:	SUNDAY DAY OF RESURRECTION	
Sequence D4:	**Christ opens the Scriptures for his disciples who rediscover him**	24:1-53

The outer sections, A and D, match. They are practically the same length. It further happens that the four sub-sections of the first section are parallel, in numerical terms, to the four sequences of section D (counting the number of signs and spaces, but excluding accents and punctuation):

Section A		Section D	
A1–A2 :	4 816	D1 :	4 742
A3–A4 :	3 862	D2 :	3 760
A5–A6 :	3 179	D3 :	2 833
A7–A8 :	4 656	D4 :	4 846
Total :	**16 513**	Total :	**16 181**

These two sections are also, particularly in fact, closely linked in terms of content. Here we are not going to explain the links[7]. Apparently very different, these two sections mention Jesus' origins, then his ends, and the two are similar as though this is normal. In the last section, even more marked in the last sequence, the sequence of the resurrection, Jesus is depicted as the one who completes the Scriptures of Israel. In the first section, his coming is prepared for not only by the final prophet, John the Baptist, but also by other prophets, Zecharaiah, who «prophesies» at length in the Benedictus, and Simeon and Anna in the Temple, and also by the older prophets, such as Malachi, who is quoted in sequence A1, and Isaiah in sequence A7, without mentioning the texts from the Torah and the early prophets.

7 See *Luc*, 982-988.

Section B has eight sequences arranged into three sub-sections:

First sub-section:	JESUS BEGINS HIS MINISTRY	
Sequence B1:	*Jesus' visit to Nazareth*	4:14-30
Sequence B2:	*Jesus' day at Capernaum*	4:31-44
Sequence B3:	*The call of Simon Peter*	5:1-16

Second sub-section:	MEN AND WOMEN		
Sequence B4:	**The doctors of the Law**	**and the Spouse of the new alliance**	5:17– 6:11
Sequence B5:	The gift of filiation		6:12– 7:17
Sequence B6:	**John the Baptist**	**and the Spouse of the new alliance**	7:18-50
Sequence B7:	The gift of fruitfulness		8:1-56

Final sub-section:	THE DISCIPLES BEGIN THEIR MINISTRY	
Sequence B8:	*The disciples called to do what Jesus does*	9:1-50

The three sequences of the first section (B1, B2, B3) closely match the three sub-sequences of the last sequence (B8)[8]. Note, particularly, that the four sequences of the central sub-section form a striking parallelism.

The four sections of the Third Gospel are organized in mirror fashion. The titles emphasize the links between the sections two by two, D with A, C with B:

A. *Christ's coming*	*prepared for*	*by the messengers*	*of the Lord*	1:5–4:13
B. Jesus establishes	the community of his disciples		in Galilee	4:14–9:50
C. Jesus leads	the community of his disciples		to Jerusalem	9:51–21:38
D. *Christ's Passover*	*predicted*	*by the Scriptures*	*of Israel*	22:1–24:53

To bring this all-too-brief summary, but one which gives a glimpse of the book's architecture, to an end, we still need to point out that the final sequence of the second section (B8) and the first sequence of the third section (C1) have many points in common, so much so that it is possible to consider this pair of sequences to be the center of the book as a whole[9].

8 So much so that one is tempted to consider them to be a single sequence.

9 See *Luc*, 976-982.

In terms of Matthew and, in particular, Mark, similar studies have been carried out by various scholars. We should mention in particular the works of Jean Radermakers[10] and Bastiaan van Iersel[11]. However, these scholars, and others, have missed out a rigorous methodological construction, to the extent that one cannot entirely trust their analysis.

There are many partial studies, and several make significant contributions. So, for example, for the central section of the Second Gospel, the most serious work is Arul Jesus Robin Muthiah's[12]. But we must repeat that the boundaries of a sequence cannot be truly established as long as the boundaries of the previous and succeeding sequence have not also been established and, logically, closely, to the very boundaries of the book. In other words, nothing is certain, until the composition of the book as a whole has been drawn out at every level of its organization.

10 RADERMAKERS J., *Au fil de l'Évangile selon saint Matthieu*; ID., *La Bonne Nouvelle de Jésus selon saint Marc.*

11 IERSEL B. van, *Mark. Reader-Response Commentary.*

12 MUTHIAH A.J.R., *Jesus, Giver of Life. Composition and Interpretation of Mark 7:31-9:50.* According to Muthiah, it is not the confession at Caesarea in the center of Mark, but the discourse on discipleship (8:34-9:1), framed by Peter's confession of faith (8:27-30) and followed by the first prediction of the Passion and resurrection (31-33) and the transfiguration (9:2-8), followed by another passage in which Jesus again predicts his Passion (9:9-13).

Epilogue

An *introduction* cannot be completed, certainly not with a conclusion —this would be a contradiction in terms. The work of this volume was to open up a path which the reader, like the author, is invited to follow. I hope to have provided the necessary tools to find one's bearings in the huge territory of the Synoptic Gospels. For many, these navigational tools are new, and it must be admitted that the lines of the new route which they enable us to follow are hardly sketched out.

This introduction was developed during the course which I have given for nearly ten years to students in the first year of the first cycle of studies at the Gregorian University in Rome. It is, however, the fruits of research undertaken more than thirty-five years ago. In 1982, I had already published a first «initiation», in which I compared, among other texts, Matthew's and Mark's settings which include «Zebedee's sons' request» and «The healing at Jericho» framing «The discourse on service»[1]. More recently I carried out the same kind of synoptic study on the accounts of the Passion and the resurrection in the Synoptic Gospels[2]. Apart from these initial analyses, a large field is still to be explored; and this is why we can say that the work has hardly begun. The fruits harvested up until now allow us to think that it is worthy pursuing this path.

Each year, students tell me that they have tried, during the course, to change the way in which they read the Gospels. They will no longer be content with a fragmentary reading, pericope by pericope; rather, they will try to carry out a unified reading, taking note of the links which tie the pericopes together, and trying to grasp the logic which connects them. This kind of reaction, repeated year after year, gives me much encouragement to continue the research. For them, as for me, the fact of being able to discover the logic of the Gospel discourse which appears in the textual composition at various levels of their organization, leads them to the discovery of a meaning which until then had been unsuspected. It also leads to marvel and appreciation at the art of each Evangelist, who are shown to be true authors, and first-rate authors at that.

The first thing to do before any synoptic work is to carry out the work to discover the composition of each of the Gospels. For Luke, I had already done this even if, of course, the analysis is always to be repeated so that it can be refined and corrected as necessary[3]. For Matthew and Mark, as for Luke, I think I have been

1 MEYNET R., *Initiation à la rhétorique biblique.*

2 See MEYNET R., *Jésus passe.*

3 See MEYNET R., «La composition du fils prodigue revisitée (Lc 15)».

able to identify the final four sequences, Jesus' instructions, trial, execution and resurrection; as in this work, I have also carried out a synoptic comparison for these texts. Like other scholars, I have studied the composition of the five debates with the Pharisees in Luke (5:17-6:11) and Mark (2:1-3:6), and of the Sermon on the Mount in Matt 5-7. The two sequences of Matt 19-20 and Mark 10 which I have analyzed here seem to be reasonably identified in their boundaries and their internal organization.

However —let me say this once again— the boundaries of a sequence cannot be considered to be certain until the boundaries of the previous and following sequence have been identified too; and thus it logically follows, until the only two indisputable boundaries of the book, its beginning, and its end, have been reached. What is more, we must add that the division into pericopes and sequences cannot be confirmed until the composition at the higher levels is carried out —first of all, the section, which brings the sequences together, and then the book, which brings together all the sections.

B1: A trap		for	the Children of Israel	3:1-8
B2: Increasing	**wealth**	*will not save*	the Children of Israel	3:9–4:3
B3: Increasing	***sacrifices***	*will not save*	the Children of Israel	4:4-13
B4: FUNERAL LAMENT		OVER	THE VIRGIN OF ISRAEL	5:1-17
B5: ***Perverse***	***worship***	*will not save*	the House of Israel	5:18-27
B6: **Perverse**	**wealth**	*will not save*	la the House of Israel	6:1-7
B7: The poison		of	the House of Israel	6:8-14

In addition to Luke, the fundamental work for us was the analysis we carried out of the book of Amos, with Pietro Bovati. In the second section (3-6) we identified seven sequences. When later we studied the section as a whole[4], the close relationship between the symmetrical sections confirmed, in an amazing way, that our division into sequences was not incorrect. To give an idea of the logic of that construction, there follows the schema of the section[5], slightly modified in its printed presentation, the better to bring out the correspondences.

In addition to other yet more important facts, note that the different names for the Israelites match the organization of the section; while in the first three sequences they are called «children of Israel» and in the last three «house of Israel», the central sequence is addressed to «the Virgin (of) Israel».

When the composition of each Gospel has been established at various levels of the text's organization, it will be possible to return to the synoptic study, but on different bases. Then we can compare not only isolated elements, but the constructions, from the constructions of pericopes to the architecture of the whole. After this purely synchronic work, it will, perhaps, be useful to examine and evaluate, from a new perspective, the different hypotheses about the history of the formation of the Gospels[6].

4 *Amos*, 225-276.

5 *Amos*, 102.

6 The results of rhetorical analysis have been presented in this work. Those who wish to take this particular exegetical work further can make use of the exercises which I have prepared for them in «*Et maintenant, écrivez pour vous ce cantique*». *Exercices pratiques d'analyse rhétorique*, available on the website of the International Society for the study of Biblical and Semitic Rhetoric (RBS): www.retoricabiblicaesemitica.org: Biblical rhetorical analysis, Exercises.

ABÛ-DÂWÛD Sulaymān ibn al-Aš'at al-Siğistānī, *Sunan*, Šarihat Musṭafā al-Bābī al-Ḥalabī, Cairo 1952.

ACHTEMEIER PAUL J., «"And he followed him": miracles and discipleship in Mark 10,46-52» in *Semeia* 11 (1978) 115-145.

AUGUSTIN SAINT, *De Sermone Domini in monte;* English translation: *Commentary on the Lord's sermon on the mount with seventeen related sermons*, The Fathers of the Church. A New Tanslation 11, The Catholic University of America Press, Washington 1977.

ALAND KURT, *Synopsis quattuor evangeliorum. Locis parallelis evangeliorum apocryphorum et patrum adhibitis. Editio duodecima ad textum editionum 26 Nestle-Aland et 3 Greek New Testament aptata*, Deutsche Bibelgesellschaft, Stuttgart 1982[12].

ALTER ROBERT, *The Art of Biblical Narrative*, London 1981.

AMPHOUX CHRISTIAN-BERNARD, see VAGANAY, LÉON.

ANGÉNIEUX JOSEPH, «Les différents types de structure du Pater dans l'histoire de son exégèse» in *EThL* 46 (1970) 40-77; 325-359.

AALMARY MARIE, *La Divine Origine. Dieu n'a pas créé l'homme*, Grasset, Paris 1993.

______, *Abel ou la Traversée de l'Éden*, Grasset, Paris 1999.

BAREILLE GEORGES, «Catéchuménat» in *DTC*, 1968-1987.

BARUCQ ANDRÉ and DAUMAS FRANÇOIS, *Hymnes et Prières de l'Égypte ancienne*, Éd. du Cerf, LAPO 10, Paris 1980.

BAUDOZ JEAN-FRANÇOIS, DAHAN GILBERT and GUINOT JEN-NOËL, *La Prière du Seigneur (Mt 6,9-13 ; Lc 11,2-4)*, Éd. du Cerf. Service biblique Évangile et vie, CEv Supplément 132, Paris 2005.

BEAUCHAMP PAUL, «Propositions sur l'alliance comme structure centrale» in *RSR* 58 (1970) 161-193.

______, Préface à R. Meynet, *L'Analyse rhétorique*, Éd. du Cerf, Initiations, Paris, 1989, 7-14; English translation, *Rhetorical Analysis*, 9-15.

______, *Psaumes nuit et jour*, Éd. du Seuil, Paris 1980.

______, *D'une montagne à l'autre, la Loi de Dieu*, Éd. du Seuil, Paris 1999.

BENOIT PIERRE et BOISMARD MARIE-ÉMILE, *Synopse des quatre évangiles en français, avec parallèles des apocryphes et des Pères*, Éd. du Cerf, I. Textes, Paris 1965; II. Commentaire, Paris 1972.

Bible de Jérusalem (La), traduite en français sous la direction de l'École biblique de Jérusalem, Éd. du Cerf, Paris 1956; *Nouvelle édition revue et corrigée*, Paris 1998.

BLASS FRIEDRICH and DEBRUNNER ALBERT, *A Greek Grammar of the New Testament*, The University of Chicago Press, Chicago/London 1961[19].

BOBIN CHRISTIAN, *L'Homme qui marche*, Le temps qu'il fait, Cognac 1995.

BOGAERT PIERRE-MAURICE, «Les Quatre Vivants, l'Évangile et les évangiles» in *RThL* 32 (2001) 457-478.

BOISMARD MARIE-ÉMILE, see BENOIT PIERRE.

BOISMARD MARIE-ÉMILE and LAMOUILLE ARNAUD, *La Vie des évangiles: Initiation à la critique des textes*, Éd. du Cerf, Initiations, Paris 1980.

———, *Synopsis graeca quattuor evangeliorum*, Peeters, Leuven 1986.

BONNARD PIERRE, *L'Évangile selon saint Matthieu*, CNT(N) 1, Neuchâtel, 1963, CNT(N), NS 1, Geneva 1982[3].

BOVATI PIETRO, *Ristabilire la giustizia: Procedure, vocabolario, orientamenti*, Editrice Pontificio Istituto Biblico, AnBib 110, Rome, 1986; English transl.: Re-establishing justice: legal terms, concepts and procedures in the Hebrew Bible, JSOT.S 105, Academic Press, JSOT Press, Sheffield 1994.

———, *Giustizia e ingiustizia nell'Antico Testamento*, photocopied lecture notes, Rome 1996.

BOVATI PIETRO and MEYNET ROLAND, *Le Livre du prophète Amos*, Éd. du Cerf, RhBib 2, Paris 1994.

BOVON FRANÇOIS, *L'Évangile selon saint Luc*, Labor et Fides, CNT IIIa, IIIb, IIIc, Geneva 1991, 1996, 2001.

BROWN RAYMOND E., *Que sait-on du Nouveau Testament?*, Bayard Éditions, Paris, 2000. English: An introduction to the New Testament, Doubleday, New York - London 1997.

CALONGHI FERRUCCIO, *Dizionario Latino Italiano*, Rosenberg & Sellier, Turin 1965[3].

CARMIGNAC JEAN, *Recherches sur le «Notre Père»*, Letouzey, Paris 1969.

Catechism of the Catholic Church, Geoffrey Chapman, London 1994.

Catholic Study Bible, The, Oxford University Press, New York 1990.

CASTELOT ANDRÉ, see DECAUX ALAIN.

COULOT CLAUDE, «Synoptique (Le Problème)» in *DBS* 13, 2005, col. 785-828.

CURTIS ADRIAN, see MARGUERAT DANIEL.

DAHAN GILLES, see BAUDOZ JEAN-FRANÇOIS.

DAUMAS FRANÇOIS, see BARUCQ ANDRÉ.

DEBRUNNER ALBERT, see BLASS FRIEDRICH.

DECAUX ALAIN and CASTELOT ANDRÉ, *Dictionnaire d'histoire de France Perrin*, Perrin, Paris 1981.

DEISS LUCIEN, *Synopse de Matthieu, Marc et Luc avec les parallèles de Jean*, Desclée de Brouwer, Connaître la Bible, Paris 1963-1964.

DUMAIS MARCEL, «Sermon sur la montagne» in *DBS* 12, 1996, col. 699-938.

______, *Le Sermon sur la montagne. État de la recherche. Interprétation. Bibliographie*, , Letouzey & Ané, Sainte Foy QC, 1995.

DUPONT JACQUES, «L'aveugle de Jéricho (Mc 10,46-52)» in *Revue Africaine de Théologie* 8 (1984) 165-181 (= *Études sur les évangiles synoptiques*, University Press, Leuven, BETHL 70A, (1985) 350-367).

ÉLIADE MIRCEA, *Naissances mystiques. Essai sur quelques types d'initiation*, Gallimard, Les essais 92, Paris 1959[6]. English transl.: *Rites and symbols of initiation: the mysteries of birth and rebirth*, Harper & Row, New York 1965.

ERNST JOSEF, *Das Evangelium nach Markus*, Regensburg, 1981; Italian translation: *Il vangelo secondo Marco*, Morcelliana, Il Nuovo Testamento commentato I (1,1-8,26), II (8,27-16,20), Brescia 1991.

FÉDRY JACQUES, «La composition selon la symétrie concentrique» in *Afrique et Parole* 57 (1980) 5-43.

FITZMYER JOSEPH A., *The Biblical Commission's Document «The Interpretation of the Bible in the Church»*, Editrice Pontificio Istituto Biblico, Studia Biblica 18, Rome 1995.

______, *The Gospel According to Luke*, AnB 28.28a, Doubleday, Garden City NY 1981, 1985.

FOCANT CAMILLE, *L'Évangile selon Marc*, Éd. du Cerf, Commentaire biblique: Nouveau Testament 2, Paris 2004.

FRAENKEL ABRAHAM ADOLF, «'Assarah Maamaroth - 'Assarah Dibberot. De la Création à la Révélation», in MÉÏR TAPIÉRO, ed., *Les Dix Paroles*, Éd. du Cerf, Paris 1995, 59-62.

_______, «Du père au Père», in MÉÏR TAPIÉRO, ed., *Les Dix Paroles*, Éd. du Cerf, Paris 1995, 305-307.

FRAINE JEAN (de), «Oraison dominicale» in *DBS* 6, 1960, col. 788-800.

FUSCO VITTORIO, «Un racconto di miracolo: la guarigione del cieco Bartimeo (Mc 10,46-52 ; Mt 20,29-34 ; Lc 18,35-43)», in LÀCONI MAURO *et al.*, *Vangeli sinottici e Atti degli Apostoli*, Editrice Elledici, Logos 5, Leumann (Torino), 1994, 213-225.

GEORGE AUGUSTIN and GRELOT PIERRE, eds, Introduction à la Bible. Édition nouvelle. Nouveau Testament, Desclée, Paris 1976.

GNILKA JOACHIM, *Das Matthäusevangelium*, Herder, HThK 1, Freiburg 1986-1988; Italian translation, *Il vangelo di Matteo*, Paideia, CTNT 1/1-2, Brescia 1990, 1991.

GOYON JEAN-CLAUDE, *Rituels funéraires de l'ancienne Égypte: le rituel de l'embaumement, le rituel de l'ouverture de la bouche, les livres des respirations*, Éd. du Cerf, LAPO 4, Paris 1972.

GRELOT PIERRE, *Évangiles et Histoire*, Desclée, Introduction à la Bible. Édition nouvelle. Nouveau Testament 6, Paris 1986.

GRELOT PIERRE, *Les paroles de Jésus Christ*, Desclée, Introduction à la Bible. Édition nouvelle. Nouveau Testament 7, Paris 1986.

GRELOT PIERRE, *Jésus de Nazareth, Christ et Seigneur*, Éd. du Cerf, LeDiv 167.170, Paris/ Montréal 1997-1998.

GUINOT JEAN-NOËL, see BAUDOZ JEAN-FRANÇOIS.

HAGNER DONALD A., *Matthew*, Word Books, WBC 33, Dallas TX, 1993-95.

HAULOTTE EDGARD, *Symbolique du vêtement selon la Bible*, Aubier, Théologie 65, Paris 1966.

HILAIRE DE POITIERS *Sur Matthieu*, II, Paris, Éd. du Cerf, SC 258, 1979.

IBN HANBAL, Abū 'Abdallāh Aḥmad ibn Moḥammad, *Musnad*, Cairo 1949.

IERSEL BASTIAAN M.F. VAN, *Mark. Reader-Response Commentary*, Sheffield Academic Press, Sheffield 1998.

Jerusalem Bible, The, Darton, Longman & Todd, London 1966.

JENNI ERNST and WESTERMANN CLAUS, *Theologisches Handwörterbuch zum Alten Testament*, Kaiser/Theologischer Verlag, Munich/Zurich 1971-1976; Italian translation, *Dizionario teologico dell'Antico Testamento*, Torino 1978. English: Theological lexicon of the Old Testament, Hendrickson, Peabody (Mass) 1997.

JOHNSON EARL S. Jr, «Mark 10:46-52: Blind Bartimaeus» in CBQ 40 (1978) 191-204.

JUSTIN *Apologies*, Études augustiniennes, Paris, 1987. The first and second apologies, Paulist Press, New York - Mahwah (NJ) 1997.

KOT TOMASZ, «Accomplir la justice de Dieu. Mt 5,17-48. Analyse rhétorique» in FRANCISZEK SIEG *et al.*, *Studies in the Bible. To Commemorate the 400th Anniversary of the Publication of Jakub Wujek's Translation of the Bible: 1599-1999*, Varsovie 2000, 73-187; reprinted and corrected at www. retorica biblicaesemitica.org: Publications in *StRh* 7, 01.02.2002.

LÀCONI MAURO *et al.*, *Vangeli sinottici e Atti degli Apostoli*, Elledici, Logos 5, Turin 1994.

LAMARCHE PAUL, *Évangile de Marc*, Gabalda, EtB, NS 33, Paris 1996.

LAMOUILLE ARNAUD, see BOISMARD MARIE-ÉMILE.

LAVERGNE CESLAS, *Synopse des quatre évangiles en français*, Éd. du Cerf, Gabalda, Paris 1986.

LÉGASSE SIMON, *L'Évangile de Marc*, Éd. du Cerf, LeDiv Commentaires 5, Paris 1997.

LEMAIRE ANDRÉ et SÆBØ, Magne, *Congress Volume. Oslo 1998*, Brill, VT.S 80, Leiden 2000.

LÉON-DUFOUR XAVIER, *Études d'évangile*, Éd. du Seuil, Parole de Dieu, Paris 1965.

______, *Les Évangiles et l'Histoire de Jésus*, Éd. du Seuil, Parole de Dieu, Paris, 1963. The Gospels and the Jesus of history, Image Books, Garden City (NY) 1970; Doubleday image books, 1970.

______, *L'Annonce de l'évangile*, Desclée, Introduction à la Bible. Édition nouvelle. Nouveau Testament, Paris 1976.

______, *Dictionnaire du Nouveau Testament*, Éd. du Seuil, Livre de vie 131, Paris 1996³. English transl.: *Dictionary of the New Testament*, Harper & Row, San Francisco 1980.

LOHFINK GERHARD, *Jetzt verstehe ich die Bibel: Ein Sachbuch zur Formkritik*, KBW Verlag, Stuttgart 1974. The Bible: now I get it!: a form-criticism handbook, Doubleday, Garden City (NY) 1979.

LOYOLA IGNACE (de), *Récit écrit par le Père Louis Gonçalves aussitôt qu'il l'eut recueilli de la bouche même du Père Ignace*, Desclée de Brouwer, Christus 65, Paris 1988. A pilgrim's testament: the memoirs of Ignatius of Loyola, Rome 1983.

LUND NILS WILHELM, *Chiasmus in the New Testament. A Study in Formgeschichte*, The University of North Carolina Press, Chapel Hill 1942; reprint, *Chiasmus in the New Testament. A Study in the Form and Function of Chiastic Structures*, Hendrickson, Peabody MA 1992.

LUZ ULRICH, *Matthew 1-7. A Commentary*, Augsburg Fortress, Mineapolis 1989.

MARCHADOUR ALAIN, *Les Évangiles au feu de la critique*, Centurion/Bayard, Paris 1995.

MARGUERAT DANIEL and CURTIS, ADRIAN, eds, *Intertextualités. La Bible en échos*, Labor et Fides, Le monde de la Bible 40, Geneva 2000.

———, ed., *Introduction au Nouveau Testament. Son histoire, son écriture, sa théologie*, Labor et Fides, Le monde de la Bible 41, Geneva 2004^{3}.

MAZZUCCO CLEMENTINA, *Lettura del vangelo di Marco*, Silvio Zamorani editore, Turin 1999.

MESSAS CHALOM, «Les dix Paroles», in MÉÏR TAPIÉRO, ed., *Les Dix Paroles*, Éd. du Cerf, Paris 1995, 17-57.

METZGER BRUCE M., *A Textual Commentary on the Greek New Testament*, United Bible Societies, Stuttgart 1994^{2}.

MEYNET ROLAND[1], *Quelle est donc cette Parole? Lecture « rhétorique » de l'Évangile de Luc (1-9 et 22-24)*, Éd. du Cerf, LeDiv 99 A.B, Paris 1979.

MEYNET ROLAND, «Au cœur du texte: analyse rhétorique de l'aveugle de Jéricho selon saint Luc» in *NRTh* 103 (1981) 693-710.

———, *Initiation à la rhétorique biblique. Qui donc est le plus grand?*, I-II, Éd. du Cerf, Initiations, Paris 1982.

———, «Les dix commandements, loi de liberté: analyse rhétorique d'Ex 20,2-17 et de Dt 5,6-21», *MUSJ* 50 (1984) 405-421 (+7 tables in appendix).

1 See www.retoricabiblicaesemitica.org: our publications, Bibliographies, Roland Meynet bibliography.

______, *L'Évangile selon saint Luc. Analyse rhétorique*, RhBib 1, I. Planches; II. Commentaire, Éd. du Cerf, RhBib 1, Paris 1988.

______, *L'Analyse rhétorique. Une nouvelle méthode pour comprendre les textes bibliques: textes fondateurs et exposé systématique*, Éd. du Cerf, Initiations, Paris 1989; English transl.: *Rhetorical Analysis. An Introduction to Biblical Rhetoric*, JSOT.S 256, Sheffield Academic Press, Sheffield 1998.

______, «Analyse rhétorique du Prologue de Jean» in *RB* 96 (1989) 481-510.

______, «Le cantique de Moïse et le cantique de l'Agneau (Ap 15 et Ex 15) » in *Gr.* 73 (1992) 19-55.

______, «"Celui à qui est remis peu, aime un peu" (Lc 7,36-50)» in *Gr.* 75 (1994) 267-280.

______, «Présupposés de l'analyse rhétorique, avec une application à Mc 10,13-52», in C. COULOT ed., *Exégèse et Herméneutique. Comment lire la Bible?*, Éd. Du Cerf, LeDiv 158, Paris 1994, 69-111 (reprinted in *Lire la Bible*, Flammarion, Champs 537, Paris 2003, 145-162).

______, *«E ora, scrivete per voi questo cantico». Introduzione pratica all'analisi retorica*, 1. *Detti e proverbi*, Edizioni Dehoniane, ReBib 3, Rome 1996; French edition, *«Et maintenant, écrivez pour vous ce cantique». Exercices pratiques d'analyse rhétorique. 1. Dictons et proverbes*, www. retoricabiblicaesemitica.org: L'analyse rhétorique biblique, Exercices, 22.09.2004.

______, «I frutti dell'analisi retorica per l'esegesi biblica» in *Gr.* 77 (1996) 403-436 (French translation in *Lire la Bible*, Flammarion, Champs 537, 163-189).

______, *Jésus passe. Testament, jugement, exécution, résurrection du Seigneur dans les synoptiques*, Editrice Pontificia Università Gregoriana/ Éd. du Cerf, RhBib 3, Rome /Paris 1999.

______, «Jésus fils de David dans l'Évangile de Luc», in LOUIS DESROUSSEAUX - JACQUES VERMEYLEN, ed., *Figures de David à travers la Bible, Congrès de l'ACFEB (Lille, 1997)*, Éd. du Cerf, LeDiv 177, Paris 1999, 413-427.

______, «Le quatrième chant du Serviteur (Is 52,13-53,12)» in *Gr.* 81 (1999) 407-440.

______, *«Tu vois cette femme?» Parler en paraboles*, Éd. du Cerf, LiBi 121, Paris 2001.

______, «Les deux décalogues, loi de liberté», www.retoricabiblicaesemitica.org: Publications, *StRh*, n° 8, 11.04.2002 (last updated: 27.09.2005).

______, «The Question at the Centre: A Specific Device of Rhetorical Argumentation in Scripture», in ANDERS ERIKSSON, THOMAS H. OLBRICHT and WALTER ÜBELACKER, eds, *Rhetorical Argumentation in Biblical Texts. Essays from the Lund 2000 Conference*, Emory Studies in Early Christianity 8, Trinity Press International, Harrisburg, Pennsylvania 2002, 200-214.

______, «La composition du Notre Père», *Liturgie* 119 (2002), 158-191; reprinted and corrected in www.retoricabiblicaesemitica.org : Publications in *StRh* n° 18, 04.05.2005.

______, *Lire la Bible*, Flammarion, Champs 537, Paris 2003.

______, «La Nativité de Jésus (Lc 2,1-20)», www.retoricabiblicaesemitica.org: Publications in *StRh*, n° 9, 26.11.2001 (last updated: 31.03.2004).

______, «Les fruits de l'analyse rhétorique pour l'exégèse biblique», in www. retoricabiblicaesemitica.org: Publications in *StRh*, n° 14, 13.12.2004.

______, *L'Évangile de Luc*, Lethielleux, RhSem 1, Paris 2005.

______, *La Bible*, Le Cavalier bleu, Idées reçues 94, Paris 2005.

______, «Es 25,10-40. A proposito del libro di Giorgio Paximadi, *E io dimorerò in mezzo a loro*», in www.retoricabiblicaesemitica.org: Publications in *StRh*, n° 21, 29.11.2005 (last updated: 04.11.2006).

______, «La composition du fils prodigue revisitée (Lc 15)», in R. MEYNET, *Études sur la traduction et l'interprétation de la Bible*, École de traducteurs et d'interprètes de Beyrouth, Sources/Cibles, Beirut 2006, 55-67.

______, *Études sur la traduction et l'interprétation de la Bible*, École de traducteurs et d'interprètes de Beyrouth, Sources/Cibles, Beirut 2006.

______, *Traité de rhétorique biblique*, Lethielleux, RhSem 4, Paris 2007.

______, *Appelés à la liberté*, Lethielleux, RhSem 5, Paris 2008; English transl.: *Called to Freedom*, Rhetorica Semitica, Convivium Press, Miami (FL) 2009.

______, see BOVATI PIETRO.

The Midrash on Psalms, Yale University Press, YJS 13, New Haven 1959.

MUTHIAH ARUL JESU ROBIN, *Jesus, Giver of Life. Composition and Interpretation of Mark 7:31-9:50*, Claretian Communications, Chennai 2005.

NANGE KUDITA WA SESEMBA, *L'homme et la femme dans la société et la culture Cokwe: de l'anthropologie à la philosophie. Une lecture des rites d'initiation*, Université catholique de Louvain, Louvain-la-Neuve 1981.

NESTLE ERWIN and ALAND KURT, *Novum Testamentum Graece*, Deutsche Bibelgesellschaft, Stuttgart 1993[27].

ORIGEN, *Commento a Matteo*, II, Città nuova, CTePa 151, Rome 1999.

ORIGÈNE, *La prière*, Desclée De Brouwer, Collection Les Pères dans la foi 2, Paris, 1977. English transl. *Treatise on Prayer*, S. P. C. K., London 1954.

OSTY ÉMILE, *La Bible*, Éd. du Seuil, Paris 1973.

PAPERON BERNARD, «Na'assé ve-nichma'», «Nous ferons et nous entendrons», in MÉÏR TAPIÉRO, ed., *Les Dix Paroles*, Éd. du Cerf, Paris 1995, 101-109.

PAXIMADI GIORGIO, *E io dimorerò in mezzo a loro. Composizione e interpretazione di Es 25-31*, EDB, ReBib 8, Bologna 2004.

PESCH RUDOLF, *Das Markusevangelium*, Herder, Freiburg 1977[2], 1980[2]; Italian translation, *Il vangelo di Marco*, I-II, Paideia, CTNT II,1-2, Brescia 1980-1982.

PONTIFICAL BIBLICAL COMMISSION, *L'Interprétation de la Bible dans l'Église*, Libreria Editrice Vaticana, Vatican City 1993.

POPPI ANGELICO, *Sinossi dei quattro vangeli. Volume I - Testo*, Messaggero, Padua 2004[14].

RADERMAKERS JEAN, *Au fil de l'Évangile selon saint Matthieu*, Institut d'études théologiques, Brussels 1974[2].

______, *La Bonne nouvelle de Jésus selon saint Marc*, Institut d'études théologiques, Brussels 1974.

ROBBINS VERNON K., «The Healing of Blind Bartimaeus (10:46-52) in the Marcan Theology» in *JBL* 92 (1973) 224-243.

ROCHAIS GÉRARD, «La formation du Prologue de Jean (Jn 1,1-18)» in *ScEs* 37 (1985) 5-44.

ROSSÉ GÉRARD, *Il vangelo di Luca*, Città Nuova, Collana scritturistica di Città Nuova, Rome 1992.

SCHÜRMANN HEINZ, *La prière du Seigneur, à la lumière de la prédication de Jésus*, L'Orante, Études théologiques 3, Paris 1965.

Sefer Ha-Hinukh, trans. R. Samuel, Comptoir du livre de Keren hasefer, Paris 1974.

SEPIÈRE MARIE-CHRISTINE, *L'image d'un Dieu souffrant (IX°-X° siècle). Aux origines du crucifix*, Éd. du Cerf, Histoire, Paris 1994.

SIM DAVID C., «The Meaning of παλιγγενεσία in Matthew 19:28» in *JSNT* 50 (1993) 3-12.

STEINHAUSER MICHAEL G., «The Form of the Bartimaeus Narrative (Mark 10: 46-52)» in *NTS* 32 (1986) 583-595.

TAPEIRO MÉÏR, ed., *Les Dix Paroles*, Éd. du Cerf, Paris 1995.

TAPEIRO MÉÏR, «Honore ton père et ta mère» in MÉÏR TAPEIRO, ed., *Les Dix Paroles*, Éd. du Cerf, Paris 1995, 265-299.

The New Jerusalem Bible. Study Edition. Darton, Longman & Todd. London, 1994.

THEODORE OF MOPSUESTIA, *Les Homélies catéchétiques*, Biblioteca apostolica vaticana, Studi e testi 145, Vatican City 1949.

THEISSEN GERD, *The Miracle Stories of the Early Christian Tradition*, T. & T. Clark, Studies of the New Testament and its world, Edinburgh 1983 (German original: 1974).

TOPEL JOHN L., «What Kind of a Sign are Vultures? Luke 17,37b» in *Bib* 84 (2003) 403-411.

Traduction Œcuménique de la Bible, Éd. du Cerf/Les Bergers et les Mages, Paris 1972-1975.

TRILLING WOLFGANG, *Christusverkündigung in den Synoptischen Evangelien*, St. Benno Verlag, Leipzig 1968; French translation, *L'Annonce du Christ dans les Évangiles synoptiques*, Éd. du Cerf, LeDiv 69, Paris 1971.

TROCMÉ ÉTIENNE, *L'Évangile selon saint Marc*, Labor et Fides, CNT(N), Geneva 2000.

VAGANAY LÉON and AMPHOUX, CHRISTIAN BERNARD, *Initiation à la critique textuelle du Nouveau Testament*, Éd. du Cerf, Paris 1986.

WÉNIN ANDRÉ, «Le décalogue. Approche contextuelle, théologie et anthropologie», in CAMILLE FOCANT, ed., *La Loi dans l'un et l'autre Testament*, Éd. du Cerf, LeDiv 168, Paris 1997, 9-43.

______, *Pas seulement de pain… Violence et alliance dans la Bible*, Éd. du Cerf, LeDiv 171, Paris 1998.

WESTERMANN CLAUS, see JENNI, ERNST.

WRESINSKI JOSEPH, *Les pauvres sont l'Église*, Centurion, Les interviews, Paris 1983.

______, *Heureux vous les pauvres*, Éditions Cana, Paris 1984.

Index of Authors

D

E

F

G

M

N

O

P

R

S

T

V

W

ROLAND MEYNET
OTHER PUBLICATIONS IN
THE BIBLE CONTEXT

Quelle est donc cette Parole? Lecture «rhétorique» de l'Évangile selon saint Luc (1-9 et 22-24), Éd. du Cerf, LeDiv 99 A.B., Paris 1979.

Initiation à la rhétorique biblique. Qui donc est le plus grand?, I-II, Éd. du Cerf, Initiations, Paris 1982.

L'Évangile selon saint Luc. Analyse rhétorique, I-II, Éd. du Cerf, RhBib 1, Paris 1988. In Italian: *Il vangelo secondo Luca*, ED, ReBib 1, Roma 1993.

L'Analyse rhétorique. Une nouvelle méthode pour comprendre la Bible. Textes fondateurs et exposé systématique, Éd. du Cerf, Initiations, Paris 1989. In Italian: *L'analisi retorica*, Queriniana, BiBi 8, Brescia 1992. In English: *Rhetorical Analysis. An Introduction to Biblical Rhetoric*, Sheffield Academic Press JSOT. S 256, Sheffield 1998.

Avez-vous lu saint Luc? Guide pour la rencontre, Éd. du Cerf, LiBi 88, Paris 1990. In Polish: *Czytaliscie Sw. Łukasza? Przewodnik, który prowadzi do Spotkania*, Kraków, Wam 1998.

Passion de Notre Seigneur Jésus Christ selon les évangiles synoptiques, Éd. du Cerf, LiBi 99, Paris 1993.

Con N. Farouki, L. Pouzet y A. Sinno, *Méthode rhétorique et herméneutique, Analyse de textes de la Bible et de la Tradition musulmane*, Dar el-Machreq, Beyrouth 1993 (en árabe): In French: *Rhétorique sémitique. Textes de la Bible et de la Tradition musulmane*, Éd. du Cerf, Patrimoines. Religions du Livre, Paris 1998.

Con P. Bovati, *Le Livre du prophète Amos*, Éd. du Cerf, RhBib 2, Paris 1994. In Italian: *Il libro del profeta Amos*, ED, ReBib 2, Roma 1995.

Con P. Bovati, *La Fin d'Israël. Paroles d'Amos*, Éd. du Cerf, LiBi 101, Paris 1994.

Lire la Bible, Paris, Flammarion, Dominos 92, 1996. In Italian: *Leggere la Bibbia*, Il Saggiatore/Flammarion, Due punti 57, Milano 1998.

«E ora, scrivete per voi questo cantico». Introduzione pratica all'analisi retorica, 1. *Detti e proverbi*, ED, ReBib 3, Roma 1996.

Jésus passe. Testament, procès, exécution et résurrection du Seigneur Jésus dans les évangiles synoptiques, PUG Editrice/Éd. du Cerf, RhBib 3, Rome/Paris 1999. In Italian: *La Pasqua del Signore. Testamento, processo, esecuzione e risurrezione di Gesù nei vangeli sinottici*, EDB, ReBib 5, Bologna 2002.

«Vedi questa donna?» Saggio sulla comunicazione per mezzo delle parabole, Edizioni Paoline, Fede e comunicazione 9, Milano 2000. In French: *«Tu vois cette femme?» Parler en paraboles*, Éd. du Cerf, LiBi 121, Paris 2001.

Wprowadzenie do hebrajskiej retoryki biblijnej (*Études de rhétorique biblique*), Kraków, Wam, Mysl Teologiczna 30, 2001.

Una nuova introduzione ai vangeli sinottici, EDB, ReBib 4, 9, Bologna 2001, 2006. In English: *A New Introduction to the Synoptic Gospels*, India Claretian Communications, Chennai 2005.

Mort et ressuscité selon les Écritures, Bayard, Paris 2003. In Italian: *Morto e risorto secondo le Scritture*, EDB, Biblica, Bologna 2003.

Lire la Bible, Flammarion, Champs 537, Paris 2003. In Italian: *Leggere la Bibbia. Un'introduzione all'esegesi*, EDB, Collana biblica, Bologna 2004.

Il vangelo secondo Luca, EDB, ReBib 7, Bologna 2003.

L'Évangile de Luc, Lethielleux, RhSem 1, Paris 2005 (Grand Prix de philosophie de l'Académie française 2006).

La Bible, Le Cavalier bleu, Idées reçues 94, Paris 2005.

Jezyk Przypowiesci biblijnych, Kraków, Wydawnictwo Wam, Mysl Teologiczna 50, 2005.

Traité de rhétorique biblique, Lethielleux, RhSem 4, Paris 2007.

Appelés à la liberté, Lethielleux, RhSem 5, Paris 2008.

A New Introduction to the Synoptic Gospels

This book was printed on *thin opaque smooth white Bible paper*, using the *Minion* and *Type Embellishments One* font families.
This edition was printed in D'VINNI, S.A., in Bogotá, Colombia, during the last weeks of the sixth month of year two thousand ten.

Ad publicam lucem datus mense junii Sacri Cordis Iesus